UNCOMMON GROUND
BIPOC JOURNEYS TO CREATIVE ACTIVISM

Other books from Write Now! SF Bay (writenowsf.com)

Essential Truths: The Bay Area in Color

Civil Liberties United
Diverse Voices from the San Francisco Bay Area

Endangered, Species, Enduring Values
An Anthology of San Francisco Area Writers and Artists of Color

Standing Strong! Fillmore and Japantown
Voices from Write Now! Fillmore and Write Now! Japantown

WRITE NOW! SF BAY

UNCOMMON GROUND
BIPOC JOURNEYS TO CREATIVE ACTIVISM

Edited by Shizue Seigel

Pease Press • San Francisco

UNCOMMON GROUND
BIPOC Journeys to Creative Activism

Shizue Seigel • Write Now! SF Bay
www.WriteNowSF.com

Pease Press
1717 Cabrillo Street, San Francisco, CA 94121
www.peasepress.com
First edition October 2022.
Printed in the United States of America.
Orders: www.peasepress.com/Uncommon Ground

Book design by Shizue Seigel. www.shizueseigel.com

Cover art: "Hope, Act, The Fight For Freedom" by Twin Walls Mural Company

Library of Congress Cataloging-in-Publication Data

Uncommon Ground: BIPOC Journeys to Creative Activism
Edited by Shizue Seigel
Library of Congress Control Number: 2022910590

ISBN: 978-1-7330590-3-9

ABOUT THIS BOOK

We honor the original inhabitants of the San Francisco Bay Area, the unceded ancestral homeland of the Ohlone, Miwok, and Pomo. As uninvited guests, we open ourselves to the interconnectedness of all things, and the responsible stewardship of Mother Earth and of all life.

Uncommon Ground: BIPOC Journeys to Creative Activism is Write Now! SF Bay's fifth anthology of Bay Area writers and artists of color. As the pandemic continues into a third year, it's clear that life as we knew it is not returning. The American Empire is in well-deserved decline, and we must evolve new ways to live in a world that keeps shifting beneath our feet.

Creative evolution is nothing new to the Bay Area. Six out of ten residents of the San Francisco Bay Area are Black, Brown, and People of Color (BIPOC). We are far more than "local color." We make essential contributions to Bay Area life and culture—we feed, care for, educate, illuminate, and inspire in vital ways, yet we remain overlooked because we value love, compassion, and justice over money, power, or fame.

Many writers and artists of color draw from life experience. We are deeply familiar with adversity and change. Our families have been tested by war, poverty, and discrimination for generations. Our DNA is suffused with profound lessons on how to cope with challenging times. And our writing is linked with daily activism in large and small ways.

In a departure from previous anthologies, I reached out to selected writers and artists and asked them to trace their creative trajectories:

What were your formative influences?

What cultural, spiritual, and community values did you grew up with?

What was the impact of family, peers, school, or other influences?

How did your perceptions of the world shift over time?

What inspired you to get into art, creative writing, and activism?

What sustains your creative practice in these turbulent times?

I invited over three dozen people. All were intrigued by the project but many had to decline or drop out because they were too busy teaching, opening a bookstore, reviewing anti-vax petitions for city commissions, pursuing wider creative horizons, unionizing, caring for new babies, recovering from cancer treatments, grieving the loss of loved ones… The list goes on. Conversations with contributors were an illuminating window into the range and severity of on-going pandemic challenges. Some declined immediately, knowing they were already overcommitted; others dropped out along the way. For the rest, it was a long but fruitful editorial process.

The birthing process was much more difficult than usual. I asked the writers to dig deep, and their responses were honest, unexpected, and illuminating, sometimes requiring multiple drafts. Production assistance was hard to find, and rising fees did not always lead to quality work. The social distancing of the pandemic has escalated the tendency to confuse the *appearance* of competence with the thing itself. Competence is not the grade, money, or job title; it's the actual skills, discipline, and hard work to get the job done.

The glamorization of the arts may fool people into thinking that words or images alone can rebuild our broken society. We must do more than spout poetry while Rome burns. What are we doing pragmatically to build something in its place? The authors of *Uncommon Ground* are providing road maps.

About Write Now! SF Bay: Write Now! SF Bay has supported San Francisco Bay Area writers and artists of color through workshops, readings and creative showcases, and publications since 2015. *Uncommon Ground: BIPOC Journeys to Creative Activism* is our fifth anthology. Intersection for the Arts has been our fiscal sponsor since 2018.

Find out more about our low-cost, donation-based virtual writing workshops for writers of color. We meet every 2nd Tuesday and 3rd Saturday of the month to share our work and build community. Open to BIPOC writers writing in any genre, at any level. Details at www.WriteNowSF.com.

About the editor: Shizue Seigel, founder/director of Write Now! SF Bay, is a third-generation Japanese American writer, visual artist, and community activist whose prose, poetry, and visual art are informed by her family's WWII incarceration and by her lived experiences in segregated Baltimore, Occupied Japan, California farm labor camps, skid-row Stockton, Indian ashrams, corporate advertising, and public housing.

Her eight books include *Distillations: Meditations on the Japanese American Experience* (Pease Press 2010), *In Good Conscience: Supporting Japanese Americans During the Internment* (AACP, Inc. 2006), *My First Hundred Years* (Pease Press 2019), and five Write Now! anthologies.

Her prose and poetry have appeared in the anthologies *(Her)oics: Women's Lived Experience during the Pandemic, All the Women in My Family Sing, Your Golden Sun Still Shines, InvAsian, Cheers to Muses, Empty Shoes,* and

My Words Are Gonna Linger as well as in *Away Journal, Soundings East, sPARKLE + bLINK, Eleven Eleven, Persimmon Tree, Whirlwind Magazine,* and elsewhere. She is working on a two-volume memoir.

She is a four-time VONA/Voices fellow, whose work has been recognized with a Jefferson Award and grants and residencies from the Jentel, Atlantic Center for the Arts, Newnan Art Rez, and Hypatia-in-the-Woods. Her papers are archived at UC Santa Barbara's California Ethnic and Multicultural Archives.

Acknowledgments: We thank the writers and artists for their thoughtful and richly varied submissions. And we also thank those who were unable to participate; your spirits are with us: Elmaz Abinader, Josiah Luis Alderete, Tony Alderondo, Sandra Bass, Tân Khánh Cao, James Cagney, Francee Covington, Jennifer Hasegawa, Leticia Hernandez, Paula de Joie, adrienne danyelle oliver, Joan Osato, Choppy Oshiro, Dena Rod, Karen and Malik Seneferu, Cindy Shih, Thomas Robert Simpson, Truong Tran, Joyce E. Young, Nancy Wang, and Robert Kikuchi Yngojo.

We couldn't have done it without proofreader Rosalie Cavallaro; administrative assistant Jennifer Banta Yoshida; typographic designer Eiselle Ty; production artist McKenzie Long; readers André Le Mont Wilson, Dondi Dancy, and Christl Perkins. We're grateful for help and advice from San Francisco Poet Laureate Emerita Kim Shuck, Anissa Malady of the San Francisco Public Library, Alison Snopek of Intersection for the Arts, arts consultant Lenore Naxon, poet and radio DJ Avotcja, Thomas Robert Simpson of AfroSolo Theater Company, and participants of Write Now! SF Bay's on-going monthly creative workshops.

Uncommon Ground was made possible with support from the San Francisco Arts Commission, California Arts Council, the Community of Literary Magazines and Presses, and the Zellerbach Family Foundation. Intersection for the Arts has been our fiscal sponsor since 2018.

Fiscally sponsored by Intersection for the Arts, a historic 501(c)(3) non-profit arts organization supporting people working in arts and culture. Supported by the San Francisco Arts Commission and the Zellerbach Family Foundation. This project is funded in part by the California Arts Council, a state agency.

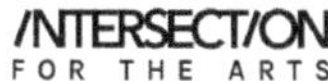
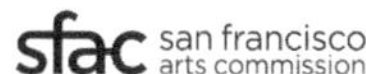
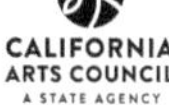
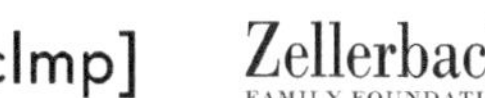

TABLE OF CONTENTS

Faith Adiele
FINDING HOME IN THE WORLD

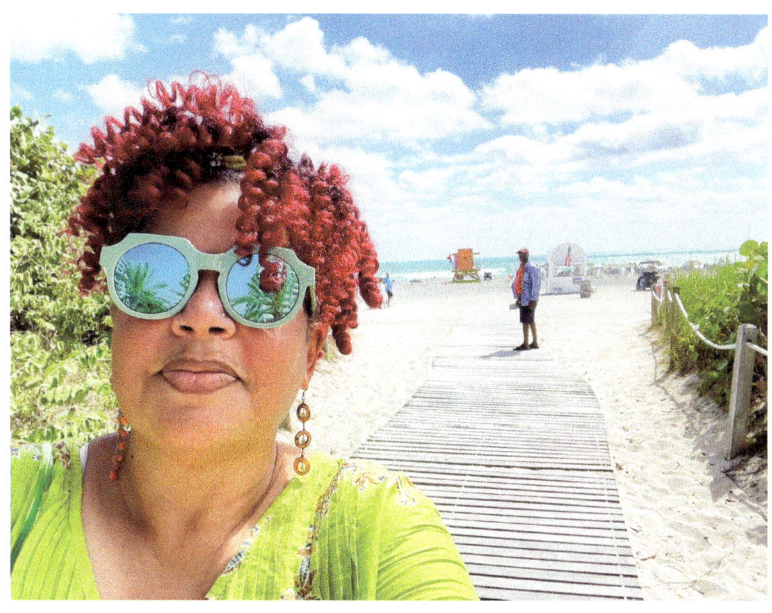

Faith Adiele is author of the memoirs
Meeting Faith, which won a PEN award, and
The Nigerian Nordic Girl's Guide to Lady Problems.
Her media writing credits include Sleep Stories for the
CALM app, two episodes of *A World of Calm*
(HBO Max) and the PBS documentary
My Journey Home. She teaches around the world,
including California College of the Arts,
San Francisco Writers' Grotto, and Left Margin Lit.
She is co-founder of BIPOC Writing Party,
an online writing community formed in response to
the pandemic and Black Lives Matter;
African Book Club at San Francisco's Museum
of the African Diaspora; and the nation's first writing
workshop for travelers of color.
www.adiele.com and @meetingfaith.

FINDING HOME IN THE WORLD
Faith Adiele

I grew up in an unlikely place, a rural valley in Washington State surrounded by dry shrub-steppe desert. To the west sprawled the reservation of the Confederated Tribes and Bands of the Yakama Nation; to the north hid the Hanford Nuclear Plant, where my grandfather worked construction; to the south meandered the Columbia River, the largest in the Pacific Northwest. Our town was composed of wealthy white farmers and ranchers, poor Latino laborers, two Chinese families descended from brothers, one Black American family, and my mixed family. We lived on a small cluster of green acreage just outside town—my Finnish-American grandmother and Swedish-American grandfather in the pastel farmhouse, my young schoolteacher mother and I in a mobile home set between the backyard and the pastures.

Though I was the only African for 175 miles, the only Black girl in school, the only brown member of my family, race was actually the least of my issues. My family were the town weirdos and unashamed about it, no matter how unpopular it made us. We were atheists and card-carrying Democrats among conservative Christian Republicans. My grandfather was active in anti-war and pro-union efforts. Mom was always challenging someone on their racism or sexism. Even my soft-spoken grandmother lobbied for the passing of the ERA and insisted on being called a homemaker, not a housewife. In the evenings the adults wrote impassioned letters to the local newspaper complaining about biased coverage. On weekends and summers, when school was out, I was "apprenticed" to different family members. I studied art making, sewing, and family history with my mummi; wood-working and tall-tale telling with my morfar; anthropology, mythology, and history with my mother. Mom read constantly—to herself and to me—and frequently spent our grocery money on books for the both of us. As a white single mother, she took her role in helping me develop a healthy racial identity seriously. Twice a year she took the Greyhound bus over the mountains to Seattle, where she bought every single book or toy with brown characters she could get her hands on. Eventually she amassed a library of 5,000 African, Asian, Latin American, and Nordic children's books.

A large part of my home-school curriculum was world religions and mythologies. In the absence of my actual father—an international student from Nigeria—I had Igbo proverbs and folktales, which taught the importance

of community. My grandparents'
Norse myths and Finnish epics
made clear the premium they put on
stoic resistance, on doing the right
thing, no matter the cost. It was my
job to stand up for the underdog
and interrupt oppression wherever
I encountered it, even if that meant
calling out my mother's school
colleagues. She would always have
my back, she assured me. Doing the
right thing was rarely the easy thing.

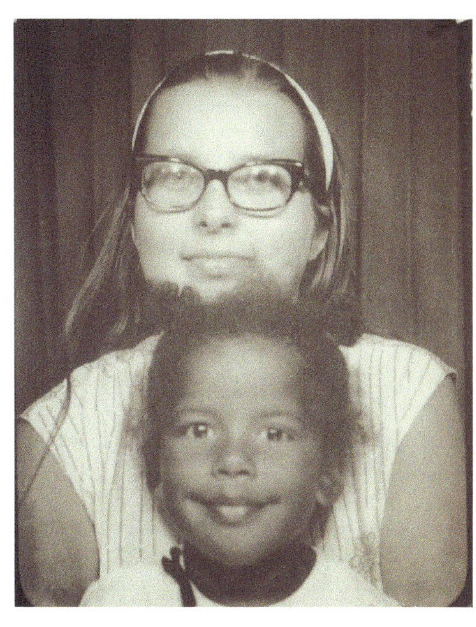

Mom also wanted me to
understand the major tenets of
the major faiths and then choose
my own path. She herself was Unitarian, and twice a year we tried a new
congregation, essentially pleasant white Seattleites with no rituals or doctrine
as far as I could tell other than a penchant for Pete Seeger songs and voting
Democrat. Truly, politics was her religion. Her white working-class immigrant
parents raised her for the class struggle. She was the first person in the family
to go to college; and there, her interest in the American Civil Rights and
the African independence movements connected her with my father. Mom
raved about how formative college had been in developing them—the only
public interracial couple on campus—as activist-thinkers. After my father's
return to Nigeria and involvement with the Nigerian civil war, she and my
grandmother immersed themselves in women's liberation. I was raised to
inherit the struggle.

I was also raised to consider the world my home. My mummi was always
talking about returning to Finland. My morfar waxed poetic about being a
photojournalist and traveling the Pacific Rim during World War II. My mom
had been prepared to move to Nigeria with my father and kept lists of the
world's great civilizations she dreamed of visiting. It also became apparent that
as a Black girl with international interests, I was going to have to leave. Any
hope of finding my people and my place lay outside my small town. And since
we were living on my mother's small-town teaching salary, I was going to have
to win scholarships if I wanted to travel or go to a good school.

I started studying abroad in high school—Mexico my sophomore year, Thailand my junior year. Mexico made sense, as I was studying Spanish (and French) in school; Thailand was a fluke. I knew nothing about the country; I was just desperate to get out of town, and after a string of disasters, the study abroad program was equally desperate to find an American student who could adapt to Thailand. This was back before American tourists had discovered Thailand, and being able to spend an entire year away from both the Western worldview and the white gaze, where people had no preconceived notions and stereotypes of who I was, was transformative, and it gave me language.

Upon my return home, I determined to continue my family's dreams. At age 60 my grandmother got her GED. In one generation, my grandparents had shifted from working-class immigrants who didn't speak English to middle-class Americans who took summer vacations. My mother and father had been the first in their families to attend college, but single parenthood derailed my mother's plans for graduate school. According to her, my father had dreamed of going to Harvard for his doctorate; he'd gained admission but couldn't afford to attend. When I won a nearly full ride to Harvard, it felt like American meritocracy at work. We belonged here.

I had been living my parents' dreams for so long that it was a shock to realize that I wasn't going to college in the 60s. An Ivy League school in New England in the 80s during the height of the investment banking craze was as far as one could get from my father's experiences at the Tuskegee Institute and my mother's experiences at the University of Washington. Greed was good; money was both politics and religion. It took a while to find my tribe. They were mostly BIPOC, first or second generation American, raised by single mothers, on scholarship, and committed to public service and social justice. I began to develop my own social justice framework, instinctively separating it from the White Savior public service model we were being taught. And when Black organizations told me gender clouded the issue and women's organizations told me race clouded the issue, I began to develop my own intersectionality and critical race analysis.

I was so invested in doing this work that I didn't pay much attention to my classes, with their reading lists of hundreds of pages by dead white men. Eventually, the spring of my sophomore year, I had a breakdown. The reasons were plentiful—the intense racism, sexism, and classicism at Harvard and in Boston; a family history of depression; a coup ending democracy in Nigeria; and my inability to live up to my perfectionist ideals. Harvard insisted that I withdraw

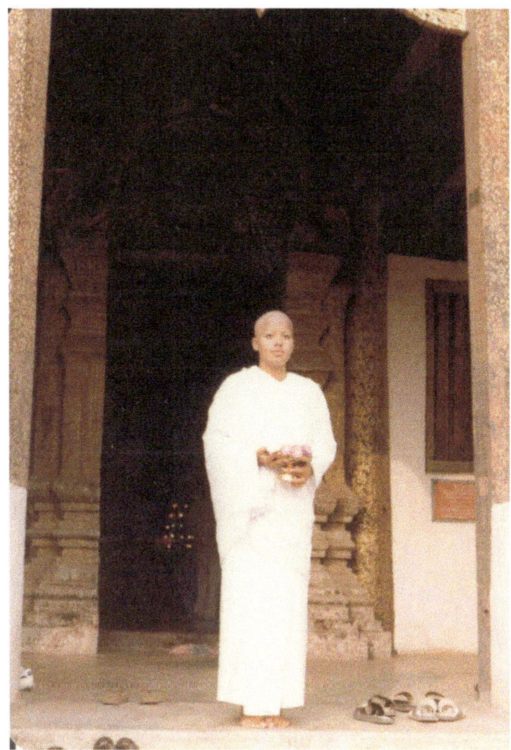

for a year, but fortunately I learned about a new study abroad program in Thailand, gained admittance, and was able to apply my scholarship funds towards this strategy to redeem myself.

I had slunk back to Thailand to lick my wounds; instead, I found myself energized by the program's fieldwork requirement. Here was the hands-on, experiential education I'd been craving at Harvard. I started studying Buddhist nuns primarily because everyone Thai told me I shouldn't, that they weren't worthy of academic inquiry. Unlike monks, who were to be revered, nuns were just women who had failed at civilian life. I was aghast; I was hooked. Though I took issue with cultural anthropology, sensing without yet having the language to critique the researcher-subject hierarchy and the mythology of objectivity, I recognized the political importance of collecting women's stories to challenge ideas of failure and intellectual worth.

In a surprising plot twist, I ended up ordaining as Thailand's first Black Buddhist nun. My advisor, a former Buddhist monk, had challenged me, pointing out the failure of Western anthropology, of outsiders coming to gawk at natives and making their careers on whatever conclusions they came to. You're asking a sociological question—why are these women choosing this demeaned profession, he stressed, and they're responding in spiritual terms—a language you don't speak. I realized I had to have skin in the game, that I had to risk and transform myself before anyone should entrust their story to me. This was another breakthrough in my thinking that has informed how I do my academic, political, and creative work.

My actual time as a nun further opened my eyes to the role of spirituality—not the harmful institutional religion I had been raised to fear—

but in a holistic political and social transformation schema. I learned not to silo political engagement and activism from spirituality from creativity from community engagement and family. They are all part of the same thing; only Western conceptions make us separate them out. Sustainability is a matter of refusing the question. Ordination demanded that I face my fears. Without this experience, it's unlikely that I would have been able at the end of my ordination to return to Harvard, graduate with honors, and soon after, win a fellowship to Nigeria. There—under a brutal dictatorship—I met my father and siblings for the first time and fought for my place in the family.

All these intersecting cultural influences, quests and failures inspired a path that combines social justice, creative writing, and teaching. My return from Nigeria sparked two more returns—one to Harvard to run a social justice program, two to my original love of writing and storytelling. Other than the ordination journal the head nun had me keep in Thailand, I had stopped writing after my first traumatic year at Harvard. Now, on a personal level, I was writing to make sense of my challenging year with my African family and biracial identity; on a professional level, I was writing to figure out how to do consensus-based

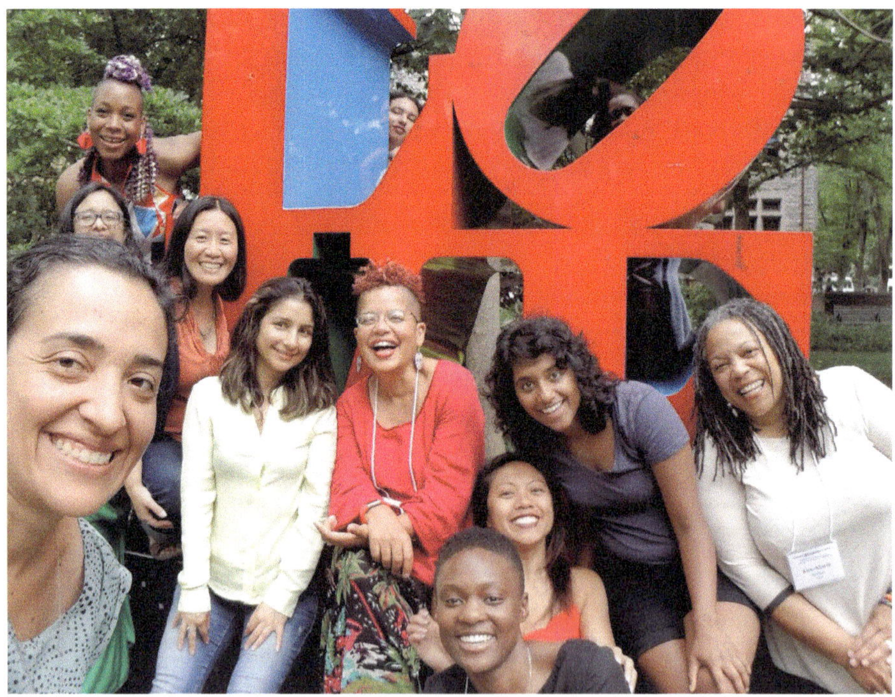

Faith Adiele with students from Voice of Our Nations (VONA)
Travel workshop, 2017.

social justice work in a truly multicultural organization. Political analysis alone couldn't do the job. I noticed that every time the collective was about to make a large policy decision, members would tell stories about themselves—where they came from, what mattered to them. It became clear that storytelling was essential for identity and for this work. A mission statement alone can't effect change. When attempting to transform organizations and society, we have to transform the individual. And it is storytelling that tells us who we think we are. And who we can become.

In developing trainings for student activists and future policymakers, I was really devising writing prompts. I started writing articles about how personal narrative isn't self-indulgent navel-gazing but civic engagement with radical potential. About the political, social, and spiritual potential of personal writing. About how de-colonizing creative writing could return it to community-based oral storytelling that has historically served a function in the world. With that, I felt empowered to put writing first and go to Graduate School to study my craft. This can be hard for those of us who come from families or traditions that view any kind of art-making as impractical, not what our parents sacrificed for. I wanted to write about my time with the nuns in Thailand and about finding my family in Nigeria, and I wanted to decolonize the teaching of creative writing, which is now what I'm known for.

To be honest, my own writing has suffered from my commitment to teaching and editing and mentoring. It's hard as a BIPOC woman to protect your time. You get asked to do so much, and if you're teaching in academia, you're always on display. People want to overwork you and then undercut your authority. It's important to find community. For a long time when I was teaching in antagonistic or unfriendly, predominantly white institutions, VONA was the one thing that would keep me sustained. For one or two weeks a year, I could see that I'm actually an excellent teacher. I could be appreciated for bringing my identity into the classroom. Students weren't saying, Oh, she's so biased, because she makes us read BIPOC authors. Or, she's not like an objective white man; she's biased because she's a black woman. VONA was the one place where I could really see my pedagogies shine, and students' writing would become incredible in just a week, and participants would also bond for life. There's nothing more rewarding than helping a young person or a novice writer have that lightbulb moment and find their voice. I find a lot of fulfillment and sustainability in creating the next generation. Hopefully they'll pass it on and be generous with others. Creating a legacy is important. Today, there are a lot of opportunities for

BIPOC writers, but when I was coming up, there weren't—especially in creative nonfiction. I had to take fiction classes, where often I was the only person of color and the only person writing nonfiction. So I was doubly exposed.

Nowadays, it's hard to imagine how challenging it was. I'm gratified that I had some part in the change but also wary. I remember when my female students didn't want anything to do with feminism; they thought they'd achieved equality. I remember being verbally abused at a conference by a famous Black woman traveler who said I was creating low self-esteem by having a travel writing workshop exclusively for BIPOC voices. So, sure, now we're experiencing a BIPOC publishing renaissance, but it's not the first time, and we'd be naive to think there will not be backlash. If we've learned anything from the 2016 election, these so-called gains and freedoms are tenuous. Don't underestimate who did the hard work to get you here, and how quickly it can all disappear.

I'm always thinking about the limited options and resources for women, Black/Brown, African peoples before me. I stand on their shoulders, so I have to pay it forward. There are so many fantastic stories and examples that have been actively erased from history by the victors. S

responsibility to exhume and honor and highlight those stories to ensure they become part of the history. This awareness of history both inspires me and sustains me in hard times. Sure, academia may be a thousand microaggressions chipping away at my soul, but I could be working in the fields or factory. Quit whining, get off the couch and get to work!

Salma Arastu
BORN WITH TWO WINGS

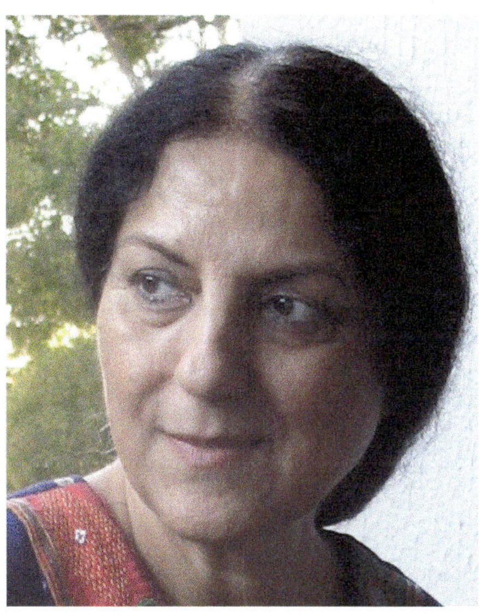

Salma Arastu was born in Rajasthan, India.
She embraced Islam and moved to USA in 1986.
As a woman, artist, and mother, she works to create
harmony by expressing the universality of humanity
through paintings, sculpture, and calligraphy.
Inspired by her Indian heritage and Islamic spirituality,
she uses her artistic voice to break down
the barriers that divide, and to foster peace and
understanding. She's had 45 solo shows nationally and
internationally and won several prestigious
awards, including the East Bay Fund for Artists and the
City of Berkeley Individual Artist Grant.
Her public art pieces are displayed in Bethlehem,
Pennsylvania, and San Diego, California. She has
also published five books of art and poetry, most recently
Our Earth: Embracing All Communities.
salmaarastu.com

BORN WITH TWO WINGS
Salma Arastu

My family was originally from Sindh, Pakistan, where my family had lived for several generations. My father was a physician and had his own practice there. In 1947, when the British left India, their holdings were divided into predominately Muslim Pakistan and Hindu India. As Hindus, my parents were forced to leave their home and other possessions and travel with their children to India by train. Initially they lived in refugee camps before settling in Ajmer, Rajasthan. I was born in Ajmer, the last of ten children.

Ajmer may be a small desert town, but the area is a great pilgrimage attraction for both Hindus and Muslims. Hindus travel from all over India to dip in the sacred waters of nearby Pushkar Lake, while Muslims travel from all over the world to visit the tomb of Khawaja Moinuddin Chishti, a Sufi mystic who died in 1230.

My father died when I was ten years old. My mother and four of us younger siblings moved to Bhilai, Madhya Pradesh in India, where my eldest

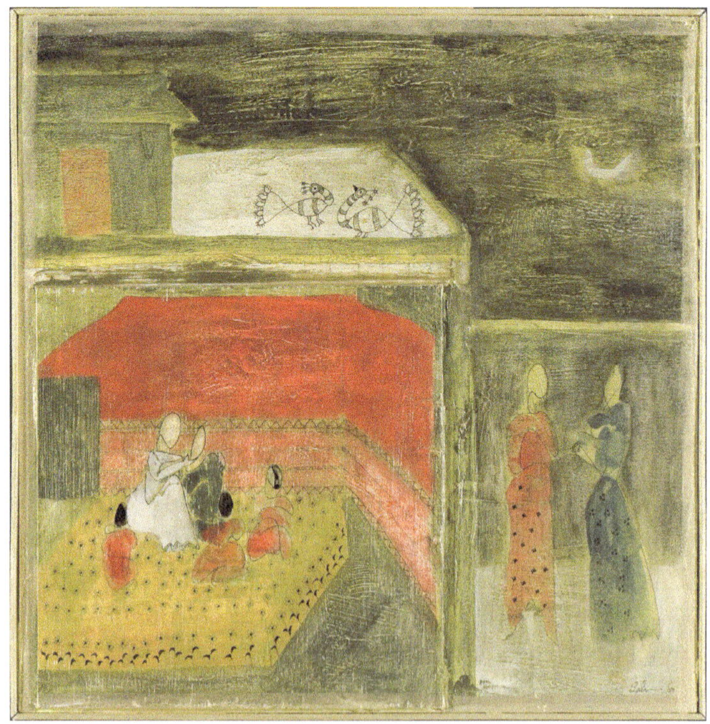

"Nighttime Stories," acrylics and pen & ink on board, 21 x 21 inches, from the series *Memory Vignettes*, 2005.

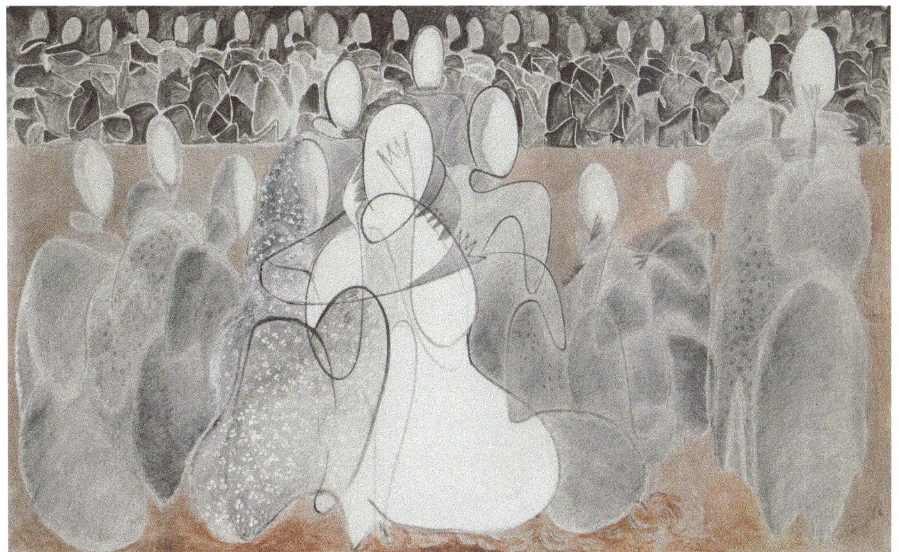

"Sharing Stories Together," acrylics and graphite on canvas-paper, 36 x 60 inches, from the series *Flow of Humanity*, 2003.

brother, an engineer, had settled and was working in the Bhilai Steel Plant. My mother was a very spiritual person. Though she was a practicing Hindu, she believed in one God, who is the source of all life on this earth and beyond. She often said that we are the children of the same God, whether we are Hindu, Muslim, Christian or Jewish.

I had complete faith in what she said, and as an adult it became my aim to bring the whole world together through my artwork and poetry.

I was born without four fingers on my left hand. My mother did not perceive this as a deformity. Before I encountered the prejudices of others, she managed to make my faith in good so strong that I grew up with confidence and gratitude. I was shy and self-conscious, but I knew that my God has created me for a special reason. That thought gave me all my strength.

I feel blessed because I was born with two wings, the love to create and a love for God. These two gifts have been sources of eternal joy and a constant flow of positive inspiration in my life. Painting became my need at a very early age. I could draw and doodle with continuous lyrical lines moving on the rhythm of my own soul. I work every day, as I have made a covenant with my Creator that I will spread the love and blessings that He has showered upon me.

Born into the Hindu tradition in my native India, and accepting Islam later on, I have enjoyed the beauty of these two distinctive traditions firsthand. I met Alam, a Muslim architect, in Fine Arts and Architecture college, and I married him because of his unconditional love for me. When I accepted my husband's religion, I knew my bond with God was the same. Only the rituals for prayer had changed. I received my mother's blessings and moved with Alam to Iran and then Kuwait, where I was exposed to a wealth of Islamic arts and Arabic calligraphy. I continued searching my identity—exploring new techniques, raising family, and traveling. The new vistas, merging with different cultures has added much texture and color to my art.

In 1986, we immigrated to the USA and landed in Bethlehem, Pennsylvania. As an artist and architect couple with two children, settling down was not easy because of financial struggles. My husband got jobs and then was laid off a couple of times. My dream was to establish myself as a fine artist here in the US; but in order to pay the bills, I started designing greeting cards. A local printer encouraged me. He printed my cards in exchange for paintings. I started searching for a niche market and gradually made up my mind to serve Islamic communities here in the US by creating Islamic greeting cards.

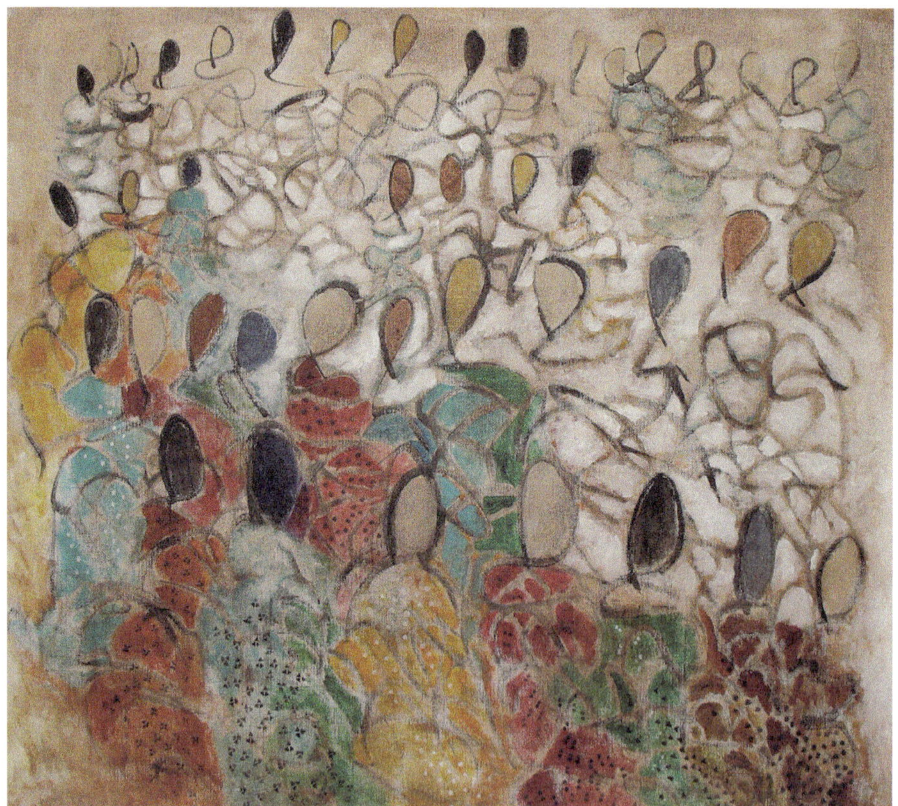

"Multitudes," acrylics and pen & ink on canvas, 48 x 48 inches, from the series *Flow of Humanity*, 2008.

My husband and my children supported me by accompanying me to conventions and community fairs, making sales, and generating mailing lists. Slowly but surely, we created a mail order business. Sales not only helped us pay our bills, but they also sustained me as a practicing artist. I was able to rent a studio and continue my artistic explorations. In the beginning, the works were abstract. I was searching through layering materials like paper, rope, and modeling paste on my canvas, and scratching, sanding, before finally embellishing with pen and ink. As I applied thin layers of acrylic paints, mystical figures gradually appeared that looked like animals or fish-like forms connected with continuous lines. Later these forms turned into gestural human figures connected with one line as groups celebrating, sharing, and communicating together.

After 9/11, I went deeper in my faith to counteract negativities about Islam. I learned Arabic, studied the Quran, and used my calligraphy skills to create large paintings of positive verses that conveyed the Quran's messages of love, reassurance, unity in diversity, and mercy for all.

Later, verses that speak about ecological consciousness inspired the project *Our Earth: Embracing All Communities*. Most recently, I have immersed myself

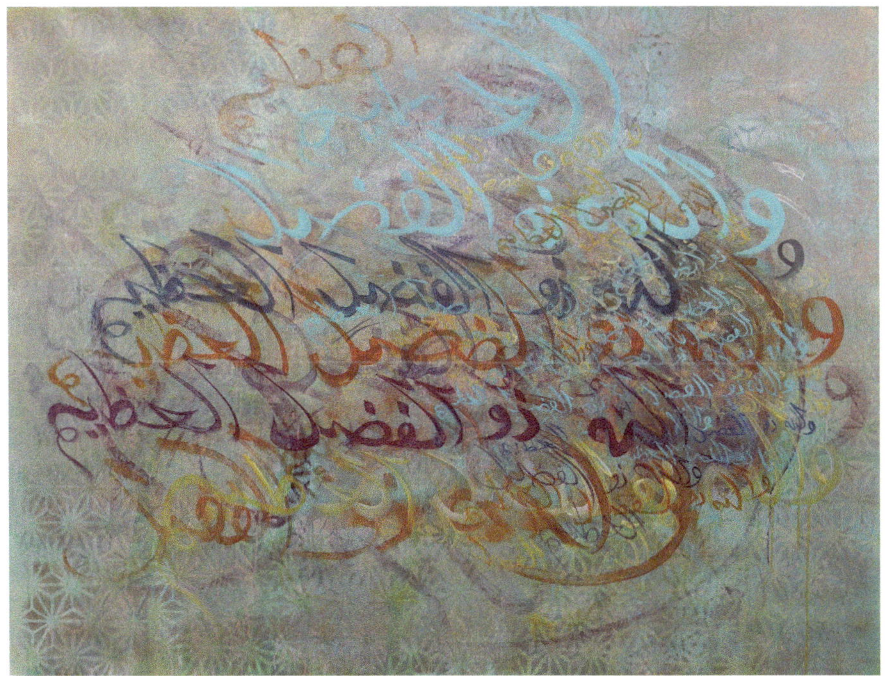

"Allah is Full of Bounties," acrylics on canvas, 52 x 72 inches, from the series *Celebration of Calligraphy*, 2016.

in deeper knowledge to find remedies to save our planet and its ecosystems. And I have discovered Mycelia—the vegetative part of a fungus, consisting of a network of fine white filaments that can break down dead plant and animal matter into soluble sugars, nitrates, and phosphates that can then become food shared with multiple organisms. A new ray of hope is rising from mushrooms and the underground network of mycelia to regenerate, activate, and heal the damaged state of our environment.

Through my lifetime of work as a painter and poet, I have arrived at the beautiful concept that oneness is not restricted to humanity only. We must achieve oneness by connecting humanity, soil, and soul. Today, I am moving forward in my attempts to bring together all humanity through Onenessprojects.com (https://onenessproject.com/). Through compassion and spirituality, we can create art, music, dance, and poetry to share and spread understanding and unity.

BEFORE I SEE YOU!

As I am arriving closer to the edge of my life
The point where I don't know what is beyond
I want to stop and fulfill my promises
To heal each soul with my love,
Removing the differences among humanity,
To save Mother Earth and her dignity,
Nurture each plant and creature
With care and sympathy,
Let me take my pen and brush
And bring out my voice with force
That tears the layers of ignorance
Holding each one in my embrace …
Oh my Lord!
Help me to fulfill my covenant with you
Before I see you!

ALLAH O AKBAR!

It is the call to my prayers
Allah O Akbar, Allah O Akbar, Allah O Akbar
I pray every morning, every day, every night
With gratitude in my heart and in my mind
God is great, God is great, God is great
The terrorist comes and hijacks this phrase of mine
Seeking Allah's help for an action not right
Allah O Akbar Allah O Akbar Allah O Akbar
And the media picks up,
Interpreting Killer God is great!
Who is giving permission to kill the innocent?
We respond with fear, hatred, and violence
Leaders rise to ban the Muslim's call to pray
Creating more chaos upon chaos
All this is happening because of our ignorance …
Allah O Akbar! Allah O Akbar! Allah O Akbar!

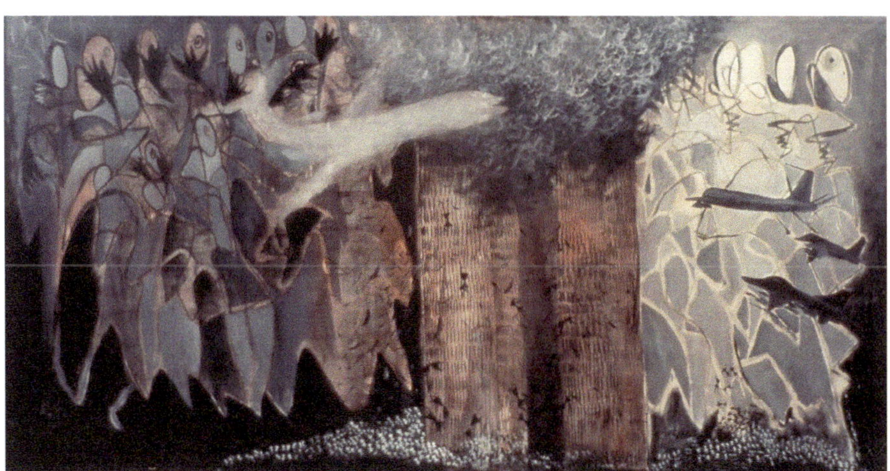

"Tragedy," acrylics and pen & ink on canvas, 48 x 98 inches, from the series *Flow of Humanity*, 2001.

OCEAN OF HUMANITY

Do not lose faith in humanity
It is a vast, limitless, spread-out ocean
It does not get dirty with a few drops of dirt at one end
On the other end,
Look at the sparkling waves gushing forward to cover it!
No evil human powers can destroy its beauty
They only cry for our attention
And invite us to advance with force and dignity
Do not shake with fear at a mere bomb blast
Or several gunshots
Rise with determination like these waves
Do not stop, as these are only warnings sent in lots
Move with intention to clean and heal
The naked wounds of humanity
Do not blame the ignorant ones
They are part of this humanity
To test our humanity
Live with patience and power to heal
It is within you, O humanity
Humanity is an ocean, life-giving and eternal
Can a few drops of evil destroy this glorious unity?

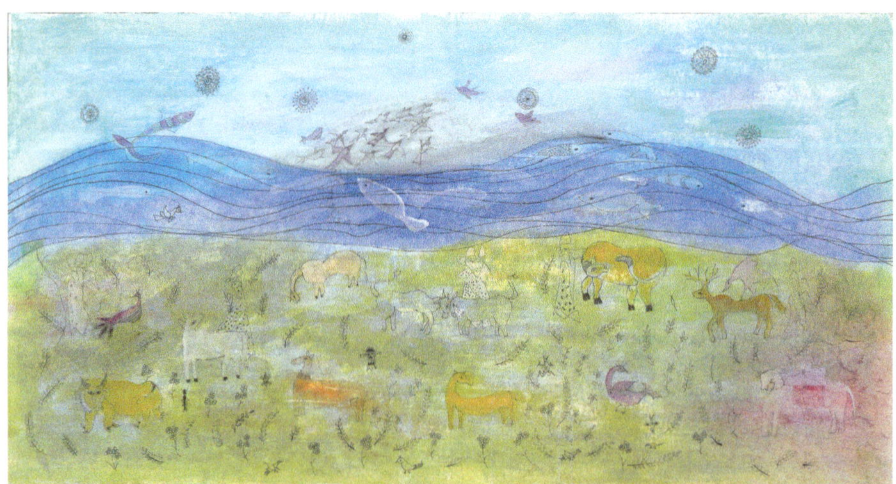

"Earth and the Sky Balance," acrylics and pen & ink on paper, 58 x 28 inches, from the series *We Are All One*, 2020.

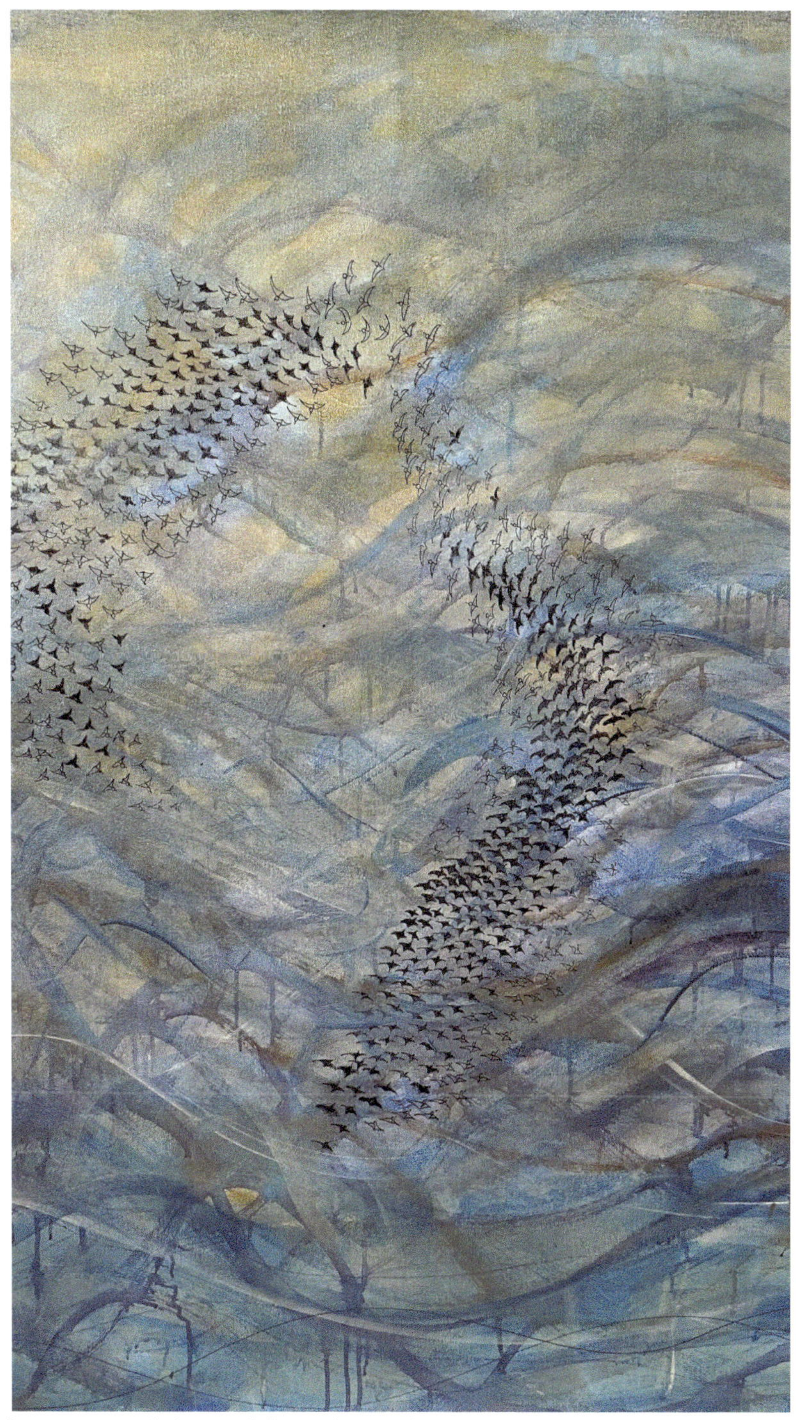

"The Waves and the Birds," acrylics and pen & ink on canvas, 52 x 32 inches, from the series *The Bay Stories*, 2022.

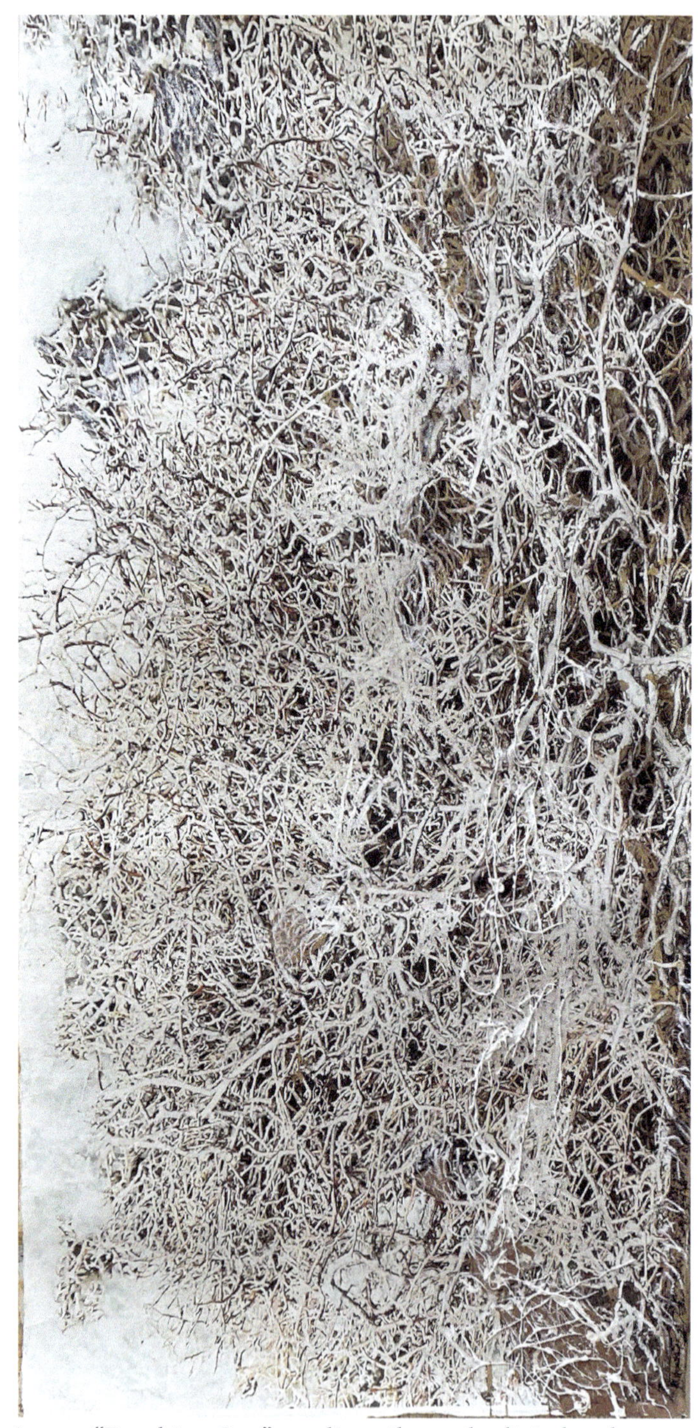

Salma Arastu, "Reaching Out," acrylics, oil pastels, digital and rust on paper, 60 x 30 inches, from the series *Energy & Hope*, 2021.

Adrian Arias
MULTIDISCIPLINARY MAGIC

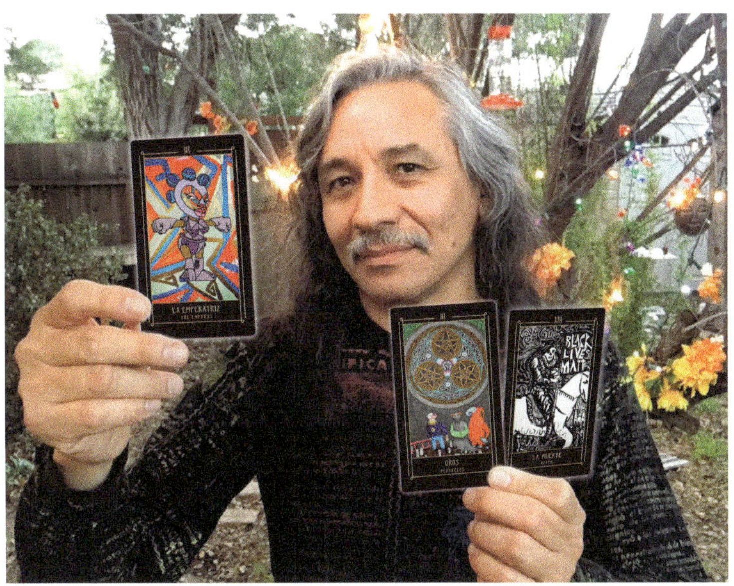

Adrian Arias is a visual artist, poet, performer, teacher, activist, and cultural promoter. He brings together multidisciplinary artists to engage in community projects with messages of social justice, racial equality, climate change, peace, beauty, health, and hope in the San Francisco Bay Area.

Born in Peru, on Mochica land, he has lived in the Bay Area since 2000. His art and performances have been featured at the Mission Cultural Center for Latino Arts, Galleria de la Raza, SOMArts Dia de los Muertos, the San Francisco International Arts Festival, and De Young Museum. He is one of the founders of MAPP (Mission Arts Performance Project) and creator of such Bay Area festivals as VideoFest, Luna Negra, and *ILLUSION* show.
Adrianarias.com

THE TRUTH OF THE CREATIVE MOMENT
Adrian Arias

Art is a tool for mental and corporal liberation, therefore, a force for social justice.

Just like my ancestors from the Moche culture, from ancient Peru, I believe in art as an expression that mixes our reality with the images created in our dreams. The Mochicas were great observers and imaginative teachers, recreating their gods, using art to inform daily life, the body and rituals to transform and create new realities.

For me, as a multidisciplinary artist and art teacher, it is important to remember that creation extends beyond the short-term physical results. The fantastic will always be written in the creative act. The Moche culture almost disappeared in 700 AD, but those of us who carry its blood continue to passionately transmit our vision of art and reality, of a community that can be brought together to create, and of individual solitudes united by an inexhaustible creative bond.

VISUAL POETRY: MURALS

My murals are usually commissioned by activist groups or institutions and by local businesses that support social justice and equality.

"River to the Sky" is a fusion between the history of the Black Hawk Jazz Cafe, Black Lives Matter, and the ancestral roots of the Ohlone peoples and my ancestral Mochica culture.

Miles Davis recorded two albums at the Black Hawk Jazz Club, April 21-22, 1961, and Billie Holiday performed there on her last West Coast club tour. These two jazz icons had very deep moments of personal struggle. Their music and art was always the engine of their existence and their passion to continue in life. I feel that it is important to invoke their presence in the Tenderloin.

Other images include California poppies—anti-inflammatory and analgesic medicinal plants that help with anxiety, nervous agitation, and insomnia. A black hawk flying in a yellow sky represents determination and

---

Previous page: Adrian Arias holding cards from *Tarot in Pandemic & Revolution*: "The Empress" by Malik Seneferu, "III of Pentacles" by William Brown, and "Death" by Adrian Arias.

"River to the Sky," at Turk & Hyde Streets in San Francisco overlooks the site of the Blackhawk Jazz Club. Commissioned by The Luggage Store Gallery and sponsored by The Someland Foundation.

clarity. Spiritually, hawks symbolize the power to control your own reality through a combination of intuitive wisdom and quick decision making—the ability to be focused and confident at the moment of creation.

An Ohlone design taken from a traditional basket represents the flow of water and the continuity of rivers, rising from earth to sky in recognition of San Francisco's underground rivers that were part of Ohlone life and culture. The zig-zag design is sister to a design from my ancestral Mochica culture.

The hummingbird connects the worlds of the living and the dead, bringing messages of joy and hope from our ancestors. Billie Holiday's earring is inscribed "Say Her Name" to mark the breaking of silence around the violation of women's rights. And huge block letters reading BLM honors the movement that began with the defense of Black lives and has grown to encompass the rights of all minorities of color.

"A Poem for the Dead," altar, *Dreams Emerging, Beyond Resilience: Día de Los Muertos 2021*, SOMArts Cultural Center.

A POEM FOR THE DEAD

Dedicated to five Latinx killed by police brutality in the U.S. and Mexico.

Mario González, 26, killed by suffocation, Alameda, California, April 19, 2021.

Victoria Salazar, 36, killed by suffocation, Tulum, Mexico, March 27, 2021.

Sean Monterossa, 22, killed by 5 shots, Vallejo, California, June 4, 2020.

Angel Zapata Hernández, 24, killed by suffocation, San Diego, California, October 15, 2019.

Claudia Patricia Gómez González, 20, killed by a shot in the head by a Border Patrol agent, Rio Bravo, Texas, May 23, 2018.

"8:46," altar, *Living Legacies: Día de Los Muertos 2020*,
SOMArts Cultural Center.

8:46*

(Read the poem with heavy breathing, pausing without breathing between stanzas)

It's hard to be an angel, but you learn.
The policeman's boot suffocating my neck for 8 minutes and 46 seconds
are the swords stuck in my body.
It's like the betrayal of love
the unexpected attack from behind.
(…)
But do I want to be an angel?
Someone made the decision for me.
The chill in my chest is endless.
When you are an angel you can feel the pain of others,
the sky and the stars weigh more than a mountain.
(…)
When you are an angel you are everywhere and nowhere
spreading your wings like swords
assisting those who are attacked by the red and blue lights.
It's hard to be an angel
but you learn.

* 8:46 refers to the time in minutes George Floyd was suffocated by police until he died.

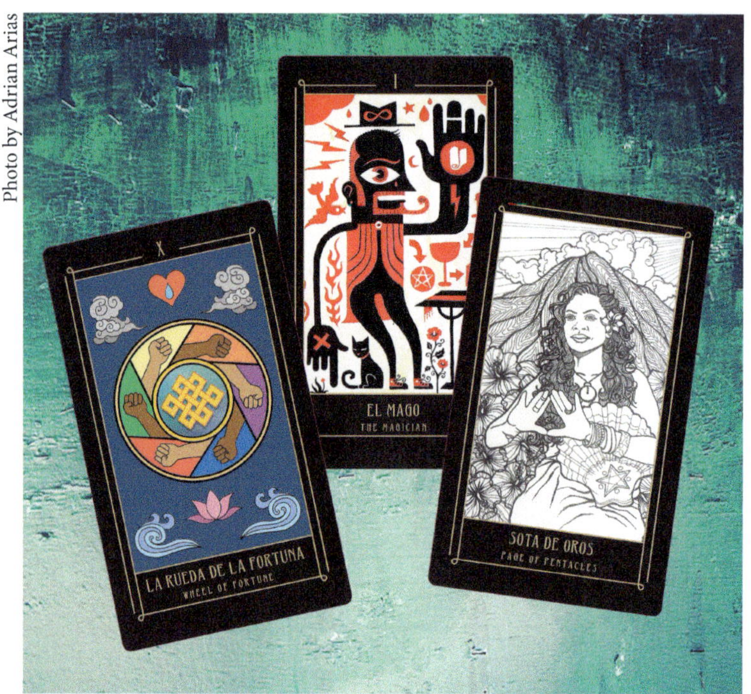

"Wheel of Fortune" by Nancy Hom, "The Magician" by Hugh D´Andrade, "Page of Pentacles" by Cece Carpio, from *Tarot in Pandemic & Revolution*.

TAROT EN PANDEMIA & REVOLUCIÓN / TAROT IN PANDEMIC & REVOLUTION

In May 2020, I had a dream that a fortune teller read Tarot to me. It was a deck with beautiful and rare images of revolution and pandemic and issues related to our time.

I decided to ask my artist friends to create this deck together, and after several months I had 78 images by 23 artists. Later I had another dream, where the fortune teller read me the Tarot, but with poems. When I woke up, I started calling my local poet friends and after a few months, 43 poets were involved. I finally found a local publisher, J. K. Fowler from Nomadic Press, to publish the deck, and Reneé Baldocchi from Baldocchi Projects to help me with all the production details. It is fantastic to have a community that understands that dreams brought into being can shift realities. Thanks to all my collaborators, I can recognize love and artwork as a revolutionary act in the middle of a pandemic.

Tarot in Pandemic and Revolution, conceived and produced by Adrian Arias, was published by Nomadic Press in 2021. nomadicpress.org/store/p/tarot

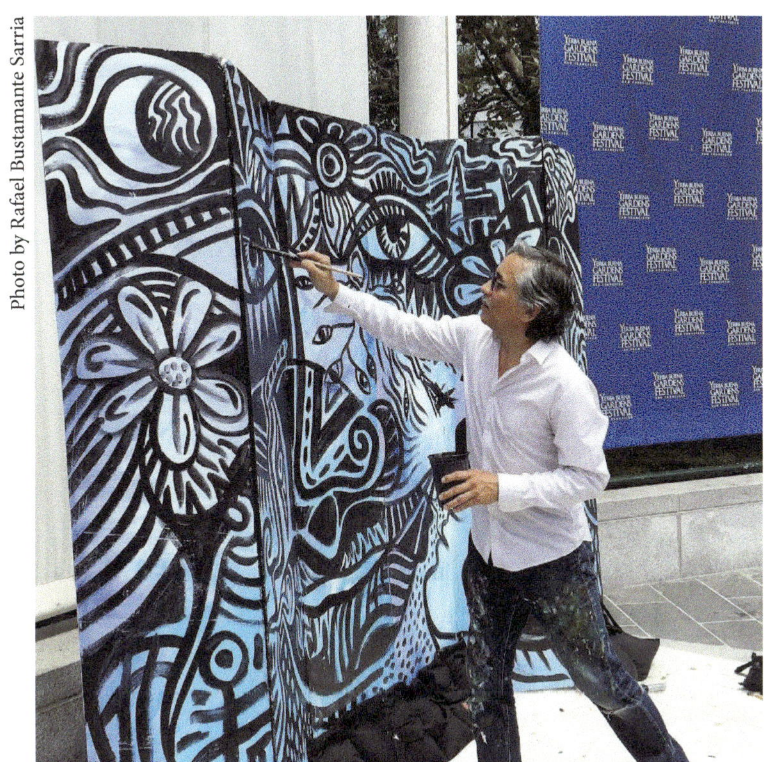

Adrian Arias live painting with LoCura Band at
Yerba Buena Gardens, July 2021.

(weaving haikus for my mother)

The map on the skin
founding treasures in the sky
kiss on the belly

you were root and time
weaving the clouds and seasons
we all are your fruit

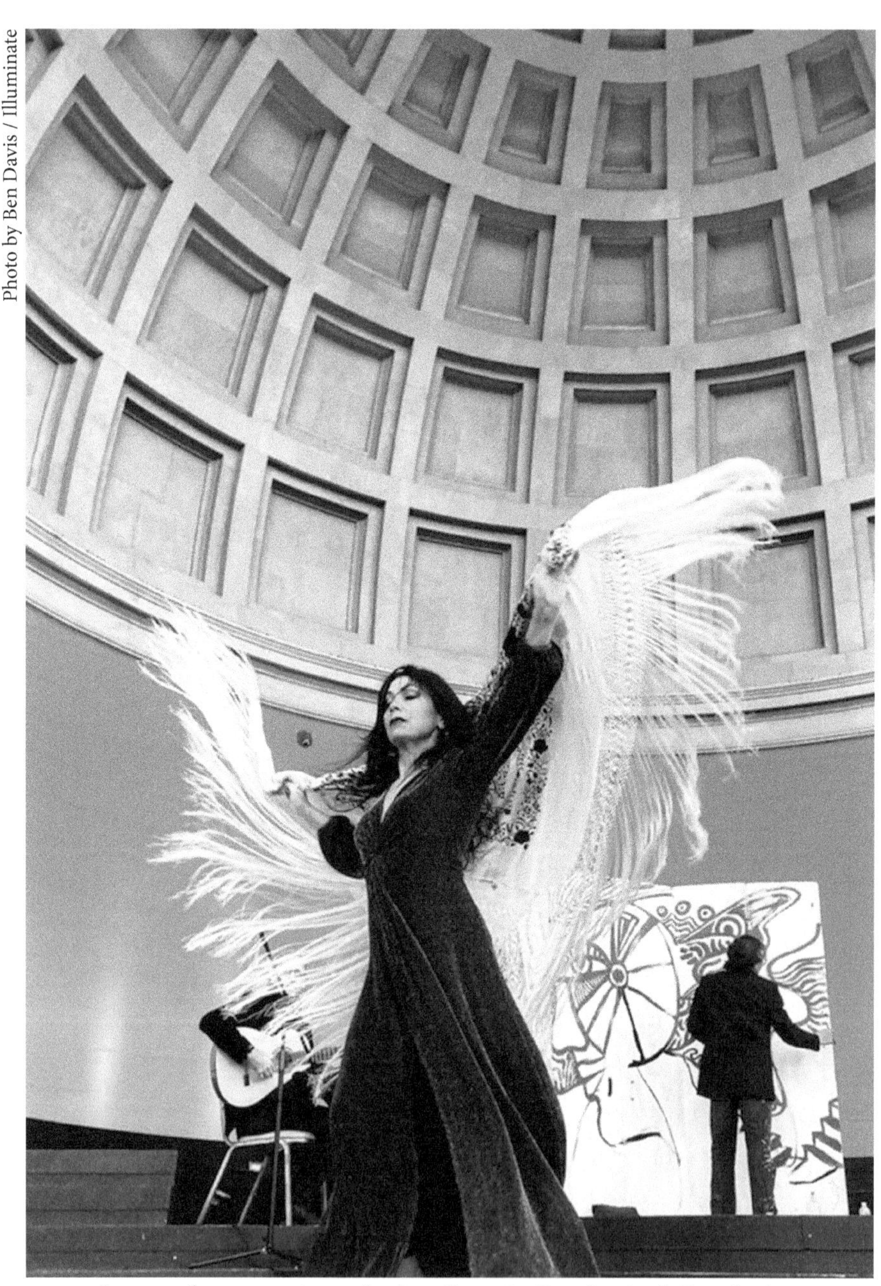

In a performance introducing *Tarot in Pandemic & Revolution*,
La Tania dances flamenco as Adrian Arias paints in the
Golden Gate Bandshell, San Francisco.

PERFORMANCES & SCORES

ILLUSION

To spark the spontaneous creativity and collective energy of fellow artists, I created the *ILLUSION* show in 2003. The show brought together about 50 artists in a large white space and invited each to create art for 5 hours inside a personal space lined with a white paper. More than 250 artists have participated in *ILLUSION* shows from 2003-2017. They have been held at the Mission Cultural Center for Latino Arts, at the de Young Museum, and at the SOMArts Cultural Center. It has been an amazing experience sharing the art, the momentum, the projects and ideas around us, as the creative process of individuals and groups. It was like a dream.

ILLUSION show 10, postponed by the pandemic, will be presented in June and October 2022 as mini Illusion shows as part of Adrian's artist residency at the Red Poppy Art House.

ILLUSION show space at the Mission Cultural Center for
Latino Arts Gallery, 2003.

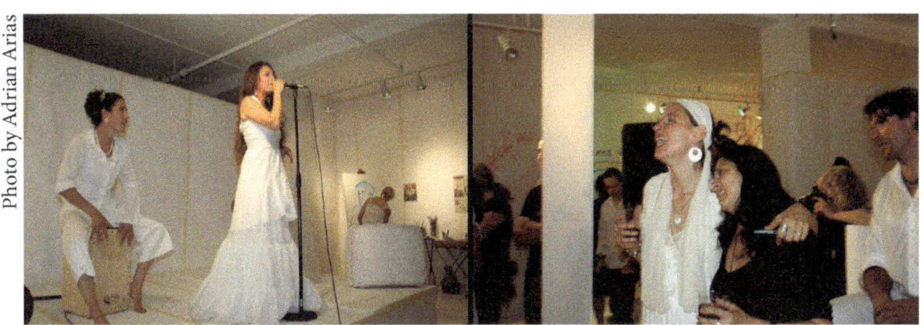

Mamacoatl and members of Locura Music, *ILLUSION* show 2005.

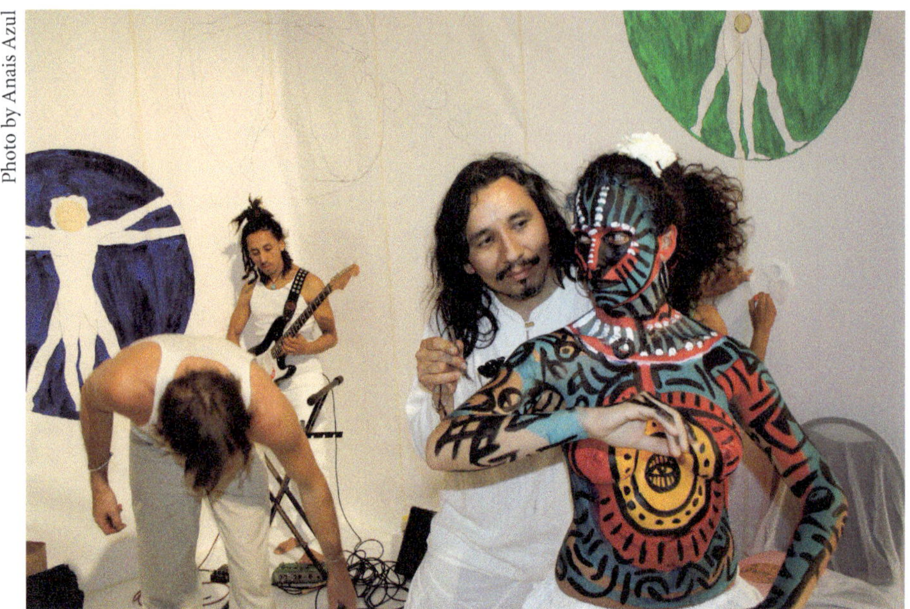

The Genie, Todd Brown, Adrian, and Sandra Durand
at *ILLUSION* show 2006, SOMArts.

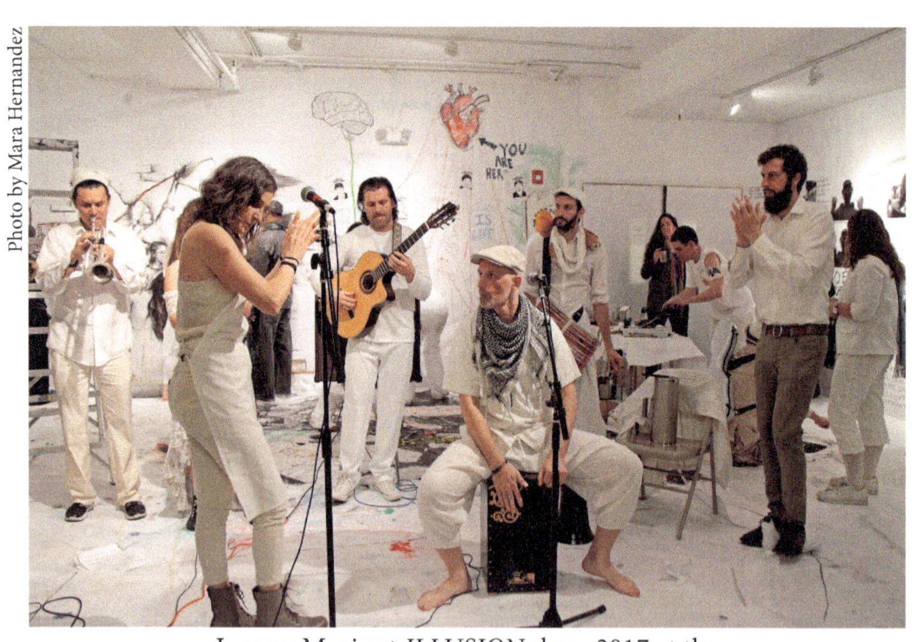

Locura Music at *ILLUSION* show 2017 at the
Mission Cultural Center for Latino Arts Gallery.

DREAMS

DREAM # 0: In this Score, the sky descends to visit the trees and the forest, turned into three bodies that dance to the rhythm of music that comes from the imagination of who dreams. The audience experiences a visual level, where they can almost touch the blue bodies with clouds, and an auditory level, with the string quartet that helps to transport them to a different reality. Dancers: Natan Daskal, Kenya Moses, and Jessica Brown Oviedo. Live music: Amaranth String quartet: Katie von Braun, Abigail Shiman, Erica Zappia, and Helen Newby. As part of the Art in Nature Festival at the Oakland Redwoods Regional Park, 2015.

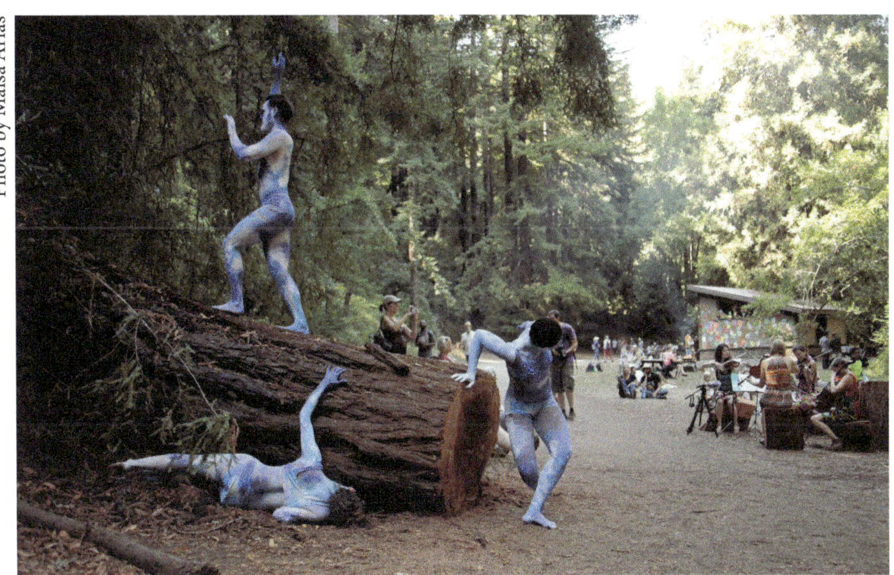

Photo by Maisa Arias

DREAM # 3: Score that explores the identity and ethnicity through a dream with the ancestors. I am dreaming that I am in this theater, telling the public about my genetic profile and the problems that arise from living in this country with 54% indigenous blood. Festival of Latin American Contemporary Choreographers, Dance Mission Theater, 2016.

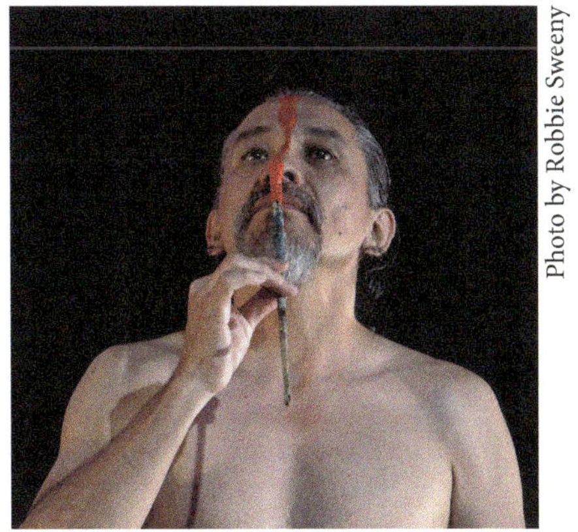

Photo by Robbie Sweeny

From 2014 to 2020, Adrian created more than 20 scores at Anna Halprin's Mountain Studio, with the Anna Halprin Lab and also independently. Many have become part of his DREAMS series.

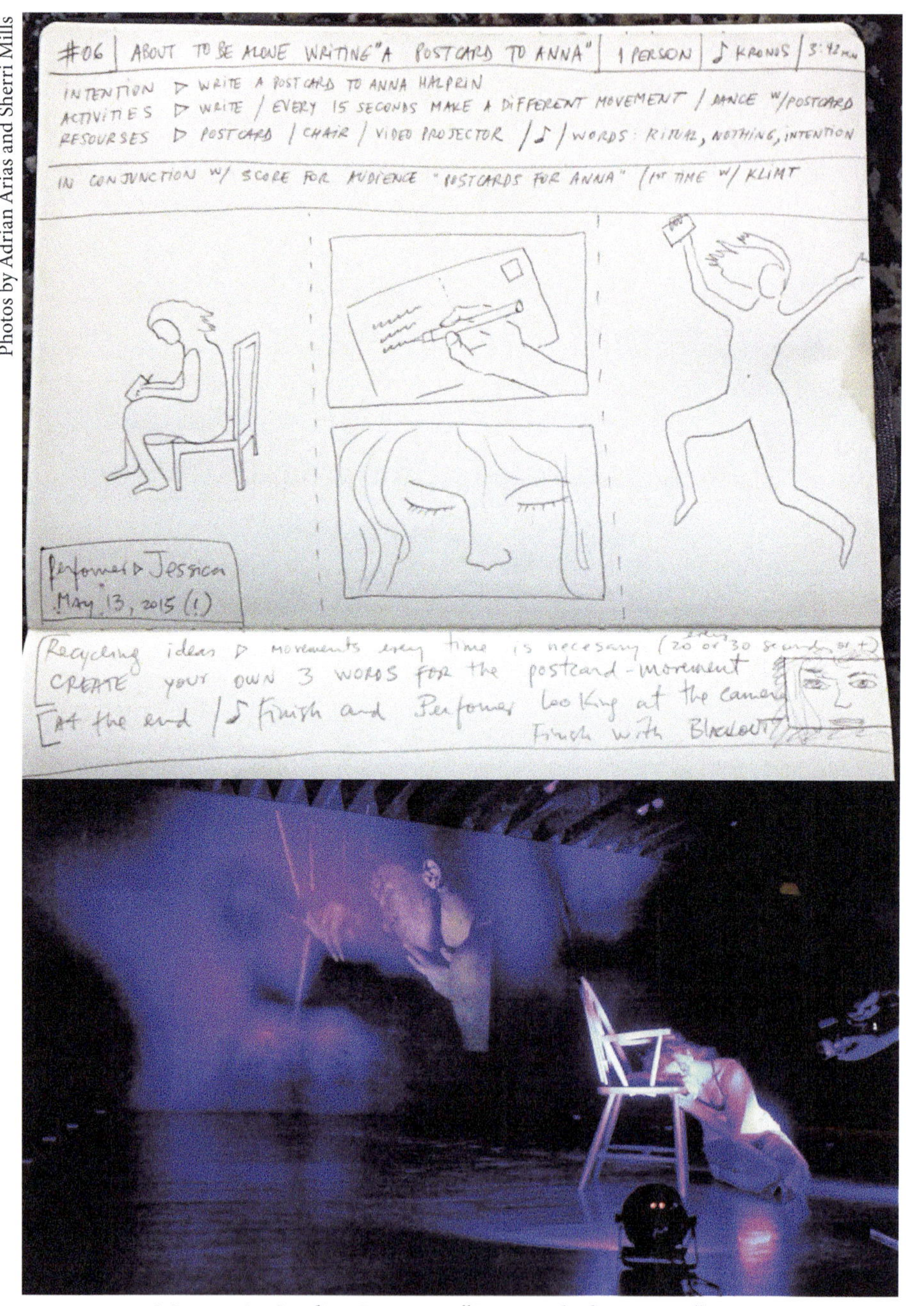

Mountain Studio. Score #6, "Postcards for Anna," 2015.

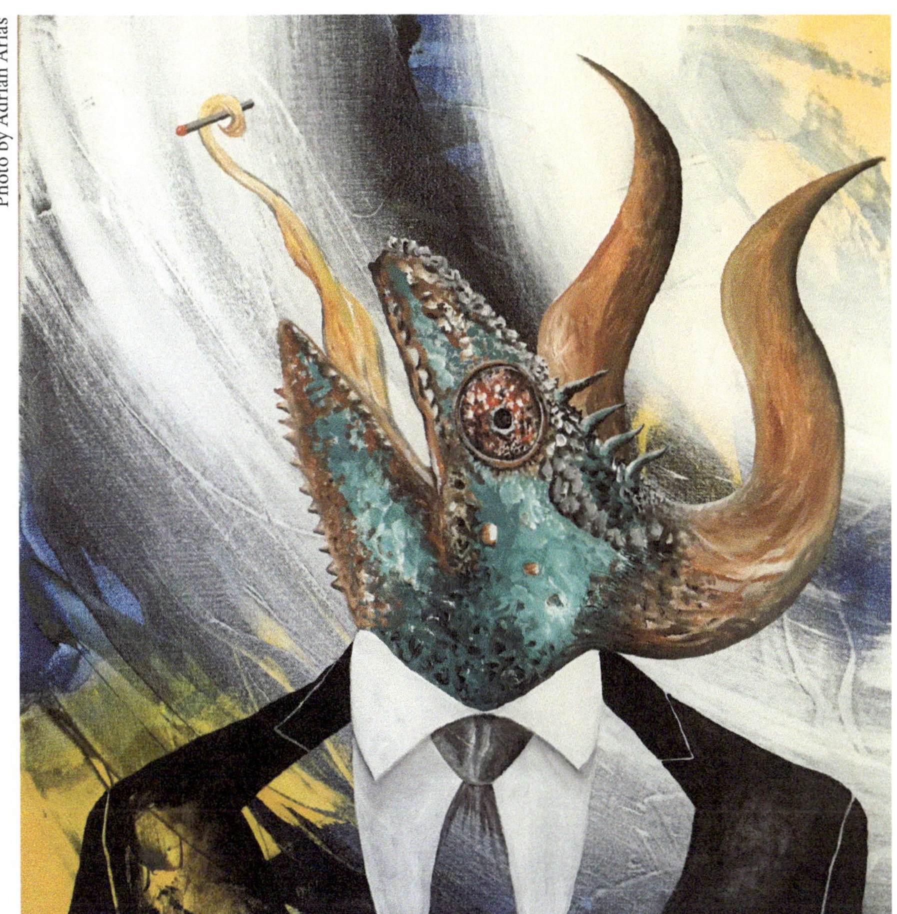

"Fantastic Animal #5," acrylic on canvas, 24 x 24 inches, in pandemic, 2020.

Painting and drawing are part of the multidisciplinary weave
that I practice to show my illusions and passions,
to get closer to the zig-zag of the symbols of creation,
those that my ancestors left me in dreams,
and to tell truths that sometimes need to be painted.
Pencils and liquid paint flowing, like imaginary fish growing in the air,
and my hands full of colors, eyes closed, eyes open.
That's my reality reinvented every day.

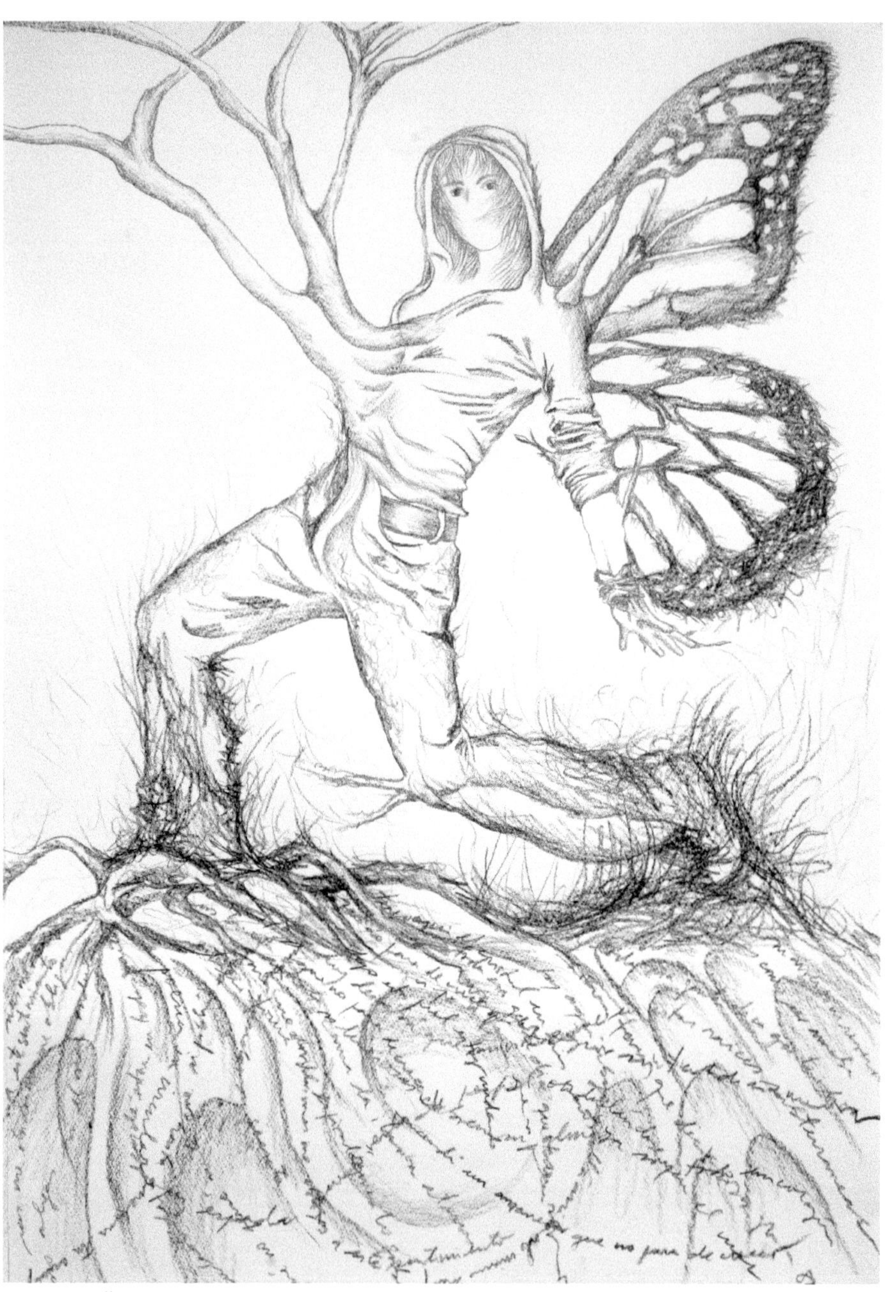

"Hip-Hop Angel," pencil on Arches 300, 24 x 18 inches, 2017.

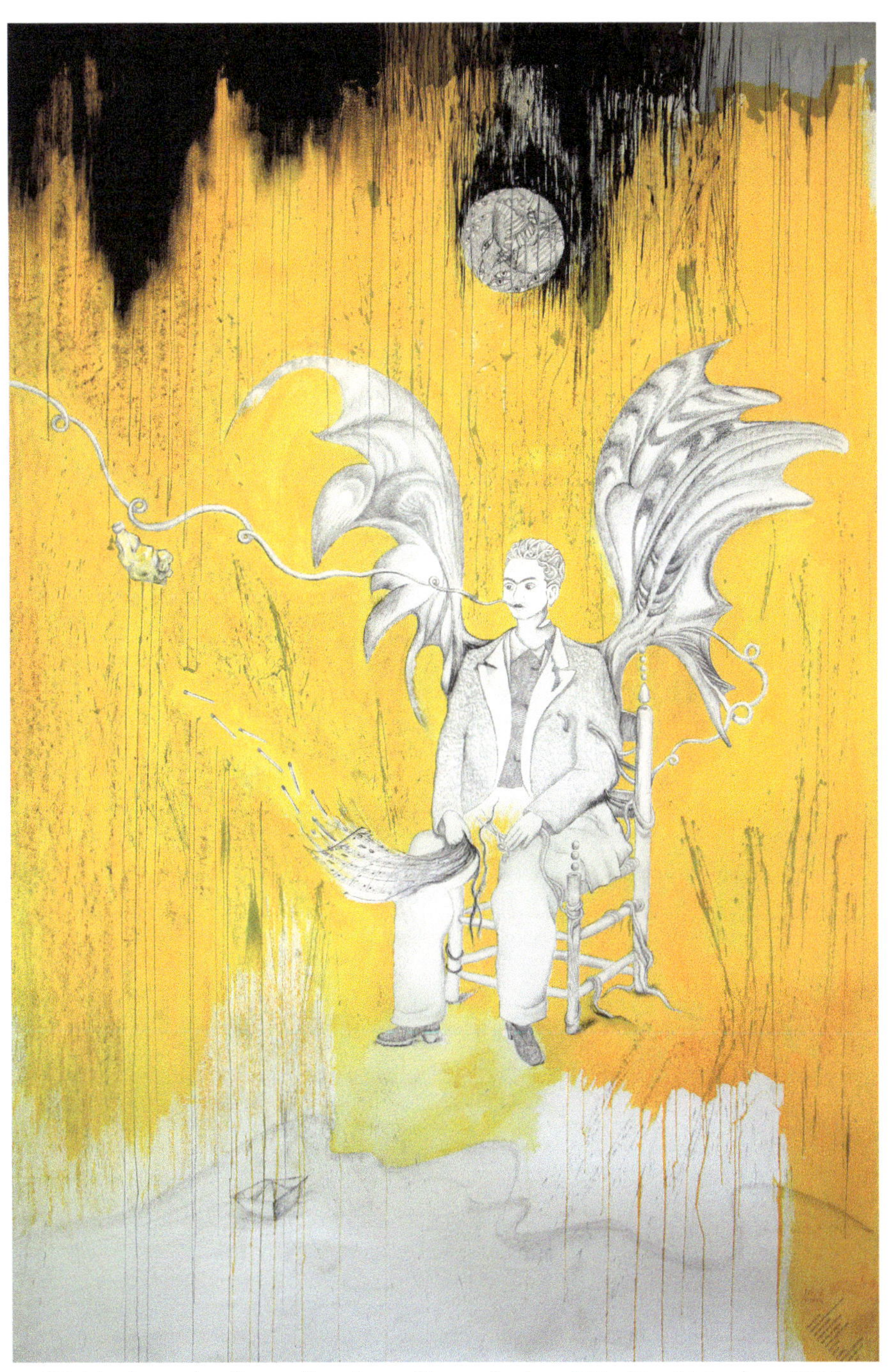

"Frida dreaming," pencil and acrylic on Arches 300, 48 x 80 inches, 2014.

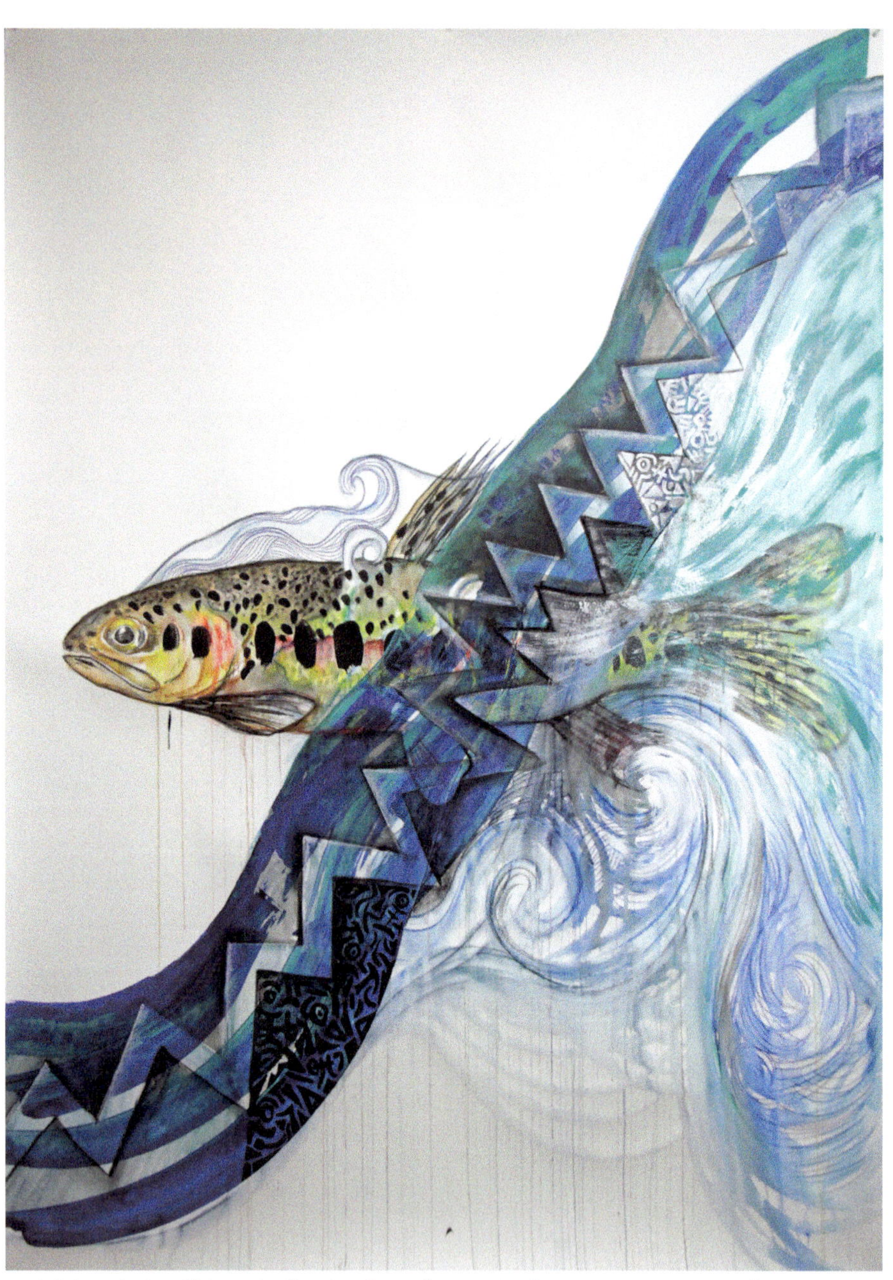

Adrian Arias, "Traveler," mixed media on Arches 300, 51 x 70 inches, 2022. Recently acquired by the San Francisco Arts Commission for placement in the Alameda Creek Watershed Center.

Avotcja
A LIFE IN POEMS

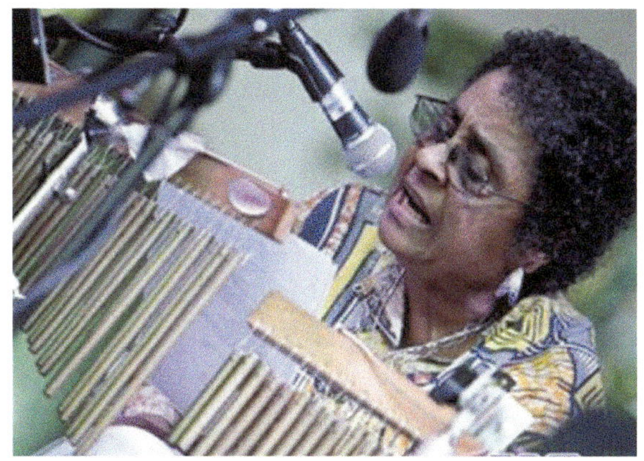

Avotcja is an award winning poet, multi-instrumentalist, and popular Bay Area DJ with weekly radio shows on KPFA and KPOO. She's been widely published in English and Spanish in the USA, Mexico, and Europe.

She has shared stages with leading poets and musicians such as Sonia Sanchez, Janice Mirikitani, Michael Franti, Rahsaan Roland Kirk, Bobi & Luis Cespedes, John Handy, Nikki Giovanni, and many others.

She's been featured at AfroSolo, San Francisco's Carnival, Asian-American Jazz Festival, New York's Henry Street Settlement Theater, and elsewhere. Her poetry and music have been performed by dance groups, and she performs frequently with her group Modúpue.
avotcja.org

CON UNA PALMA EN EL ALMA
Avotcja

Nací
Ahogando en un Lago de lágrimas
Encarcelada
En la locura de la Ciudad de Nueva York
Nací una Poéta enojada
Frustrada
Una Chiquitita
Nadando por el cemento
Una Jibarita de la Ciudad
Vagabundeando por las Calles duras
Detenida
una grandisima maldición
Nacida
Por falta de la belleza de la naturaleza
Erá
Una Chamaquilla atrevida
Mi vida perdida
En un mundo encementado
Desesperada, pero optimista
Un enigma metaforica
Con una Palma en el alma
Y
Una Pluma en la mano

Los Ancianos me dijieron
Cuando erá un sueño
Mi vida fue escrito en un Poema ancestral
Y
Como una Flor rompiendo el cemento
Nací
Una fuerza irrefrenable
Floreciendo
Como un rayo de esperanza
Adentro de
Miles de los desmoralizados
Vení
Un ensueño llena de picardía
Volando
Una Bomba de palabras

Y
Una ternura poética
Llegué con una Palma llamandome
Y una Pluma cantando mi nombre

Nací
Tirando Poemas melodicas
A mi manera de curar la locura de la Ciudad
Ablandando corazónes perdidos en egoísmo
Y
Rompiendo el cemento
En la mente de la insensible
Ahorita … hoy día
Me encuentro una Jibara de la Ciudad
Tirando Flores alquimisticas
Una soñadora, vieja pero rebelosa
Con una pluma en la mano
Y
Una luz irrefrenable

Vengo
Una tejedora de palabras
Con Poesía escrito en mis huesos
Yo soy una viejita atrevida
Una luchadora romantica
Siempre
Rompiendo el cemento, armada con creatividad
Una Jibara de la ciudad soy yo
Con
Un fuego encendido en el corazón
Apasionada, profunda, decidida
Caminando
Andando a cámara lenta
Mi Pluma en la mano
Y
Una Palma en el Alma

Yo soy
Una Poéta hasta el fin
Cansada sí, pero
Todavía
Tirando Flores poéticas

Y
Metaforas picantes que cantan con sabor a
Sofrito y el Coquí
En la esquina de mi vida
y
La esperanza
Este regalito te doy
Una medicina mística hecho a mano
Una Ofrendita
Pá dar a luz a un nuevo amanecer

———————————

WITH A PALM TREE IN MY SOUL

I was born
Drowning in a lake of tears
Imprisoned
In the madness of New York City
I was born an angry Poet
Frustrated
Just another Baby Girl Child
Swimming through the concrete
A City/Country Girl, a Hick
Stuck
a colossal curse
Brought on by the lack of Nature's beauty
I was
An all up in your face little Girl
Life lost
In a World covered with concrete
Hopeless, but hopeful
A metaphoric puzzle
With a Palm Tree in my Soul
&
A Pen in my hand

The Old Folks told me
When I was just a Dream
My life was written in an ancestral Poem
&
Like a Flower breaking through the concrete

I was born
An unrestrainable force
Blossoming
Like a ray of hope
Among the of thousands of demoralized Folks
I came
Full of unabashed lofty idealism
Exploding
A Bomba of words
&
A poetic tenderness
I arrived with a Palm Tree calling me
And a Pen singing my name

I was born
Throwing down melodic Poems
My way of curing the madness of the City
Softening hearts lost in the hardness of egotism
&
Breaking up the concrete in the minds of the hardhearted
Right now … today
I find myself a City/Country Girl
A magical Flower tossing Conjuror
A Dreamer, old but rebellious
With a Pen in my hand
&
An unstoppable glow

I come
A word Weaver
With Poetry written in my bones
I'm a sassy old Lady
A romantic Warrior Woman
Always
Armed with creativity & tearing up the concrete
Still just a City/Country Girl
With
A fire burning in my heart
Passionate, profound, determined
Walking
Moving in slow motion

My Pen in my hand
&
A Palm Tree in my Soul

I am
A Poet to the Day I die
Tired?
Yes I'm tired, but
I'm still tossing poetic Flowers
&
Spicy metaphors that sing to me
Like
The unmistakable taste of
Sofrito & the unforgettable voice of the Coquí
On the corner
Of
My life & hope
This little gift I give to you
A handmade mystic medicine
An offering
To give birth to a brand new Dawn

Taurean Horn Press; First edition (January 2, 2013)

IN LINDA'S HOUSE
World of Our Queen Mother Linda Hill,
First Lady of The House Of UGMA

Pianist/Composer/Arranger/Community Activist Horace Tapscott was an undeniably brilliant catalyst for change & an innovator of the highest order. Tapscott was an ingenious musical magnet, but Linda Hill was not only his main disciple, she was his right arm & his friend. She was always "the" one who was always there & "the" organizer behind the Organization. Tapscott said she was the most talented woman he ever knew & called her Lino. I say, she was an unavoidable power source & an off the Richter scale Piano player's Pianist. Linda was a strikingly beautiful, big boned, dashiki wearing, head as bald as a baby's behind example of African American pride. I always remember her wearing the biggest hoop earrings I had ever seen. Linda scared most folks to death, but she introduced us to the true interdependence of life!

Linda was a for real Amazon. She was also a no nonsense, straight shooter & an unassuming motivator. It all began in her small apartment. Her place was so full of Music & big dreams that we never thought of it as just an apartment. It was the center of existence. It was our umbilical cord. Home was always "Lino's Pad." And it was her house & her dedicated quiet brilliance that was the true glue that held us all together. And believe me when I tell you she was no ordinary glue … she was a one of a kind type of Sistah. She was a professional Nurse & a full time Mother & that background manifested itself in every move she made. Even though she was not much older than most of us & a lot younger than some of the others, she was our Mama!!!

Linda was stronger than metal & as soft as was necessary whenever it was necessary to be soft. The woman was tough! She had to be or we would have never survived, because we were one strange unlikely group of characters … a whole lot of "anything you wanna." We came to L.A. from everywhere & every thing. We were high class, middle class & a whole lot of no class. Music, the Word, the Dance, our Art was our religion & the sacredness of sound was our only common denominator.

And Music … our Music was everywhere. Music bounced off our every thought & action. We played Music before we ate, while we were eating & then had to have some more Music for dessert. Music was our one & only reason for being alive. It crawled all over the ceiling & was the floor we walked on. It lived in between every board of the floor. Came in out of every corner. Rolled in melodically off the roof top & drifted like a magical spell out of every window.

Linda's house was alive with our Music & we lived to immerse ourselves in its beauty. A beauty full of the mysterious unfolding enchantment of the rebirth of ourselves.

We were obsessed … a wild bunch of creative fanatics. We had been deliberately hand picked … a select crew of chosen people. Some were chosen by fate … some by Horace … others by Linda & eventually by other Musicians. There were so many great Artists that came through UGMA it would take forever to mention them all. But a few of my favorites were Leroy Brooks-Drums, "Black Arthur" Blythe-Alto Saxophone, Jayne Cortez-Poet, Adele Sebastian-Flute, Red Calendar-Bass & Tuba, brothers Butch Morris-Cornet & Wilbur Morris-Bass, Bobby Bradford-Trumpet & Cornet, Ray Draper-Tuba, John Heard-Bass, Rickey Kelly-Vibes, James Newton-Flute, E.W. Wainwright Jr.-Drums & Multi Percussion, John Carter-Alto Sax & Clarinet, Azar Lawrence-Saxophones, Lester Robertson-Trombone, Michael Session-Saxes, David Murray-Tenor Sax & Bass Clarinet, Percy Smith-Artist, Ojenke-Poet, & Everett Brown Jr.-Drums. I was brought into the family on the sly by my friend & brother, Drummer Bill Madison. I can still see & hear us when we had two Guitars, three Basses, two full sets of Drums, a couple of Pianists, a Tuba, a Flute, a Singer, a Dancer & several Saxophones & Trumpets on stage at the same time playing our hearts out. Arrangements straight out of Heaven. Sounding tight, like we were one instrument. We were no joke!!! We were a whole brand new breed … running away from the massive, but lucrative boredom of the Los Angeles studio trivia & a racist Musicians Union. Some of us were "hope to die" traditionalists taking that tradition to a whole new level. Others were coming straight out of the Avant-Garde & played unconventional Musical Masterpieces on traditional & not so traditional instruments. All of us were rebels in search of our own voices.

We took our Music out into the Streets, the Parks, into Public Schools, Libraries, Community Centers & Churches. We played everywhere the people were, including innumerable Festivals & Night Clubs, but we always came back home. Home was where the action was! We made Music every single day non-stop on soda bottles, played intricate polyrhythms on Linda's kitchen pots, Pablum boxes & anything else we could get our hands on. And Music bounced off everything, crawled up out of the alley in back of her house & fell out of the sky like comets & shooting Stars. And like clockwork, amazing tunes came racing out of the uncharted universe of our imaginations. Music was the language of our Souls, the blood in our veins. Our Music was a life force all its own. And Linda's house was the center of our existence … the home of The Pan Afrikan People's Arkestra … The House of UGMA (The Underground Musicians' Association). Linda's place was the nursery that gave birth to it all. And even when we outgrew the confines of Linda's small South Central apartment & moved over to Percy's wonderful large house on Figueroa, Linda came & remained our Matriarch.

Everyone talks (and rightfully so) about Horace Tapscott & the UGMA, but none of it would have happened without Linda. Linda … a big beautiful dark chocolate Piano playing singing giant of a woman. Linda … Linda Hill … Linda the High Priestess of The Pan Afrikan People's Arkestra & UGMA. Linda … an ebony Queen, who opened her heart, soul & home to a musical movement. A woman who's faith, love & home gave us a home & helped create a dynasty, an unstoppable wave of brave new school Musicians. Yes, it was the strength of Horace's dream—The magical pull of Papa Horace … he was the magnet that pulled us in. But it was the Music & the organizational magnitude of our Matriarch Linda that was the loving glue that held us together & kept us whole.

Thank you will never be enough. I'm still just another hard working Artist … a Musical Poet. Just another number in a long parade of the multitude she helped to create. I have nothing to give to repay the debt for all she gave, but the gift of this short story. It's my way of making sure the world will never forget her & her contributions to the history of this great American Art Form called Jazz. It was from the womb of her house that musical history was disemboweled & reformed & traditional miracles bathed in pride were reclaimed & reborn.

The healing powers of Music ran all over the ceiling of Linda's house like it ran all over our lives & was poured into our hearts with every sound from the streets that brought us to her door.

And a brand new seriously dedicated army of Music Makers was forever changed.

THIS SISTER AIN'T QUITTING!!!
or
LIFE DODGIN' THE MARGIN OF ACCEPTABLE RISK

Been living my life on borrowed time
Going to sleep exhausted & I still wake up feeling tired
Beat up & almost knocked down from doing the MS* shuffle
Got tossed around, tricked, caught up & sucked into
What could be my own demise, disguised by
An innocent looking smile on the iron jaws of science
(And any fool knows that science never lies)

But one taste of truth
Forced me to look at their toxic delusions & BLAAAM!!!
I opened my mouth & saw the fake beauty of
All that Mercury staring back at me
Sitting there … just as cold & bold as it wanted to be
An enemy had moved in & made itself at home in my teeth
I was caught, entrapped by a medical fantasy, a Venus Flytrap &
Now all "their" pretty mercury's really got a hold on me

Even after all my shuckin' & jiving & ducking & denying &
Trying to make every kind of outlandish bargain with God
There's still no place I can hide, 'cause
I'm still waking up tired & still finding myself riding
In the Margin of "their" Acceptable Risk
Acceptable? … By who's definition?
Marginal? … Compared to what?
Me? … Are "they" really talking about me? … Not this Sister!!!
Uh, Ugh! … Can't be! … Not me! … But who?
Watch your back, cause there's always some mad scientist
Cooking up some new strange brew in his cauldron of doom &
Dr. Strangelove wants to try it all out on you

"Oh no, can't be!" … "Not here in the land of the free!"
"That kind of stuff just doesn't happen today! But…….?"
Dodging the Margin is acceptable … to who???

When science is God, the margin gets hazy
It's a racket … A scam! … It's a multi-million dollar game
The whole concept is inhumane, it's madness, completely insane
It's crazy!!!

"The Margin of Acceptable Risk"
Is anywhere the powers that be, want it to be &
They want "it" anywhere there's a profit to be made, it's all about
Money, money, money all the way to the grave
Like the so called benevolent syphilis experiment in Tuskegee
Only this time "their" experiment is me &
It's as moveable & obscene as a corporate baron's morality &
As clean as the untested "miracle" of "their" Estrogen dreams
As unasked for & unnecessary as the cruel gift of Agent Orange &
As evil as dumping on unsuspecting Farmworkers
Sitting like ducks, stuck, getting sprayed picking crops
This is a nightmare in real time!!!
And unfortunately, this time it's my time

The "Margin" is a very profitable lie … it's as sick, as sick can go
Look at me, I'm living proof, all this drama ain't no joke
It's anything "the scientific community" claims it to be &
It's whatever "they" claim it to be & as long as it's done for
"Their" financial gain, in the name of "their" progress &
The only real casualties are you, our neighbors & friends & me
Seems to be, The Margin of Acceptable Risk is
Whatever "they" can get away with & "they" get away with it
All the time!!!!!!!

So here I be … still tired … almost whipped
Caught up & all wrapped up
Locked in the temple of some invisible "madman's" technology
Just one more insignificant waste of "their" corporate space,

Another loud mouth expendable Artist
A "marginal" target sitting in the center of "their" bullseye
But, I refuse to go out living my life like some sacrificial lamb
In The Margin of "their" Acceptable Risk
Just a new age human receptacle, a toxic waste dump on legs
Hidden away in some unethical, but
Scientifically acceptable deception

I don't know what "they" been smokin, but my life ain't no joke &
As long as there's one of us strong enough to write this Poem,
I'm gonna be a thorn in all "their" self righteous myths
This Sister wasn't born to quit & even though
I still wake up tired & MS may steal some of my fire,
I plan to live my life right up 'til the day that I die & I know
MS may eventually get the best of me, but until
The White Citizen's Council unanimously elects
A Blue/Black man Imperial Grand Dragon of the Ku Klux Klan
The Margin of Acceptable Risk will continue to be
Completely unacceptable!!!!!!!

Acknowledgments

"In Linda's House" and "This Sister Ain't Quitting!!!" were previously published in *With Every Step I Take,* Taurean Horn Press, 2013.

Lorraine Bonner
FOR WHICH I HAD NO WORDS

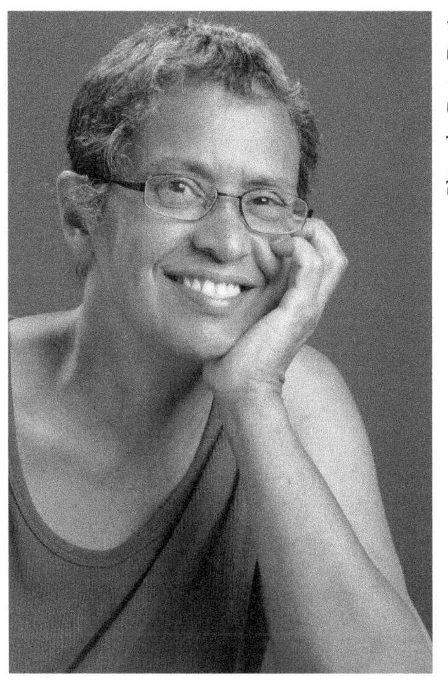

Lorraine Bonner was born in New York.
She had an early aptitude for science and eventually
became a physician. At the age of 38,
suppressed memories of severe childhood sexual abuse
began erupting into her consciousness.

Although she had had no training in art,
within a few years she was drawn to clay,
using it to express experiences and feelings for
which she had no words. Gradually the clay began to
expand her understanding, placing what had
happened to her in the larger context of planetary
betrayal and exploitation.
lorrainebonner.com

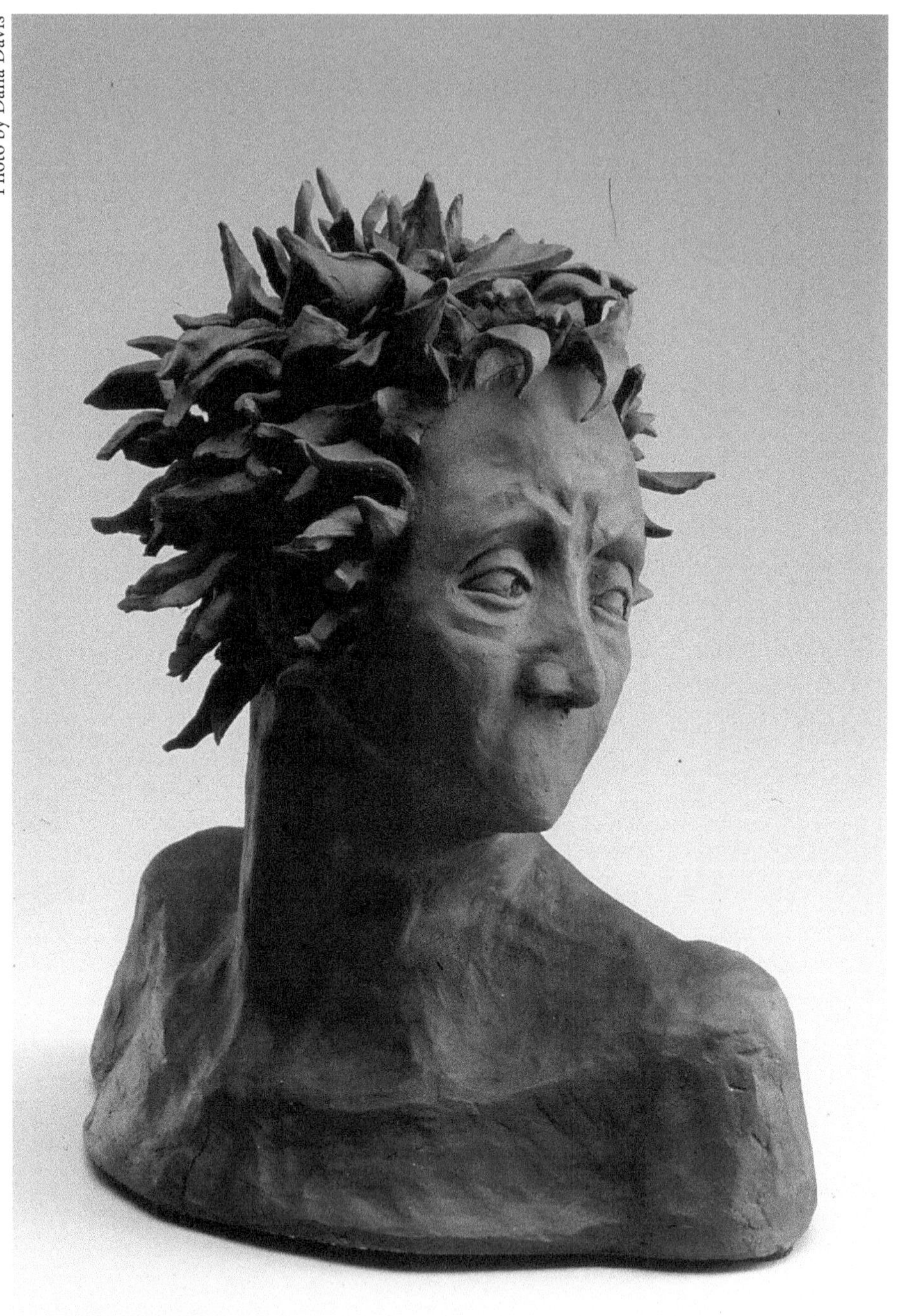

"Inescapable," clay, 15 x 14 x 8 inches, 2003, from the *Perpetrator* series.

SOMEWHAT LONGER THAN BRIEF BIO
Lorraine Bonner

I came up in New York City, in a part of the borough of Queens called Jamaica. The first day of kindergarten we had to draw a picture to identify our cubby. I think I drew some kind of stick figure, but the kid next to me drew this intricate spider web. I looked at his and looked at mine, and knew in that instant that he was an artist and I was not. After that, I never even tried.

I did write all through elementary and junior high. The adults were supportive; in this Black community I was one of the "Talented Tenth" on whom the hopes of the race were pinned. But when I got to high school, one of a tiny minority in an all white school, my writing wasn't good enough, and I stopped.

I had always been interested in science. I spent a couple of summers in a high school biology program at a top research facility in New York. I began to dream of a career as a researcher in molecular biology and winning a Nobel Prize for uncovering the secrets of immunity.

The guidance counselors in high school had been supportive, but when I got to college I realized I was on my own, an even tinier minority in a vast sea of whiteness. At the same time I realized there was something wrong with me, nothing specific, but insistent. In early childhood I had practiced self-injury. I began again in college. I cared nothing for the social interactions that seemed so important to the people around me. I acted normal, but inside I was hiding. I did start writing again.

By the middle of my junior year, I could no longer hold it together and dropped out of school.

Things got worse, but I was able to keep writing. I thought I was going to die, and if I did, it wouldn't matter if I wrote or not, but if I lived and kept writing, I would be a better writer. After a year I went back to school and was eventually admitted to a mental hospital. In the hospital I began writing poems, which I showed to no one.

When I got out of the hospital I got a job as a reporter for a Black weekly newspaper. It was the first time I had an editor, someone who cared about my writing. They were paying me to write better, and I was eager to learn. I remain grateful to have had this opportunity. This job also opened my mind to the revolutionary fervor that was gripping the Black community in those days.

But I was also getting restless and tired of the East Coast. I wanted to go to California.

One day I met two young Black men who had been traveling cross country and were about to return home to California. I decided to go with them. I ended up living in a redwood forest in Sonoma with one of them, going to classes at Sonoma State, and living an idyllic hippie lifestyle. We decided to have a baby, but soon after I got pregnant, the estate we were living on as caretakers was sold and we were evicted.

Like everyone we knew, we were studying socialism, especially African socialism. We were homeless, on welfare, and feeling bitter about a country that would permit the eviction of a pregnant person. We decided to get married and find a better place to have our baby.

My husband was an anthropology major and was able to arrange for our trip to be a field study. We chose Tanzania because at that time it was practicing the purest form of African socialism, known as Ujamaa. When we got to Tanzania I was about seven months pregnant, and our daughter was born in Dar es Salaam, the Harbor of Peace.

We lived in the African part of the city and worked on becoming fluent in Swahili. When the baby got a little older we traveled around the country, studying Swahili, living on financial aid, and writing back reports on our observations.

As our daughter approached her first birthday, we had to decide whether to stay in Tanzania or return to the US to pick up the struggle. I knew I could not get back into research, but I thought I could probably go to medical school. My husband was uncertain but was considering law.

We made our way back to the West Coast, and I started medical school as our daughter was turning two. We had another child at the end of my second year. During my third year I learned to meditate, but I didn't have any time to write.

After my internship year I took a class in journaling, which opened me up to writing all over again. I developed a daily writing practice and one year wrote a poem a day. As I began working as a doctor, I wrote a book about my experiments attempting to practice medicine collaboratively with my patients.

Eventually I began to realize that my marriage wasn't working and we split up. Soon after the separation, at a meditation retreat, I got a memory of my father molesting me as an infant. Over the next few years more and more memories came—of torture, other men, other children, cameras.

My life was torn apart. I didn't know who I was anymore, who my parents were, how did no one know what was going on, how had I survived? At the same time, other elements of my life now made sense: the self-injuring I did as a child, or the breakdown in college.

I couldn't work and I had to stop meditating. I plunged into therapy, body work, groups—I read everything. There wasn't much relief.

Then a friend gave me a bag of clay, and little figures started emerging from my fingers telling things I had no words for. I started getting interested in the clay itself, and the clay led me to an understanding that what had happened to me was a microcosm of much larger systems of exploitation. My personal was political. I had become an artist after all.

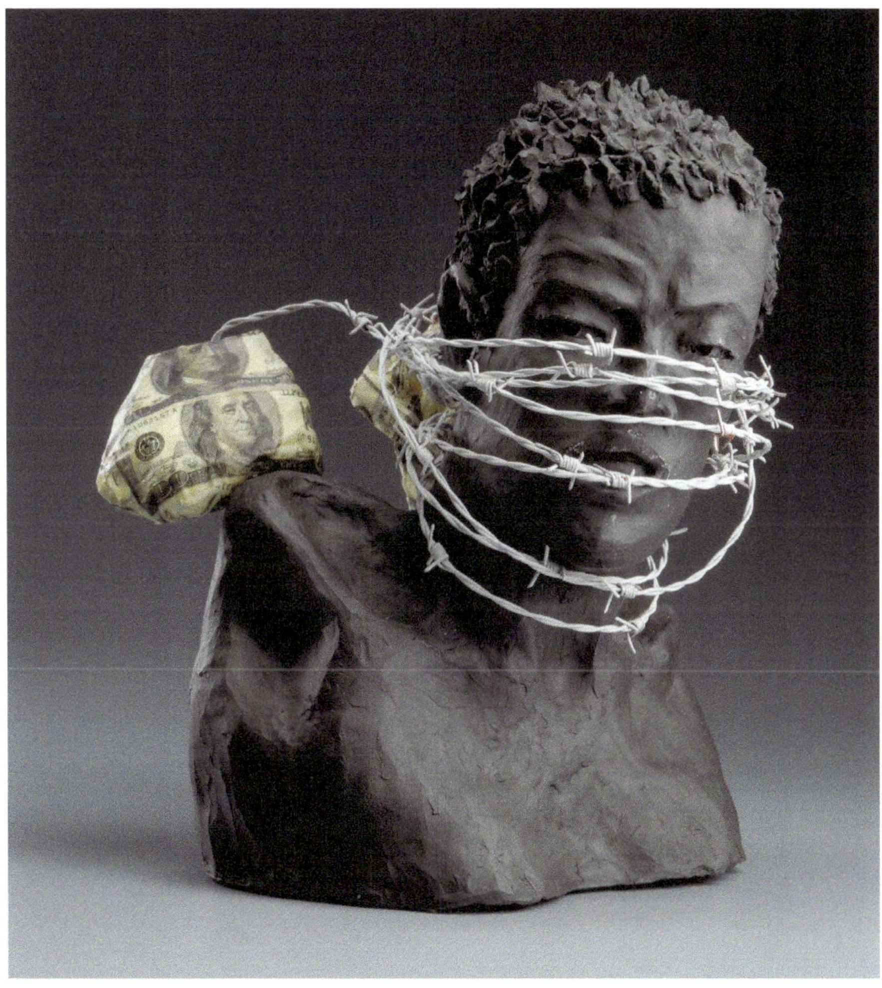

"Benjamins," clay, barbed wire, $100 bills, 16 x 11 x 15 inches, 2010, from the *Perpetrator* series.

IN RESPONSE TO TRAUMA

I began doing art in response to trauma. The earliest work became the Perpetrator series. A perpetrator is not some bad guy in a cop show. I use the term perpetrator to mean someone who has betrayed a trust. Since social living is based on trust, a perpetrator is by definition, anti-social. Born or made? I say both.

I have studied the perpetrator, in the external world and internalized in my own mind. I have memories that live in my body like stones. My mind and heart have been fragmented. Sometimes when I try to express my feelings of hurt, rage and frustration, I end up hurting myself. It feels like there is no escape, and what I am feeling, the whole world is feeling. I was desecrated as a child, whole nations have been enslaved or exterminated, the Earth herself is torn open, her beautiful creations destroyed.

It wasn't always like this. We know from the memories of indigenous elders that there was a time when people lived in harmony with one another and within the world. We see it in disasters, such as when people who have been forced from their homes form encampments, and simply help one another.

But there are those who are insatiable, believing that their god has given them the right to devour everything and everyone, including every one of us here today. Theirs is a religion of supremacism, white over black, male over female, mind over body, human over the Earth. They dull our minds with

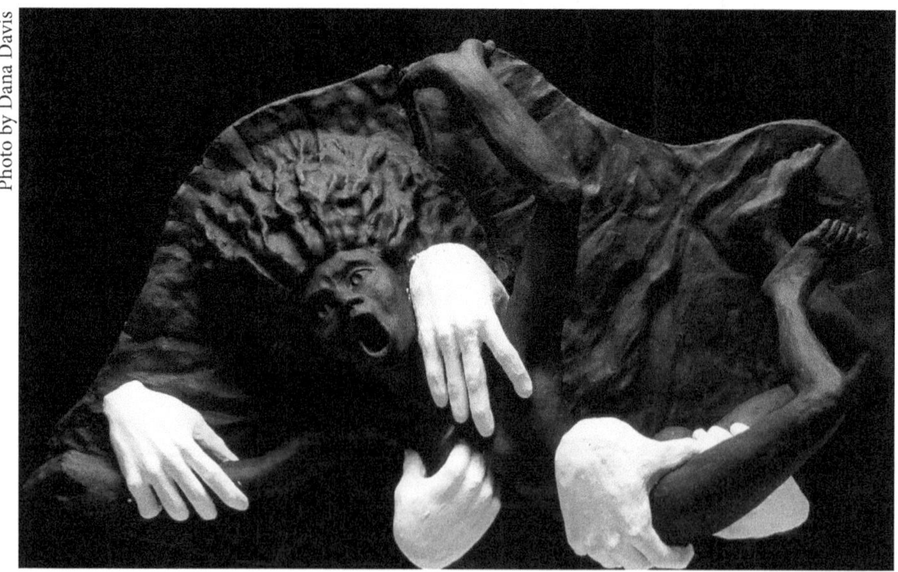

"World Trade," clay, 8 x 30 x 20 inches, 2002, from the *Perpetrator* series.

drugs and flickering images on screens, which we accept, because it eases the pain a bit. They tell us that theft and violence and lies are part of human nature, but we know this is not true because we hate lies and theft and violence.

When I learned about trauma, I realized that just as I had internalized the perpetrator, I could also extract him—pull out these supremacist lies and see them for what they are. I began looking and listening for new sources of information, for comrades along the way. I became an explorer in a new vision of the world.

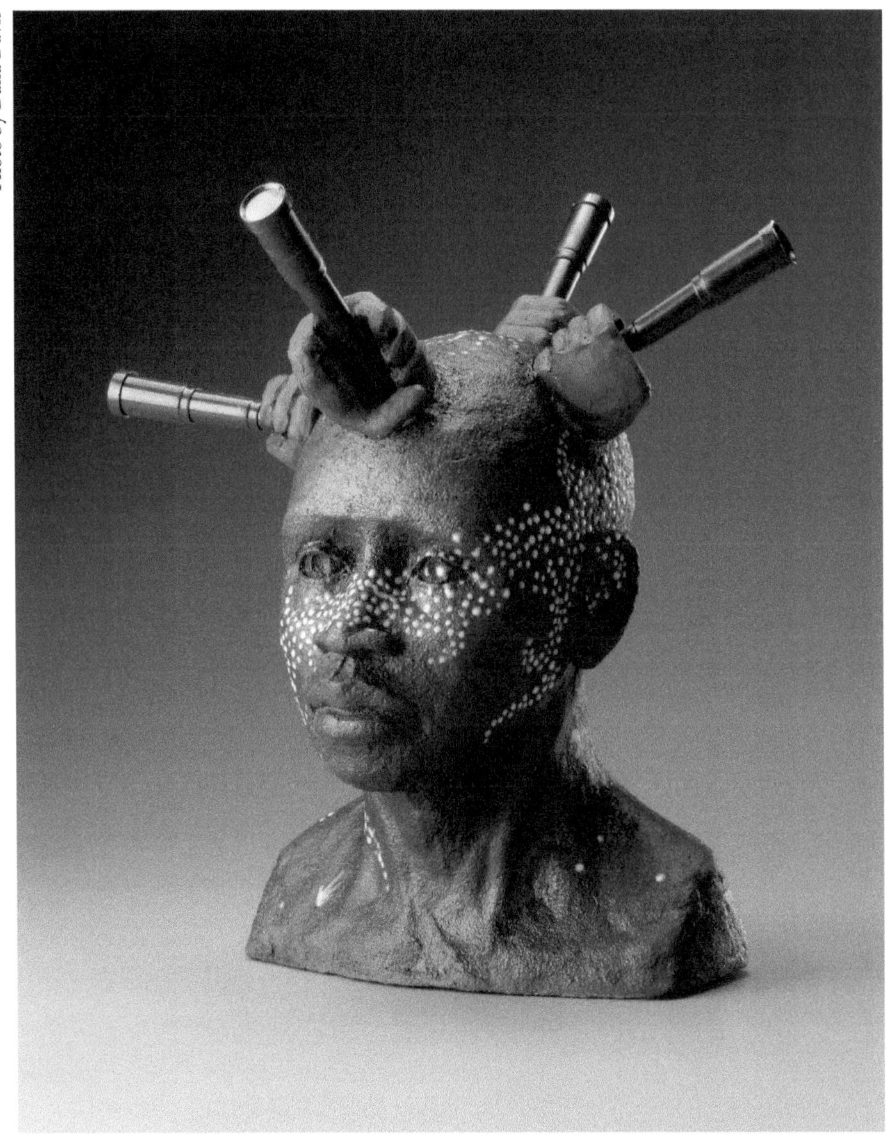

"Explorer," clay, telescopes, glow-in-the-dark paint, 14 x 10 x 10 inches, 2009.

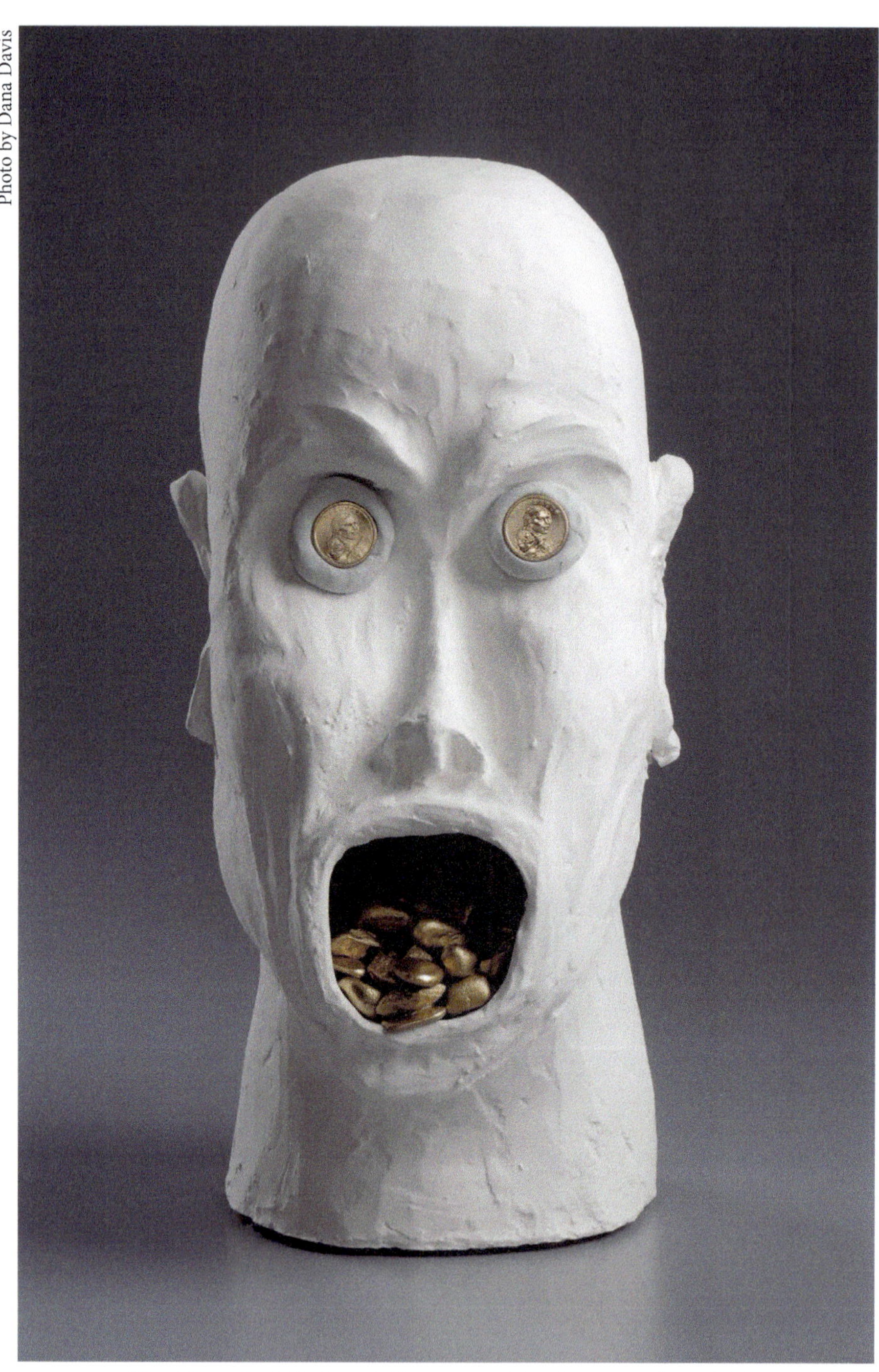

"Eat Your Gold," clay, dollar coins, 18 x 9 x 11 inches, 2011.

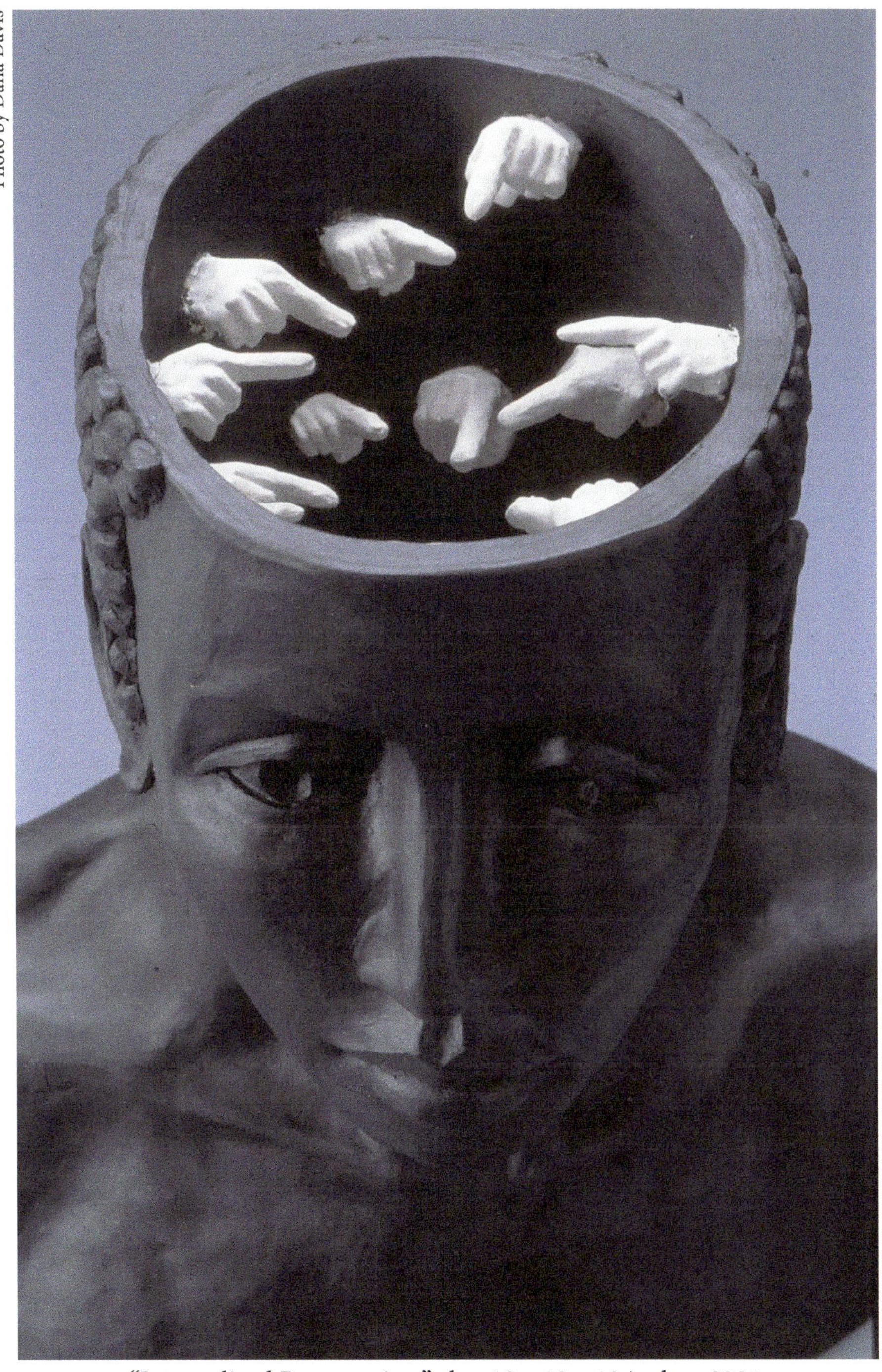

"Internalized Perpetration," clay, 13 x 13 x 10 inches, 2001,
from the *Perpetrator* series.

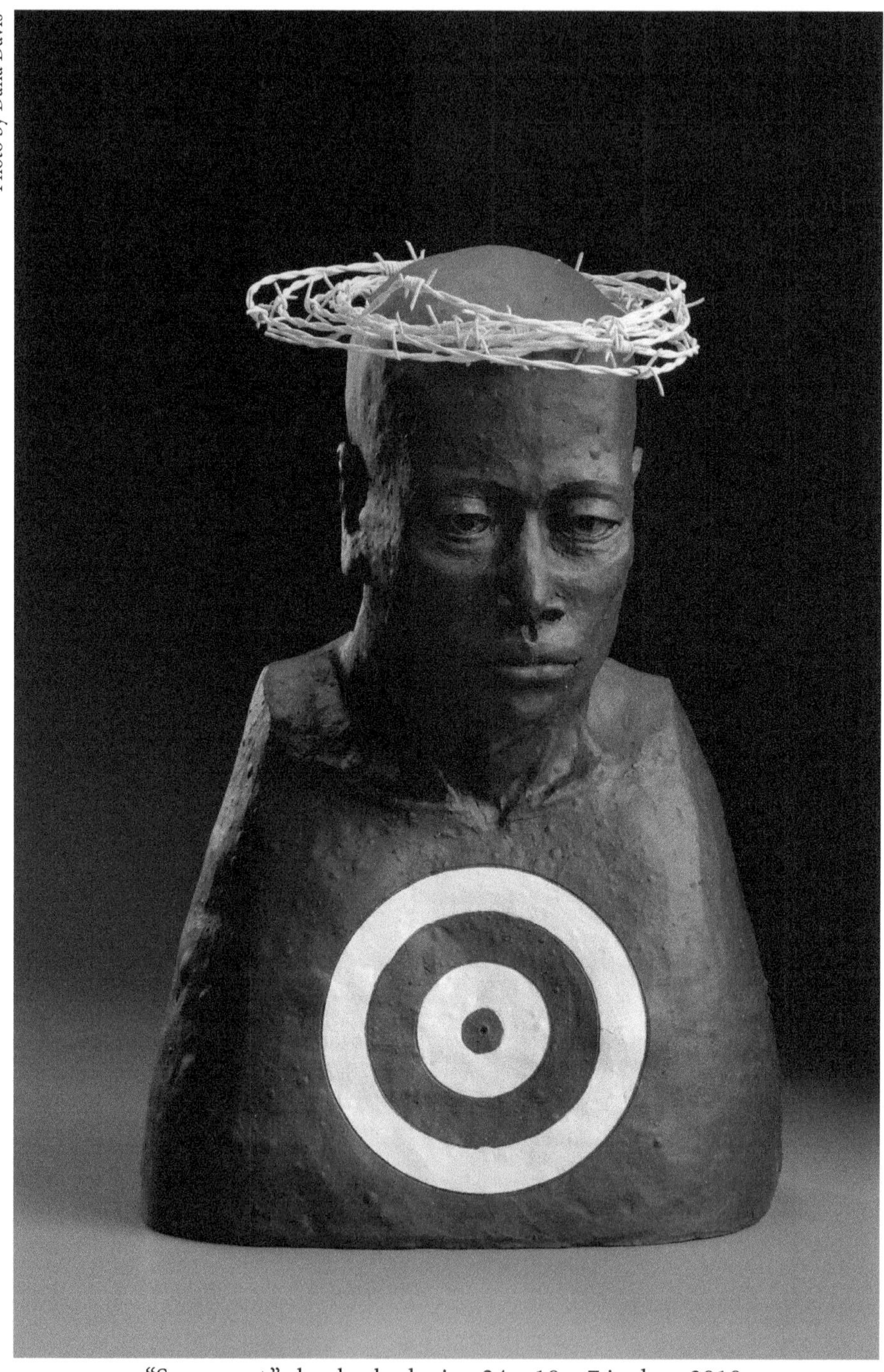

"Scapegoat," clay, barbed wire, 24 x 10 x 7 inches, 2010,
from the *Perpetrator* series.

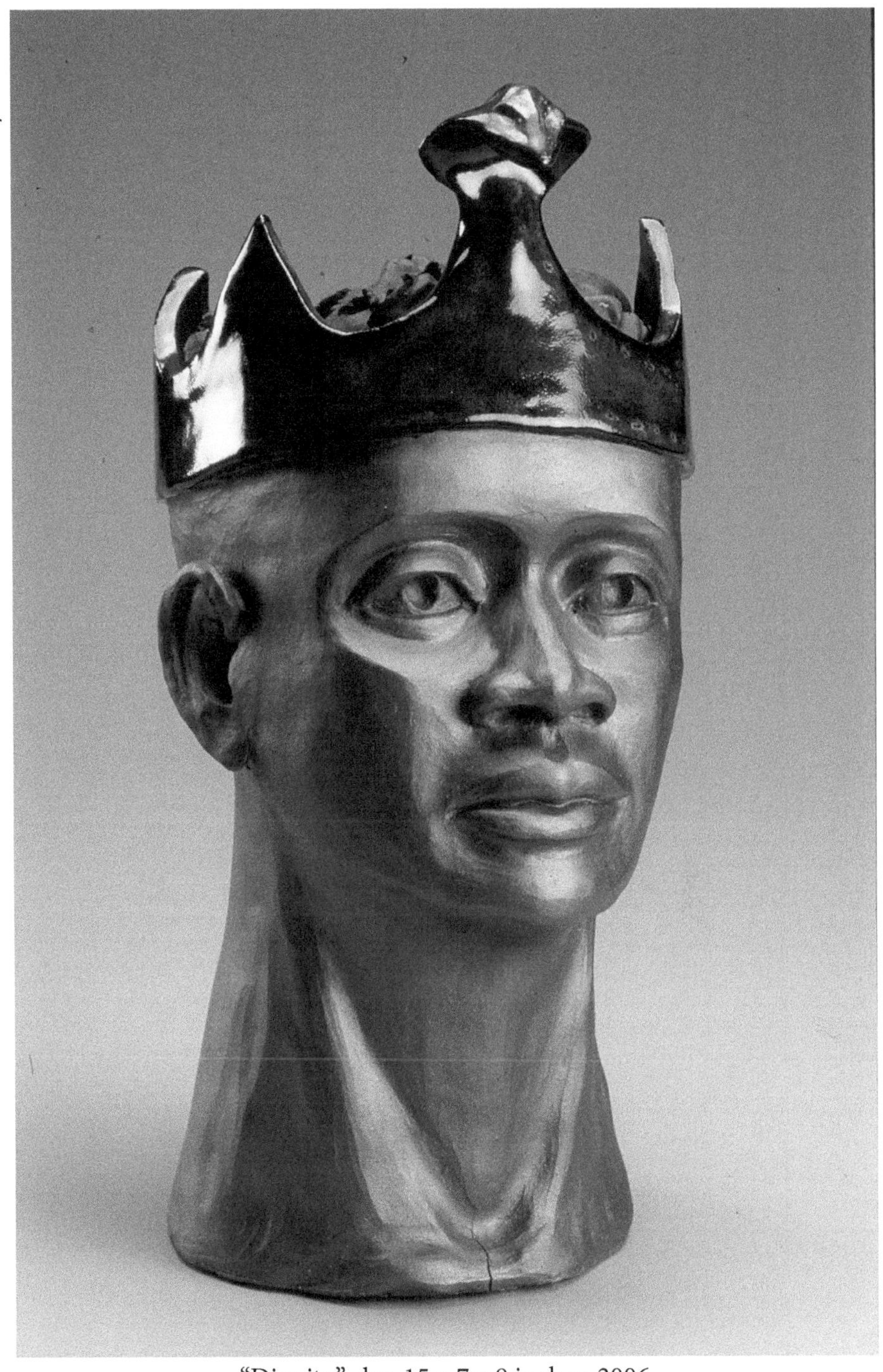

"Dignity," clay, 15 x 7 x 9 inches, 2006.

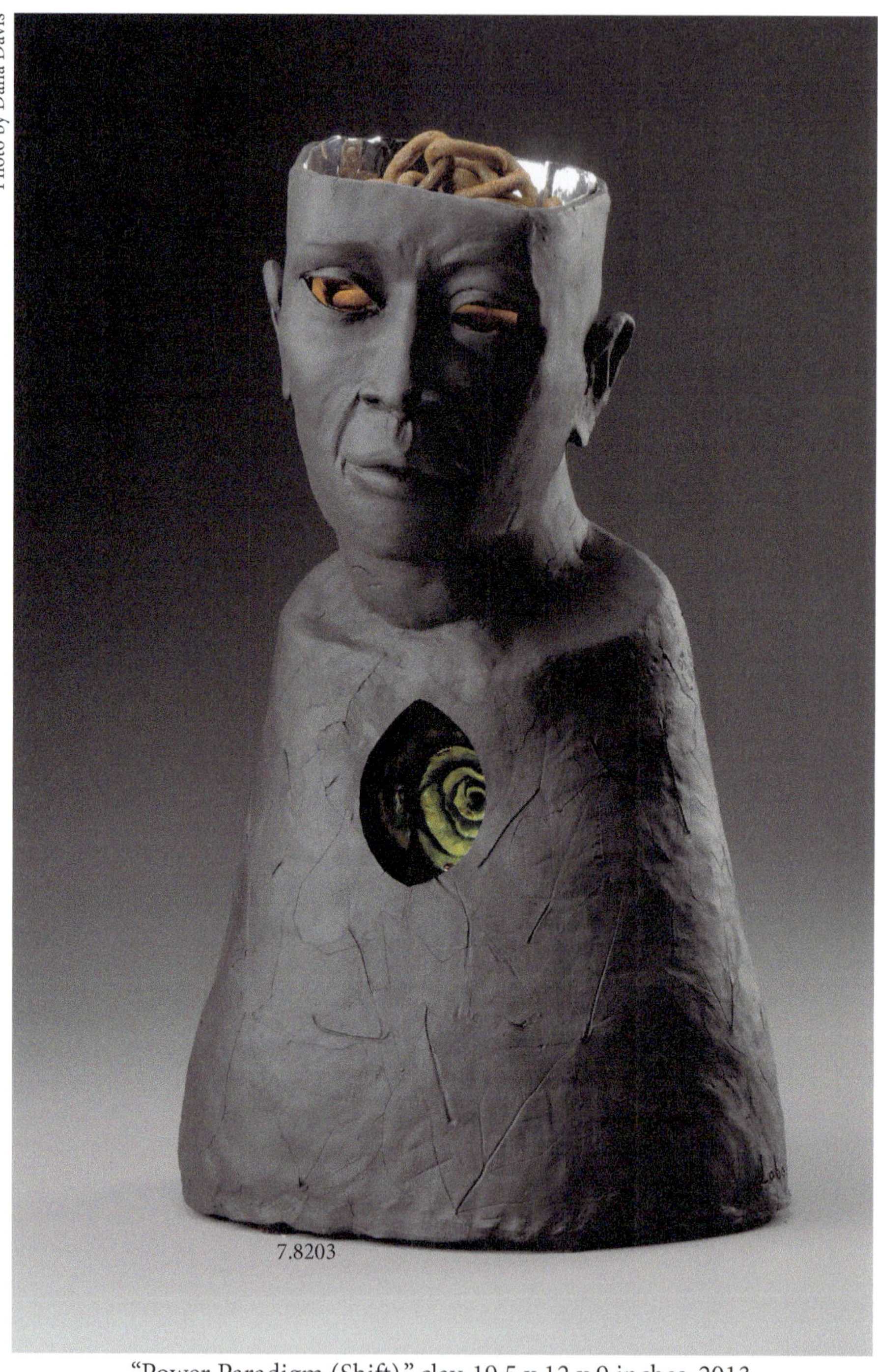

"Power Paradigm (Shift)," clay, 19.5 x 12 x 9 inches, 2013.

I had been using black and white clay for the perpetrator series, but clay comes in many shades of brown, from very light to very dark, tinged with reds or yellows. I began experimenting with different colors of clay. The piece "Multi-Hued Humanity Frees Black From the Weight of White" showed me I was on the right track.

The first time I showed this piece, a young man, whose skin was a luscious cocoa color, protested that it looked as if Black people have no agency in our liberation. I pointed to one of the clays in the hand and said, this color is you, we are all these hands. This foot is not Black people, these chains are not white people. We are all, regardless of our social labels, so-called white people, so-called black people, all of us part of a multi-hued humanity.

I returned to the ceramic supply stores again and again, sampling various colors of clay, figuring out how to build with them so the colors would be both discrete in some places, merged in others, so that anyone walking up to the sculpture could find their own skin color somewhere in the piece. Many of the sculptures gave me poems:

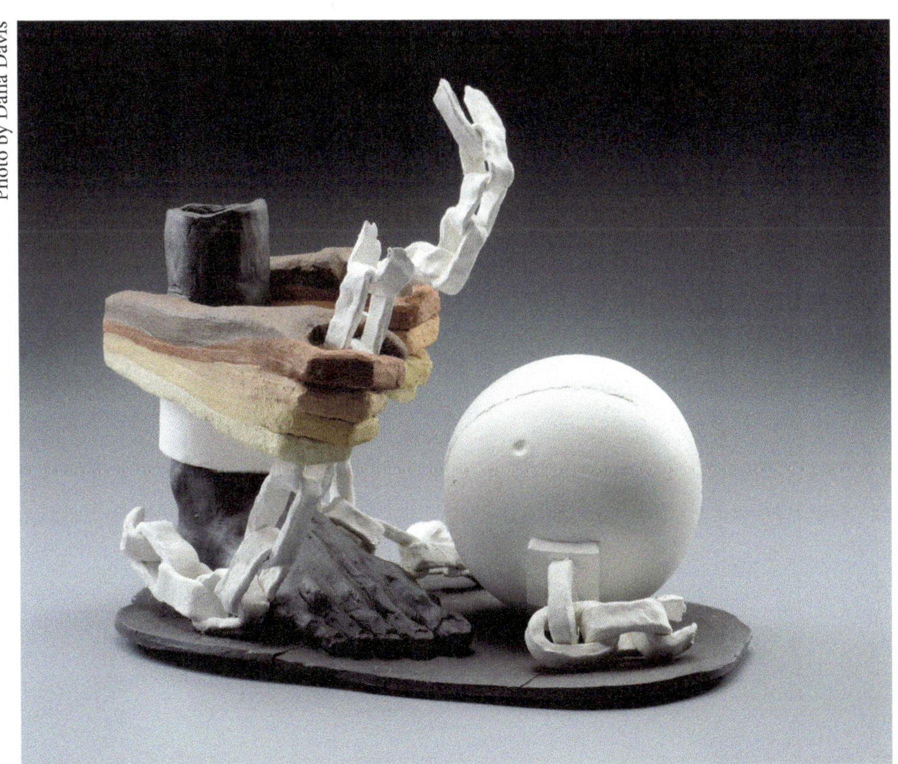

"Multi-Hued Humanity Frees Black from the Weight of White," clay, 13 x 18 x 12 inches, 2014, from the *Multi-Hued Humanity* series.

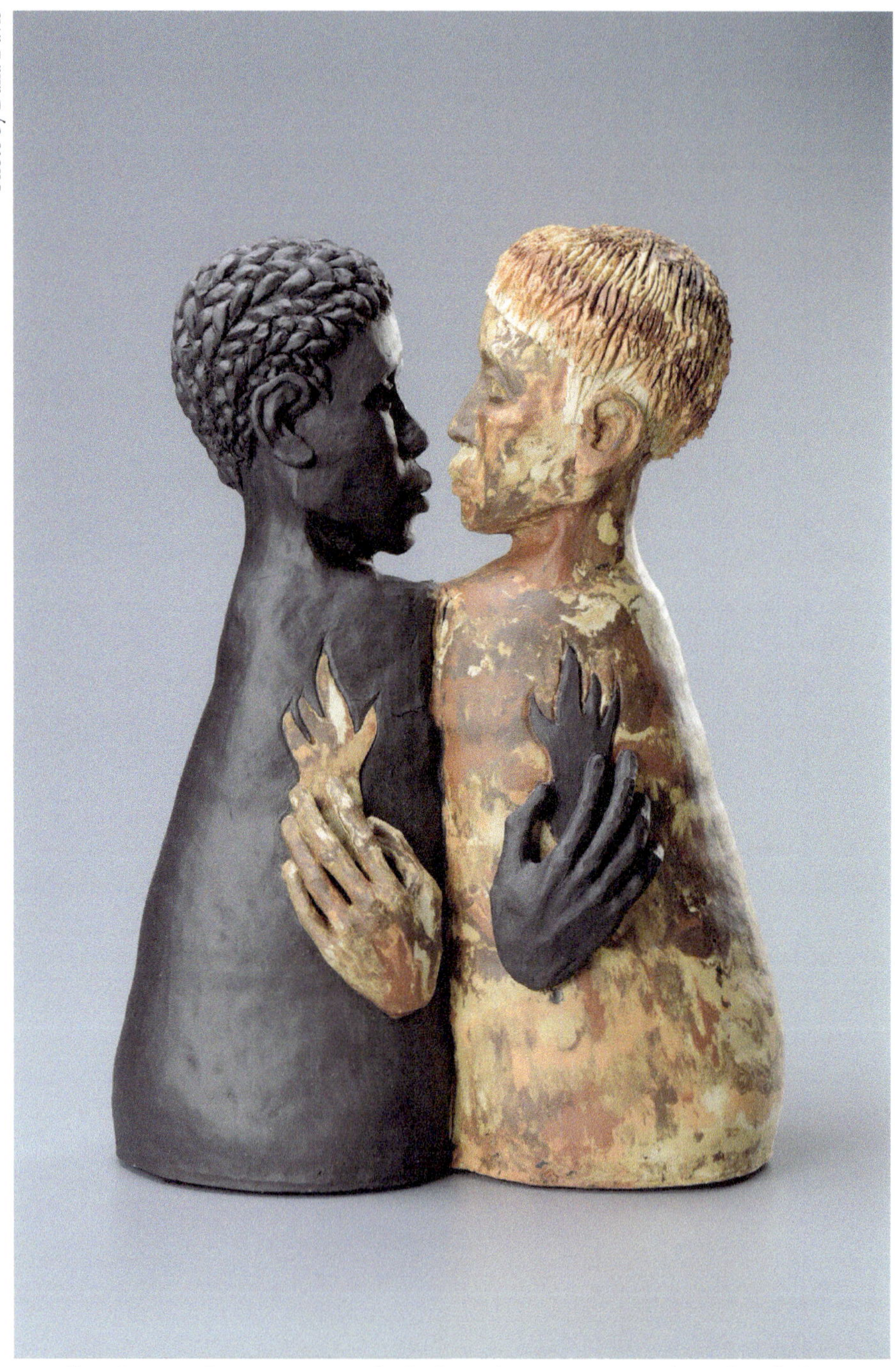

"Multi-Hued Humanity and Black Embrace in Mutual Healing," clay,
21 x 15 x 8 inches, 2015, from the *Multi-Hued Humanity* series.

MULTI-HUED HUMANITY EMBRACE IN MUTUAL HEALING

In the beginning was the Dark
silent and infinite
there was no god
Light arose and entered Dark
and together
they created Everything in Time

In time, Everything created us:
A rainbow of browns
Deep dark umber to pale rosy beige
Multi-hued humanity
Multi-gendered, multi-abled, multi-tongued
Children of Balance

No one knows why a gang
burst out of the family rainbow
tagged white
all over every home and mind
Beat down Black
treated Earth like dirt
treated dirt as if
it were not their mother

Who are these people?
We multi-hued struggle to find
a name for them
The gang claiming white

How lonely they must be!

They burn the ground
As they back away

The Multi-hued Humanity work is so aspirational. I loved the hopeful potential, but honestly, it was hard to sustain. Events, including some health issues, pointed me in a different direction.

I began exploring the Japanese art form called Kintsugi, in which broken ceramic pieces are repaired with gold, in keeping with the Japanese tradition of celebrating and even enhancing flaws and brokenness. I realized that both my medical and artwork have grown out of my traumatic childhood, and began reflecting, as I have many times, on the many artistic and spiritual contributions people of African descent have brought to all of humanity.

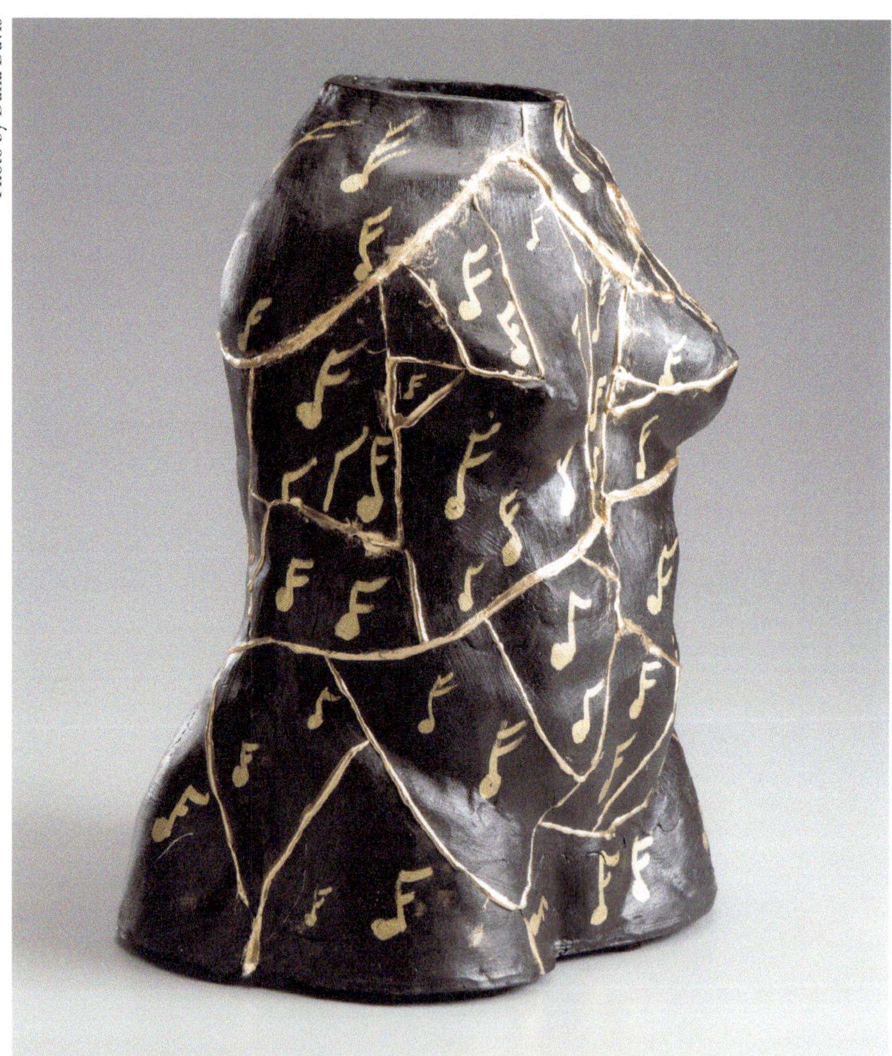

Lorraine Bonner, "Mending: Birth of the Blues," clay, gold, 15 x 11 x 9 inches, 2021, from the *Mending* series.

Karla Brundage
MÉLANGE: MY TRUTH, MY PLACE

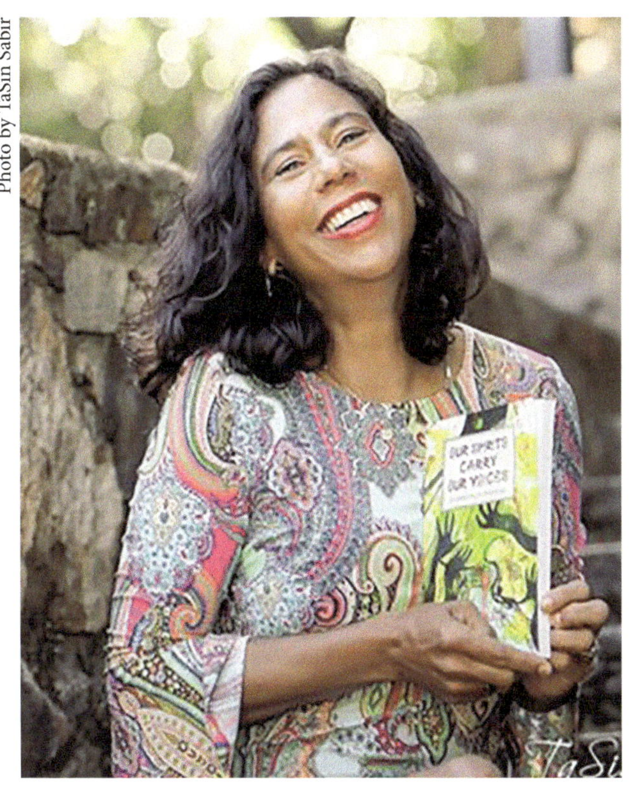

Karla Brundage is a Bay Area based poet, activist,
and educator with a passion for social justice.
She believes that in order to restore balance to earth,
racist structures must be dismantled.
A Pushcart Prize nominee, she is the author of
Swallowing Watermelons and
Mulatta—Not so Tragic. Her work is
found in *Konch, Hip Mama, sPARKLE & bLINK*,
and *MiGoZine*. She is the founder of West Oakland
to West Africa Poetry Exchange.
karlabrundage.com.

MÉLANGE: MY TRUTH, MY PLACE
Karla Brundage

Growing up mixed race in Hawai'i sounds like a cliché, except for my particular mix. In the Hawai'i of the '70s, being part Black and part Caucasian was far from the normal mélange of exotic combinations that are part of the western psyche found in the remote Pacific. While "hapa" is a word commonly used in Hawai'i for those of mixed heritage, this term has traditionally excluded "popolo" (Black) folks. As a child, I was unaware of this, and identified as hapa until I learned that being hapa meant Asian and/or Hawai'ian and white, so my basic tag line became half Black and half white. I did not account for any shades or remnants of miscegenation. I did not account for subtleties of ancestry. Most people wanted to know why I was brown and why I was not then of a commonly understood phenotype. My mathematical solution seemed to put all the inquiries at rest. Eventually I learned there was a term for my specific combination, mulatto. I embraced it fully.

I have been asked why I do not identify as Hawai'ian. Simply put, I am not Hawai'ian. Hawai'ian people are the descendants of the indigenous inhabitants of the Hawai'ian islands who trace their ancestry to Tahiti. My family is from Alabama via slave ship via West Africa and the Congo; and from upstate New York, via Germany and the Protestant Reformation. I also have a number of indigenous ancestors originally from the Powhatan territory now known as Virginia.

This may be why I became a writer.

In sixth grade, I began to caw like a bird in class. I would suddenly become stiff, stare into space, and then my mouth would open and I would shout "caw caw" like a raven. This phenomenon had many impacts on my identity and how I was perceived. My neighbor who was eleven at the time and recently arrived from Samoa, told me that she believed I could be a witch. This was an identity I loved and also embraced. We spent hours wandering the rugged mountains collecting popolo berries, which created a purple dye, and "red berries" (Ardisia), mashing them up with other fruits like pomegranates. We made potions in bottles that we found on the beach which had floated over from distant lands such as Japan, China or even Russia.

My sudden bird calls and moments of staring into space prompted the teacher to send me to the principal or nurse the first couple of times—until she realized I really did not remember at all what was happening and that my class disruptions were not deliberate. One day the cawing stopped, my eyes rolled back into my head and I had the first of many grand mal seizures. I can remember my teacher dragging me by one arm to the principal's office as I kicked and screamed after coming to consciousness. My life's goal became to be seen as "normal."

But I was not normal, I wore my hair in cornrows and was called the "n" word, people always apologized to me before saying the word "Black" or worse, and also I did not speak pigeon, the local dialect in my small community. On the long walks home from school, I was bullied until I learned to become a bully for survival.

In class and at home, I read early in life and enjoyed spelling quizzes. One of my most fraught memories was in third grade, when it occurred to me that if I could learn new vocabulary I could train my tongue to speak pigeon. I wanted to fit in, to be accepted in our small plantation town. After a couple days, our beloved teacher (it is important to note here that she was of Hawai'ian descent), pulled me aside in the class and sat me on her lap. She said something I will never forget. It changed my future, but also further alienated me from my community. She said, "Karla, you have so much potential. I do not want to hear you speaking pigeon. All these kids in here," she made a sweeping gesture towards my classmates, "none of them are going anywhere, but you are. If you start to speak pigeon, you will never go anywhere." A cloud of darkness enshrouded me as I comprehended these words, this threat, from a mentor and teacher that I greatly admired. My mother had also scolded me for trying on this new tongue. Kids laughed at me when my mouth could not form the words. So I put language learning in a box and locked it up. I think this also has impacted my ability to speak French or Spanish as well as Russian.

Things have changed since then.

My mother is a poet, professor, and political activist. Her story and life inspired me. Kathryn Marie Waddell Brundage Takara, daughter of Lottie Younge and William Henry Waddell, IV, grew up in Tuskegee, Alabama.

My white father, Frederic William Brundage, spent the last 40 years of his life writing and rewriting a memoir about his marriage to my Black mother in the '60s, as well as the rise of the counterculture generation and finally, after his second divorce, his decision to leave society completely and live off the grid. His memoir does not mention me or my birth at all. However, he always told me that he felt that part of his decision to marry my mother and have a mixed race child was to participate in the creation of a new race, effectually to change the world. Was this my burden or his?

My mother comes from a long line of activists and resistors, but not revolutionaries. Our family is the type that penetrates the system. We have our reasons. My maternal grandfather had been the only one of eight children to receive a formal education. He attended Lincoln University and was a roommate with Langston Hughes for a semester, and then the University of Pennsylvania where he became one of two Black veterinarians in his time. He met my grandmother, Lottie Younge Waddell, in Tuskegee when he was working with George Washington Carver. He participated in the founding of the Tuskegee Institute School of Veterinary Medicine, and made some good friends there, including Tuskegee Airman General Benjamin O. Davis, who became my mother's godfather.

Lottie was orphaned when her father died at a young age, and her mother Maude (my great-grandmother) found herself a widowed mother of three. They moved to Ohio where Maude either passed for white or did not. She became the manager of a boarding house and eventually was murdered by a jilted lover. This tragic history soiled my grandmother's past and scarred her self-perception. But after her marriage to my grandfather, who was an upcoming star, she thrived in the high society of Tuskegee. They embraced the Jack and Jill upper middle class of Black life. My mother lived a charmed childhood, filled with birthday parties, ballet classes, and the best education money could buy, but this was also the 1950s and '60s. The Civil Rights Movement was brewing.

It was due to a *freedom ride* in which Wesleyan University students visited the historic Black Tuskegee Institute (now Tuskegee University) that my parents met and fell in love. My maternal grandparents were both professors at the time. As faculty, they hosted one of the Wesleyan students for Thanksgiving dinner. My mother was home from Tufts for the holiday. After a whirlwind romance and courtship, my parents were married in 1963. My father later shared with me that he wanted to "see what Black people were like." I would imagine he used the word "negroes" at the time. He told me more than once that he wanted to know what "they smelled like." I always found that strange.

My mother always spoke of her fear of the South—of whites and the violence of snakes, dogs, and lynching in the greater state of Alabama. She lived in a cocoon of sorts in Tuskegee; it was a safe haven. It makes me sad that her discovery of the vile ugliness of racism came from her father-in-law, who called her "nigger" and disowned my father when they married. Grandfather

Brundage was a fall-down alcoholic who threatened to kill everyone in the wedding, which took place in Boston, a haven for interracial marriages at the time. Loving vs Virginia (the ban on interracial marriages) would not be passed until 1967, the year of my birth. My parents fled, first to France on a Fulbright awarded to my mother and later to U.C. Berkeley where they protested the Vietnam war, joined the free speech and free love movements, and had me in the summer of love—August 1967, not long after Martin Luther King, Jr., proclaimed from the steps of Sproul Hall, "America has brought the nation and the world to an awe-inspiring threshold of the future … And yet we have not learned the simple art of walking the earth as brothers and sisters."

There is no way I can divorce this loaded history from why I became a writer. When I read Obama's book *Dreams of my Father*, I felt like I was reading my own story.

Before I was born, however, my parent's divorce began to take shape. My mother, an only child, attended the historic Chambliss Children's House School, located on the campus of Tuskegee Institute, along with Carol Lawrence, Lionel Ritchie, and Kathleen Neal, who would soon be the wife of Eldridge Cleaver of the Black Panthers. Like Booker T. Washington, my mother's family had always favored working for change from the inside; but this approach would change for my mother in 1966, when she was still abroad in France. That was the year her first cousin, Sammy Younge, Jr.—who was more like a brother to her—was shot in the head and killed by an elderly gas station attendant for using a "Whites Only" bathroom in Macon, Alabama, late one Monday night. Sammy, a U.S. Navy veteran and Tuskegee student, had joined SNCC (Student Non-Violent Coordinating Committee) to help with voter registration. He was confronted by the attendant outside the gas station who after a brief scuffle shot him. In an effort to protect the family from further harm, this violent death was something we never spoke about in family, much like the murder of my great-grandmother Maude. Sometimes, I wonder if this desire I have always had to write comes from a desire to understand the truth of the world around me, to uncover painful secrets.

Bereft, my mother found herself in a marriage with a white husband whose family was deeply racist. These seeds were planted and grew. Even though I was born, I could not save the doubt that sprouted on both sides. My father resented my mother's budding activism, as he had been disowned in the marriage, and my mother had descended into her own sorrow and anger about racial politics in the United States. They moved to Hawai'i to try to save the marriage, but even in that "interracial haven," they were challenged by the chaos of an unsteady world. My parents drifted apart and divorced when I was three, in 1970, both marrying again soon after the divorce. My father married my baby-sitter, who was a beautiful Korean law-school student and my mother married a young Japanese surfer who had been her student. Neither of them ever moved away from Hawai'i.

This is the world I was raised in. A world in which I had no voice, no culture or history, and no connection. When my grandparents arrived to help my mother raise me, I clung to them like the passion fruit vine.

Concurrently, my mother had become an activist in the islands, working on the military bases to do interventions (now called social justice workshops) when Black soldiers were discriminated against. She co-founded a Black Cultural center and helped bring the Martin Luther King Jr. Parade and Kwanzaa celebrations to the state of Hawai'i. She most notably became the first Black professor in the newly formed Ethnic Studies program at the University of Hawai'i where she created all the Black studies courses and curriculum. She worked tirelessly with multicultural students and athletes, many of whom were Black. She organized shows and pageants redefining Black beauty by featuring natural hair styles and African clothing. She became a cultural icon in the community, whose work inspired other leaders such as Haunani Kay Trask. Often compared to Malcolm X, Trask was a charismatic leader of the Hawai'ian Sovereignty Movement and a founding director of the Kamakakūokalani Center for Hawai'ian Studies at the University of Hawai'i at Mānoa.

I started writing when I was at Vassar College. It was the 1980s, hip hop was still called rap by some, and in New York it was everything. Madonna was wearing a bra in public, Mork (Robin Williams) was saying *nanu nanu*, we wore overalls and truly believed that nuclear war was imminent. South Africa had not been fully divested, the war on drugs and the crack epidemic were in full swing. I mostly started writing because, when I arrived at Vassar College, I thought I was Black. Or I thought I was half Black and half white. I had never really been forced to choose my race. All my life I had been choosing not to choose: my race, one parent or set of relatives over another. Some parts of the decision were easy—like choosing my maternal grandma and papa over strangers who had refused to acknowledge my existence, but at Vassar the stakes seemed to increase. To say I was Black meant entering a geographic and cultural territory I had little lived experience in—Black America. Being Black meant some kind of behavior or way of being that maybe I had not learned to emulate. Just as

I had not spoken pigeon English, I had not spoken Black English or attended Black churches. I'd known only two other Black people in my high school and one in my elementary school. Choosing Black, to me, felt natural carnally—as I had always embodied my Black body—and historically—as I understood my place in the world as my mother and father had both shared in their own ways. I certainly fell legally into the category of Black by blood quantum; but to choose Black, what did that mean to my day to day? To choose white, however, felt completely impossible. I definitively and concretely have always known that I am not white; that was an impossible choice.

All my poems in college were about rainbows. I loved green and purple. Girls in my short stories cut themselves with razor blades and slammed doors on the faces of those they loved.

My college professors called my writing cliché. But I kept on scribbling down notes … I am so depressed … Why don't you love me … Who will ever love me … blue and black, black and blue … never black and white.

I credit Black Barbie for pushing me over that edge, my leap into the world of poetry. Very much like Toni Morrison's protagonist, as a child, I wished for blue eyes like my father. In Hawai'i, surrounded not only by Hawai'ians, but by the iconic surfing culture dominated by surfing magazines and Hollywood portrayals, the standard of beauty for men and women was bronzed, blond, and blue-eyed beach surfers accompanied by admiring beach bunnies. For that reason alone, I hoped and wished that my eyes would turn blue.

My mother, in her way of empowering me to see a different standard of beauty, bought me a Black Barbie when I was probably around nine. I rejected this doll. The way a young child does, I hated the doll. There was something about her that spoke "bad" to me. It was not until I became a mother and teacher myself that I learned about Drs. Kenneth and Mamie Clark's famous "doll tests." These experiments conducted in 1940's with Black and White dolls, revealed the psychological damage caused to Black children by white supremacist standards of beauty ('www.naacpldf.org/ldf-celebrates-60th-anniversary-brown-v-board-education/significance-doll-test/). As a young child, despite my upbringing and historic heritage, when playing with friends, my Black Barbie was the bad sister, the ugly duckling, and even the man.

Toni Morrison's *The Bluest Eye* inspired me to revisit my own sense of self-worth. In response to a prompt, I wrote on my experience with my Black Barbie. The intention was to show how as a young Black woman, I was coming to terms with other standards of beauty. The Black Barbie had an afro like my mom, and dark skin. I had light skin and straight hair. My phenotype fit an exotified Eurocentric standard of beauty.

This was never more apparent to me than when I was in college. I was not easily accepted in the Black community, and also not really part of the upper-class white culture at Vassar, an Ivy League sister school to Yale. However, my writing was not up to par. My message was lost in my own blind spot. My rejection of Black Barbie, which I saw as tragic, could also be interpreted historically as the way lighter skinned Blacks have "passed" or distanced ourselves from our darker skinned family members.

My poem about self-love was also about colorism; and there was a firestorm of comments in the news and around campus. I was energized by the controversy. Despite the anger the poem provoked, I felt seen for the first time by the Black community that I so longed to be accepted by. After this poem, there was another incident surrounding an unpublished article I wrote investigating racism and colorism on campus. This incident ended up with an intervention by Black alumni and a resurgence of activism around racist incidents at Vassar College. I joined the gospel choir and Black Student Union, protested Apartheid, and cut off all my hair. Previously, I'd been on the periphery, taking classes, volunteering at Green Haven maximum security prison, minoring in Education and Africana Studies. I had not been seen or accepted. I was mostly just that light skinned girl who "thought she was white." But when I wrote, spoke out—even when I was misunderstood—suddenly I began to make sense to people.

1989, the year I graduated, was the year *Fight the Power* took over the repeat of all of our brain waves, along with Spike Lee's *Do the Right Thing*. N.W.A. had just dropped "F**K tha Police" and KRS 1 started a Stop the Violence movement. After graduating, I got in a white van with my white boyfriend, his sister, and her dog, and we drove across North America. My destination: Oakland. "I want to find my Black roots," I kept saying. I am not sure why I needed to look further than my own family, but at that time, Oakland, chocolate city, land of the Black Panthers, was calling me home.

In Oakland in the '90s, Black people and folks of color were bee bopping around town in our oversized overalls—hair out. In Oakland in the '90s, Black on Black crime was on the decline (having peaked in the late '80s). In the news with giant metropolises such as Brooklyn, Chicago, the Bronx, and Compton, was Oakland: population 372,242 and 43% Black. (For some perspective, in 2020, Oakland's population was 440,646 people and 23% Black. In the

'90s 163,256 Black people lived in our city—down to 101,348 now. And our homeless population is 60% Black.)

When I arrived in Oakland, I kept hearing a voice saying, "I want to find my people." I was not really sure what that meant, but I also knew it meant Black people. One of my first memories was of meandering through the city in the deep east (maybe 83rd and Bancroft), looking for myself. I found Uhuru House, a small building painted red, gold and green with fist bursting through a flag, and the outline of a panther stenciled on the wall. I entered the building tentatively. "Can I help you?" a soft male voice enquired. "Can you tell me about your work," was all I could think of to say. I mean, I couldn't really ask him to help me find myself. "Yes, we are working to stop the epidemic of drugs and violence plaguing our community. We have a meeting tonight." I went to the meeting and to several more—listening … absorbing … The youth, I learned, included myself, but also did not include me. I had grown up in a relatively safe land and had a college education. "What can I give back?" I asked, "How can I help?"

I can see now why the community did not immediately embrace me. Who was I trying to help? Who did I think I was? At Uhuru, I learned what I had been wondering about for a long time—that colorism is something you are born into. It is completely out of your control, until it isn't. I learned this the hard way, when one day I stood up in the meeting to say something about the ways we can support youth. "I think … "

"No one in here wants to hear what this yellow b*** has to say!!" someone said from the back. And all of a sudden I was back at Vassar, back at that moment in the cafeteria when I heard women mutter "She think she white," under their breaths as I walk by. I sat down and stayed silent for the rest of the meeting. I never went back.

I literally walked the streets looking for myself. Every day, I woke up and looked for something, but I did not know what it was. The world was spinning out of control and I did not know where I was going. Finally I called home. My mother said, go see Barbara Christian, a founding professor of Black Studies at U.C. Berkeley. Barbara took me under her wing and introduced me to Opal Palmer Adisa. These two powerful women along with Amahra Hicks embraced and mentored me. My mother arrived in town and introduced me to Ishmael Reed, QR Hand and a lot of powerful leaders, writers and artists. But it was Paradise, aka Richard Moore, who brought me into the Oakland poetry scene. Richard was looking for someone to help him start readings at the then Ohana

Center on Telegraph. We made posters, called folks on the phone, and hosted weekly readings. Through Paradise, I met Wanda Sabir, Avotcja, Keith Adkins, and Robert Henry Johnson, who eventually brought me to the San Francisco world where I met Nikki Byrd who was involved in Rhodessa Jones's Medea Project.

Poetry is where I found my community in my 20's. Through poetry I met the father of my daughter when we created a performance art piece, *Earth Peace*, focusing on Black People loving the earth. This environmentalist focused choreopoem featured the work of Azibuike Akaba, Keba Konte, Abji Jibril, and other Bay Area artists.

My desire to share love and joy through writing doubled down when I became a mother. When my daughter, Asha (hope), was born, I was only 25, but I stood pregnant and proud on the stage of the Women's Building in San Francisco in a red unitard in 1993 along with Michael Franti and others raising funds for CAMP. Asha also joined me on stage in Rhodessa Jones' Medea Project in 1994, as I recited the words, "Can you push again? Hell yeah? And I did." Celebrating black love, joy, and motherhood. I was topless and nursing her.

Over the past thirty years, I have taught writing in public and private spaces and given workshops in Oakland, Hawai'i, New York, Zimbabwe, Ghana, and Cote d'Ivoire. By sharing with students the sense of empowerment one finds when opening the pandora's box called voice, I've been allowed to witness the myriad ways that writing can change lives.

I also run a small non-profit called West Oakland to West Africa (WO2WA), which seeks to promote cultural understanding and facilitate a Sankofa (return to the ancestors) through poetry. What I learned in Cote d'Ivoire is how an accurate history of Black people has been lost not only here in the United States, but in West Africa as well, due to the colonialism of the educational system. Many young people in Ghana and all over West Africa have embraced hip-hop, spoken word, and rap as an art form. In the U.S. we are taught that modern rap arises from the West African griot tradition. But West Africa youth are not taught this. So we in the U.S. learn our connection to Africa through hip-hop and Africans learn their connection to America through hip-hop.

This is the healing necessary for reclaiming our humanity and our roots. WO2WA hopes to play a small role in using writing to create connections, teach history and empower people to use their voices for social change.

This is why I write.

Charles Dixon
REACHING FOR SKY

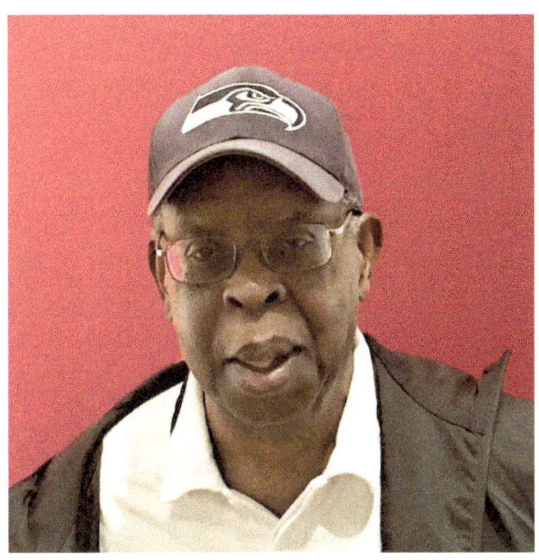

Charles Dixon grew up in an African American community
in Philadelphia. He is the oldest of six children
born to parents who fled the tobacco fields and racism
of southern Virginia to find refuge in the
"City of Brotherly Love."
First in his family to attend college, he earned
a BS in Chemistry from Lincoln University,
a historic Black university, in 1962.
His 1970 Wharton MBA was the key to a career
in sales, marketing, promotion, and
corporate development with a major high-tech
Silicon Valley corporation. For years he traveled nationally
and internationally and gained
a unique perspective on self, community, and the world.
He now lives in San Francisco
where he uses his passion and expertise to support the
Fillmore's African American community.

RUSTY RUF: GOTTA RUN MORE THAN YOUR MOUTH
Charles Dixon

The first 15 years of my life, I attended elementary and junior high school within 3 blocks of my house in Nicetown, a predominantly Black neighborhood in North Philadelphia. I'd grown sick and tired of not having the opportunity to ride the bus, trolley or subway to a foreign destination in another part of Philadelphia, so I applied to and was finally accepted at a high-caliber, predominantly Jewish high school located 5 miles away—and 1 block away from my father's part-time second job.

I got more than I asked for. The new school's instructors gave us four hours of homework each night. And my father felt that since I was so talented and could navigate the subway system, I could now work his second job 2 school days a week. On those days, I would leave home at 5 in the morning, catch the subway, work 2 hours cleaning bowling lanes, walk down the hill to school, go to class, return home, deliver newspapers, and finally study.

Needless to say I was a mental wreck, but I could not tell my father that homework, school, jobs were too much. I would've only gotten the routine lecture from a migrant sharecropper's son who found greater opportunity in the North. "Son, I wish I had your opportunity," he'd say. "I did not go to school for one year because we were so poor I could not afford a pair of long pants." He often quoted a famous local college dignitary, "There are acres of diamonds at your feet; all you have to do is pick them up." I was sure my father would misdiagnose my predicament and had no solution for my fragile mental state.

My small world was being destroyed. English was not a problem because I loved to read, but Math was another issue—a big issue—and Geometry a bigger issue! I didn't know the difference between a right angle and a left angle, much less an axiom and a theorem, and I saw no reason on earth for proofs. This new kind of math was poised to ruin my life, limit my stick ball games, and place me in the insane asylum.

I played my last survival card: my Scoutmaster Rufus H. Cox, or "Rusty Ruf" as the kids in my troop called him behind his back. Mr. Cox was a machinist by profession, but my father called him "the smartest man in Nicetown—smarter than the ministers, doctors, lawyers, number runners, and politicians that laid claim to the title.

Mr. Cox devoted all his spare time to Troop 134. He planned challenging activities for his two dozen "knuckleheads" and watched over our academic and moral growth. "There is no reason for you to go to school unprepared," he stated, so he held open tutoring sessions on any subject at his dining room table every night from 7 to 9 pm.

I rang his bell one night to alert him to my rapidly approaching nervous breakdown. "I want to transfer to an easier school." Mr. Cox shook his head and laid a calming hand on my shoulder. "Don't worry, we can do this. Together."

For the entire school year he tutored me in Plane and Solid Geometry. My grade went from a fat F to B+. If we could not solve a problem during our evening sessions, he worked on it late that night and relayed the solution to me the next morning. I became the class math wizard. There was no problem I could not solve—or should I say, Mr. Cox could not solve. Geometry was the make-or-break moment of my young life, and Mr. Cox saved me from a fate worse than death: another "When I was your age" lecture from my father.

Mr. Cox offered unselfish assistance—financial, educational, and emotional—to a group of young knuckleheads. His inspirational presence, spiritual depth, and wisdom were unmatched. They continue to guide my moral compass and work ethic. Like W.E.B. DuBois, he believed we were all members of the "Talented Tenth." To his mind, we all had innate intellectual and academic potential worth molding and nurturing. Throughout college, business school, and a long career, I remembered what Rusty Ruf taught me: "You gotta run more than your mouth to get somewhere. It's not a level playing field, so you need to jog during the day, and train late into the night to leap hurdles."

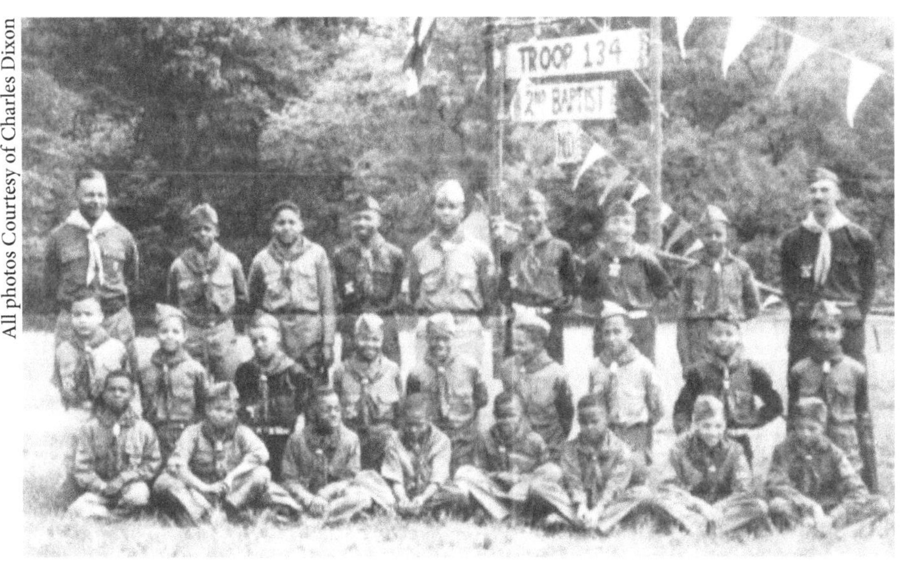

TOUCHING THE CEILING

Having taken mainly technical courses to obtain my college degrees, I decided after I moved to Cali to round out my education by taking art and social studies courses at the local community college. The first course I took was Philosophy 101, which introduced me to Plato's "Allegory of The Cave." In short, Plato states that people's world view is controlled by their environmental, cultural, and developmental influences—good and bad. Like prisoners seeing carefully curated shadows on a cave wall, most people perceive what their society allows them to see. My African American reality is based, good or bad, on what I've been exposed to (racism), what I've been taught (by my parents and community) and what I've internalized (through love and relationships). Much of what we perceive as reality are stereotypes generated by the dominant society, and our reality can change based on new input. Recently my understanding of stereotypes was shaken by trusted and irrefutable new input.

Initially in my writing, I wanted the reader to understand me—my own journey from poverty to corporate life from a minority perspective. Recently, I was reminded it was about much more than me when I got an e-mail of two African American comedians impersonating famous personalities. I thought the skits were excellent and forwarded them to friends. One, a psychologist, replied they were "right on." A week later, I forwarded another skit by the same comedians impersonating two ladies gossiping in church. The psychologist sent a stern reply. Males dressing in drag was emasculating, he declared, and the church women's exaggerated behavior perpetuated the stereotype that Blacks were over-emotional, unregulated, and couldn't be trusted in leadership positions! I had to stop and think. Why had I not viewed the stereotypes as offensive?

My mind flashed back to a college classmate, Donald Lambright, whom I remembered as a quiet, unassuming, peace-loving advocate for social justice—someone you would never consider a threat to society. He was the son of Lincoln Perry, better known as Stepin Fetchit. In the mid-1930s, Perry became the first Black actor to earn a million dollars through his many screen portrayals of the "Laziest Man in the World." Lambright, his son, achieved his own fame in 1969. While driving on the Pennsylvania Turnpike, he killed three people, including his wife and son, and wounded fifteen more before turning the gun on himself. I've always believed that this horrendous deed—and his final act of suicide— were desperate attempts to break free from his father's powerful depictions of African Americans as lazy, low IQ, nonreactive, sleepy and powerless.

Then I watched the PBS documentary[1] about Sammy Davis, Jr. that outlined the success, tragedy, and racism that Sammy experienced as a black entertainer from the '30s though the '70s. He had to perform in black face as a child, was chided for impersonating white entertainers, and received death threats for committing the ultimate sin of marrying a white woman.

I again reflected on the stereotyping that I had played out, been a party to, or witnessed without a thought—instances that paid the bills but impeded my professional progress in the end. I'd been focused on "touching the ceiling," reaching my highest individual potential as a Black man—without much thought to the larger social implications.

During the '60s and '70s, young males in my Black Philadelphia neighborhood expected to be drafted. We didn't know anything about college deferments or other ways to avoid the draft. We just assumed, if called, you proudly served! Before my high school graduation, I overheard my white classmates privately weighing options to avoid that fate. One possibility was to join the National Guard, which in those days stayed close to home to protect the community from an impending Viet invasion. They talked about joining the New Jersey unit because Pennsylvania's was at maximum enrollment. Another option was to become a conscientious objector and be ostracized like Muhammad Ali and lose all income. Or you could bribe your doctor into saying you had flat feet and could not walk over a mile. All these options seemed implausible to most young African American men, who dreamed and strived to enter the middle class. They still saw military service as a path to advanced education.

I was lucky enough to survive the early draft calls, but following college graduation, I reported to my local draft board and was classified as 1A—draft eligible. I had landed a job as a research analytical chemist at a local company. I was the only African American in the group. I was an oddity at the time, an early beneficiary of a growing affirmative action movement and the death of Jim Crow. During this era, I saw a popular magazine cover depicting a young African American man carrying a briefcase. He was attired in a white shirt, tie and suit jacket, but from the waist down, he wore athletic shorts and basketball shoes. The caption, heralding the inclusion of African Americans into the corporate mainstream, declared, "Every Company Needs One." I felt honored to be the needed one, but embarrassed by my new title and by the implications of the cover picture, which were quite literal. Every week at the conclusion of

---

1. *Sammy Davis, I Got To Be Me* on PBS *American Masters* series (2019).

our weekly staff meetings, my manager made me demonstrate my standing jump by leaping up 11 feet to touch the ceiling.

The research lab was housed in a secluded mansion in suburban Philadelphia. Every day, I boarded the commuter train to work. On my first day, I was befriended by two older African American women who worked as domestics for wealthy suburbanites. Seeing that I was young and naïve, these ladies took me under their wing. Every day, they saved me a seat and passed their used newspaper to read on my 25-minute journey. On a fateful October day, I picked up the newspaper and read, "Kennedy is calling up another 50,000 troops." I was shaken, knowing I would soon be on my way to Vietnam trenches.

I gave my employer a "heads up" so that they could start looking for my jumping replacement. The Director of Research nodded and said he'd get back to me later that afternoon. It was almost quitting time when a man called from the corporate office. He introduced himself as a retired Army Colonel, and said he would try to get me a critical skills deferment. He quizzed me about my duties—the mundane, repetitive task of analyzing daily gas samples. He felt satisfied that my work, even as a newbie, was technical and a grade above the janitorial staff. "How do you like your job," he asked. "This is the best job I've ever had," I could say sincerely—actually it was my first full-time job aside from delivering newspapers. A week later, I received a copy of the letter he wrote to my local draft board, stating that I was an integral part (really?) of a key research team working on high performance plastics for jet aircraft. A month later, the draft board granted me a deferment.

I continued to ride the commuter train with the two ladies for another two years! Every day I read the war headlines about atrocities, growing outrage, and U.S. missteps. I reflected on how a chance seat on a commuter train played a role in preventing me from becoming a hero or casualty of a needless war. The kindness of people like my scoutmaster and those kind commuter ladies made a difference in my life.

I thought about my parent's history and legacy—the narrative passed on to me as a black male. I reflected on my past and current views of the world and the dominant culture's evolving view of minorities. I had once thought that touching the ceiling would show my white coworkers that I could do anything they could do and better. Now I realized that my technical skills were average, and all that my high jumps accomplished was to show I was an excellent representation of the magazine caricature. I was reaffirming long-held majority beliefs about black athleticism— not black intellect.

It was embarrassing to think how oblivious I'd been to white privilege and microaggressions. Then I realized in my parents' generation, corporate jobs were denied Negros. A good-paying occupation for a Black man with a college degree was sleeping car porter. My parents migrated to Philadelphia in the '30s. Their objective was to find employment and survive, holding tight to faith of a better day. My educated mother accepted a sleep-in job as a domestic for a wealthy lawyer. My sharecropper father's first job was as a pin boy in a bowling alley! Due to racist beliefs in government and major corporations, skilled, good-paying jobs were simply not open to Negros. It was not until the '40s and WWII that a labor shortage and a presidential decree created increased employment opportunities for African Americans. And it was not until the mid-'60s and the civil rights movement that the housing market was desegregated.

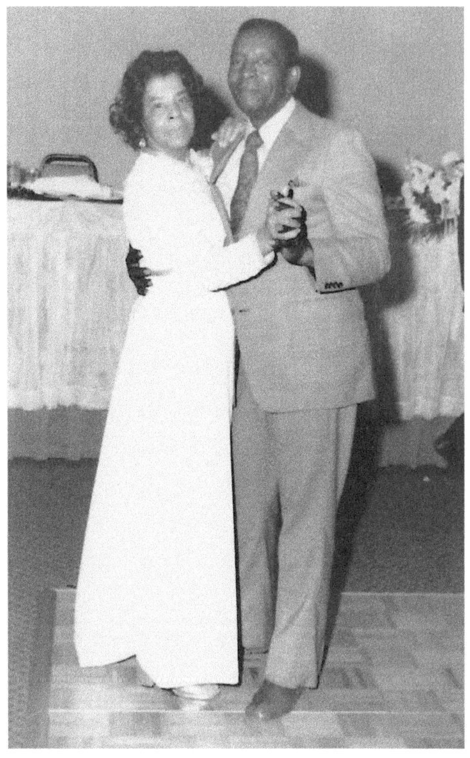

Stepin Fetchit, Sammy Davis, Jr., Donald Lambright, and my parents all moved the needle of American progress, although some of their actions could be viewed in a negative light. Fetchit accepted degrading movie roles "to feed the people I loved." Sammy Davis performed in Blackface as a child to feed his uncle and father. Lambright's tragic end illuminated issues of internalized oppression, rage, and armed resistance. Now, I realize that touching the ceiling was buffoonery, but it allowed me to continue my struggle and to fight for equity in pay and status. The two comedians, after a successful run, have now separated, and are working on larger projects with larger paydays.

When my friend challenged my reaction to the comedic skit, I chose not to brush it off. Thinking deeply about my own perceptions of and reactions to stereotyping has changed my reality, and it will keep changing. I hope yours does, too.

PLEASE CALL

In 1971, I had suddenly become a limited, valued, high demand, corporate commodity: an African American MBA from a top tier business school. I had quickly outgrown my current position as product manager at our east coast facility and had requested greater responsibility and reassignment to San Francisco. I now aspired to hold a top managerial position in this Fortune 500 company—my next planned career move!

I rolled into the Silicon Valley plant on a cold rainy day in early February 1971 with high expectations. I was eager to start in my new high visibility position. My new assignment was to develop the market for business computer applications and data models which in turn would increase the company's market share of computer software and hardware sales. My transfer instructions were to report to the personnel office for orientation, introductions, and expense monies. As Janice, a petite, congenial, and attractive office receptionist greeted me, I thought, If this is what Cali has to offer, I'm all in!

Janice was well dressed, five one, bowlegs, cute ankles, and radiating Blackness. She took in my Italian cut suit and understated tie as she casually inquired about my flight from the East Coast. "I hope you're happy with the hotel we booked for you." I was naively impressed by her warmth, not realizing that of course she would have been privy to my file and interview report. She would have known about my MBA, my career path, and my hefty new pay increase. Professional Black men were not exactly a dime a dozen in the corporate world in those days.

Roscoe, assistant personnel manager at the San Francisco location, had met me on a company college recruiting trip. Welcoming the idea of a peer in his home office, he facilitated a successful invite, interview, and job offer.

Now he gripped my hand warmly. "Welcome aboard." He quickly gave me the lay of the land regarding: housing, my position, and the office pecking order. Then he invited me to a weekend party that he and his wife were hosting. I thanked him for his hospitality, pocketed my fat expense check, and proceeded to leave.

On the way out, I stopped at Janice's desk to thank her for her assistance and check out her smile again. She casually directed the conversation to my likes and dislikes, then let me know she was single. I responded with, "We need to continue this conversation over lunch." Roscoe witnessed my lingering exit and found a reason to leave the office with me. As the office door closed, he said, "I don't want any drama in my office." He then stated with emphasis: "Leave Janice alone."

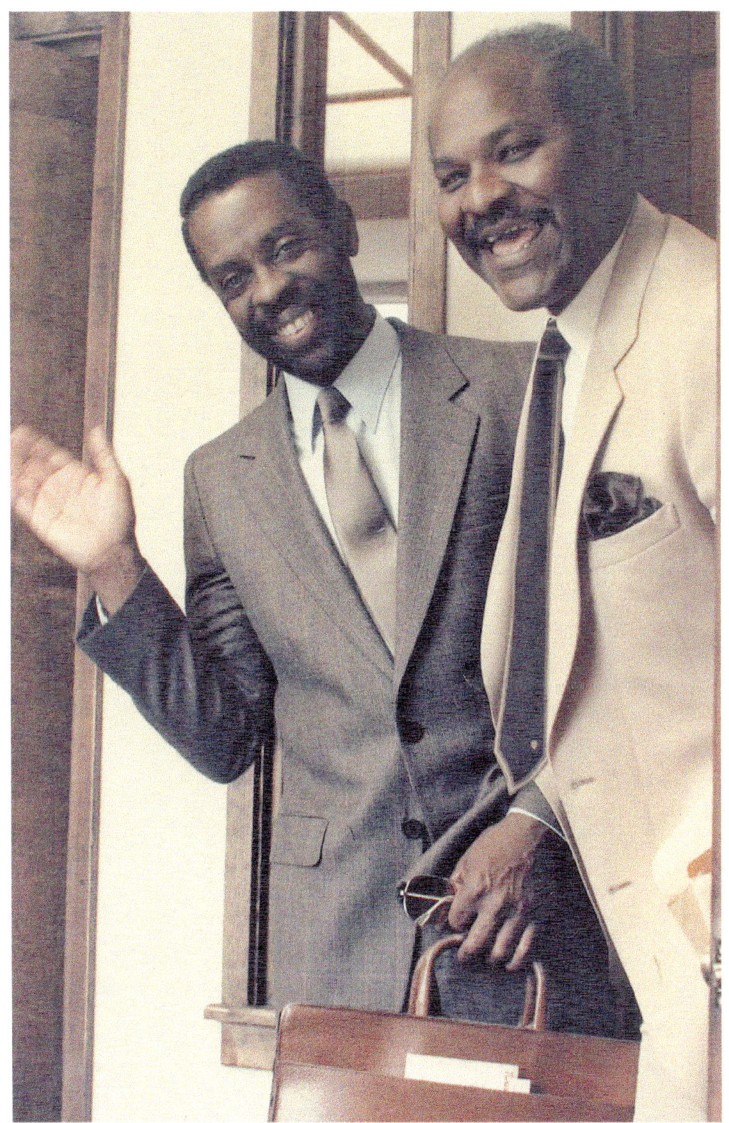

My new position entailed constant travel for the next six months. My assignments were to 1) foster information dissemination and exchange among elite business school professors in the emerging field of computer business application models, 2) start a publishing company to widely disseminate the information of these new and exciting computer applications, and 3) hold one of the first symposiums of its kind in France to inform the world of the innovative work and to persuade educators to buy computers. To accomplish the above, I traveled nationally and internationally, and saw San Francisco and my apartment only on weekends.

During my first month, I heeded Roscoe's advice concerning Janice, since I felt that he knew something that he did not want to share. She must be involved with someone else, I concluded. However, Janice kept calling, calling, calling, and I finally decided I would take her out. We clicked and during the next months we would see each other on a regular basis when I was in town. All I wanted was weekend companionship and she amply filled the requirement, but I kept in mind Roscoe's words and attempted not to give all my energy to the relationship.

After a successful symposium, and European vacation, I settled down in my new surroundings and focused on Janice's bowlegs. We dated more often, but we stalled at every other week. Janice would leave on Sunday happy and laughing, but during the week she appeared withdrawn and uncaring. But then, the following week, she would re-enlist for another weekend and the love dance would begin again.

While traveling, my plant needs, correspondence, and requests were handled by a group secretary and by Brenda, an intern, who was placed under my mentorship and supervision. Brenda and I became fast friends. I viewed her and treated her as if she were my baby sister. "Baby Sis" was warm, articulate, humorous, and acted as my in-house liaison when I was traveling. Brenda's most important asset, however, was access to ladies' room gossip. During one of Janice's withdrawal periods, I was at my desk, depressed and consulting my "Player Strategy Playbook" to prepare for my next Janice encounter. Brenda noticed my mood and asked, "What is your problem?!" I confided that I'd been dating Janice for several months with the same hot/cold results. Brenda said calmly, "Roscoe is dating Janice, I thought you knew. I recommend that you stop confiding in Roscoe and confront Janice!"

Christmas came and I went home for a short visit. On my outbound flight I was seated next to an attractive artist from Sacramento. After a five-hour flight of enjoyable conversation, we deplaned in Philly, I gave her my phone number and suggested we do lunch the next time she traveled to the Bay Area. Three weeks later, the artist called and asked if she could visit for the weekend. The following Monday morning, Roscoe asked, "How was your weekend?" I gave him an exaggerated X-rated version of my weekend encounter and threw in, "We spent Sunday afternoon in downtown San Francisco, ending in a stroll through Union Square." Tuesday, Janice would not speak to me. She finally called on Friday and told me the reason: "I saw you in Union Square last Sunday, arm in arm with another woman!"

A few weeks later, I asked Janice to lunch and confronted her about Roscoe. I chose a small secluded restaurant near our work location which was our favorite. After the main course and before dessert I stated, "There's no way I can continue to see you when you're already in a dead-end relationship with a married man." Janice was stunned that I knew. "I'm so sorry! I like you a lot, and it's not like I enjoy the situation with Roscoe. I didn't know he was married at first, and then got pulled into a thing because he kept saying his marriage was on the rocks and he needed comfort." She looked at me beseechingly with those big brown eyes. "I'm a single mom, I can't afford to lose my job …." After that lunch, Janice and I no longer dated, but we remained friends. As for Roscoe, I found ways to create social and professional distance without jeopardizing my career.

Many decades have passed. Recently, out of the blue, Janice left a message on my answering machine. "Call me, call me! Brenda gave me your phone number." I assume Baby Sis knows more than I do about the female psyche and gave up my number for a reason—reengagement, closure or just to reinvigorate bathroom gossip.

Will I return Janice's call?

TROUBLE MAN

"I come up hard, baby
But now I'm cool
I didn't make it, sugar
Playin' by the rules."
—*Marvin Gaye*

When I entered Trouble's new office for the first time and heard the lyrics of Marvin Gaye's song 'Trouble Man" playing, I should have known to exit left. However, I first met Trouble when he was a research engineer at the prestigious high-tech company where we both worked. He was an African American in his early twenties, billed as a boy wonder. He appeared serious and was well respected by his fellow engineers. He carried newspaper and scientific articles of his high-school science awards in his briefcase along with his lunch.

In 1984, I left the company because of a long running feud with my racist manager concerning a single over-budget item charge of $50—after a successful $8,000 national sales meeting that I chaired. When I refused to eat the charge, he bombarded me with a host of "issues," past and present, closing with an accusatory,

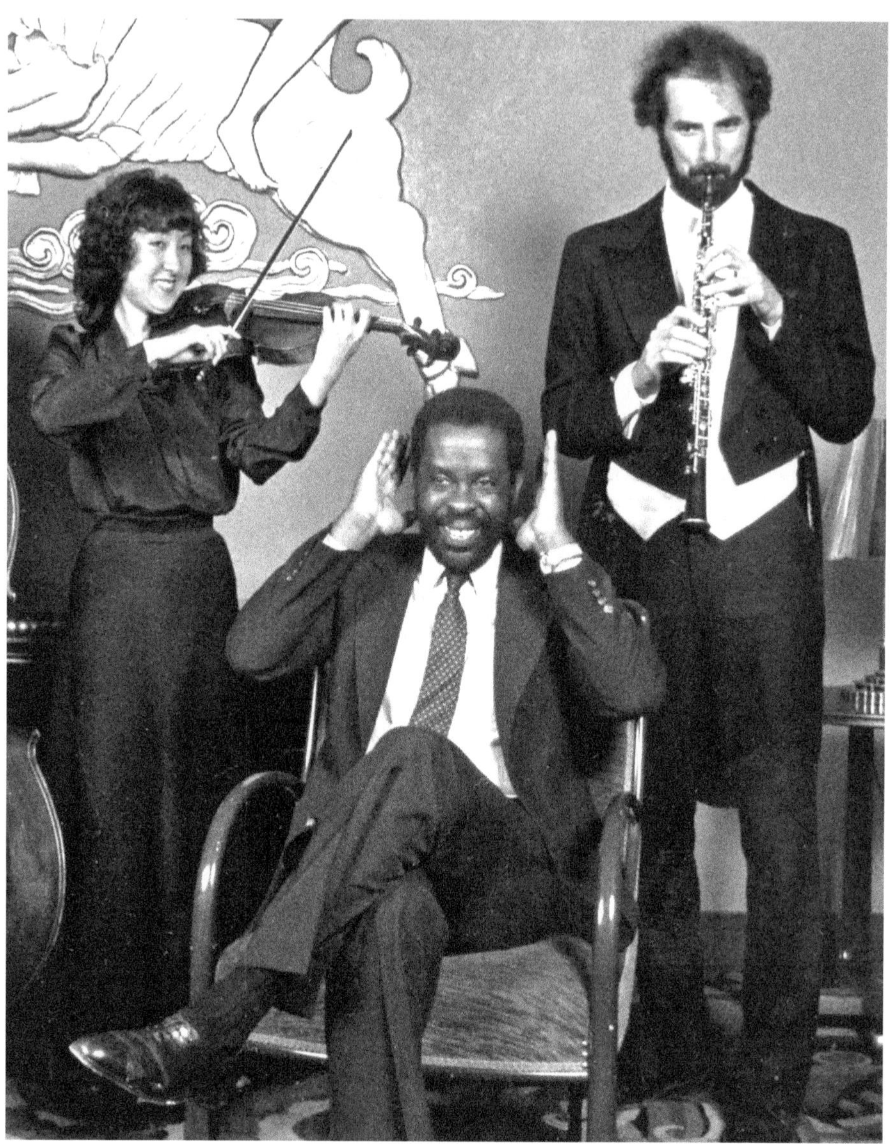

"How can you afford to wear a starched shirt to work every single day?" I snapped, and exited the meeting with the retort, "All I have to do in this world is stay Black and DIE!" Knowing I would be shot at dawn by HR for walking out on my boss with a remark like that, I resigned from the company—leaving with retirement benefits, a BMW, an upscale apartment, and enough savings to last a year. Shortly afterwards, Trouble approached me and invited me to work for his startup as marketing manager. He showed me several products that he claimed were his designs with patents pending. I felt confident the products would revolutionize the infant personal computer market.

I agreed to work for Trouble for stock and a small salary. On my first day, I met my fellow cast of characters. Dolly, the cute part-time secretary, and full-time middle-aged swinger with the best X-rated weekend stories. Jesus, the company's evangelist accountant, who always had a positive outlook and demeanor. And Trouble's affable cousin Muscle—everyman, bodybuilder, playboy and ladies' man—who had just left the army. Muscle handled everything that fell through the cracks (security, errands, comedy). We all got along well initially, and in the early days we seemed to be on the start of a great journey. However, my relationships with Trouble and Jesus were the first to sour as I began having suspicions and fears about the company's success.

At the time, I was living in Oakland with my girlfriend, and commuting to Silicon Valley daily. In my new position I had to put in late hours. Trouble suggested that on long workdays I stay at his house and sleep on his couch. I accepted the offer, but soon discovered that Jesus and Trouble slept together in a king-size bed—not for sexual reasons, but so that Jesus could fuel Troubles' ego and paint rosy pictures of product and venture success. The arrangement seemed odd, but I'd heard stories of creative geniuses having strange needs and bedfellows.

My first reality check came a few weeks later, as I was sitting at my desk. A white interloper walked in and asked how product sales were going. "I can't answer that question because I don't know who you are or why are you're standing in front of my desk." He quickly entered Trouble's office and returned a few minutes later and stated, "I designed the products you're selling, and I want to collect my royalties!" He explained that he worked at a nearby computer chip company and had developed these products based upon his insight, curiosity, and technical information he'd gained as a member of the "Homebrew Group," a collection of hotshot personal computer hobbyists that included Apple founder Steve Jobs and Trouble. After the man left, I confronted Trouble. He sheepishly confirmed that the man's claims were true. "The next time he comes into the office, be more courteous. Give him an overview of the marketing effort and what we're attempting to do."

A few weeks later, we had a problem getting an advertising company to create ads for our new products (since we had little up-front money). We finally found an advertising company in Monterey that was willing to develop the advertising content in exchange for a stake of the company. The owner of the advertising agency "Simple" was convinced that Trouble was the Black Messiah. He said that Player, a principal investor in his agency, would like to buy a stake in Trouble's venture as well. Trouble met with Player, who said,

"This is a venture I'd like to take under my belt and guide to greater wealth than you can dream of."

In hindsight, we all should have known something was strange because Player traveled in a chauffeur-driven limo but never picked up a meal tab. He wore white shoes, a red shirt, and a large white cowboy hat; and he claimed he had at one time dated Marvin Gaye's girlfriend "Tammy Terrell." Player announced he was immediately pulling all his money out of his LA investments to invest in Simple's advertising company and Trouble's start-up.

On the weekend of the transfer of monies, Player invited Simple and his top management and their families to LA for a celebration dinner party. The day of the celebration, with the agency's management and their families sequestered in LA waiting for the evening gala dinner and the receipt of the big check, Player and his family skipped town, but not before robbing all the ad executives' homes. He left no forwarding address.

When I returned to our office on Monday morning, I was the only one there. I called Simple to find out how the great weekend went in LA. I needed to know how much money they'd be placing in Trouble's account. "Player never showed up." Simple reported. "We were stuck with the travel, hotel, and dinner bills. Not only that, we came home to find that our homes had been ransacked and Player is nowhere to be found." Trouble had not yet arrived at the office, so I rushed to his house to tell him the news. His place was deserted. Later, Muscle called to say that as soon as he heard the news from Simple, he and Trouble had packed up all their goods and driven to Texas to seek refuge and employment with one of our buyers. I was left holding the bag—a big bag of unpaid creditors!

The landlord's office was right downstairs from the office space Trouble was renting. He was familiar with the work I'd been putting into the company, so when I informed him of my dilemma, he thought for a minute, then said, "You're a good man; I trust you. I can carry you for a while, but you need to get everything together."

I went to the product developer, the white boy I'd yelled at, and told him what had happened. He said, "Don't worry, I'll support you in your new effort." I immediately found a lawyer, formed a new company and called it Obsidian—a black volcanic mineral that is 1000 times sharper than steel and used by the Aztecs for open heart surgery. After numerous attempts, I found an investor that agreed to invest $200,000. I was back on my feet and in the game again. Simple reported the crime to the Monterey Police, and they interviewed me.

They caught Player and brought him promptly to trial. As for Trouble, I didn't hear from him for several years. Not until after, he'd re-invented himself in Southern California—still playing "Trouble Man."

Four years later, I was sitting in a garment clothing factory in New York City, signing off on a large merchandise order for a major televised boxing event. The owner shared with me her excitement about her upcoming meeting with a potential investor that her lawyer had been introduced to at a weekend party in the Hamptons. She waved towards the waiting room, which was visible through her office window. To my surprise, the new investor seated in the reception area was Player—bold as brass. I said nothing to the owner, but at the close of our meeting, I hurried through the waiting room with my face turned away from Player. Since I no longer had a beard and afro, and was dressed in an Armani suit not in the Silicon Valley formal wear of jeans and Tshirt, he did not recognize me.

I immediately called the Monterey police, to confirm I had not witnessed the second coming of Christ, but a jailbird who'd served his term. Then I called the owner to alert her that this was an investor to ignore and went to the nearest bar for a stiff drink.

Black success is always hard to come by. I had to remind myself, "Don't hate the Player—hate the Game!"

Acknowledgments

A version of "Rusty Ruf" was first published in *Standing Strong! Fillmore & Japantown,* Pease Press, 2016.

Rafael Jesús González
RIFFS ON A POEM

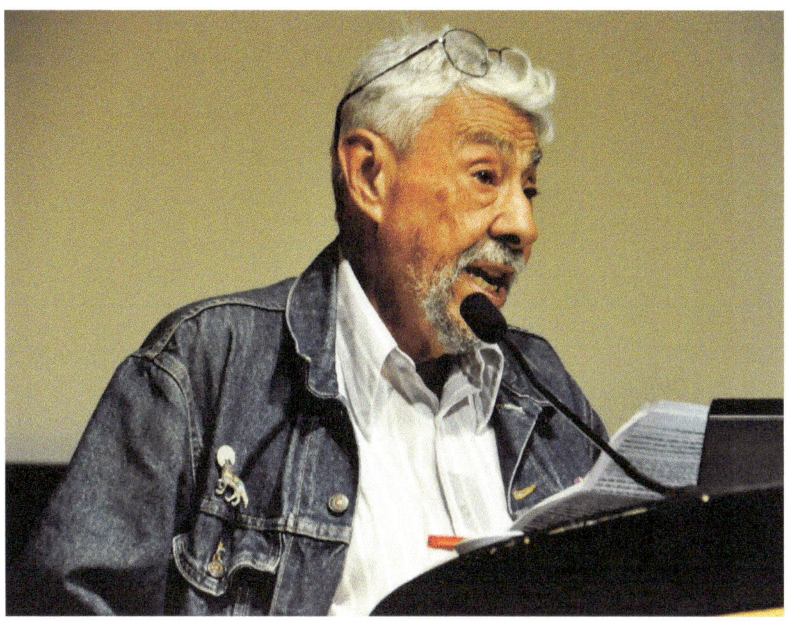

Rafael Jesús González, a professor of
creative writing and literature, taught at several
universities before he settled at
Laney College in Oakland, California,
where he founded the Department of Mexican
and Latin American Studies in 1969.
Four times nominated for a Pushcart Prize,
Rafael was honored for his writing by
the National Council of Teachers of English in
2003. He received a César Chávez
Lifetime Achievement Award in 2013 and one
from the city of Berkeley, California, in 2015.
Rafael is Berkeley's first Poet Laureate. He can be
reached at rjgonzalez@mindspring.com.

A UNA ANCIANA
Rafael Jesús González

Venga, madre—
          su rebozo arrastra telaraña negra
          y sus enaguas le enredan los tobillos;
apoya el peso de sus años
en trémulo bastón y sus manos temblorosas
empujan sobre el mostrador centavos sudados.
¿Aún todavía ve, viejecita,
la jara de su aguja arrastrando colores?
          Las flores que borda
          con hilazas de a tres-por-diez
no se marchitan tan pronto como las hojas del tiempo.
          ¿Qué cosas recuerda?
Su boca parece constantemente saborear
los restos de años rellenos de miel.
          ¿Dónde están los hijos que parió?
¿Hablan ahora solamente inglés
y dicen que son hispanos?
          Sé que un día no vendrá
          a pedirme que le que escoja
          los matices que ya no puede ver.
Sé que esperaré en vano
          su bendición desdentada.
Miraré hacia la calle polvorienta
refrescada por alas de paloma
hasta que un chiquillo mugroso me jale de la manga
y me pregunte:
          — Señor, jau mach is dis? —

TO AN OLD WOMAN
Rafael Jesús González

Come, mother—
>your rebozo trails a black web
>and your hem catches on your heels,
you lean the burden of your years
on shaky cane, and palsied hand pushes
sweat-grimed pennies on the counter.
Can you still see, old woman,
the darting color-trailed needle of your trade?
>The flowers you embroider
>with three-for-a-dime threads
cannot fade as quickly as the leaves of time.
>What things do you remember?
Your mouth seems to be forever tasting
the residue of nectar hearted years.
>Where are the sons you bore?
Do they speak only English now
and say they're Spanish?
>One day I know you will not come
>and ask for me to pick
>the colors you can no longer see.
I know I'll wait in vain
>for your toothless benediction.
I'll look into the dusty street
made cool by pigeons' wings
until a dirty kid will nudge me and say:
>"Señor, how mach ees thees?"

RIFFS ON THE POEM "A UNA ANCIANA / TO AN OLD WOMAN"
Rafael Jesús González

Coming home from my stint in the U.S. Navy in 1958, I enrolled under the G.I. Bill at the University of Texas El Paso which was then named Texas Western State College of the University of Texas. After classes, I worked at my father's small general store named Gonycia (abbreviated for González y compañía) which sold toiletries, school supplies, toys, notions, and sundries, in el Segundo barrio, the working-class neighborhood closest to the U.S.-Mexican border.

From my experience working there came my poem "A una anciana / To an Old Woman" in 1959. I had formed a bond with a regular customer, a very elderly woman who often consulted me about embroidery floss to match or complement the colors of her exquisite embroidery. Beyond that, the poem is a work of my imagination. She did not trail a rebozo nor trip on her hems, nor did she pay for her purchases with "sweat-grimed pennies." She could see well enough and our discussions of colors were purely aesthetic. I embellished her image for my own purposes as a writer and imagined a situation which might or might not have been hers to present a problem that had (has) always concerned me: assimilation.

I was born and raised in El Paso, Texas, with family across the Río Bravo in Ciudad Juárez, Chihuahua, and identity increasingly became a problem. Spanish was my first language and, until about the mid 1960s when I became Chicano, I was simply Mexican though I knew that I was a citizen of the United States of America. Even today, when I am asked "What are you?" my immediate response is "Mexican" though when I am more alert, I will say "Chicano." Though when am asked "What is your citizenship?" I do not hesitate.

I did not learn English until I was seven at Lamar Public School and at first it was not easy. I was already doing some basic reading and writing in Spanish and the unpredictable sound of the same letters in English confused me. I was in the dark most of the time. One day my mother with my little brother walked me to school and went on to my grandparent's house a few blocks away. I found myself in a totally empty playground, doors of the school closed. I was terrified. I walked back home to an empty house. I sat on the porch confused, afraid, lonely until my mother and grandmother came with my little brother and covered me with abrazos and kisses. A holiday had been announced by the teacher, but I had not understood.

It did not help that we were punished if we were heard speaking Spanish in the classroom, the halls, or the playground. If we asked a classmate, "¿Qué dijo la maestra?" we were made to stand in a corner or kept after school. I have the distinction of having failed first grade. I did excel in drawing and coloring and I recall a kind teacher, Mrs. Hall, in fourth grade who praised and encouraged me. But the principal recommended that my parents take me and my brother Arturo (two years younger that I) to Bailey School for "retarded" children.

My father did so and the principal at Bailey School who could not have kept us there more than thirty minutes or so, told my father that we did not belong there, and recommended that we change schools. My parents went into debt and bought their first and only house so that we could change districts and go to Morehead Public School where our problems vanished. (Two teachers stand out: Mrs. Patricia Robinson, art teacher, who spoke excellent Spanish and would invite a few students to her home on weekends to draw and paint. And Miss Mary Hignett, English teacher, with whom I became friends in my college years until her death.)

By then in 1950 I was adjusted, acculturated if you will; I was not assimilated (which to me has connoted being chewed, swallowed, and digested). For me, language has been a touchstone of assimilation. Mexican Indian me had long been assimilated; my maternal grandfather Papanito, don Diego González Sosa, except for his color and features and his saying that we were indio spoke no indigenous language to indicate it, but only a formal castellano. Mexican mestizo me not so. I was blessed with parents, Jesús F. González of Coahuila and Carmen González Prieto of Durango, (brought to the U.S. at 13 and 12, respectively) who always insisted that we speak and write both Spanish and English. I took Spanish courses throughout high school and graduated from college with a degree in English literature with enough hours in Spanish literature for a double major. In an irony of fate, I have spent most of my life as a professor of English in universities and colleges.

Resisting assimilation is a struggle, especially in an empire that imposes its hegemony (military, economic, political, linguistic, cultural) on the world. All my life I've had to defend even my name. Folk who should know better insist on spelling Rafael, Raphael (the ph does not exist in Spanish), leaving out the accents in Jesús and González, and spelling González with an S. And some have had the effrontery to address me as Ralph, among them S. I. Hayakawa, a Japanese-Canadian immigrant linguist, adamant opponent of bi-lingual education and founder of the English-only "U.S. English" movement to make English the official language of the United States.

Of course, assimilation involves much more than one's name and one's native tongue. The pressures to assimilate are great in the U.S. and it is accomplished by and to degrees by whatever one undertakes: schooling, profession, political activism—social involvement. But, as with the conquest of the Americas, it is to be resisted. The question is, to what degree. For me a line of identity to be respected is my name and my mother tongue though I recognize that some of my Chicanx compatriots most resisting assimilation were given English names at birth and taught only English by parents eager to assimilate to try to save their children from the virulent discrimination, racism, endemic to the U.S.

Two major reasons for my coming to San Francisco Bay were its community college system and the rich racial and ethnic variety of its people. At Laney College, Oakland where I taught for thirty years, many of my students spoke Spanish, Ebonics, Cantonese, Japanese, Tagalog, Pachuco, Nahuatl, Quechua, a Maya language, and other tongues too many to list. In my classes, I always emphasized that I would teach Standard English, not as a substitute for the language or languages they already knew but simply as another one to be added. In many places and situations such as in their home, 'hoods, church, their native tongue would serve most excellently well. At the same time, in other places such as academia, work, politics, the bank, Standard English would be a tool to open doors otherwise closed to them. Beware of and avoid false dilemmas, I would say to my students. When asked if I wanted vanilla or chocolate ice cream, I would reply, yes, please, I will have both.

The mulish, sometimes vehement, resistance to bilingual education in the U.S. used to puzzle me. Each language is a world in a shared Earth, a particular way of shaping a reality, an adventure of human consciousness. Why deny children a second language at an age when they could so easily learn it? Why insist upon ignorance?

It now puzzles me less. Exceptionalism, like narcissism, is a fragile identity intolerant of variety, of comparisons. It prefers one world in its image, its own brand of reality, its hegemony. Exceptionalism insists on "purity" of race, politics, religion, culture, language, and so on. Jealous of its own borders, exceptionalism does not hesitate violating those of others. It insists on assimilation—or else. Language is arguably the single most important aspect of identity not only of nation but often of social class. The goal of teaching classes only in Standard English in public schools is of course standardization, homogenization, assimilation which are prerequisites of the nation state in which the Anglo-American is viewed as the ethnic standard.

I am not partisan of the nation state; I much prefer the multinational state, and much as there is resistance to it, historically violent and genocidal, the U.S. is in fact such. I am not a nationalist. When asked my citizenship, I would most likely now reply, "of the world." Or Berkeley (destined to borders, the dividing line between the city of Berkeley and the city of Oakland runs right through the middle of my house so that I fix breakfast in Berkeley and eat it in Oakland.)

I am a denizen of the border; I grew up disbelieving in borders. I like differences, am tolerant of contradiction, comfortable with paradox. I like distinctions but I also like the blending, the diffusion, shades and hues. I understood when my customer the old lady asked for hilaza matizada (variegated floss) for her embroidery.

As to my writing, my refusal to sacrifice my Spanish no less than my name, makes me heir to two muses, congenial sisters, and I will not forsake one for the other. I never know which will speak to me first, but as soon as one gives me a line, a phrase, a verse, the other will immediately give me its equivalent in the other tongue, a dialogue, a discussion that affects each version so that almost all of my poems are unique pieces in two tongues, neither version the translation of the other. Editors most often do not understand bilingualism and ask which version is the translation of the other, which should be set in italics. It seems to disconcert them when I say neither. And even more when I insist that neither should be individual words in the body of the text.

I might also note that though I respect blending, I also like distinctions and that I write in both fairly Standard U.S. English and fairly Standard Mexican Spanish, each separate and distinct. I am afraid that this not only speaks to my identity, but also to my schooling, and perhaps my class. Such be the Chicano I am.

But the kid in my poem "A una anciana / To an Old Woman" must be answered his question: Demasiado mijo, mucho muy demasiado; too much, much, much too much.

RIFFS SOBRE EL POEMA
"A UNA ANCIANA / TO AN OLD WOMAN"
Rafael Jesús González

Regresando a casa después de mi servicio en la marina estadunidense en 1958, me matriculé bajo la ley GI en la Universidad de Texas El Paso que entonces se llamaba Texas Western State College of the University of Texas. Después de clases trabajaba en la tiendita general de mi padre llamada Casa Gonycia (abreviatura de González y compañía) que vendía artículos de tocador, útiles escolares, juguetes, artículos de mercería y artículos varios el Segundo barrio, el barrio de clase trabajadora más cercano a la frontera mexicana-estadounidense.

De mi experiencia trabajando allí vino mi poema "A una anciana / To an Old Woman" en 1959. Había formado amistad con una cliente frecuente, una mujer muy mayor que a menudo me consultaba sobre la hilaza de bordar para combinar o complementar los colores de su exquisito bordado. Más allá de eso el poema es obra de mi imaginación. No arrastraba rebozo ni tropezaba con su bastilla ni pagaba sus compras con "centavos sudados." Podía ver bastante bien y nuestras discusiones sobre los colores eran puramente estéticas. Coloreé su imagen para mis propios fines como escritor e imaginé una situación que pudiera o no ser suya para presentar un problema que siempre me había (ha) preocupado: la asimilación.

Nací y me creé en El Paso, Texas con familia a través del Río Bravo en Ciudad Juárez, Chihuahua y la identidad se convirtió cada vez más en problema. El español era mi primera lengua y hasta los mediados de los 1960s cuando me convertí en chicano, era simplemente mexicano aunque sabía que era ciudadano de los Estados Unidos de América. Aun hoy en día cuando se me pregunta "¿Qué eres?" mi respuesta inmediata es "mexicano" aunque cuando estoy más alerta digo "chicano." Aunque cuando se me pregunta "Cual es tu ciudadanía" no titubeo.

No aprendí inglés hasta los siete en la escuela pública Lamar y a principio no fue fácil. Ya leía y escribía básicamente en español y el sonido impredecible de las mismas letras en inglés me confundía. Estuve en la oscuridad la mayor parte del tiempo. Un día mi madre con mi hermanito me acompañó a la escuela y se fueron a casa de mis abuelos a unas cuadras de distancia. Me encontré en un patio de recreo totalmente vacío, las puertas de la escuela cerradas. Estuve aterrorizado. Caminé de regreso a una casa vacía. Me senté en el portal confundido, asustado, sólo hasta que mi madre y abuela vinieron con mi hermanito y me cubrieron de abrazos y besos. La maestra había anunciado un día de fiesta pero yo no había entendido.

No ayudaba que fuéramos castigados si se nos escuchaba hablar español en la aula, los corredores o el patio de recreo. Si le preguntábamos a un compañero de clase, "¿Qué dijo la maestra?" se nos hacía pararnos en un rincón o nos detenían después de la escuela. Tengo la distinción de haber reprobado el primer grado. Sobresalía en dibujo y pintura y recuerdo a una amable maestra, la Sra. Hall en cuarto grado, que me elogió y animó. Pero el director recomendó que mis padres nos llevaran a mi y a mi hermano Arturo (dos años menor que yo) a la Escuela Bailey para niños "retrasados."

Mi padre lo hizo y el director de la Escuela Bailey que no pudo habernos tenido allí más de treinta minutos, le dijo a mi padre que no pertenecíamos allí y recomendó que nos cambiáramos de escuela. Mis padres se endeudaron y compararon su primera y única casa para que pudiéramos cambiar de distritos e ir a la escuela pública Morehead donde nuestros problemas desaparecieron. (Dos maestras se destacan: la Sra. Patricia Robinson, maestra de arte que hablaba excelente español e invitaba a algunos estudiantes a su casa para dibujar y pintar. Y la Srta. Mary Hignett, maestra de inglés, con quien hice amigo en mis años universitarios hasta su muerte.)

Para entonces en 1950 me había ajustado, aculturado si quiere; no fui asimilado (lo que para mí tiene la connotación de ser masticado, tragado y digerido). Para mí, el lenguaje ha sido una piedra de toque de asimilación. El indio mexicano yo había sido asimilado durante mucho tiempo; mi abuelo materno Papanito, don Diego González Sosa a excepción por su color y facciones y su decir que éramos indio no hablaba lengua indígena para indicarlo sino solo un castellano formal. El mexicano mestizo yo, no así. Fui bendecido con padres, Jesús F. González de Coahuila y Carmen González Prieto de Durango, (traídos a los 13 y 12 años respetivamente) quienes siempre insistieron en que habláramos y escribiéramos tanto en español como en inglés. Tomé cursos en español durante la escuela secundaria y me gradué de la universidad con un bachillerato en literatura inglesa con suficientes horas en literatura española para una doble especialización. En una ironía del destino, he pasado la mayor parte de mi vida como profesor de inglés en universidades y colegios.

Resistir la asimilación es una lucha, especialmente en un imperio que impone su hegemonía (militar, económica, política, lingüística, cultural) en el mundo. Toda mi vida he tenido que defender aun mi nombre. Personas que deberían saber más insisten en escribir Rafael, Raphael (la ph no existe en español), omitir los acentos en Jesús y González y escribir González con S. Y algunos han tenido el descaro de dirigirse a mí como Ralph, entre ellos S. I. Hayakawa, un lingüista japonés-canadiense, firme oponente a la educación bilingüe y fundador del movimiento "Sólo Inglés" para hacer el inglés el idioma oficial de los Estados Unidos.

Por supuesto que la asimilación implica mucho más que el nombre y la lengua materna de uno. Las presiones para asimilarse son grandes en los EE.UU. y se logra grado a grado por lo que sea que uno emprenda: educación, profesión, activismo político, participación social. Pero, como con la conquista de las Américas, se debe resistir. La pregunta es, ¿en que medida? Para mí una línea de identidad que se debe respetar es mi nombre y mi lengua materna aunque reconozco que algunos de mis compatriotas chicanos que más se resisten a la asimilación se les dieron nombres en inglés al nacer y se les enseñó solo inglés por padres ansiosos por asimilarse para tratar de salvar a sus hijos de la discriminación virulenta, el racismo, endémico de los EE.UU.

Dos razones principales por las que vine a la Bahía de San Francisco fueron su sistema de colegios comunitarios. En el Colegio Laney, Oakland donde enseñe durante treinta años, muchos de mis estudiantes hablaban español, ebonics (dialecto africano-EE.UU), cantonés, japonés, tagalo, pachuco, náhuatl, quechua, un idioma maya y otras lenguas demasiadas para listar. En mis clases siempre enfaticé que enseñaría inglés estándar, no como un sustituto del idioma o idiomas que ya conocían sino simplemente como uno más para agregar. En muchos lugares y situaciones, como en su hogar, barrios, iglesia, su lengua materna serviría excelentemente bien. Al mismo tiempo, en otros lugares como la academia, el trabajo, la política, el banco, el inglés estándar sería una herramienta para abrir puertas que de otro modo estarían cerradas para ell@s. Cuídense y eviten los falso dilemas les decía a mis alumn@s. Cuando se me pregunta si quiero helado de vainilla o de chocolate, respondo que sí, por favor, tomaré de los dos.

La resistencia terca, a veces vehemente, a la educación bilingüe en los EE.UU. solía desconcertarme. Cada idioma es un mundo en una Tierra compartida, una forma particular de formar una realidad, una aventura de la consciencia humana. ¿Por qué negar a l@s niñ@s un segundo idioma a una edad en la que podrían aprenderlo tan fácilmente? ¿Por qué insistir en la ignorancia?

Ahora me desconcierta menos. El excepcionalismo, como el narcisismo, es una identidad frágil que no tolera la variedad, las comparaciones. Prefiere un mundo en su imagen, su propia marca de realidad, su hegemonía. El excepcionalismo insiste en la "pureza" de raza, política, religión, cultura, idioma, etc. Celoso de sus propias fronteras, el excepcionalismo no vacila en violar las de los demás. Insiste en la asimilación—o bien. Se podría decir que el idioma es el aspecto más importante de la identidad, no solo de la nación, sino a menudo de la clase social. El objetivo de impartir clases solo en inglés estándar en las escuelas públicas es, por supuesto, la estandarización, la homoeneización y la asimilación que son requisitos del estado nación en el que el anglamericano se considera el estándar étnico.

No soy partidario del estado nación; prefiero mucho más el estado multinacional, y por mucho que haya recistencia a él, históricamente violenta y genocida, los Estados Unidos es en hecho tal. No soy nacionalista. Cuando me preguntan mi ciudadanía, lo más probable es que ahora responda, "del mundo." O Berkeley (destinado a fronteras, la línea divisora entre la ciudad Berkeley y la ciudad de Oakland pasa justo por el medio de mi casa así que preparo el desayuno en Berkeley y lo como en Oakland).

Soy habitante de frontera; crecí sin creer en las fronteras. Me gustan las diferencias, soy tolerante con la contradicción, cómodo con la paradoja. Me gustan las distinciones pero también me gusta la mezcla, la difusión, las sombra y los matices. Entendí cuando mi cliente la viejita me pedía hilaza matizada para sus bordados.

En cuanto a mi escritura, negarme a sacrificar mi español no menos que mi nombre, me hace heredero de dos musas, hermanas congeniales y no abandonaré la una por la otra. Nunca sé cual me hablará primero pero en cuanto una me da un verso, una frase, la otra inmediatamente me da su equivalente en la otra lengua, un diálogo, una discusión que afecta a cada versión para que casi todos mis poemas son piezas únicas en dos lenguas, ninguna versión de la otra. Los editores a menudo no entienden el bilingüismo y preguntan que versión es la traducción de la otra, cual debe estar en cursiva. Parece desconcertarlos cuando digo que ni la una o la otra. Y aun más cuando insisto en que tampoco sean palabras solas en el cuerpo del texto.

También podría notar que aunque respeto la mezcla, también me gustan las distinciones y que escribo tanto en inglés estadounidense bastante estándar como en español mexicano bastante estándar, cada uno por separado y distinto. Temo que esto no solo habla de mi identidad sino también de mi enseñanza y quizás de mi clase. Así sea el chicano que soy.

Pero hay que responderle a la pregunta del chiquillo en mi poema: Demasiado mijo, mucho muy demasiado; too much, much, much too much.

Acknowledgments

The English version of "Riffs on the Poem 'A una anciana / To an Old Woman'" was first published in *English Quarterly*, Vol. III, no. 5, May 2022, of the National Council of Teachers of English.

The poem "A Una Anciana / To An Old Woman" was first published in *New Mexico Quarterly*, Vol. 31, No. 4, 1961.

Mark Harris
VISUAL DIARY OF LIVED EXPERIENCE

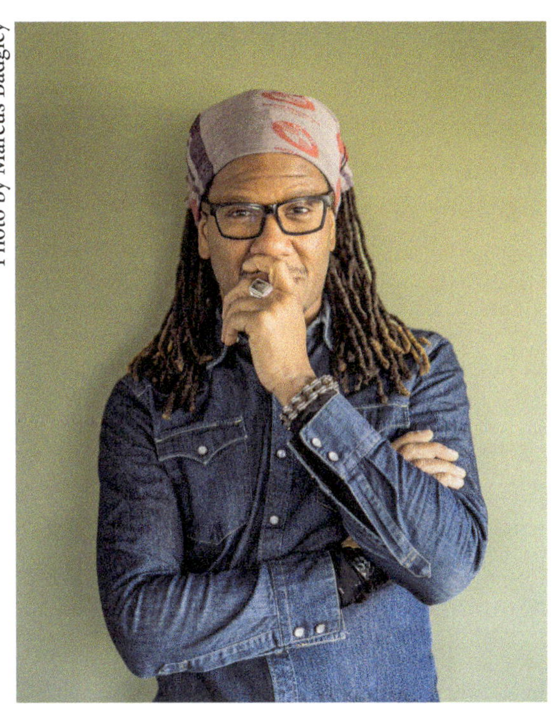

Mark Harris is an award winning artist, activist, and educator.
He has combined his passions for art making and activism
to create visually compelling work that he uses
to engage his audience on issues facing society today.
He has established a strong independent voice
and is one of the San Francisco Bay Area's most
controversial artists. The *Metro Silicon Valley News*
called his work "brilliantly subversive."

His evocative, elegant, and dynamic creations have caught
the eye of international and domestic art collectors alike.
A native of Durham, North Carolina, Harris grew up in Atlanta,
Georgia, and now lives and works in San Francisco, California.
www.artofmarkharris.com

VISUAL DIARY OF LIVED EXPERIENCE
Mark Harris

Creating art has given me a sense of comfort and identity since an early age; it's how I process the world around me. The people, places and events that profoundly affect me are what fuel my work. My desire as an artist is to fully explore and express my emotions related to these influences, rather than simply illustrate them.

When I was 7 years old, I asked my father to draw a picture of a horse. What he created looked like a badly drawn box on stilts. I told him it didn't look like a horse to me, and he responded by encouraging me to find a picture of a horse I liked and then draw it until I was happy with it. That's exactly what I did, over, and over, and over again. This simple interaction with my father is what sparked my lifelong interest in creativity; in essence he gave me my first drawing assignment. From that point on I drew as much as possible each day. After horses I began drawing sports figures, then hot rod cars, and then characters from comic books. Throughout my youth I drew as frequently as I could about the things that interested me most.

By the time I reached my late teens I'd become distracted by the pursuits of young adulthood, and I stopped creating altogether. After graduating high school, and a short stint in Junior College, I spent the next five years doing various corporate jobs in and around Atlanta. In 1996, I began feeling a desire to return to my creative roots, so I enrolled at the Art Institute of Atlanta. I worked full time while I studied, but dropped out after two quarters to take a job in the financial printing industry in Tampa, Florida. I lived there three and a half years before moving to the Bay Area in the year 2000 for a job in Palo Alto. I continued working in financial printing for another year, which helped to further solidify my desire to leave my corporate existence for a more fulfilling life. Then one afternoon in late spring of 2001, I found myself in a meeting with my boss and the human resources manager. Their message was simple and to the point, the "Dot Com" bubble was starting to bust, and the company was cutting back. I was offered a choice of taking a $20,000 cut in salary and keeping my job, or being laid off with two weeks severance. They gave me 24 hours to decide.

The decision was a no brainer for me. I'd become increasingly dissatisfied with working 9 to 5 in corporate America, and I wasn't about to continue doing it for $20K less. By this point I had a strong desire to live my life differently. I wanted to do something that would allow me to explore and use my creativity. I returned to work the following day and said no thanks to the pay cut.

At that moment I made a life-altering decision to leave a comfortable yet unfulfilling corporate job and pursue my dream of becoming a full-time artist. I had no idea how or if this would come to pass. Instead of focusing on the how, I sat down with my journal and wrote out my heart's desire for the kind of artist I wanted to become.

Then I began to paint every day, without fail, over, and over, and over again. I approached this new chapter of life with the same curiosity and excitement I had as a seven-year-old boy when I started drawing. Over the past 22 years I've maintained that deep curiosity about life and artistic expression, and I've continued to practice my craft while exploring different mediums. The result is a body of work that is a visual diary of my lived experience as an African American man in the United States of America. These experiences are illustrated in various styles from cubist, to abstract expression, to collage— all artistic expressions of the various people, places, and events that have profoundly affected me.

My current body of work was influenced by the murder of Michael Brown and the civil unrest that followed in Ferguson, Missouri in August 2014. These events had an enormous impact on me emotionally and artistically. For the past eight years my work has been focused on issues of social justice, specifically examining themes of police violence and the doctrine of white supremacy in the United States. Currently I combine aspects of photo collage with painting and traditional collage to create mixed media works on wood panel. Each work presents an alternative narrative to the status quo by using text, juxtaposition, and mid-20th century advertising imagery. My intention is to engage and inspire my audience while throwing a "glitch" into their perception.

We are living in an unprecedented time of social change and the evolution of humanity. The circumstances we find ourselves in here in the United States provide fertile ground for the collective conscious to reimagine a more just and equitable society. I believe that my art can be a way to help facilitate that change.

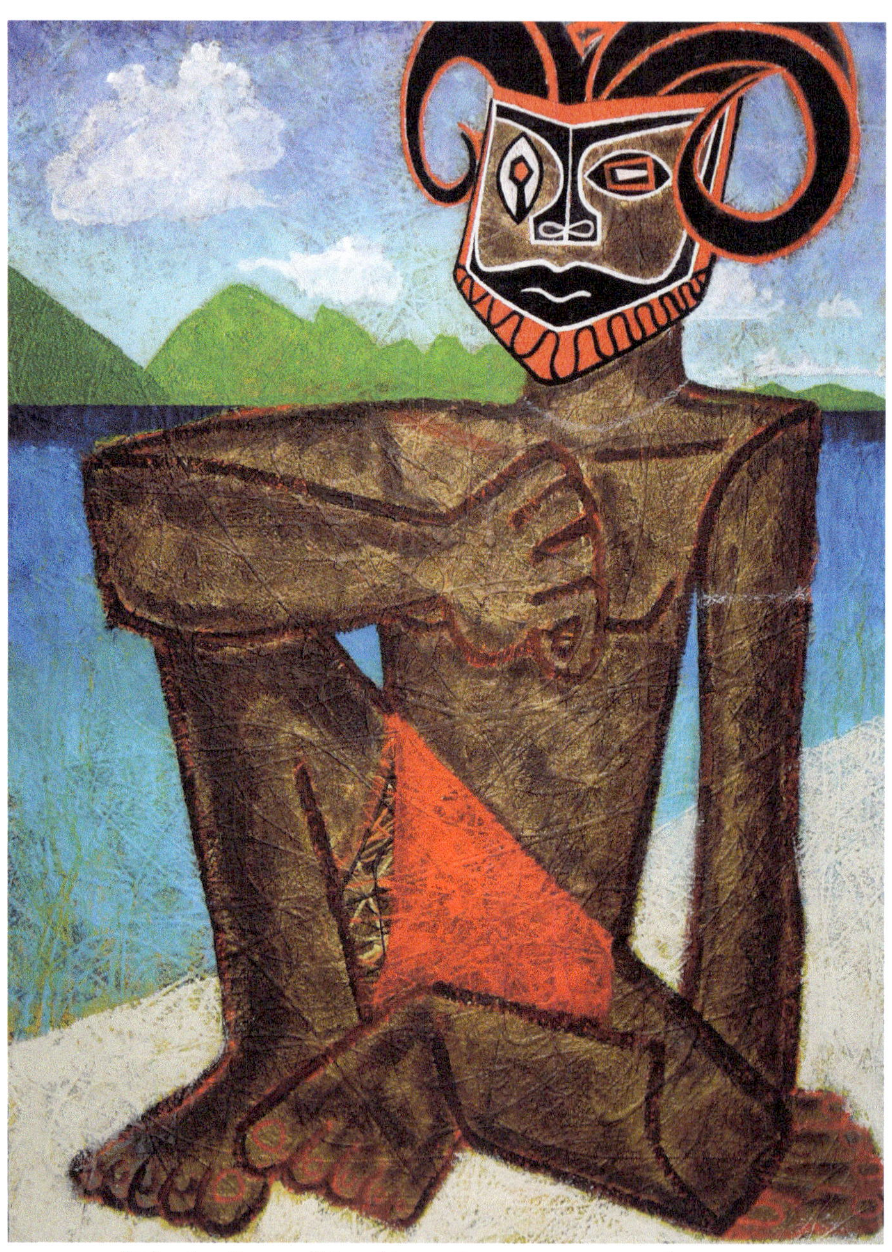

"Warrior Repose," Acrylic on Canvas, 36 x 48 inches, 2009.

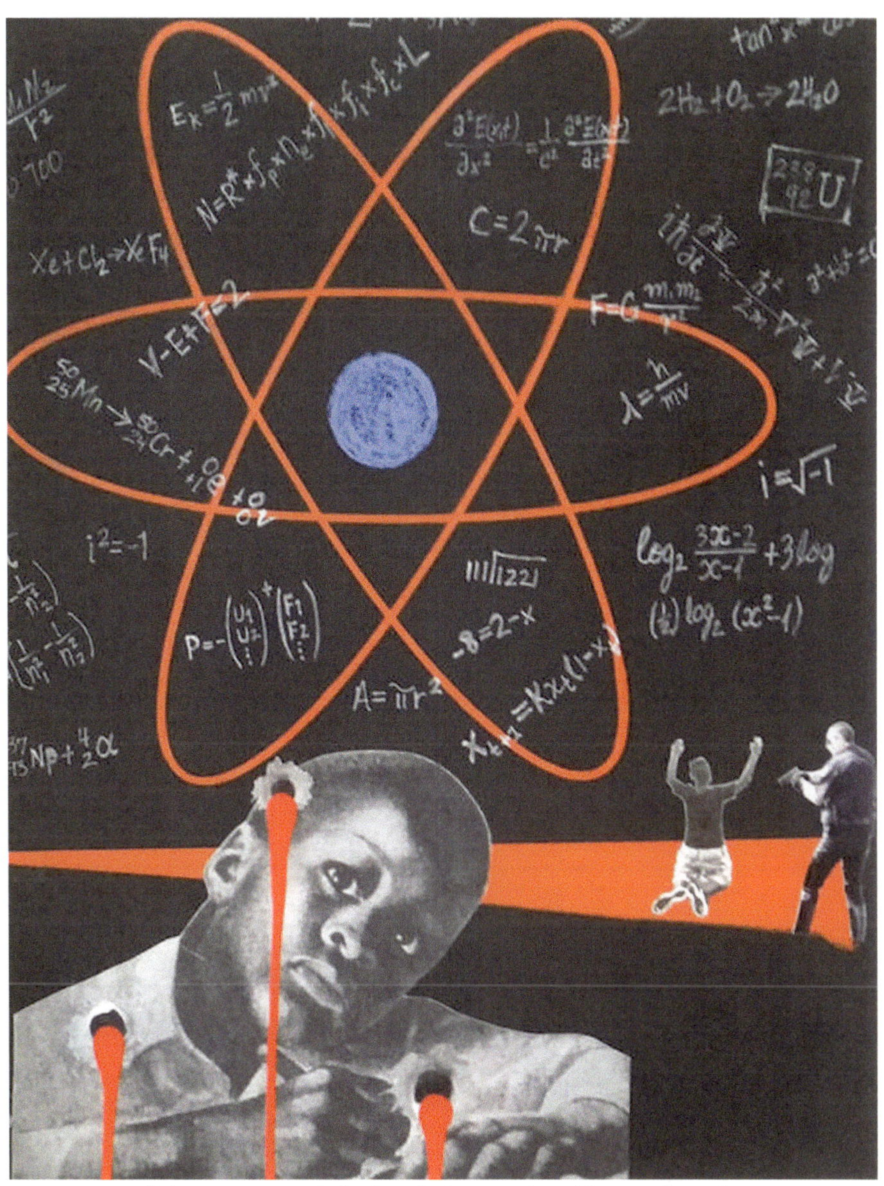

"To Be Young, Gifted and Criminalized," mixed media
on paper, 16 x 20 inches, 2014.

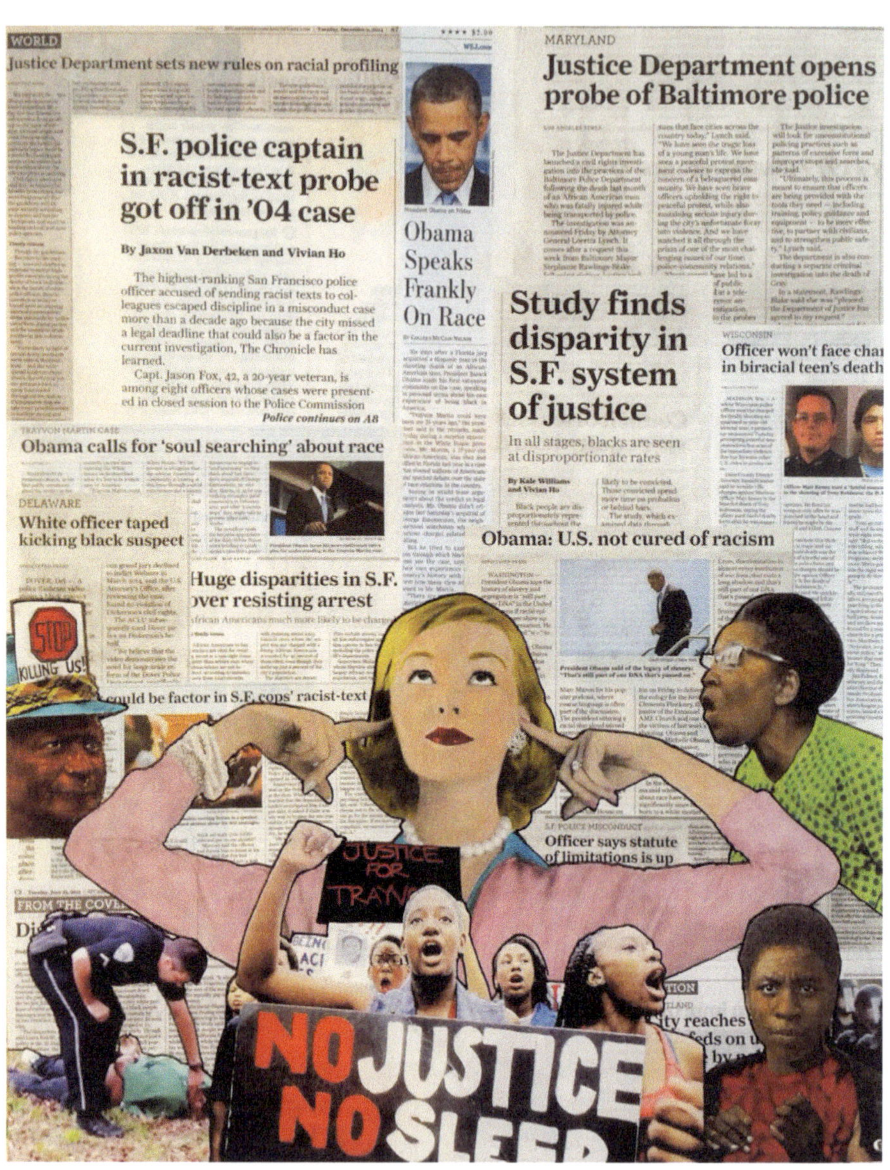

"Tuned Out," mixed media on panel, 30 x 24 inches, 2015.

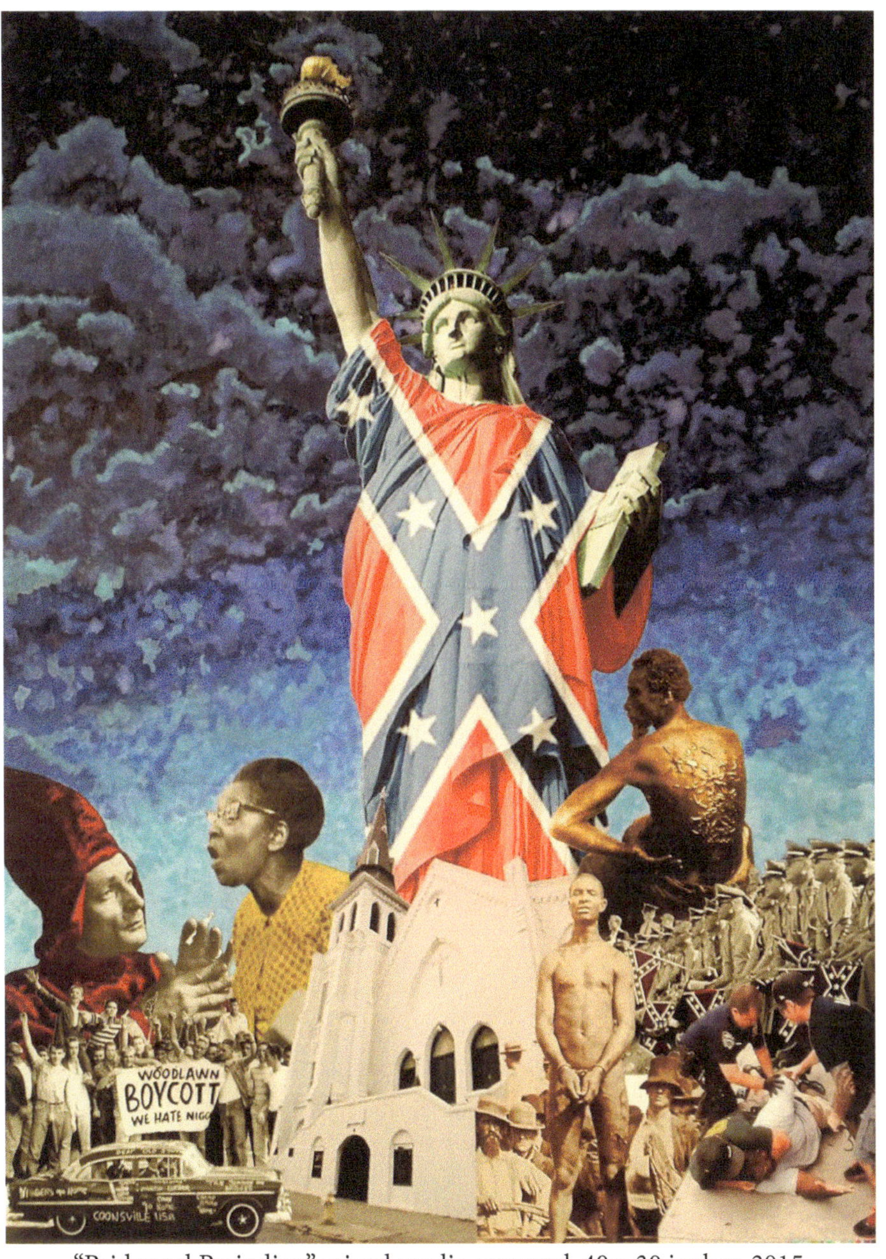

"Pride and Prejudice," mixed media on panel, 40 x 30 inches, 2015.
Response to Charleston church massacre.

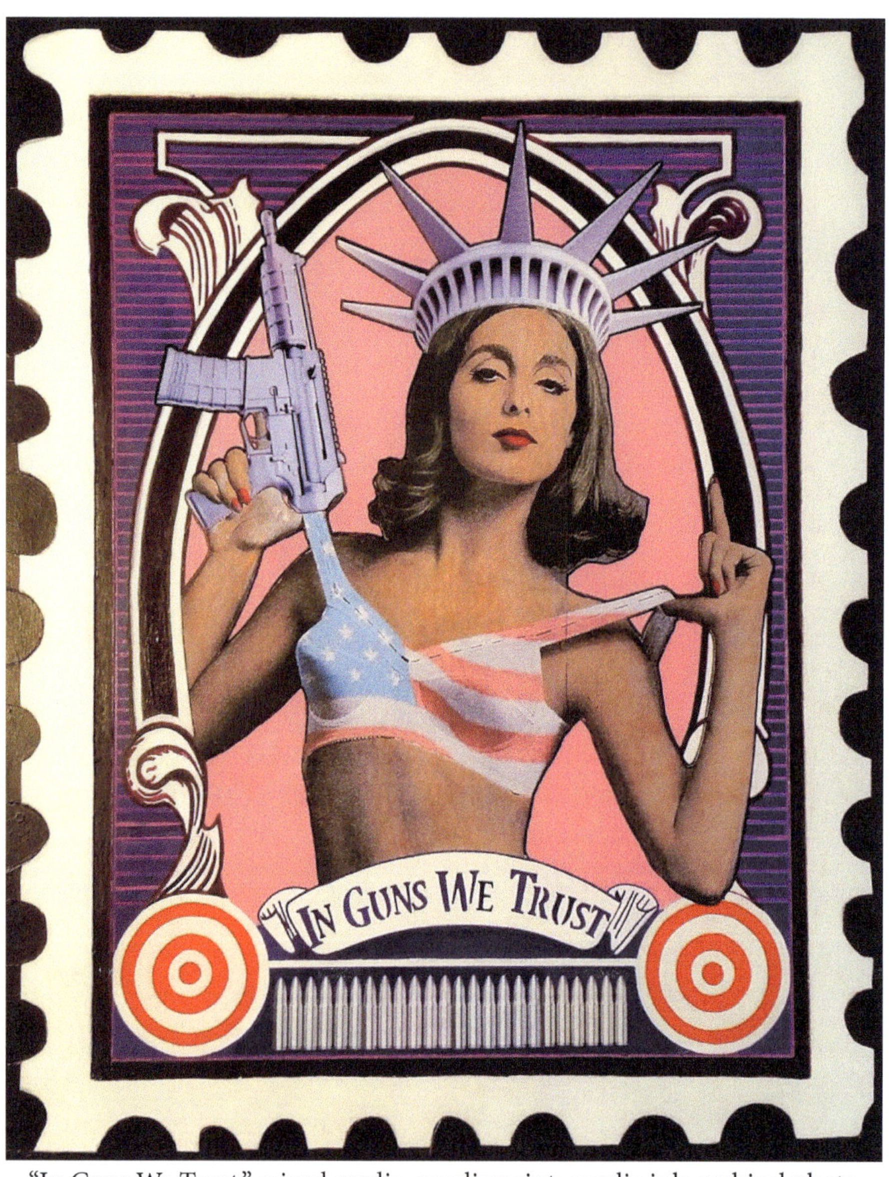

"In Guns We Trust," mixed media, acrylic paint, acrylic ink, archival photo paper, and vinyl, 30 x 24 inches, 2015. Response to America's love of guns.

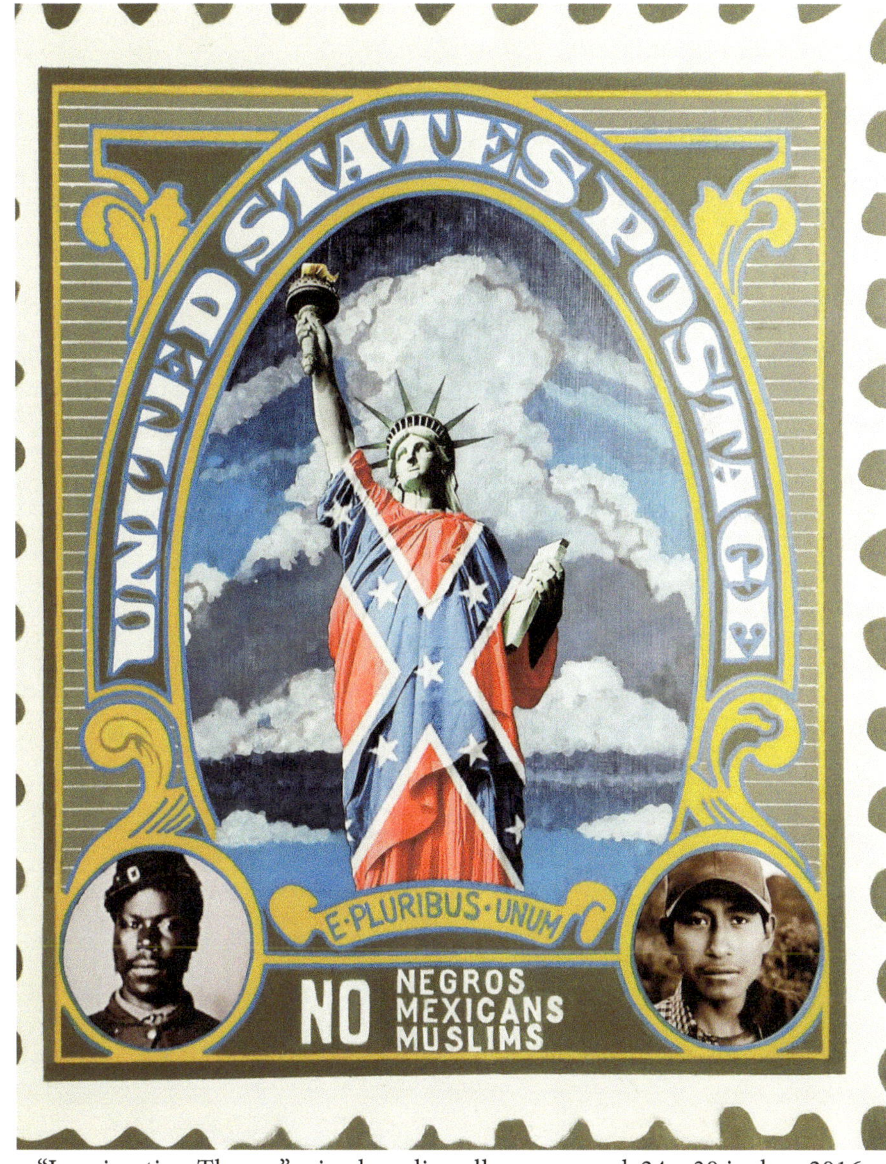

"Immigration Theory," mixed media collage on panel, 24 x 30 inches, 2016.

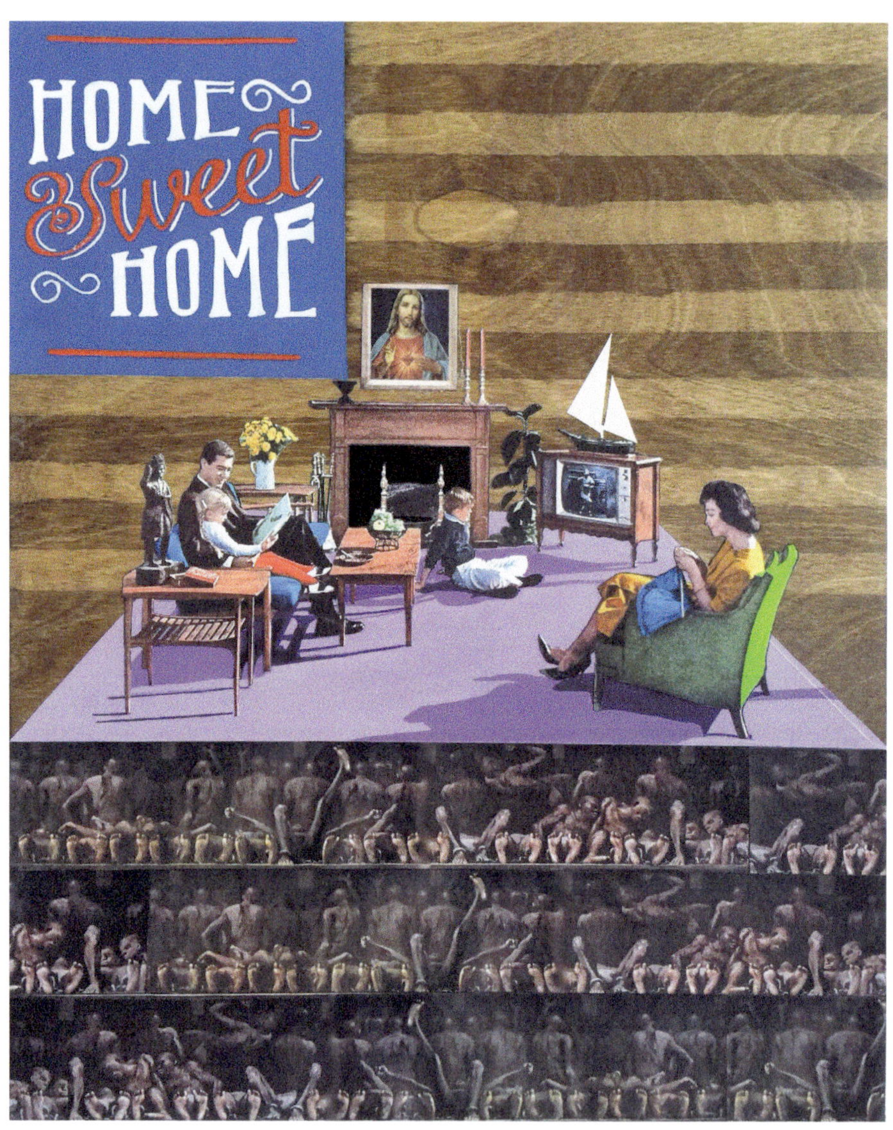

"Den of Iniquity," mixed media on panel, 20 x 24 inches, 2016.

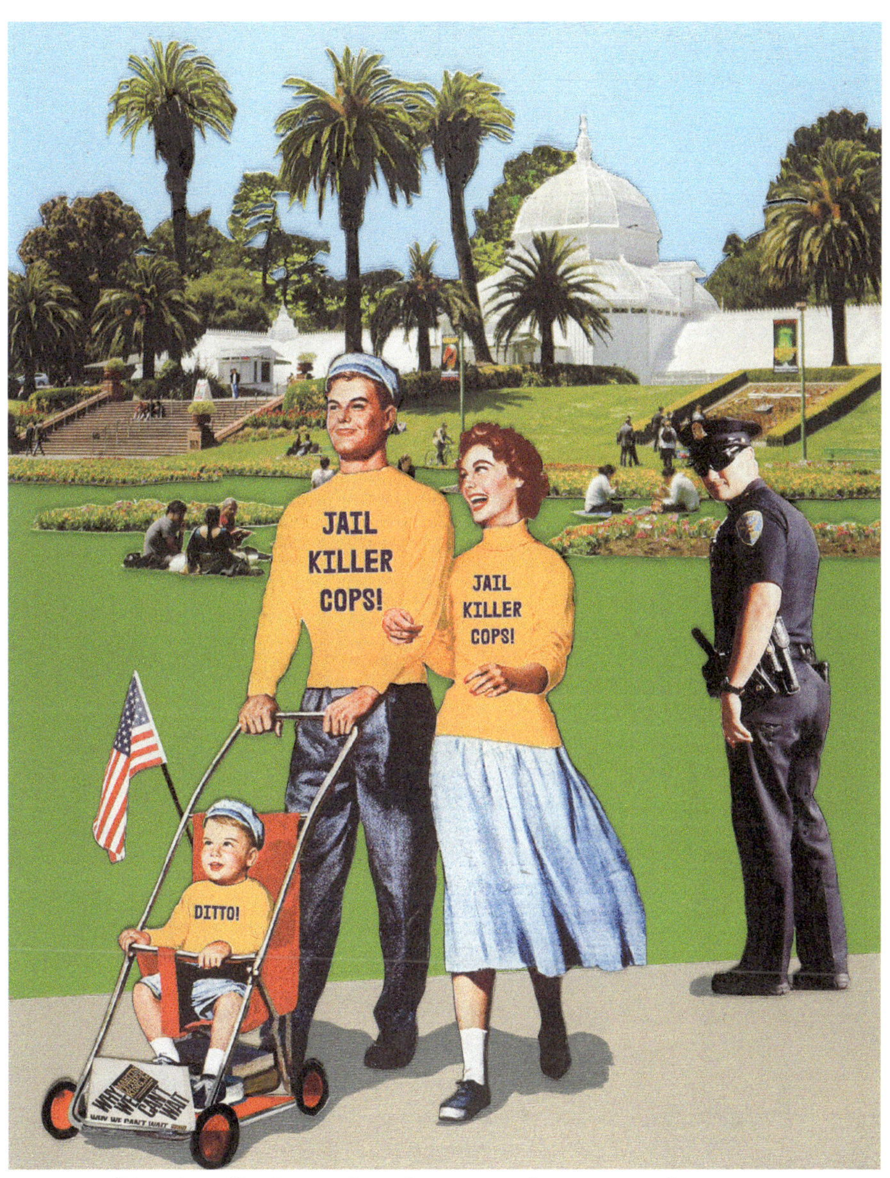

"Family Affair," mixed media on panel, 16 x 20 inches, 2021.

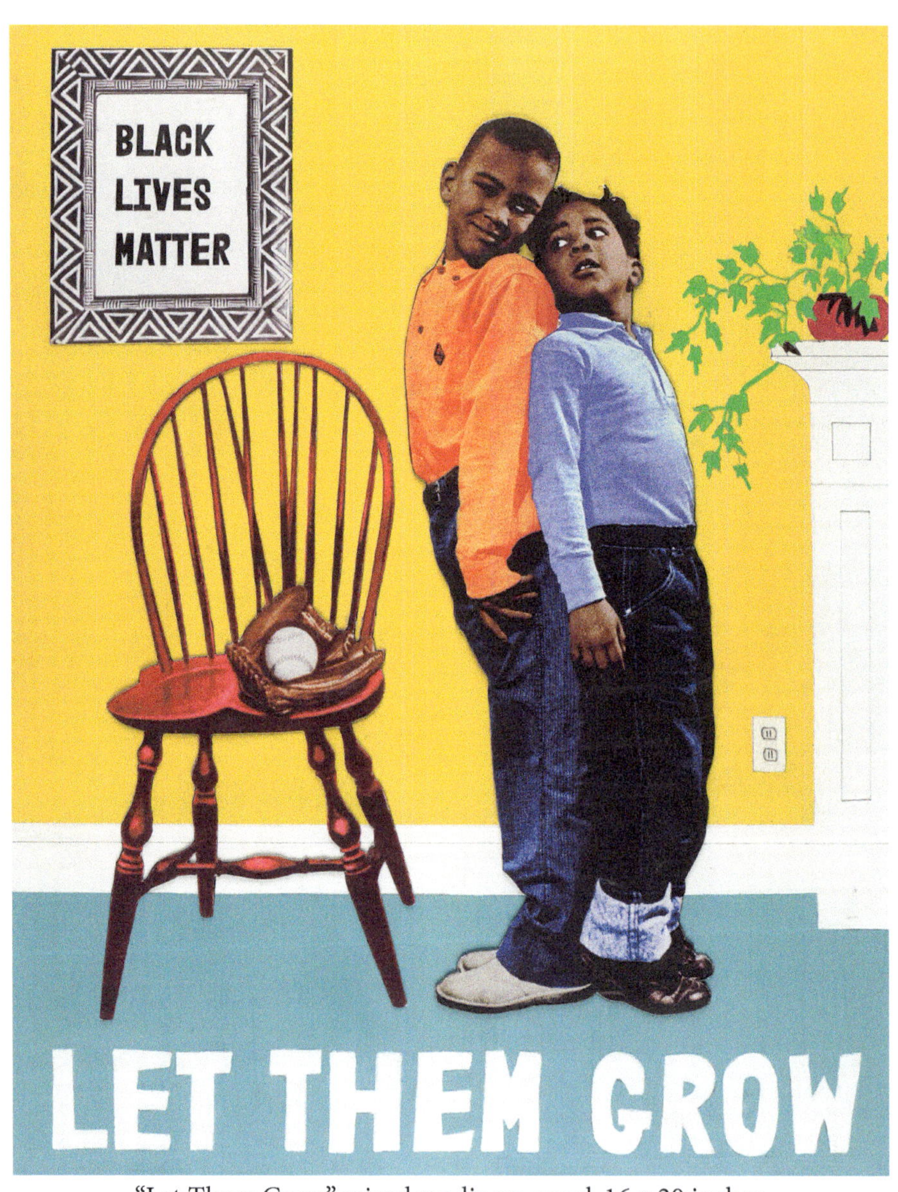

"Let Them Grow," mixed media on panel, 16 x 20 inches,
study for *Exploratorium Stories of Change* exhibit, 2021.

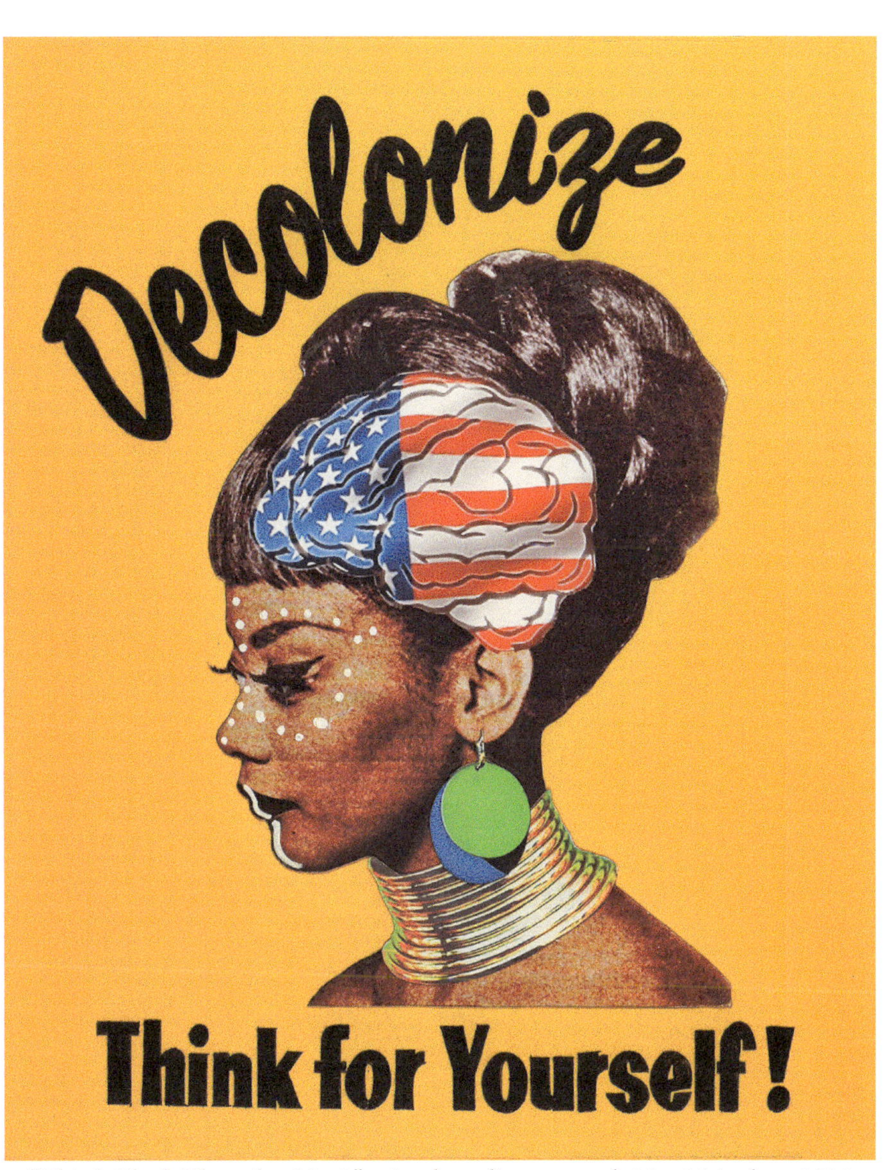

"Think Black Thoughts No 1," mixed media on panel, 16 x 20 inches, 2021

Acknowledgments

"Den of Iniquity" was previously published in *Endangered Species, Enduring Values*, Pease Press, 2018.

"Pride and Prejudice" and "In Guns We Trust" were previously published in *Essential Truths, the Bay Area in Color*, Pease Press, 2021.

C. K. Itamura
CIRCUITOUS PATHS OF THE YONSEI

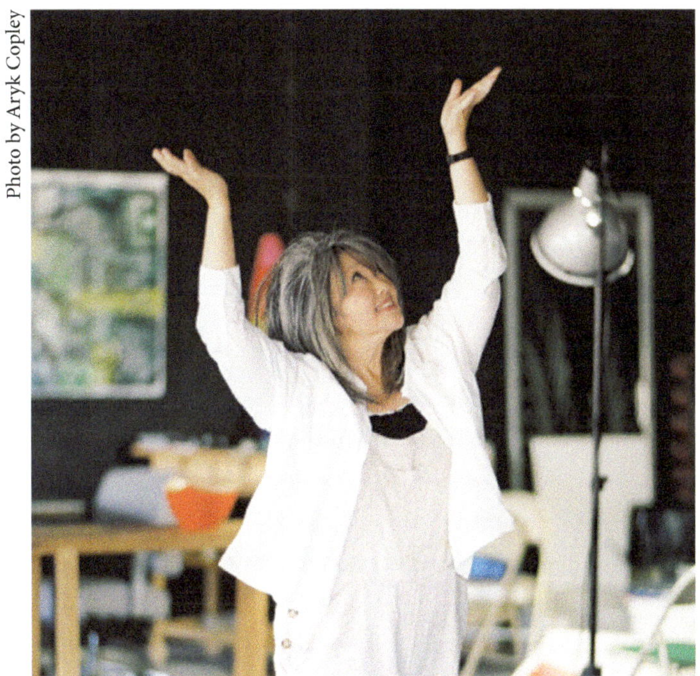

C. K. Itamura is a Yonsei interdisciplinary artist based in Sonoma
County, California. Her conceptual, visual, performance, and
community engagement art is fused with the aesthetic
of Nikkei traditions and serves to engage diverse multicultural,
intergenerational audiences in the exploration of observation,
contemplation, and expressive imagination.

C. K. is a recipient of the 2019 Discovered Awards for Emerging
Visual Artists and artist residencies at The Imaginists,
Chalk Hill, and In Cahoots. She is a co-founder of Book Arts
Roadshow and a former director of San Francisco
Center for the Book. She has served in directorial, managerial and/
or production roles for live theatrical performances, live events,
concerts and festivals, radio shows, and video productions.
peachfarmstudio.net

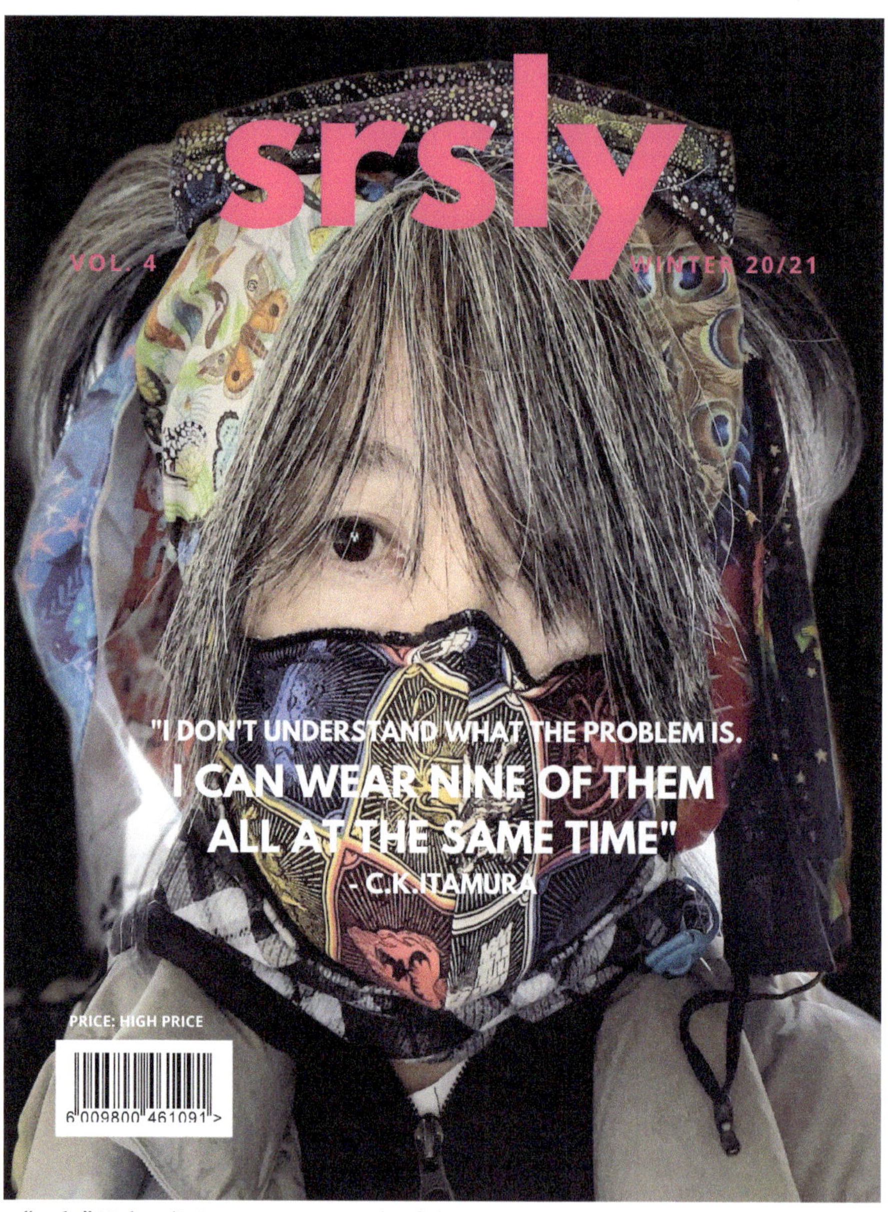

"srsly," Vol. 4 (Winter 2020-2021) of the *covers* series, photography and text, digital assemblage printed on metal, 2021.

Image is a selfie of C. K. at home, first thing in the morning, wearing nine masks. "I don't understand what the problem is."

CIRCUITOUS PATHS OF THE YONSEI
C. K. Itamura

I am a child of *Sesame Street, The Electric Company, The Lone Ranger,* and *ZOOM*, a television program for kids that has nothing to do with video conferencing and everything to do with being your own cool, interesting, and unique self.

I am also the child of *Hello Kitty, Speed Racer, Ultraman,* and *Zatoichi*, the blind swordsman who is a sort of gambling, Zorro-esque massage therapist, and I am also Yonsei. No, not Beyoncé. Yonsei, as in the Japanese diasporic term used, particularly in North America and Latin America, to specify the great-grandchildren of Japanese immigrants. Perhaps you have never thought of Japanese people as having had a diaspora and have never considered what being of Japanese ancestry means now, over a century after the opening of Japan to the West and the Big Migration, but many of us still keep track: Ichi-Ni-San-Yon-Go, 1-2-3-4-5. Issei, Nisei, Sansei, Yonsei, Go, 1st, 2nd, 3rd, 4th, 5th generation. My parents, both Sansei or 3rd-generation grandchildren of Japanese immigrants, influenced my path to the arts in very different ways.

My dad's expectations of me were, I suspect, heavily influenced by the losses he experienced in his early childhood: the forcible removal of his family from their Sacramento Valley home; the loss of their farming livelihood, all their belongings, and their community. In 1942, Executive Order 9066 forced my 4-year-old dad, his 9-year-old brother, his mother and father, and all other Americans of Japanese ancestry living in California and along the west coast, to be incarcerated in "The Camps," with only one suitcase of their belongings each. He and his family remained in Tule Lake until 1946.[1]

Dad was 8 years old and his brother was 13 when they were released from Camp. The two of them grew-up farming peaches with their parents. Always at the mercy of how weather, insects, and all varieties of fruit-tree disease might affect the blossoming, growing, and harvesting seasons, the family had no

---

1. Tule Lake was one of the 10 camps operated by the War Relocation Authority (WRA) from May 27, 1942, to March 20, 1946—the period of Japanese-American incarceration where 120,000 Japanese-Americans were forcibly removed from their homes and communities and incarcerated. Tule Lake began as a "relocation camp," then became a "segregation camp." It was the last WRA (War Relocation Authority) camp to close, remaining in operation seven months after World War II ended. https://www.nps.gov/places/tule-lake.htm

benefits, no financial security from season to season, and no guarantee from year to year that things would eventually turn out okay.

Throughout it all, his parents, my Grandpa and Grandma, discouraged him from speaking Japanese and insisted he speak English instead because he was an American and they lived in America. Years later, in order to prove his family's Americanness and put his own patriotism on display, he, his brother, and so many of their peers, enlisted in the United States Marine Corps. After serving and being honorably discharged from the military, he worked a string of odd jobs—doing watch repair, working as a graveyard-shift janitor, and owning his own small one-man barbershop—before getting married, having three daughters, and eventually achieving his dream: getting a job working for the United States Postal Service. He believed wholeheartedly that working for the U.S. Postal Service was the best job in the world.

My dad made it abundantly clear to me: money was not to be wasted on going to college. Rather, I should get a job with the United States Postal Service, as he did. "Good pay. Overtime pay. Double time for working on holidays. Paid sick and vacation time. Medical insurance and pension," he enthusiastically repeated to me countless times.

When I complained that I didn't want to work for the U.S. Postal Service and tried to explain that I wanted to go to college and learn how to be an artist instead, his reply was always the same: "Okay. If you don't want to work for the Post Office, UPS is pretty good too. And you can still save all your money for emergencies."

I was born in San Francisco but raised for the greater part of my childhood in Sacramento. I played on basketball, volleyball, softball, and soccer teams; had my own blue-marbled bowling ball; and played pinball, PacMan, and Space Invaders.

I am also a kid who performed Fuji-No-Hana odori in my silk kimono and threw wrapped hachimakis into the audience at my first public performance. I played the card game Hana and the war game Go with my mom. I went to Sakura Gakuen to learn Nihongo, how to speak, write and read the Japanese language. I folded paper cranes in the back seat of the car out of the origami my mom kept stashed in the glove box; watched sumo wrestling on TV with my cousins; dressed in cotton yukatas to dance at the annual Obon festival; and with ojuzu in hand, made an offering of incense at the Buddhist Church every Sunday.

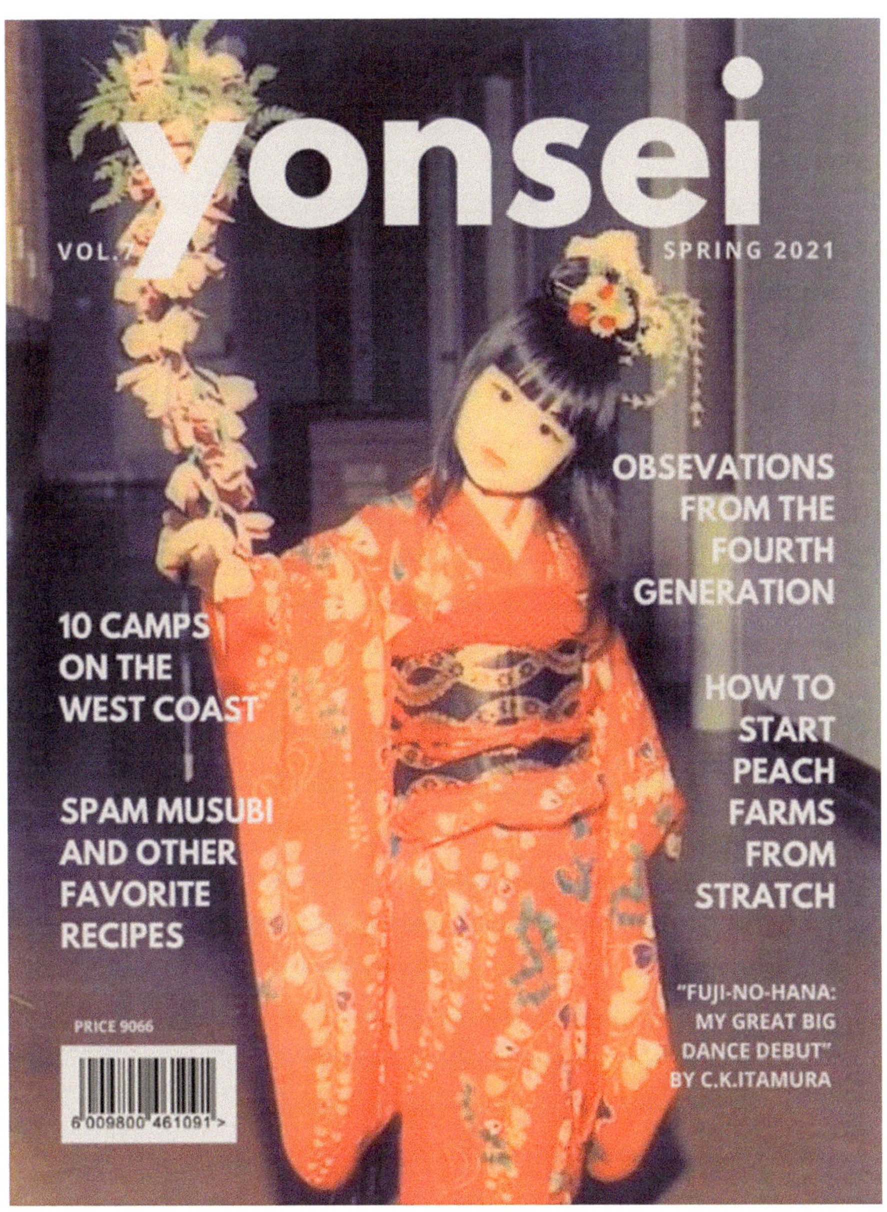

"yonsei," Vol. 7 (Spring 2021) of *covers* series, photography and text, digital assemblage printed on metal, 2021.

Image of C. K. (age 6) in the backstage hallway just before her debut stage performance of "Fuji-no-hana" ("Flower of Mt. Fuji").

Born and raised in Hawai'i, my mom had childhood experiences that were quite different from my Dad's. Her family lived in a quiet cul de sac on the island of Oahu in a small house that her Otosan, who worked as a carpenter, had built. The main room of the house had tatami mat floors, shoji screen sliding walls made of wood and rice paper, and a small low table on which to place ikebana. Meals were eaten on a wooden board placed over low risers with zabuton—thin, cotton-covered cushions—placed all around on the floor to sit on. The newspapers and magazines in the house were all in Japanese. Her family spoke only Japanese and she herself learned to speak English as a second language when she started elementary school. As an adult, all her phone calls with her parents and the handwritten letters she sent to and received from them via Airmail were in Japanese.

My mom was 2 years old in 1941 when Pearl Harbor was bombed on the other side of the island. In the aftermath of the bombing, all Hawai'i residents were subject to close military oversight, yet her family and about 158,000 other residents of Japanese descent—more than one-third of the territory's[2] population—did not face mass removal and imprisonment as their mainland counterparts did. They never experienced losing all they had worked hard for. Their loyalty was never questioned, so they continued with the customs and traditions their parents and grandparents brought with them from Japan. Unencumbered by fear or shame about their Japanese heritage, they were free to express their innate creativity in their daily lives and in community endeavors. To them, art wasn't set apart as something done by artists.

When I was growing up, my mom was a suburban housewife who played guitar and sang American folk and pop tunes around the house. She made paper mâché masks and puppet heads, and sewed costumed bodies for the puppets so that her daughters could produce shows in the wooden puppet theater her otousan, father, constructed in the living room. Her kitchen-and-bathroom-tile-installing oniichan, older brother, created a mosaic garden at his home and created mosaic statuary, walkways, and fountains throughout. Her anichan, younger brother, a lineman for the telephone company, took portraits of family members and built a dark room to pursue his interest in photography. Her homemaking okaasan, mother, sewed matching dresses for her daughter and granddaughters out of store-bought fabric and used bundles of fabric scraps she received through the backdoor of a Hawai'ian shirt factory to make quilts she gave as gifts.

---

2. Hawai'i was a territory of the United States from 1900 'til 1959 when it became the 50th state.

I am an adult who found myself working for a bank when I was 20 years old and then a database company for about 18 years because of good pay, paid sick, vacation and holiday time, regular raises, job security, health insurance, and 401(k). I am an adult who discovered, while working on an 18-month database project for the San Francisco Opera, that people could and did make a living in the arts. I am an adult who wanted to do what they were doing and who realized that I would need to quit the work I was doing in order to make room on my calendar, in my brain, and in my body for this other way of existence to enter my life. I am an adult who built upon the practical skills I learned in the corporate world. I added to it the spirit of observation, contemplation, and expressive imagination, and blended it with the Nikkei[3] aesthetics that dwell within me. I have for the past 20 years found my way by working with theater companies, music festivals, film and record companies, and art organizations, and in my own art studio. I learned that it is possible to dream, and to learn by doing, discovering with each new job a little more of what is needed to achieve these dreams, and finally being in position to create art which is personally fulfilling.

I am an adult who enthusiastically participates in the rituals of osoji and seiri, deep cleaning and decluttering the house on New Year's Eve to bring the year to a close and to welcome in fresh energy and new possibilities. I am an adult who buys omiyage while on vacation to give to friends, prefers to open gifts in private, wraps gifts and food in furoshiki, including my own bento box packed with lunch for outdoor adventure days. I am an adult who washes gohan until the water runs crystal clear, cooks a gluten-free version of Golden Curry from scratch, and routinely makes miso soup with dashi, wakame, and tofu, and adds little bits of tamago and green onion on top.

I am Yonsei. As I write this, I am 58 years old, just two years younger than my Sansei mom was when she died from cancer. My Sansei dad passed away three years ago. Now, after decades of puzzling things together, I have a new understanding of what senzo-ni-kansha-shimasu, "thanking ancestors" means.

---

3. Nikkei means "Japanese ancestry." It is a word that encompasses people all around the world who have Japanese heritage, but who do not live in Japan. https://www.bctf.ca/whats-happening/news-details/2021/06/11/culture-through-history-getting-to-know-nikkei-in-canada.

When I was a child, I thought we thanked the ancestors because without them, my grandparents, parents and I would never have been born. Now I realize that "thanking ancestors" also means thanking them for the Nikkei values and strengths and for modeling hard work, ingenuity, creativity and craftsmanship. Their example set me on the long and circuitous paths that continue to lead me to knowledge, experience, and appreciation to pour into my art, my life, and my community. Arigatōgozaimasu!

DRESS CODEX (2015)

Explore pockets of memory, beneath the layers of lessons learned, find yourself. Memories of diverse encounters with women encapsulated in dress forms made of paper.

Two women: an elderly French doctor who after spending a lifetime helping those less fortunate, wants to die now that she is crippled and can no longer climb mountains and lead the active life she loved; and an art patron who fell on hard times and now lives in her van struggling each day to find a place to park the van overnight each night and a place to take a shower each day.

My grandmother who always hung laundry outside on a line between two lichee trees on sunny days and in the garage between two support beams on rainy days.

Walking through a shopping mall and being inundated by signs of a [fashion] industry that profits heavily off of women through the use of heavy doses of psychological manipulation.

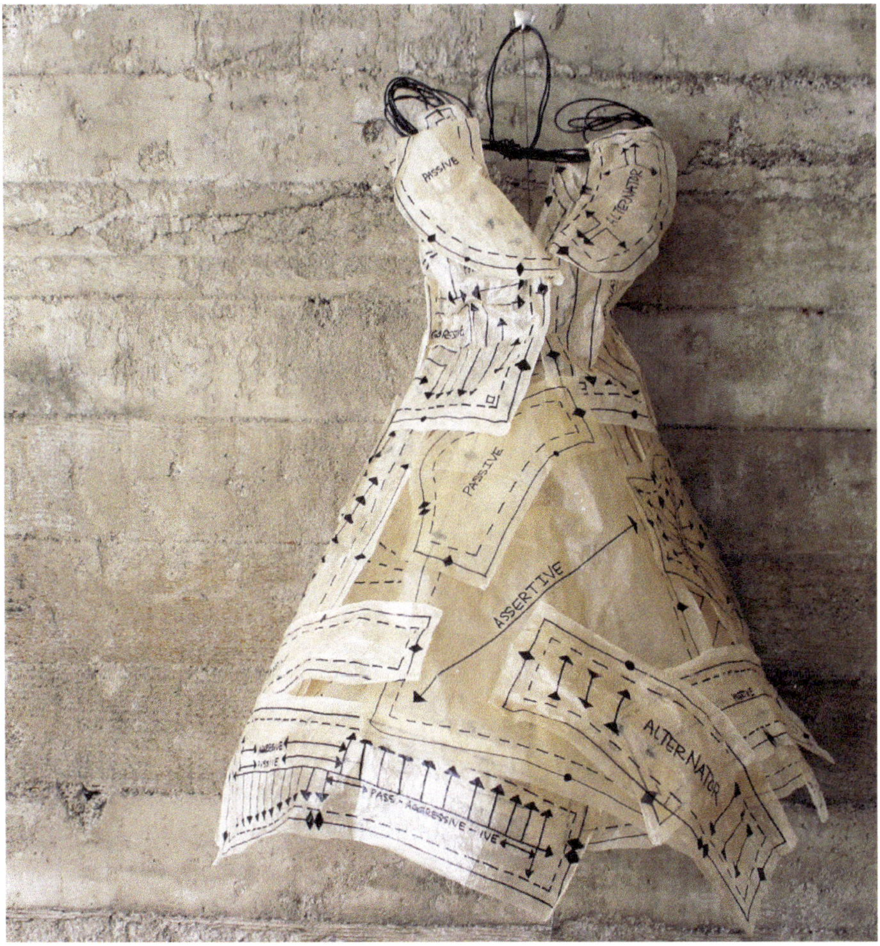

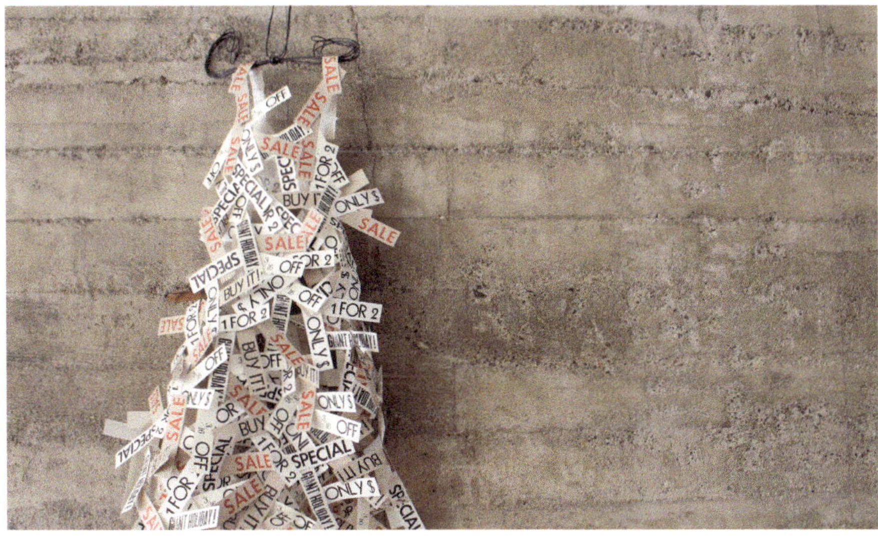

PASSIVE
ALTERNATOR
PASSIVE
ASSERTIVE
ALTER NATOR
PASS · AGGRESSIVE · IVE
SALE
SALE
SALE
OFF
SALE
SPECIAL
SPECIAL
BUY IT!
ONLY $
SALE
OFF
1 FOR 2
BUY IT!
ONLY $
1 FOR 2
OFF
SALE
SALE
OFF
BUY IT!
ONLY $
1 FOR 2
SALE
OFF
SPECIAL
1 FOR 2
BUY IT!
SALE
SPECIAL
ONLY $
SALE
OFF
BUY IT!
1 FOR 2
SPECIAL

12 STEPS TO FREE

A Post-theater performance
Conceived, Written and Created by C. K. Itamura
Commissioned by The Imaginists, 2020
Performed by You

Inspired in part by Maslow's Hierarchy of Needs, a theory in psychology proposed by Abraham Maslow in 1943.

Self-contained play for one actor, in five acts. Includes script, artist notes and props created as a limited edition of 90 signed and numbered objects.

Production Locations: In a public place. In front of a mirror. In your head.

Distributed to "Bedrock Donors" (aka "Bedrockers") of The Imaginists via United States Postal Service First Class Mail.

Debuted in October 2020 for an indefinite run.

Playwright / Artist Notes
So long as a person is kept in a state of constant struggle, unable to achieve or complete any combinations of Scenes from the first four Acts, they will remain under the control of, obedient and indebted to those who retain the power to gain from and perpetuate the conditions. Those on the subjugated end of this construct, by design rarely reach Act Five where the Scenes of "achieving creativity," "transcending," and "realization of freedom" are possible. Even if some are successfully able to elude the gauntlet of oppression, the process continues mechanically, repeating efficiently to create and process the next generation of indentured and enslaved subjects anew, and the next and next generations thereafter.

What systems are currently in place that create levels of desperation, division, danger, disenfranchisement, and [fear of] death? What circumstances ultimately instill fear, deny freedoms and subjugate entire populaces? What individual personal values and behaviors play a part in perpetuating subjugation on successive generations of beholden?

Q & A: https://www.peachfarmstudio.net/q-and-a-12-steps-to-free
What will YOU work for?

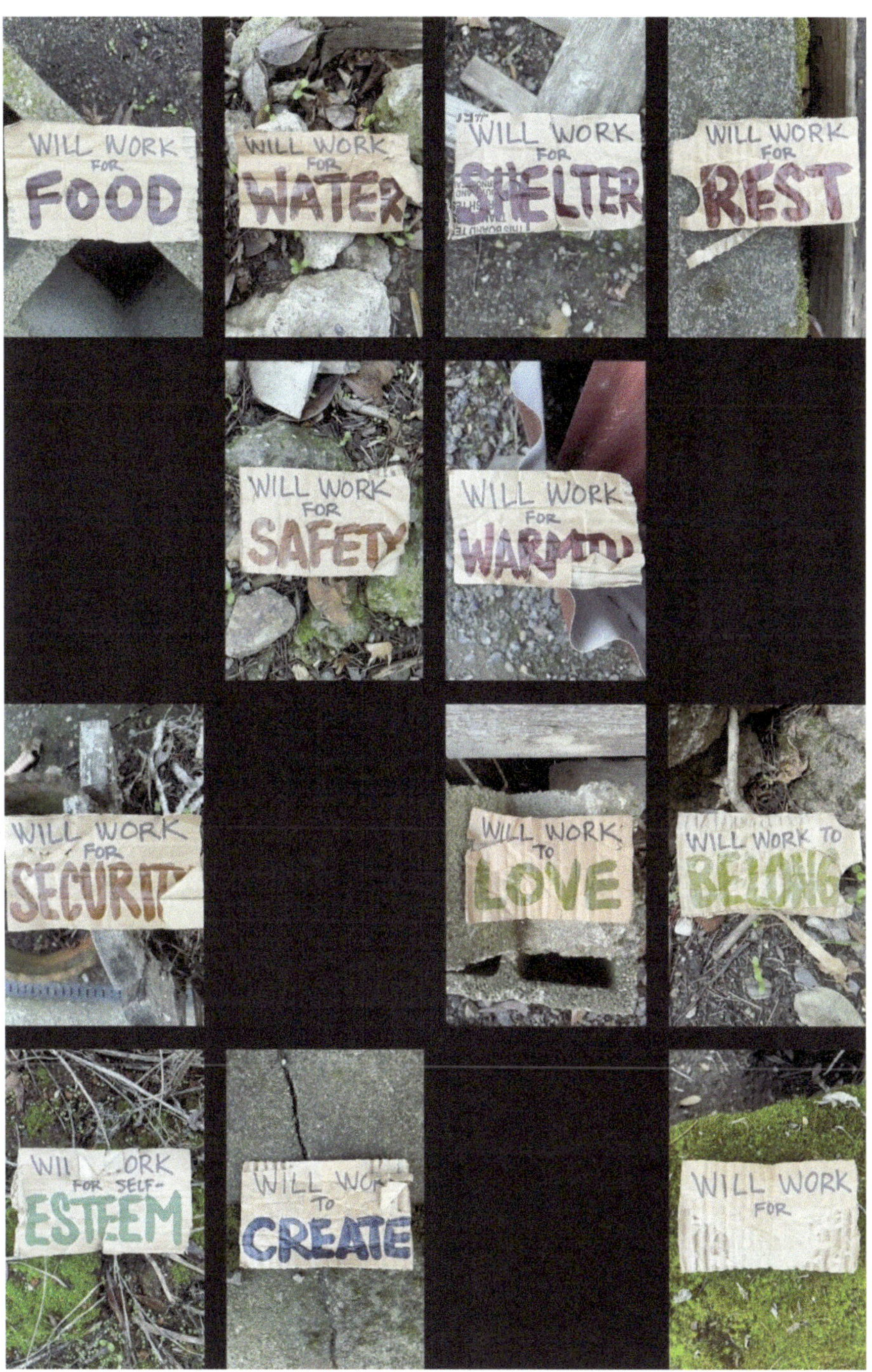

"12 Steps to Free."

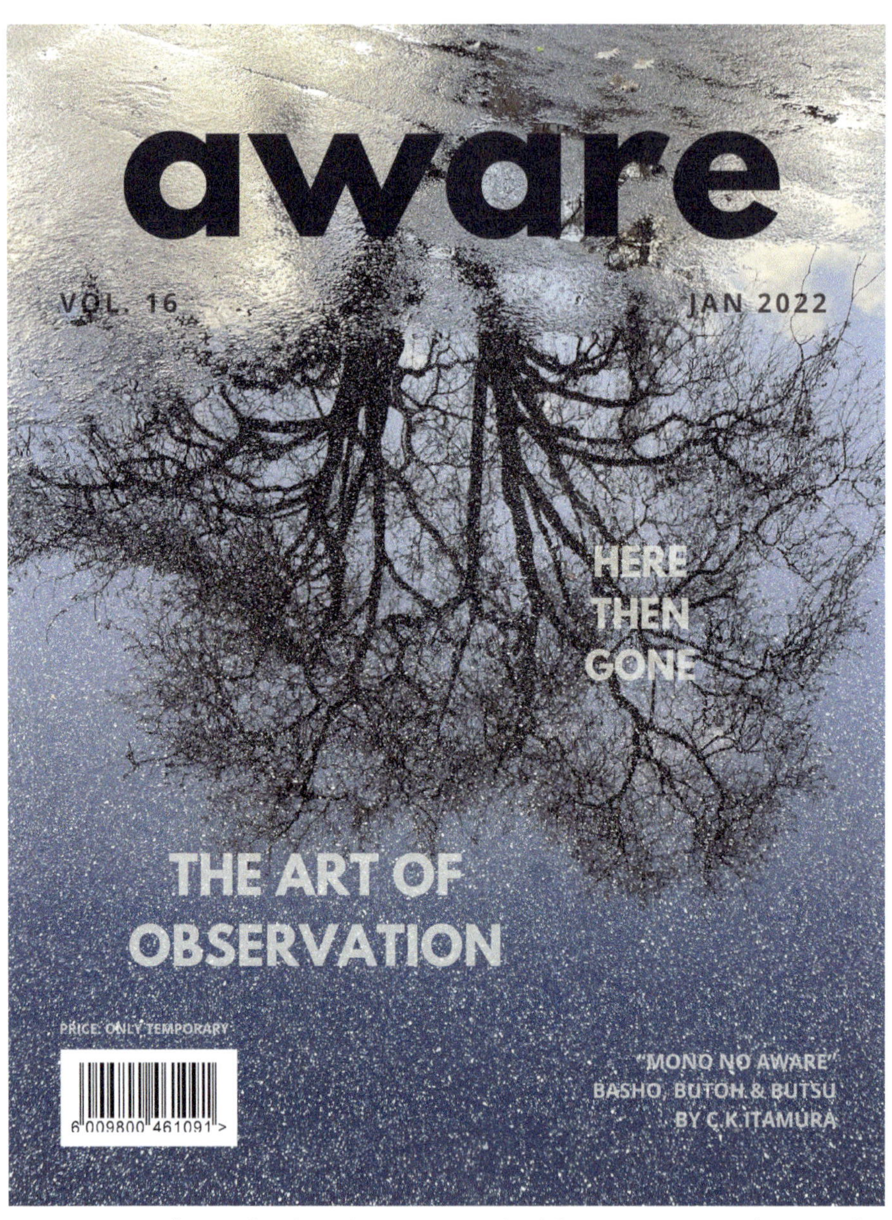

C. K. Itamura, "aware," Vol. 16 (January 2022) of the *covers* series, photography and text, digital assemblage printed on metal, 2021.

When the world seems upside down, closer inspection reveals things to be just as they are, where up is down and down is up, and snow and stars are one and the same with simply being grounded.

Tehmina Khan
BECOMING A POET: A LOVE STORY

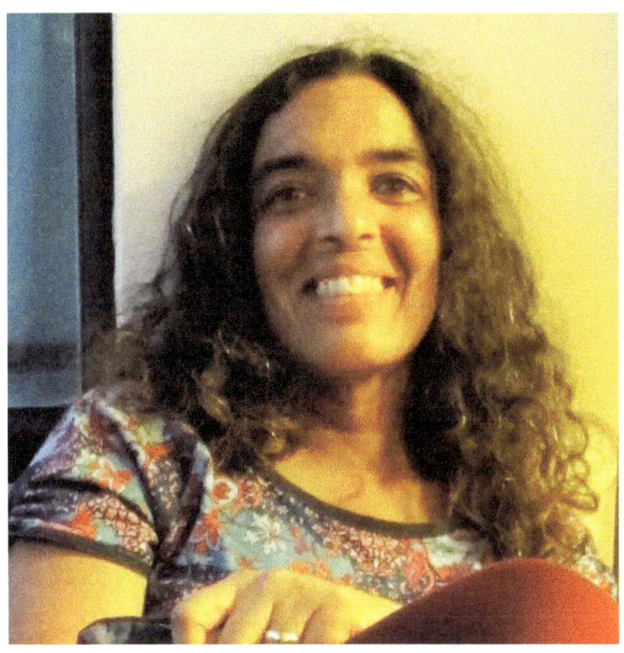

Tehmina Khan is a daughter of Indian immigrant
scientists who has spent her adult life writing,
teaching, resisting, and mothering.
She has taught science to preschoolers,
citizenship to octogenarians, and
literary translation to elementary school students.
She now teaches English and Interdisciplinary
Studies at City College of San Francisco,
where she defends everyone's right to a quality
education. Her work has been published in *Poets11*,
OccuPoetry, *CCSF Forum Magazine*,
Civil Liberties United, *The City is Already Speaking*,
Essential Truths, and *Muslim American Writers
at Home*. She lives, works, rides her bicycle, and
loves on unceded Ramaytush Ohlone land.

BECOMING A POET: A LOVE STORY
Tehmina Khan

December 15, 2021

Dark and cold outside, I'm sitting at the front of my classroom while the students take their final exam. We've been reading bell hooks' *All About Love* and have been exploring what love looks like to each of us—its complications and contradictions. We've learned to see love as a verb—as something we practice with intent. bell hooks states that love is "the will to extend oneself for the purpose of nurturing one's own or another's spiritual growth." The students are creating their final exam in any form they like. They can draw, write a poem, write a letter, create a collage, or write an essay. We've been meeting in person, masked and distanced, while most of the college is still online. For the past eighteen weeks, we have talked about family dysfunction, cycles of abuse, strict parenting, addiction, and career paths. bell hooks tells us that the will to power and the will to love cannot coexist, so we consider how we can choose love in the face of power. We have shared poems, songs, and images. We have brought our loved ones into our Day of the Dead remembrance, in which one student told us about her late husband who died of cancer at age 22, and another told us about friends killed by the military in Burma only a few months ago. I am thinking about all we have shared, about their stories, about their own inquiry into love, and about the growth and expansion of their writing, and by extension, mine One by one, students finish and leave. As I begin packing up, one of the students gives me the news: bell hooks died today. I feel my world spin rapidly and go still.

> We study love together
> in pandemic times, in masks
> dark outside, light within

1988

I begin reading bell hooks' *Talking Back*. She writes as a Black feminist, claiming her own voice, naming the white supremacist patriarchy. As a young Indian Muslim child of immigrants, I have been thinking about where my story connects with history. I think about colonialism, immigration, and racism. In her book, I see my own struggle. I see my own heart. Coming out of a childhood of silence and alienation, I see a way forward for me, my words, my voice.

1967

"Zenena tired," the last words my older sister speaks before she withdraws into herself. She speaks of herself in the third person. Zenena for Zarina. We will call her Zeno. She stops speaking as I am born. I am the newborn no one worries over.

1969

Early flashes of memory take me to Northern Ireland, where we live for two years. A red dog. A trailer where we live temporarily. Roses. I do not know which memories are mine and which are constructed from what my parents tell me. Ireland becomes a place of the imagination, a secondary place of belonging. My parents find themselves outsiders to the beginnings of "the troubles," a conflict not theirs. This also will capture my imagination.

1970

I do not know what autism is, only that I talk and Zeno does not. She is older and bigger than me. My parents have hired a speech therapist who comes to our apartment in Salt Lake City and sits with Zeno trying to teach her to repeat sounds. Zeno and I go to preschool together. I make two drawings, one for her and one for me. One afternoon, I watch my preschool teacher write on a piece of paper. I take a piece of paper and draw zig zags in red crayon, intrigued by the mystery bound up in lines on a page. I am told that I learned to talk and never stopped, but I am also shy. I don't say anything to new people, especially adults.

> I use words but she does not.
> What does this mean?
> What does she want to say?

1972

I take the school bus from University Village, where we live, to Beacon Heights Elementary. Two of my friends, Mohja and Mujeeb, ride the same bus. We are all in kindergarten. My teacher is a tall white woman who wears dresses and shoes with heels. She says my name in a weird way. She asks me to say something in my language and for Mohja to say something in her language and to see if we understand each other, even though we are from different countries with different languages. We learn to read from a book about Dick and Jane and Spot. She tells me I color too slowly.

Zeno goes to a different school for special kids. I think this means it's a school for kids who don't talk. I am not special. I talk.

The bookmobile comes to University Village and I go there and get a library card. I am with other kids and no grown ups. I check out books. I'm not sure how I choose them. Mommy reads books to me every night. I love reading books with her. Zeno sits with us too but does not understand.

> books and freedom
> a window to another world
> curled up with my mom

1972

We have Islamic School in the small community center at University Village. Tariq Uncle recites suras and we repeat after him. I like the sounds of the suras. Maysoon Auntie teaches how to say the sounds of the Arabic alphabet. I like saying qaf and 'ain, sounds that come from the back of the throat. I like it when we all pray together. Tariq Uncle tells us that there are angels on our shoulders. We can't see them, but they are there. They watch us and write down all the good and bad things we do. If we are good, we will go to heaven and in heaven we can do or have anything we want. "What would you like to do in heaven?" he asks us. Some kids say they want to fly. Others want to swim like a fish. "I want my sister to talk," I say. "Will she talk in heaven?"

> Who am I with Zeno?
> What does it mean to talk?
> to not talk?

1973

I can read big books now. I read the same books over and over because I love to be inside them. I can be the kids in the book when I read.

1973

Daddy is going to India. I'm not sure what India is, but it's where we are from. It's where all my beautiful clothes come from and Mommy's saris. Ammam and Pappa come to stay with us while Daddy goes to India. I imagine India is a big shopping center filled with beautiful things we can't find here.

1974

Mommy is in the hospital having a baby. My parents have been trying to convince me that we all want a boy, but I want a girl, a sister. Daddy calls us at Rafia Aunty's house. "You have a sister." I am happy. We are three girls now. Her name is Usma.

This is the year we leave Salt Lake City and University Village for California. Zeno's new school teaches her sign language. Mommy and Daddy have special meetings at the school so they can learn too. We all learn sign language. Zeno can tell us when she's hungry or angry or if she wants something.

1975

We move to a house in Santa Clara with a backyard with big trees. I beg my parents to get a cat. A girl in my class has a mother cat with kittens that need homes. His name is Mulligan and we call him Mullie. He's white with a reddish nose, paws, and tail—a red point Siamese. I pet him and play with him. I am so happy.

I walk two blocks to school every day. My teacher tells my mom that I'm not doing all my reading assignments. I don't tell her that I'm bored, that we did the same readings last year in second grade. The teacher tells my mom about a new program at a school across town. She says I need more structure. Mommy thinks this is a good idea so next year she will drive me to school and then take Zeno to her special school. All my life, I will resist structure.

1977

I love reading books. I love to read books that make me cry, and I read these books over and over again and cry. In *Little Women*, when Beth dies of Scarlet Fever, Jo is so full of sadness. I can't say it makes me feel good to be sad, but it does something to me. I feel more like myself, like my own deep sadness can breathe.

1978

Mullie gets sick. The vet says he has cancer and will die. I cry and cry. Mommy doesn't want to put him to sleep. She says it's not right. Allah will take him at the right time. I make a bed for him, putting a pillow in a box. He moves more slowly and eats less. One night, all he does is sleep. He is on my bed. I pet him. Every time I leave the room and come back I check for his heartbeat. Around midnight I don't feel it anymore. I tell Mommy. We both cry.

I write my first real poem, a poem that says what I feel. I count syllables and search for rhymes. It's a long poem about Mullie in rhyming couplets. Mommy shares it with some of my aunties. It makes them cry. I feel a little better in my sadness. I can release my sadness with my words. I can make people feel things with my words.

> A girl's tears drip ink onto a page
> creating a poem and more tears.

1979

The hostage crisis is on TV every day. People wear yellow ribbons and wave flags. Mexican kids in the neighborhood call me Eye-Rain-ian. I'm the only Indian kid at my school. My other Indian and Muslim friends live further away, about fifteen minutes' drive, in Sunnyvale or San Jose. Each of us is alone at our schools unless we have brothers or sisters. It occurs to me that if Zeno were normal, we would be in the same school. She would be ahead of me. She would teach me things.

> Sometimes I want to be a different person
> Understanding the unspoken secrets around me

I am in love. I pine and agonize over a boy who lives down the street, who is funny and smart, though not as smart as me and my friends. I ride my bike past his house. I dream. I write in my journal about these feelings inside, feelings that I'm not supposed to have. In Islamic School, we learn that it is haram to like boys, but I do like boys.

This is the beginning of the Great Unrequiteds—a projection of a longing inside me. I write when I am in love, when I am longing. I am beginning to feel things intensely—anger, fear, love, desire …

Next year, I will become friends with the boy and those feelings will dissipate into the air and attach themselves to someone else.

Unrequited love—such deep girlhood longing
What I want is what I already have hidden in my depths

1980

I audition for "Free to Be, You and Me" at the Santa Clara Junior Theater. Everyone gets a part, and I have a few lines. I fall deeply in love with being on stage. A bigger and louder way of telling stories, with my body among other bodies. I want to be seen! I want to be heard! I feel for the theater what I felt for the boy I liked last year—a passion, an obsession.

The joy of being loud
eyes and ears turned toward me,
in the company of an ensemble—we speak in chorus.

1981

The science club takes a backpacking trip to Pt. Reyes. The fragrance of the air, the birds, and my legs carrying me forward bring me into a new relationship with my body. I am not strong or athletic. I am the last kid picked on sports teams for PE. I am the last kid to learn the dance steps for a play I'm in. I carry forty pounds of gear on my back, and I walk five miles on the trail to the campsite. I am the last kid to get to the campsite, but I am in awe that my body—small, round, brown, and female—can do this.

We are going to India for the first time. Mom and Dad can only go for three weeks, but Mom suggests that I go for the whole summer. Dad thinks it's a bad idea to let me travel alone. But I want to go. I am on a plane for twenty-four hours, with stops in New York and London, before landing in Bombay. I spend a week with Khair Aunty in Bombay and then three weeks with Ammam and Pappa in Hyderabad. India is both strange and familiar, or perhaps strange because it's familiar. I don't speak Urdu, but I learn a few phrases. I like the way people speak English in India and go between English and Urdu. I like the food. I feel at home, part of a bigger family, a place that is mine. Mom, Dad, and Usmi come a month later. Zeno's teacher has agreed to take care of her while they're gone. I'm sad when it's time to leave.

When we say "back home," we feel a gravitational pull
holding us to an earth we were not born to

1981

I begin to learn Spanish. It feels familiar, like I can express myself more clearly than I can in English, even though I have limited vocabulary. Something about the sounds and the rhythms say what I feel. This is a beginning. I will study Arabic, Hindi, and Urdu, and find myself in each language, new words, new rhythms.

Life beyond English, like leaving Kansas in black and white
for Oz in technicolor with witches, ruby slippers, and flying monkeys

1983

I audition for the summer musical and get cast as chorus. Everyone who does not get a leading role is chorus. A brown girl cannot get cast as a lead, but beyond that, I do not understand the stories. The stories express a culture and a sensibility that is not mine.

1984

South Africa is in the news, and so is Berkeley, where students are protesting apartheid and building a shantytown in the plaza to demand that the university divest from South Africa. I want to go there—to Berkeley, to the world.

I am a straight-A student. I'm good at math, science, English, and Spanish. I'm okay at music. But I'm bored. I can take tests, solve problems, and write essays. I'm good at doing what I'm told. My parents want me to be a doctor or a scientist like them. Mom says medicine is the best career for a woman. I'm good at science, and I love my physics class, but that's not where I want to go. I am thinking about writing and journalism.

To change the world with a story
that connects to other stories.
Power to the people!

1985

In Berkeley! At last! My adult life beginning. I read books, learn Arabic, drink coffee, and go to rallies. I wander down Telegraph Avenue to used bookstores and used record stores, searching for new words and new sounds.

> A world of ideas, events, and stories
> in this city beyond book learning
> a passion

1987–88

I am living in Cairo for a year and the world becomes both big and small. Forming words and phrases in Arabic brings me into a new self, a self that is more real than my English self, even though I struggle for the right words. I feel safe here as a young brown Muslim woman, safer than I did in Berkeley. I travel on weekends or school breaks alone or with friends. We go to the Sinai, Alexandria, Luxor, Aswan, and the oases. I love traveling alone, speaking Arabic, meeting new people.

The last of the Great Unrequiteds is a French Canadian whom I meet in Aswan on a Felucca trip to Luxor. He visits me in Cairo and we explore different parts of the city. He tells tall tales and makes me laugh. He leaves and I pine for him. He is the best of the Unrequiteds.

I come into my identity as a Muslim woman. There are many ways to be Muslim, not just what they taught us in Islamic School or Muslim Camp. In Cairo, the college students have parties with music, alcohol, and hashish. They have boyfriends and girlfriends. Couples walk hand in hand along the Nile. I can find my own way of being Muslim, a way that is freer, less anxious.

> Egypt is the Mother of the World
> Man fears time, but time fears the pyramids
> If you drink from the Nile, you must return
> To live along a great river is to feel yourself flowing out to sea.

1988

I return to Berkeley and protest for El Salvador, South Africa, Palestine. I have fallen in love with a man who loves me back, but he's far away, and it doesn't last.

1990

I graduate from Berkeley with an interdisciplinary degree in Humanities. I have taken literature classes in English, Ethnic Studies, and Arabic departments. I begin to write poems after reading Dennis Brutus and Mahmoud Darwish, poems of protest and affirmation of my own complex identity.

After taking a Third World Film class, I decide to go to film school. Ousmane Sembene, Satyajit Ray, Lino Brocka. These films show me the world. This is what I want to do! Create a world, a vision for liberation.

1991

I learn in film school that resources are finite, and some projects get funded and others do not. I am asked to define my audience, and I don't know how. I know my classmates are not my audience, and I know the funders are also not my audience. I am baffled by the trivial work that gets praised—work that says nothing in clever ways. How many ways are there to say nothing? Film is an unforgiving art and all-encompassing art: sound, image, movement, color. I can immerse an audience in what I want them to see.

> light projects through celluloid pictures
> colors dance across a screen
> a window to another world.

The Gulf War begins, and I immerse myself in protest. With other young people of color, we form Roots Against War linking war and imperialism to racism, sexism, and homophobia at home. We are loud. We are fierce. We dance in the streets. "Hold on, wait a minute, let us put some color in it! Roots, roots, roots against war!"

I write a long protest poem "Tales for a Desert Storm," which laments the bombing of Baghdad, of Shahrazad and the Thousand and One Nights—a civilization built on stories. I perform it at rallies and readings.

1992

I get a job as a paraprofessional teaching assistant at Francisco Middle School. They hire me specifically to work with Arabic-speaking kids. The kids are Yemeni and Iraqi, all boys and one girl. They live in the Tenderloin. I help them with their English, translate documents for their parents, call parents when things go wrong. I enjoy getting to know these kids and their families.

1995

At film school, they make us compete against each other. They've established a new MFA program and they tell us we need to reapply for a limited number of spots. I know I am not one of the darlings of the program. I cannot come up with a new way of saying nothing. I speak of colonialism, trauma, and liberation. I am not selected.

1996

I get a job at the Chinatown Campus of City College of San Francisco. I help Chinese immigrants prepare for their citizenship interviews. I've always come to Chinatown as a tourist, but now I come to the inside of this place. The students are mostly older people, who need to become citizens in order to keep their benefits after Clinton's new welfare law. They practice telling me their names and addresses. They practice answering the hundred US history questions. When they pass their interviews, they come back to tell the class about it. I feel closer to my own history as I work with these older immigrants. When I walk through Chinatown, I feel like I belong here, like I can live here, in San Francisco. I can make a home here.

Ammam dies in New Jersey a month before she was going to come to California. I wish I could have brought her to Chinatown, to this city within a city.

> Stories upon stories
> in languages not my own.
> So much I don't know but learn to love anyway
> in a time of loss.

Epilogue

I feel betrayed by the Gatekeepers of Cinema. I leave the motion picture. I return to the poem, where the resources are abundant. Myself and a Pen. Myself and a Voice. Publishers and editors are gatekeepers, but they cannot stop us from creating the work. I do not study creative writing. I don't want to be workshopped. Instead, I turn to comparative literature and read widely and closely across time and place, creating my own poems in conversation with these texts. I start a family, create a home in San Francisco. I write best in community, one poem in conversation with another. I teach poetry and translation to children. I learn to write from abundance, not scarcity, from a desire to expand, not a desire to control. I don't fall hard and fast for poetry, as I did for film and theater, allowing the medium to intoxicate me. Poetry is the companion waiting for me to return, like the man who loves me back and becomes my family. I cultivate this love. I nurture it and it nurtures me.

> A world in a poem: roses and thorns
> love and grief
> I offer you a mirror reflecting your eyes
> and mine

Tureeda Mikell
FOSTER CARE CHRONICLES AND BEYOND

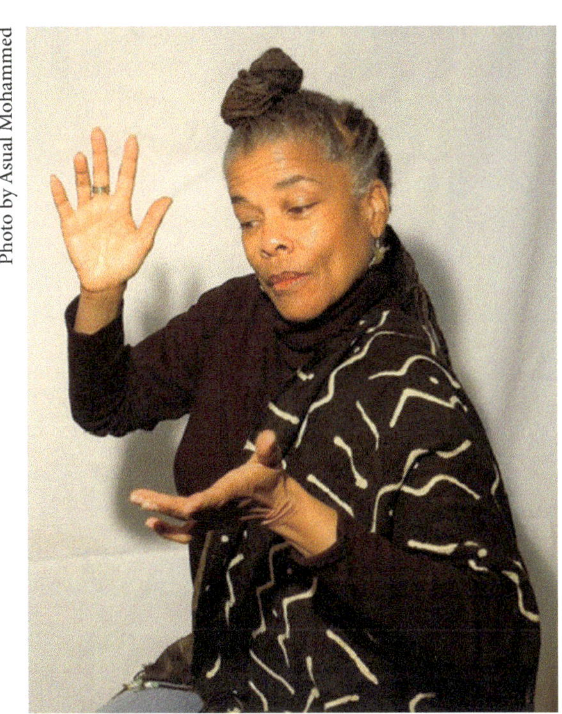

Tureeda Mikell, Story Medicine Woman, is an award-winning
poet whose work has been published in many languages.
She was cited as an "Activist for Holism" by an
Iranian doctorial scholar. She has published 73 anthologies
of classroom writings authored by at-risk students.
She is also a UC Bay Area Writing Project Fellow;
the author of *Synchronicity: The Oracle of Sun Medicine*,
nominated for the California Book Award;
and the co-author/curator of EastSide Arts Alliance's
Patrice Lumumba Anthology (Nomadic Press). She was
Oakland Museum Poet In Residence 2006 and
was recently named 2022 Poet-in-Residence at the
Museum of the African Diaspora.

FOSTER CARE CHRONICLES AND BEYOND
Tureeda Mikell

I come from
Star bird bees honeysuckle nectar apricot fruit trees
Schwinn bike races skates piano dance lessons girl scouts
The wonder of flowers opening and closing by night's star lights
and family fishing on Berkeley pier before laws needed
to make the bay a garbage dump

I come from watching Mama be afraid of snakes on TV
living room dances with daddy, her cooking canning
magic potions of brilliant yellow corn tomatoes from his garden
chow-chow relish and black-eye peas that outlive her in the pantry

I come from recalling her warning me when I was ten.
"Life for you, may not be peaches and cream"
before going back to the hospital a second time
From dawn's light materializing Mama in my bedroom
Dressed in her favorite suit, kissing my forehead
Though somehow I knew she was still in her hospital room

I come from witnessing Mama's slow death
A sheep among wolves living buy-bull's word tool
dying of Lupus, a wolf disease depriving her body
of oxygen and daddy losing his mind
  leaving three baby girls behind
    "She's gone home,"
      church ministers say

I'm from watching little sister's eyes
Staring at the door waiting for mama's return
Waiting for hugs caress to nurture love lost
Mama's never coming back home
  Not to this side of the veil

I come from Daddy being haunted by Mama
Seeing her in every room of our home
Moving from east Oakland to north
A new secret harbors cruelty
Rape, death threats, becoming obese
Stuffing my body from feeling empty
alopecia: balding, aphasia: refusing to speak. I'm 11.

I come from Child Protective Services
Lie detector test and detectives asking about
the color of my dress, yes it was yellow
but detector said, no, I lied.

I come from Bell's Palsy my body making
another decision without me
Left side of face paralyzed from
the first night CPS dropped us off at the cottage
Up that steep winding road

I come from information overload
Watching younger siblings digest dislocation
No Mama, no Daddy, now weird looking big sis
Removed twice from family homes.

I come from the Cottage Sunday Chapel
where the Old English proverb
"Children are to be seen and not heard."
And buy-bull verse
"Suffer little children who come unto me"
remove chunks of my heart and frappe it in a blender
consume it in my face as though I were blind
without sense or unable to comprehend
the dimensions of their decisions

I'm from finding a place among other girls
11 to 15 years old confused as me
One Black, one Latin, one Jewish and one White

recalling their abuse, dipped in boiling pots,
birthing father's baby, mother forcing daughter
to be her father's lover, and father having sex
with three of his four daughters

I come from foster homes, alma mater thrones
San Francisco's turbulent 60s and the irony of
Bell's Palsy staining my face
Courts separating me from younger siblings
Soul sore and misery soars, living in a
rat infested alley between Webster and Fillmore
and Whitey's on the moon

I come from shades of family skin
Judged bad abhorrent sin of Ham
Middle sis nut-brown skin and black eyes dismissed
Accepts guilt of being less than our little sis
Olive tone and hazel-brown eyes
She runs away hiking from Vallejo
to San Leandro back to the Cottage
where she felt no judgment
She was braver than me
finding her way from foster's cruelty

I come from learning the race game
attending church every Sunday
wearing a natural denied by
Foster mother that said I couldn't go inside
The Church with my hair looking like that
From weighing the force of an adult bully
contradicting the will of a god she thinks
made my mane a mistake!
Extension cord whooping couldn't tame
muscular springs to lay down their crown of glory

I come from poetry rising up out of me
War and violence sign of life times changing
How do we stop it? When will it end?
When will people start getting back together again,
asked Marvin
From Martin Luther King coming to our church
Macedonia Missionary Baptist on Sutter in S.F.
Coming to help us receive liberty and justice, until
bomb threat disrupts the congregation and
Dr. King's call for freedom's ring is postponed.

I come from survival
Young teen dazed amazed under dark heavy haze
Tired of paying toll at a bridge to nowhere,
I come from choosing to let go, until visions of those
far worse off than me intercede
Without food a roof thin cold and little clothing

What's going on, What's going on, sang Marvin

I come from new strength breaking death sentence
Holding on, set free, speaking up for myself
Finding my social worker refusing shit
from foster mother or anyone else though
beatings, bed wettings, sexual abuse continue
I come from moving through it!
from learning my body was pissed off
releasing guilt for my Holy walk!
18 years old grown on my own in Oakland
Receiving last check from foster home
Got to find a place to live
Younger sisters still wards of the system

I come from finishing high school by myself because
F Mother enthused by her foster care wealth needs me to
babysit her flock of working mothers, CPS, and stable

of women's children owned by a pimp.
While she shops, I miss too many days of school

I come from applying for funds to attend college
being refused, no reasons why
just a few breakfast tickets to get me by

I come from a government that spends
19 million dollars for toilets in space
to keep shit from floating in the sky
while I resort to liberating books to free my mind
Taking to heart what Dr. King said
"Sometimes you must break the law to uphold justice."

I come from never giving up and the song
"Searching I'm searching I'm searching I'm searching …"
applying to nursing program and getting in
everything paid for—books, uniform and monthly stipend

I come from believing Mama had my back from the other side

From wanting to make a home
Meeting my daughter's father learning
The act of giving birth is an act of war
Educating her in public, private, and home school
protecting her from hidden agendas denying her fuel to learn

I come from attending Laney and Merritt rage
Fist raised in fight for human rights
Panther Ten Point program
Black Power Black Power, saying it loud
I'm Black and I'm Proud

I come from Emmett Till, Four little girls
blown-up in a church, Malcolm X, Medgar Evers,
Martin Luther King, JFK, Robert Kennedy murdered

It's the KKK, an elder says
The death of my innocence dissolving everyday

I come from witnessing
San Francisco State agents of change
Merritt College in the East Bay
Fight for ethnic studies, our military:
Huey Newton, Bobby Seal, H Rap, Amiri Baraka,
Sister MacKenya, Angela Davis, Stokely Kwame Ture,
Little Bobby, George Jackson, private Jimmy Garrett,
Erica Huggins, Emory Douglas, Fred Hampton and … and

I come from music that kept me moving
"War, huh, what is it good for …"
"Don't call me Nigga, Whitey
don't call me Whitey, Nigga …"
I come from had to get Sly
And sometimes Stoned—
Hot fun in the summertime
Motown and Stevie Wonder
 Living for the city.

I come from fighting to live
And living to fight the termites
killing my family tree softly day and night
I come from wanting to know answers why
Classes in cultural, physical, and political sci,
Anthropology biology sociology chemistry music and
Muntu reconnecting my circle broken.

I come from the audacity of hope
 supplying artillery's artistry
 to shoot down what they think I be!
Moving mountains, bitches!

I come from Black Panther clinic volunteers
 dedicated teens to 20-something rotating

homework, between patients studying under
Black Drs. Tolbert Small and Eddie Newsome
On-site Black physicians teaching us how to
Screen for diabetes, Sickle cell, check for
high blood pressure, assist in prenatal care.
I come from Director Smitty carrying out
the methadone program helping to clean up
epidemic of heroin addiction purposely placed
in our neighborhood to weaken Black Power base

I'm from making alterations from altercations
—23 years after volunteering at the George Jackson clinic,
The *Tribune* calls asking,
"How many guns did you have at the Black Panther Clinic?"
  and reporter not asking
"How many services were provided?
How many programs were implemented?
How many doctors or healthcare workers volunteered?"
Not even wondering why we'd put into practice such a program
With so many hospitals in our community.

I come from PTSD
Got to keep it moving
Dropping the BS
Trusting Kwame Ture's message
"Education in this country make you stupid
But what is worse, it makes you arrogant in your stupidity
Revolution is coming whether you want it or not."

I come from Niecy
"Black Butterfly sail across the waters
   tell your sons and daughters what the struggle brings"

From G's gravity of matter
Auguring deaths of father and both younger sisters
From holy-be names come-around go-around frames
Circling bowl echoing sounds bound in rhythm

Rockin' 360 circuits mocking red rings
members memory missed trees green
Carting gold graphs marking soul our raff's mystery
I'm from Nirvana hands wheeling fingers round knife
Wielding blade round wood sculpting image
Ancient speech reviving Gye Nyame

I come from track and trace 'til done
Go back and fetch it coccyx tales won
 from West Africa's birth print copy sell
 and give as was given in baptism
 of RNA DNA helix spring from S.F. beach
 blue sky music inscribing
saltwater tide's swelling my infant breath
Rebirthing red purple gold jade bliss
New day insisting I head east on Geary
through tunnel under Fillmore

I come from eyes magnified right by 3-foot-tall-wide
Gye Nyme sign my soul was told to materialize
two weeks prior!
from ancestral speak saying
We see you, recognize you
Watched you grow in Western Addition
Foster home two blocks away
in old Victorian whose backyard faced
rear of the Booker T Hotel … you were
a suicidal teen wanting to give up living
until you heard

Hold on, hold on, …
A change gonna come.

I come from third eye opening
Seeing folk worse off than me
No food, no roof, bone thin cold exposed
I rose!

From smells of piss dead fish,
  beatings, bed wettings,
    death threats and rape
      foster brothers and sisters
        assault and battery
          where the rat man
            would set traps, and
              Pick up dead rats

Witnessing hells dwelling once here
  Razed and replaced by
  Family of Gye Nyame
    Andinkra reeds sitting on
      Safeway's walkway awning
        Waiting my arrival

I come from their smile
Welcoming my come-around go-around trial

I am Lotus child transformed
 reborn from act of 54 bones
   Holding on and on and on until
     Sun rescued dawn

I come from Gye Nyame
  Except omnipotent power
    Fear none!

Acknowledgments

"Foster Care Chronicles," parts I-III of VIII will be published by *Colossus* in 2022.

Josué Rojas
DOUBLE CONSCIOUSNESS

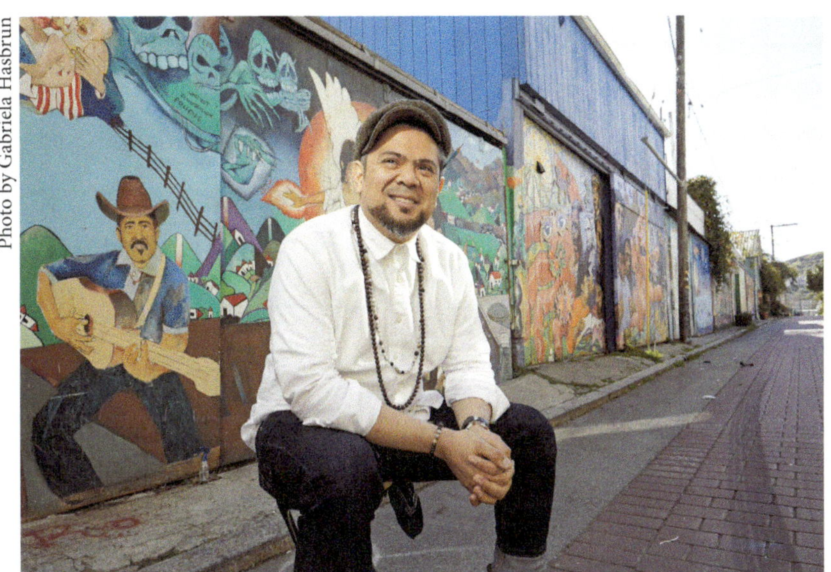

Josué Rojas was born in 1979 in San Salvador,
El Salvador. He was raised in San Francisco,
California, where he was introduced to the arts
through mural painting.

Currently, his painting takes many forms.
His working approach is nimble, encompassing
watercolor-sized paper and book-sized paintings,
canvas, and large-scale murals.
His work arises from intrepid experimentation and
play, illuminating social blind spots through an
interplay of the poetic, tragic, and often humorous.

Rojas holds a BFA in Painting from the California
College of Arts and Crafts and an MFA in Painting
from Boston University. He now lives and works
in San Francisco.
www.josuerojasart.com

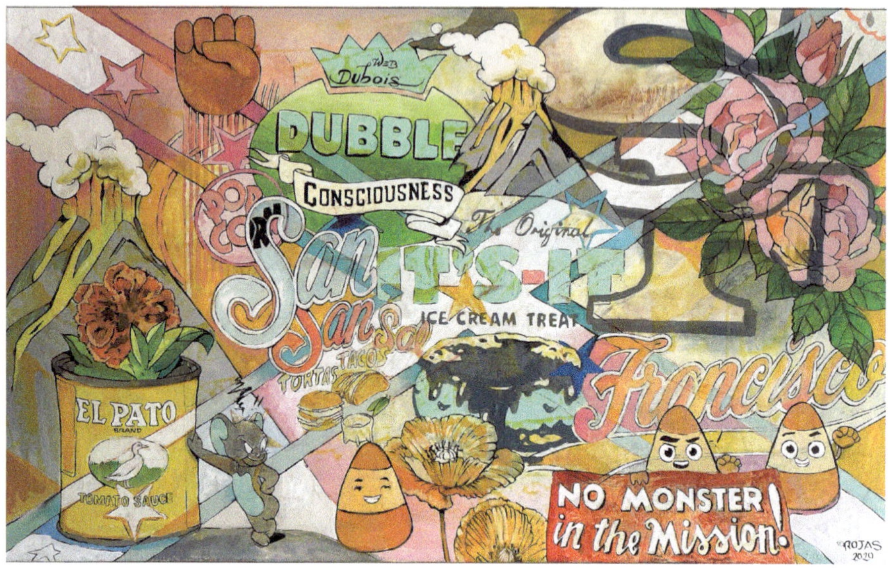

DOUBLE CONSCIOUSNESS
Josué Rojas

I am a socially committed visual artist whose creative vision centers on a public and studio practice that mixes visual language(s) + critical consciousness. The work is informed by a bicultural and bilingual experience as well as by 20+ years of arts leadership in the Bay Area working with public art & media. I feel an artist should serve not only as the "conscience of their era" but also as a positive conduit, infusing values of "right relationships" into the public imagination.

Four pieces—"It's It: Double Consciousness" (2019), "Golden Gate Junction: Starburst" (2021), "Golden Gate Junction: Blue Bayview" (2021), and "Somos Bruce" (2022)—are related works which demonstrate how I utilize pop-culture references, recognizable imagery, cartoons, comics, sports logos—and break their traditional settings, remixing them alongside emojis, Central American folkloric patterns, abstraction, and elements of graffiti. The pieces are a playful dance in acrylic, spray paint, and drawing, where fine art meets the streets. I am fluently bi-lingual in my life, in form and content. As such, I use multiple cultural entry points by design.

As an artist, I seek to blend forms. Developing my own aesthetic in the work is a challenge, especially in a place as saturated as the Bay Area where so many incredible, original artists are making dynamic new work.

Amongst all my influencers, including great artists of many eras, cultures and genres, is the influence of my family. Chief among them is my mother, María Esther García, who raised four boys alone—while maintaining her identity as a creative. As an immigrant raised in an immigrant household, I grew up in a home filled with faith and vibrant cultural experiences that I now value above all. Navigating two worlds strengthened what W.E.B Du Bois dubbed "double consciousness," as I was often put in a position where self-reinvention was necessary. This is the stuff of artists.

I am a product of the local public arts community. It has been my initiation into the practice of art as community activism.

I worked for the past four years, until recently, as Executive Director of San Francisco's own Acción Latina, proud publisher of the award-winning *El Tecolote Newspaper*. Established in 1970, it is California's longest-running bilingual newspaper. Acción Latina's mission is to promote cultural arts, community media, and civic engagement as a way of building healthy and active

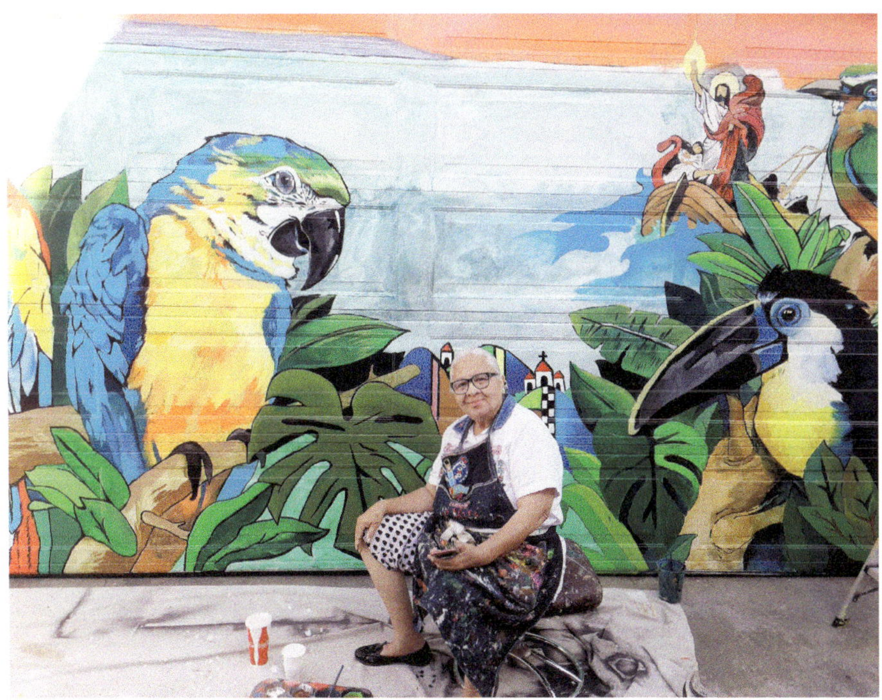

María Esther García (Ms. M.E.G.) painting an untitled mural with her son in Balmy Alley. Her painter's apron features a hand-beaded hummingbird.

Latino communities. The organization's work centers on the empowerment of the local community via media, arts, and culture.

For five decades, Accion Latina has proven to be a positive force in our community with a remarkable imprint in arts, journalism, and intersectional, intergenerational cultural work. It's worth noting that *El Tecolote*'s archive spans 50 years of historical memory for the Latina/o/x community, a treasure which no other San Francisco institution holds. As the leader of this organization, I learned invaluable lessons of curation, culture-building, and arts leadership in communities—particularly in the Latinx, migrant, and refugee communities in San Francisco (to which I myself belong).

Now, as an independent artist, I seek to implement these hard-earned lessons in my practice going forward. A deep love for San Francisco keeps me here, contributing to its thriving creative culture via public works. I center my work around the community process, often interviewing residents, gathering investigations, feedback and real-life narratives that tell the intersectional story of the place.

I have been fortunate enough to reap the benefits of growing up in a place like San Francisco and in particular the Mission District, where art is a way of life. I feel public artists hold a responsibility to the residents of the communities where their works are made. This is our mandate. This is my process and my intended approach with my work going forward.

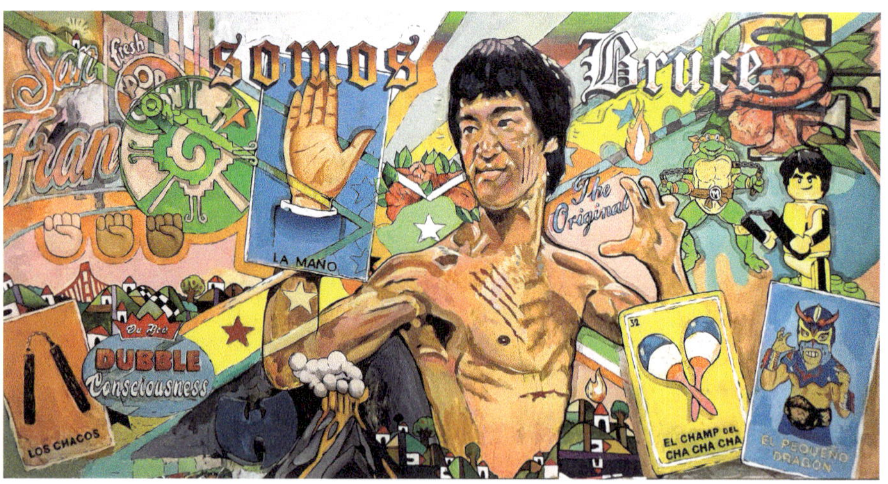

"Somos Bruce," acrylic, ink and multimedia on canvas,
80 x 40 inches, 2022

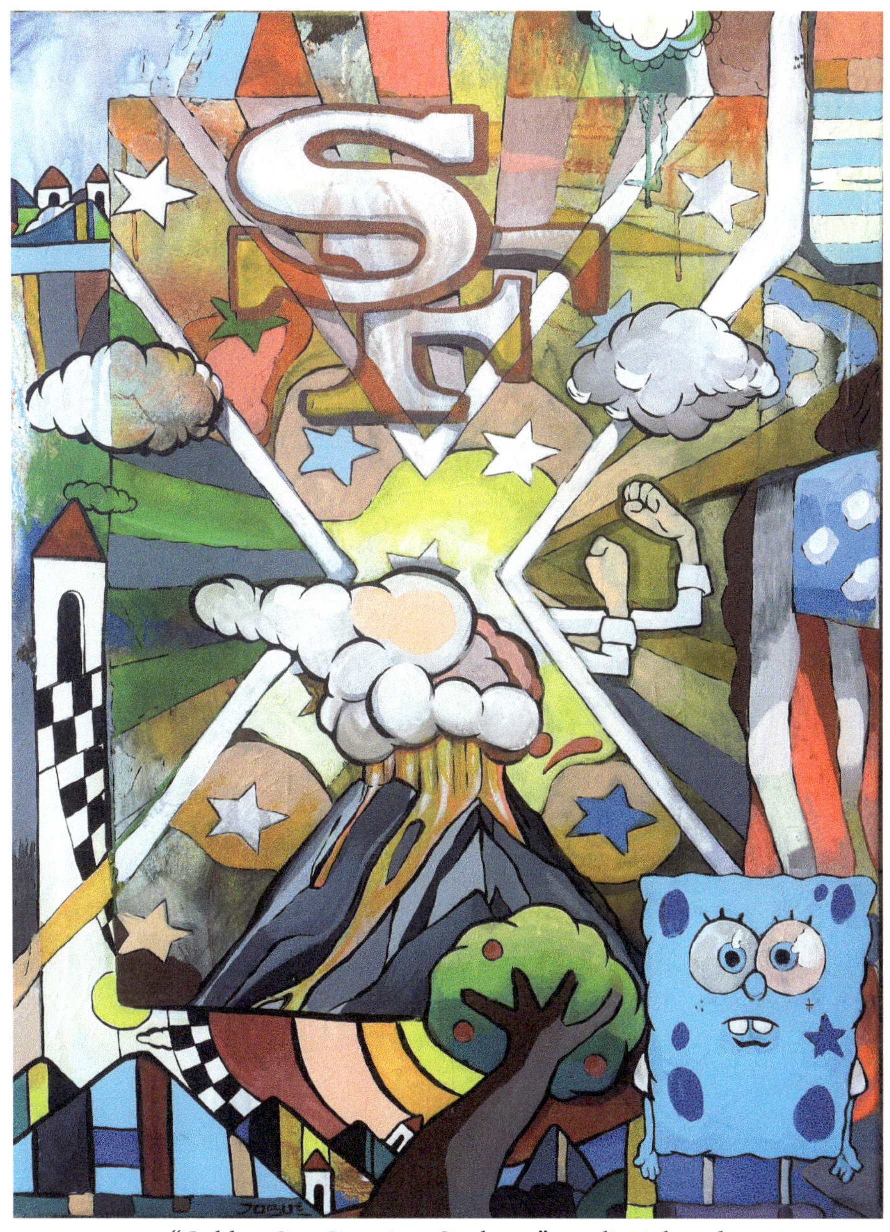

"Golden Gate Junction: Starburst" acrylic, ink and
multimedia on canvas, 30 x 40 inches, 2021

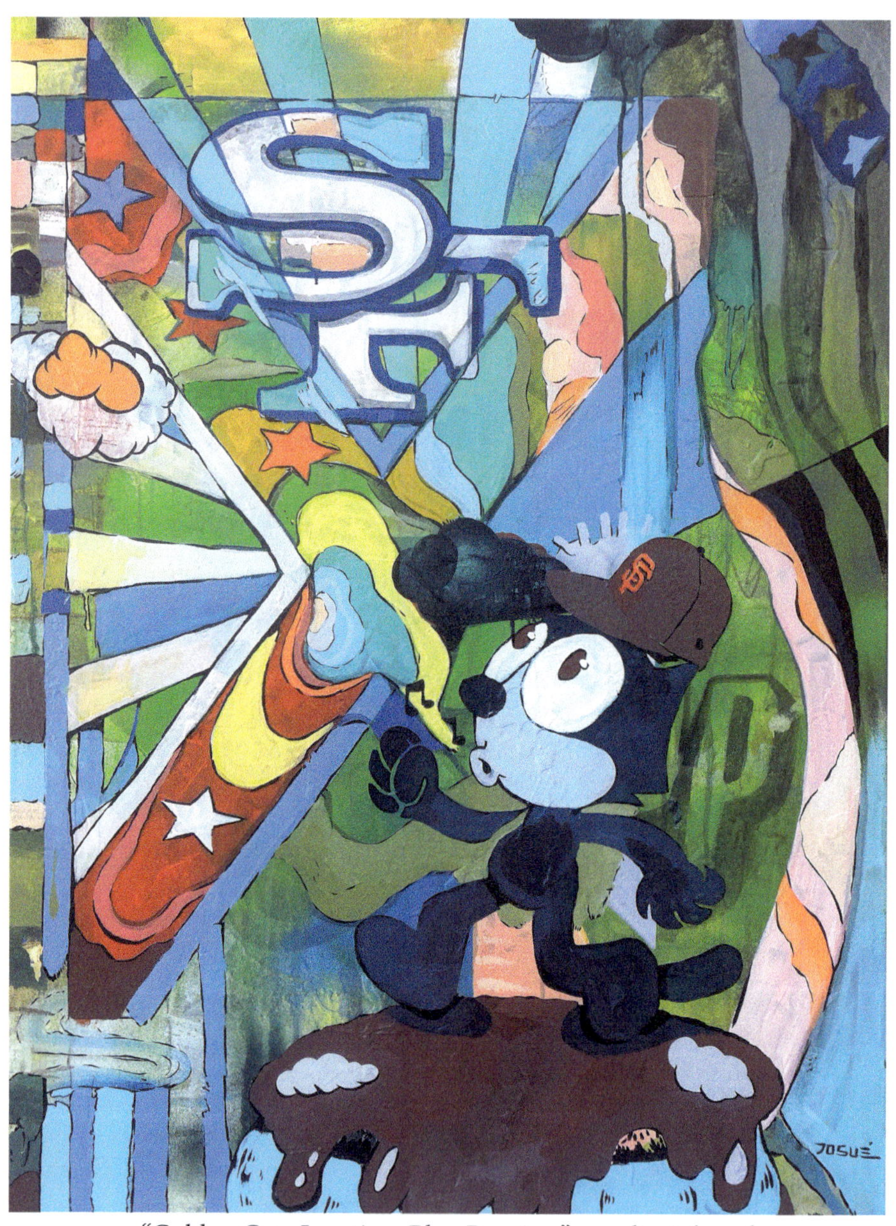

"Golden Gate Junction: Blue Bayview," acrylic, ink and
multimedia on canvas, 30 x 40 inches, 2021

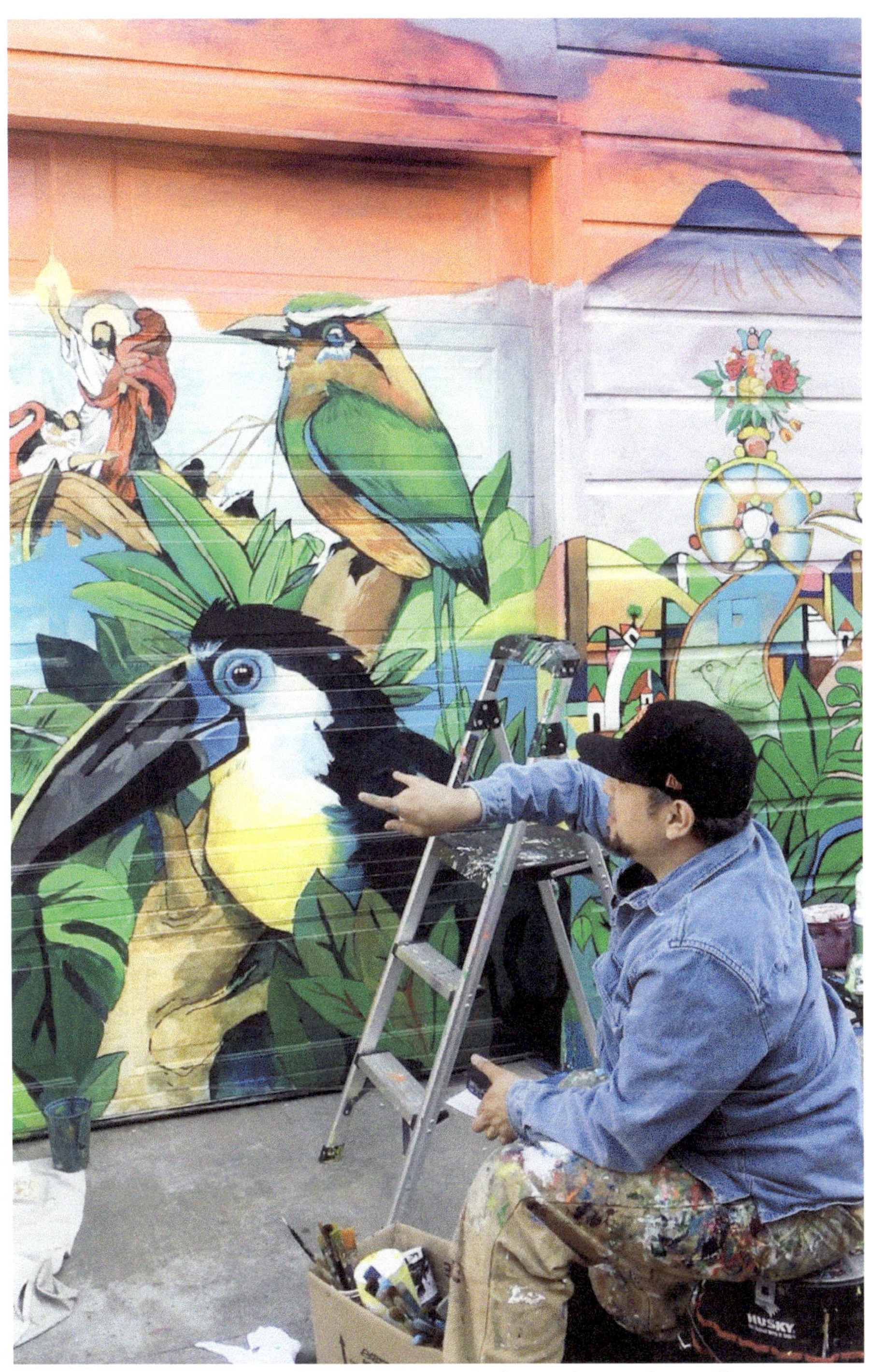

Josué Rojas working on an untitled mural on Balmy Alley
spearheaded by his mother María Esther García (Ms. M.E.G.).

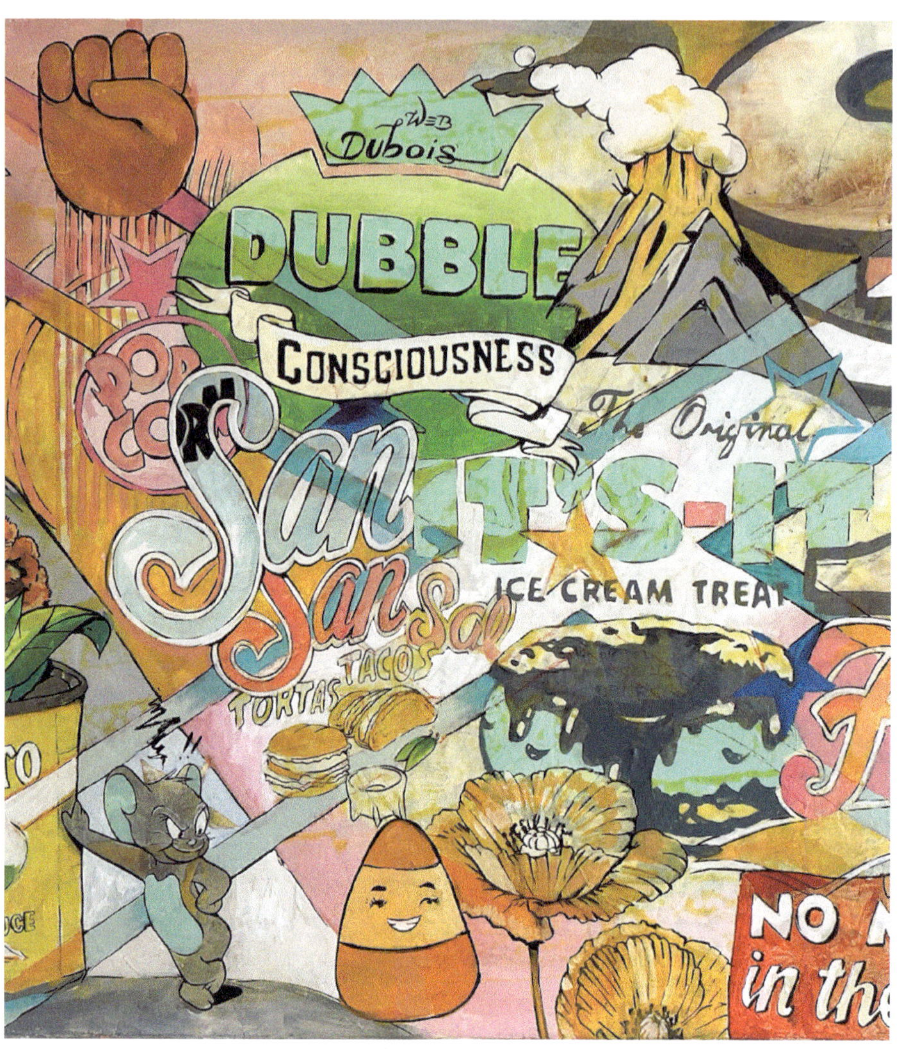

Josué Rojas, Detail: "It's It: Double Consciousness."

Wanda Sabir
CHOOSING MY EDUCATION

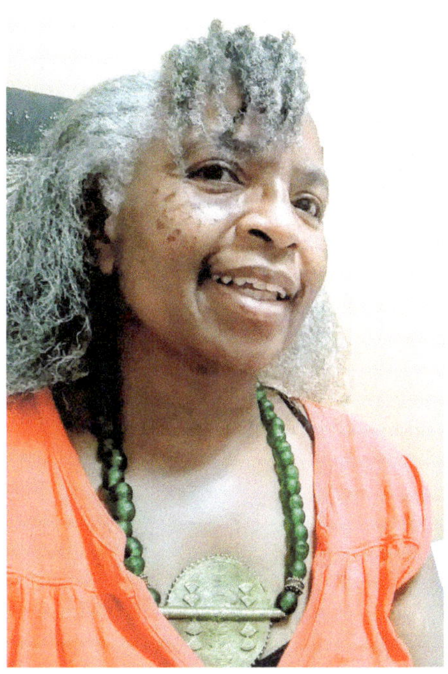

Wanda Sabir covers Black arts and culture in print, radio,
and the web on Wanda's Picks and in a column
in the *San Francisco Bay View* newspaper.
She is a Depth Psychologist, with deep roots in the
bayous of Louisiana where she was born.

Her interests and expertise are trauma
and trauma healing—the Maafa, specifically
ancestral memories, dream tending, and the use of art
and guided Appreciative Inquiry (AI) to stimulate
those forgotten conversations, especially
among Diaspora descendants. She holds
a Master's Degree in Writing from the University of
San Francisco and teaches at College of Alameda.
wandaspicks.com

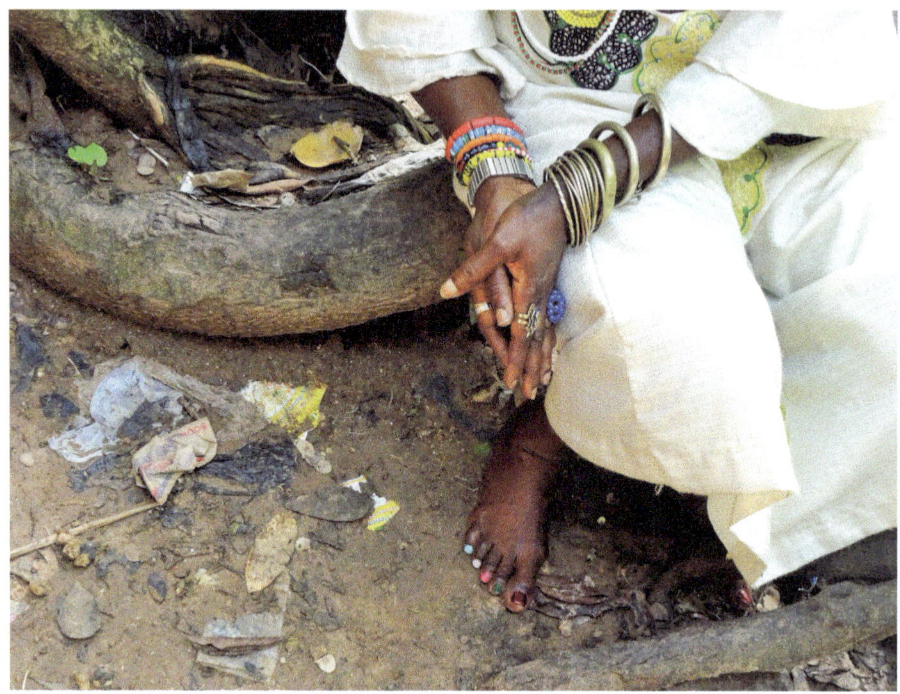

"Ifa Divination@ Oṣun River," digital photograph, 20 x 30 inches, 2018.
Oṣogbo, Oṣun State, Nigeria.

SUGAR WATER LIBATION

for Mama Makeda, Cousin Sweet and all Sweet Wom(b)en
Unnamed, but Remembered

Ladies: *"Drop your sweet wom(b)en in the river to bathe"*
We pour libations today for the sweet wom(b)en
Sweet now
Sweet intentions yesterday
Sweet even when bitter winds blow … cold
She, warm desert air we return to when our insides get to churning

INTERCHANGE

At a time historically when conversation is for the most part a lost art,
I am amazed that the only people talking are
    those trapped next to each other on flights
Or in prison cells on lockdown, or on sinking ships
    once the last lifeboat is filled.
Conversation is not the penalty for isolation, but often it feels as such.

GROWING UP BLACK IN SAN FRANCISCO
Wanda Sabir

In Memory of El Hajjah Nebeehah Sabree Shakir (1949-2015)

They were impressive, like the sisters in Terri McMillian's *Waiting to Exhale*. Their presence was a cool breeze, a breath of fresh air. I thought of them as giants, Amazons in a San Francisco desert. Fillmore and Geary an oasis of Black culture—Elijah Muhammad our guide.

It was 1974, and we worked at Muhammad University of Islam No. 26, which was housed in that yellow brick building at Fillmore & Geary that is now the Fillmore Auditorium. There was Sister Nabeehah (Corliss), Sister Munira (Linda), Sister Marva, Sister Rashidah (Joyce 5X), Sister Sharifah, Sister Bayinna, Sister Aeeshah Clottey (Patsy), and Sister Mahasin (Leslie). Then there was Sister Izola in the kitchen and the Lieutenants and Junior Lieutenants, of whom I was one. We were directed by the Vanguard Lieutenant and Sister Captain, who reported to the minister.

I remember wearing a hot pink, two-piece uniform: culottes and tunic, and showing off our drill steps—we were hot in more ways than one! We'd have drilling competitions in front of the entire community; sometimes other Vanguards from other mosques would compete with us. I don't remember losing. On Saturdays we'd have bake sales and oratory contests where we'd memorize chapters from the Messenger's (Elijah Muhammad) books and see who had memorized the longest passages. We would also share original work. I recited one essay about the illusion of time. Both girls and boys were encouraged to show off academically and were praised by the ministers and other adults. We'd have sleepovers at friends' houses where we'd dance the latest dances and stay up all night talking. The next day, we'd get up early, put on our dress-white uniforms and go to the mosque where we'd serve shifts as greeters and security in the women's check room.

As a junior lieutenant, I also supervised and patted down the women and girls who needed a second check. There were never any incidents while I was on duty, and I never found any weapons, but when we trained, we planted weapons on each other—knife-like and gun-sized objects. Many of us also trained in karate. We were a sharp and confident youth group.

We also had a nursery where mothers could nurse their babies and feel more comfortable. For guests who needed more modest clothing, we had nice clothes they could borrow.

It was a family-friendly environment. We respected ourselves and each other, especially our visitors whom we wanted to feel most welcome. When I was 12, I wrote a letter to the Hon. Elijah Muhammad in Chicago to request an X. Afterward, I was officially emancipated from the vestiges of plantation life. Wanda 2X meant I was the second Wanda in our community to get an X. We went to the front of the assembly and the minister welcomed us into the community. Though my knees were shaking, I was really excited, and I beamed when everyone applauded. I might not know what my ancestral family name was, but "Oliver" was given back to the slave master.

My brother wasn't doing well in public school, so when the Muslim school opened, my parents wanted to send him. But they weren't sure they could afford to send both of us right away. I really wanted to go. I made all A's in school but it would be so wonderful to be with my peers, other girls and boys who dressed like I did and worshipped like I did, too. I was tired of being around kids who treated me differently. I was so happy when my parents were able to pull their funds together and I got to go to Muhammad University of Islam No. 26. The building accommodated the school perfectly. Carpenters built classrooms in the lower auditorium where we prayed and where the Wednesday night and Sunday afternoon meetings occurred. A library was built upstairs in the dining area, and there were partitions installed along the balcony. These smaller cubicles were where students met for classes.

I was so excited! I was in the first graduating class. Class valedictorian at 15 years old. After graduating, I was hired as a teacher. Assistant Director Brother Sunni Ali Shabazz wanted to get me into the University of California, Berkeley, but my father didn't think I was old enough, so I waited until I was 17, almost 18. I enjoyed working at the school. I learned to teach writing from the trainings by one of the assistant directors, Dr. Fatimah Ali.

Sister Nabeehah, one of my mentors, taught third grade. I had her younger son in my class—cute, energetic Dawud. I liked him and he liked me. This is important in a relationship between an unruly child and authority. We never talked about it; I didn't label him or ask to read his file. He and I just understood what was reasonable to expect. He couldn't sit still for long periods of time—what child can? There were others like Dawud—siblings Marcus and Sultana, who dealt with things children shouldn't have to face, like abuse and homelessness. I tried to fortify my students with enough love to face the world outside our time together.

The boys met in the morning and the girls in the afternoon. When I started teaching, my first grade class met in the dining room across from the kindergarteners. I think the other elementary classes met on the balcony, I just don't remember how we divided the space. I don't recall hearing them or being annoyed. Downstairs were classrooms for the older children like my brother. (Now when I enter the Fillmore Auditorium, I can remember classrooms along the far wall, now gone, and the checking rooms to the far left where the bar is now.)

I wouldn't say I was playing at teaching, but I didn't have teacher training. In retrospect, I was teaching as an intern, in the same way as on a post-slavery plantation, where students graduated and then shared what they knew. My first mentor-teacher was just across the room from me, teaching pre-kindergarten. I supplemented what she demonstrated with the methodology my mother successfully used at home to help my brother. At eight or nine, he had trouble reading, so she used phonetics; whole-word vocabulary; and flash cards, books and other materials we bought at teacher supply stores. I used the same strategies with my students. My job was almost a family affair. My parents supplemented my salary and helped me with purchases.

Reading lessons formed the basis of a curriculum which also included: African and world history, mathematics, and composition. Our textbooks were often the writings of the Hon. Elijah Muhammad. I remember my biology teacher using photosynthesis as a metaphor for black consciousness, the light— Allah, Subhanahu Wa Ta'ala. The breath is spiritual life. The Messenger always spoke of spiritual death and how light or truth is what would awaken our people from slumber. He said we were, "Blind, deaf, and dumb to the knowledge of self."

My education was supplemented by classes at the Academy of Sciences in Golden Gate Park, the de Young Museum, and trips to the library. We had an extensive Black history library at home and my father quizzed me on the material. I think it helps that I didn't attend Muhammad University until after seventh grade in public school. I was a smart girl, tested and placed in the gifted and talented classes. My talent was writing, but I also liked math and science. I could also draw very well. I had aspirations to be an architect, a medical illustrator, and a billboard sign painter. My parents cultivated these talents with books and classes and field trips. My mother took me to concerts and later bought tickets so older sisters (like Sister Joan) could take me. One highlight was seeing Alvin Ailey and Dance Theatre of Harlem at the

San Francisco Opera House. I think I could have become much more—and I have accomplished a lot—had I not had to fight so hard against racism in the dominant society and the patriarchy inherent in the Nation of Islam.

When I had my own children, I was determined not to sacrifice them for the "cause." I would prepare them for, and try to mitigate, the harm to their fragile Black souls as they navigated educational institutions where whiteness is normative. I almost lost my younger daughter to this, but a watchful and committed staff at her preschool embraced her and our family. We were able to rescue our little Black girl and give her tools to continue to rescue herself, as this cultural deficit within the midst of academic plenty would continue through higher education. TaSin got a BFA in Fine Arts Photography at the California College of Arts and Crafts. It was the same fight for my older daughter, Bilaliyah, who continued on to graduate school and graduated with a BA in Women's Studies and Psychology and a MA in Education at Cal State East Bay.

We wonder why our children fail to thrive. I know my success is directly related to the love I received in the Nation of Islam. Though underprepared academically when I entered UC Berkeley, I quickly excelled because I had superior preparation in Black consciousness and Black confidence—I knew I was capable. This self allowed me to navigate an often hostile terrain and later prepare my daughters for the battle inherent in this suspect space—America, a place which even today negates or denies Black greatness, especially Black female greatness.

When I attended MUI, all the female leaders and teachers were really young. Later, I was surprised to realize they were in their 20s—at most ten years older than I, sometimes less. In my youthful eyes they looked so big and strong and able to do so much. Sister Nabeehah Sabree Shakir kind of scared me. She had a college degree and taught in Oakland public schools. She understood the value and challenges of Black English, so after she left Muhammad University of Islam, she advocated for supplemental education for children who needed help with Standard English. She developed the Standard English Proficiency (SEP) Program. Black students could learn the cultural and historical value of Black English as well Standard English. SEP also provided resources for teachers who viewed Black English as "bad English" or slang. Sister Nabeehah testified in Congress in 1996 during the national controversy over the concept of "Ebonics" as a distinct language. Later she started her own school and mentored many children and their children until she died in 2015 at 67.

When I was accepted into UC Berkeley, I saw how academically underprepared I was. I had to run to catch up that first year and had to repeat English 1A and English 1B before I could write a decent freshman essay. I didn't learn about thesis sentences and argument until studying for a Master's in Writing at the University of San Francisco.

While I am supportive of independent schools, I am not supportive of schools which do not make Black children competitive and academically competent. What distinguished those early years at MUI is the concept of positive Blackness. We grew up in the 1970s when negative associations with Blackness were not directly challenged, yet we felt the biases in subtle ways. This is why I had wanted to go to a Black school so badly.

The teachers at MUI loved us. My brother had been failing in public school. He might not have gotten complete academic preparation at MUI, but the love and support gave us both confidence that we could do anything. After all, the Black Man is God of the Universe and Black Woman, Mother of Civilization. Potential was present in our very DNA. We could create a new world again in a blink of the eye. We were capable—more than capable. So we did not answer to anything except signifiers which we recognized. We were not what America said we were. Our history was larger than the slavery episode—a great moment for the West, but not for us. We proved our greatness once again in the present age by not only surviving but thriving.

Black people are magnificent! This is what we learned in Brother William's math class, Sister Arifah's architecture class, Sister Munirah's English class. My classmates went on to become attorneys, college professors, models, authors, filmmakers, clerks, security guards, and chefs. Muhammad University was renamed Sister Clara Muhammad School and relocated to Oakland at 47th Avenue and Bond. I taught there briefly, but the legacy began for me in San Francisco at Muhammad University No. 26, of which I am a proud graduate.

A PARTICULAR MEMORY

I am a transplant from a country called New Orleans. We arrived in San Francisco on a Greyhound bus, mother disheveled, brother crying, Dad waiting for us at the bus terminal looking proud yet scared. Reunited for the first time in months, I couldn't recall this big man who hugged me like I was an anchor in a sea too shallow to hold us all. It would be a rocky journey, our vessel full of holes only liquid paraffin could plug. Not necessarily seaworthy, we stayed aboard the plywood flotilla until it capsized one day. That day we stood up, grabbed our belongings and decided to try living on land—at least it didn't move as much—or so we thought.

Earthquakes followed us from Oak to Page, from Page to Brookdale, from Brookdale to Tioga, from Tioga to Granada, from Granada to Holloway, from Holloway to Mariposa, from Mariposa to *skid road*. The fissures were deep, and each time the holes were a bit harder to climb out of.

There were no hands reaching into the chasm to grab our waving ones, nor any bodies lining the cliffs to prevent our falls. We just adapted and got good at walking in our sleep, scraped knees and hurt elbows, twisted ankles and dislocated tenure in a *Dream* we'd applied for, yet were denied. We grew to accept this norm—if we were to make it, it would be on our own.

No one cared about us San Francisco transplants from a country called New Orleans. Our Black lives definitely did not matter to anyone except us.

I spent my time writing poetry, memorizing chapters from *Message to the Black Man*, and thinking about *The Fall of America*, which couldn't happen too soon if that could make my family safe. With my words I fashioned a place where Black men like my daddy could find vessels large enough to hold them and their families, spaces where they were able to stretch and grow and be free.

The shackles that rattled, the ball that he tripped over, and the dimly lit room he was assigned to kept him trapped. The doctors kept telling him, "It's all in your mind," but the failed job applications and rental agreements were shredded sheets we used to cover our shame each night.

My father's Blackness was a liability. Yet, it was not just his Blackness, it was his undeniable Blackness, coupled with an unshaken pride that populated a dirge the angels would sing when sober enough to lift their wings. It was an uneasy life for a Black girl, the eldest of two. I wish I'd been more like my little brother, who fought all the time for justice. It was a justice too blinded by our Blackness to ever weigh in positively for our dad. But Daddy never gave up, even when he could no longer see—Miz Justice's scales a bleak outline on a horizon too distant to matter.

HOW I MOVE: DANCING DIASPORA ONE TERRITORY AT A TIME

When I started traveling to continental Africa in 2009, I was 51. At 50, I'd vowed to not let another year pass when I was not getting to know my people— wherever they were in the world. I spent the next ten or more years traveling

Africa and the African Disapora, exploring—what was to me—unmapped territory, one connection at a time. These connections were crucial because I had to rely on my own finances and connections.

The first opportunity came at the Association of Black Psychologists Convention, where I met Mouhammadou "Pape" Niang and his mother, Mame Ulimata Diouf, daughter of the famous mystic, Mame Fatou Seck. Pape said that if I went to Senegal, I could stay with his family in Rufisque, a city just outside of Dakar. Then, Walter Turner, host of *African Today*, KPFA (94.1 FM) introduced me to his friend, Coumba Toure, whose mother Suzanne Toure (on Walter's recommendation) invited me to stay with her in Dakar. She was a former schoolteacher and single mother with a house, servants, and lots of patience. She was a destination for Diaspora Africans. Coumba, who lived in Mali, also kindly made a list of people to call and see and places to visit.

I became what I call a fly-by-the-seat-of-my-pants traveler. I'd buy my ticket and figure it out later (literally). This attitude involves a lot of trust. I always make sure I ask someone here at home to connect me with someone there; however, after that, the arrangements—where I go, who I see—are in flux.

I always have a place to stay confirmed; however, how I get to that place is often not—I have found myself stranded in airports waiting. On my second trip to Senegal, I was cheated out of all my cash, because of course, the trip to the King's Hotel cost everything I was holding. Luckily, I was able to bunk with a friend, Dr. Runoko Rashidi, the late scholar, until he left town, and then the Senegalese government, under President Abdoulaye Wade, took up the tab and then moved the Diaspora folks to an Artist Village built just for those attending the World Festival of Black Art and Culture (FESMAN 2010).

I made a lot of mistakes while traveling, some irreparable, but that did not stop me from apologizing and trying to stay connected to the lovely people I met. I've exhibited photos of my trips, and when I sold any that included friends and acquaintances, I sent them the money. It was a small way to pay back their hospitality and kindness.

We might have been strangers but they often felt as if they might have been relatives or neighbors from the distant past. Suzanne has freckles, so I saw my face in her face. Learning that her mother, her grandson and a young village girl from the village were staying with her, my daughter, TaSin, gave me jeans and fashionable clothing to take to her. I took my friend Pape shoes and a computer.

Suzanne's daughter, Coumba, ran the Ashoka West Africa office in Dakar. The office manager, Binta introduced me to Ashoka Fellows in The Gambia when I told her I was traveling there. I also met a couple fellows in Dakar. These innovators showed me how they were using Ashoka resources to develop projects for sustainable—often economic—change in their communities. The projects I saw focused on women and youth. Badara Dioup used solar energy to light his village at night, and by day he showed youth how to make agriculture profitable. Youth were leaving home for the city and starving. Why not bring the technology into the village? By developing agribusiness, the youth could have the best of both worlds. What I also loved about this village and others in The Gambia was women in leadership. His chief was a woman who was really cool.

In The Gambia, I also visited Mame Fatou Ben's elementary school. When the kids go home, the school opens up as a community computer lab. Back in Senegal, I visited the Ghanaian author, Ayi Kwei Armah (The Beautiful Ones Are Not Yet Born), whom I first met at UC Berkeley. He now lives in Popenguine. The King's summer home is unique to this location as is Armah's PerAnkh where he coaches youth to pass qualifying exams for high school and college. Without this academic help, these young people would have no hope of access to professional skills. Another woman I met, from America, trains girls who did not pass these exams in entrepreneurial skills. I met her while in Touba City to visit the holy mosque for the African saint and revolutionary Cheikh Amadou Bamba, who resisted French colonialism through fasting and prayer.

Senegal is my African home. It was the first place I visited and the country where I saw the potential for positive change—one person, community or village at a time. I was to travel to a deeper, more painful place when I visited Ghana in 2016 and 2018.

RETRACING THE TRADE

When I decided to go to Ghana, West Africa, it was to see the famous slave dungeons: Elmina and Cape Coast. I also wanted to retrace the slave route from the northern most part of Ghana to the south. It took two trips to complete the journey. I'd like to return for a third trip to meet the indigenous people along the route—stopping at all the dungeons to see what stories remain of the journey so long ago.

Before I visited Ghana, I'd been to Gorée Island in Senegal; it stirred no ancestral energy. I felt nothing inside, except intellectual horror at the solicitude paid to the French tourists. Of course, this trade in Black kinspeople was terrible; however, it would not be until I was led into the Ghanian dungeons several years later, in the company of Seestah IMAHKÜS Njinga Okofu Ababio (One Africa), a Diaspora mother of the continental drift, that I could I truly feel a tangible lingering trauma.

I felt welcomed, certainly seen, in Ghana; but even then I felt no immediate inclination to release the hurt. I didn't feel safe enough to let my imagination or blood memories travel into spaces I might have difficulty returning from. The trade in African ancestors is a deep ravine or tunnel I am still trying to find my way from. I was born into this legacy—at once strong and bold and tenacious. I think I needed congestion and confusion, consternation and unknown fear, tears or anguish to enable release.

As I walked the fort, I was outside my body—an animate corpse looking into holes and bed chambers, then into cells for the unruly rebellious ones who never left the tombs. My feet felt adhered to sticky, blood-soaked floors, feces caked—I didn't fall down, yet felt pulled into a darkness I used my phone flashlight to illuminate.

Many visitors—and staff— assumed the nonchalance of the disaffected: "You feel too much," the uniformed guides and guards said as European descendants of the perpetrators walked silently nearby, many with African descended wives or girlfriends.

Elmina is one of many slave dungeons along the Gold Coast, in Ghana, West Africa. The edifice is weathered, haunted by memories visitors carry in suitcases past customs—inheritance spilled between this location and that to enter a land beyond our ancestors' wildest imaginations. Neither prey nor indigenous predators knew the cost of this severance, breach, hole filled with Black bodies, which from then to now, do not matter. Value has always been a negotiable yet tangible notion among traders in Blackness, especially once the commodities were no longer worth the dollars[1] they were printed on. Drowned, repatriated, imprisoned, worked to death and then recycled—Black memories are stirred here—this space both sacred and profane. Elmina is a gravesite. We visit to put flowers on the mounds, to feed the wandering ghosts, to pour water on stained walls, dash on floors, leak into tunnels.

We walk these hallowed chambers where our ancestors suffered fates worse than death, because despite the casualties, many captives lived. They

---

1. www.albany.edu/jmmh/vol3/facevalue/facevalue.html. www.thedailybeast.com/when-dixie-put-slaves-on-the-money

didn't live long, but they reached outposts in the Pacific and Caribbean, Indian and Atlantic oceans where they wrote a new Black chapter.

There are no return tickets to Elmina dungeon and other way stations. The exit migration was one way for most descendants. There is mystique and lore attached to these geographic spaces. We fantasize about homecomings. Pilgrimages. Alex Haley's *Roots* is the prototype. And for some, there is this welcome. For me, there was none.

I was seen as a reverse negative. White woman in Black face.

157 years after the end of the Civil War, I, an African Diaspora descendant, question landmarks like Elmina that lament, reinjure and sanctify victimhood— slave dungeon a stop on a Black History Reeducation Tour. What legacy does this promote? Reparations? Land? Healing from the MAAFA spelled out? Are such sojourns a path to reunification? Or do they perpetuate the myth that African Americans are what was left, forgotten, discarded. We are the fragile egg the Sankofa bird holds gently in its mouth. Akwaaba! It is up to us to make ourselves welcome as we undertake a journey of healing that may take many, many visits.

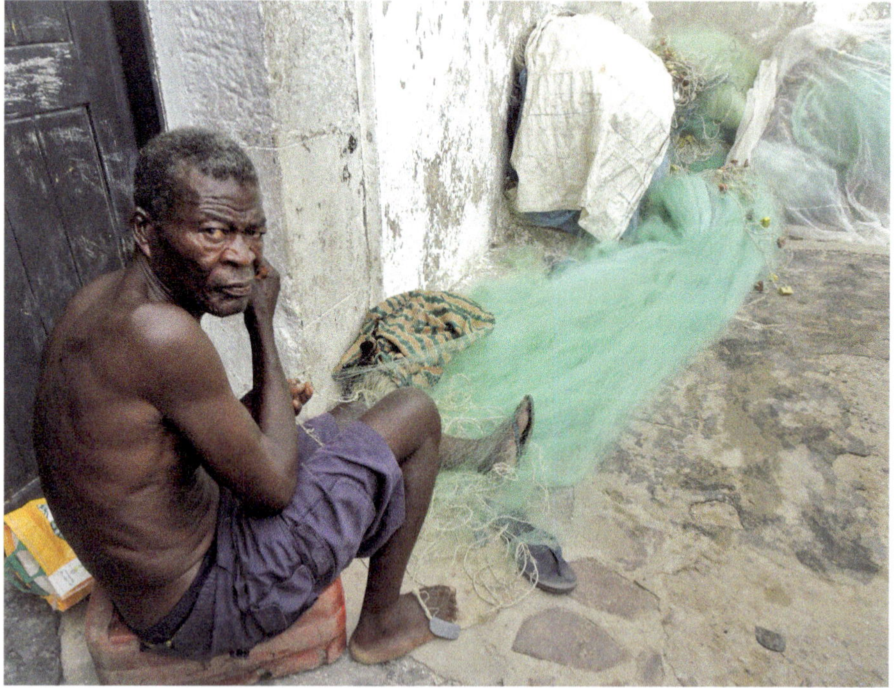

"Seated at the Door of No Return," digital photograph, 24 x 22 inches, 2016. At Elmina Slave Dungeon, the old man reflects on the author's presence with skepticism and a bit of wonder.

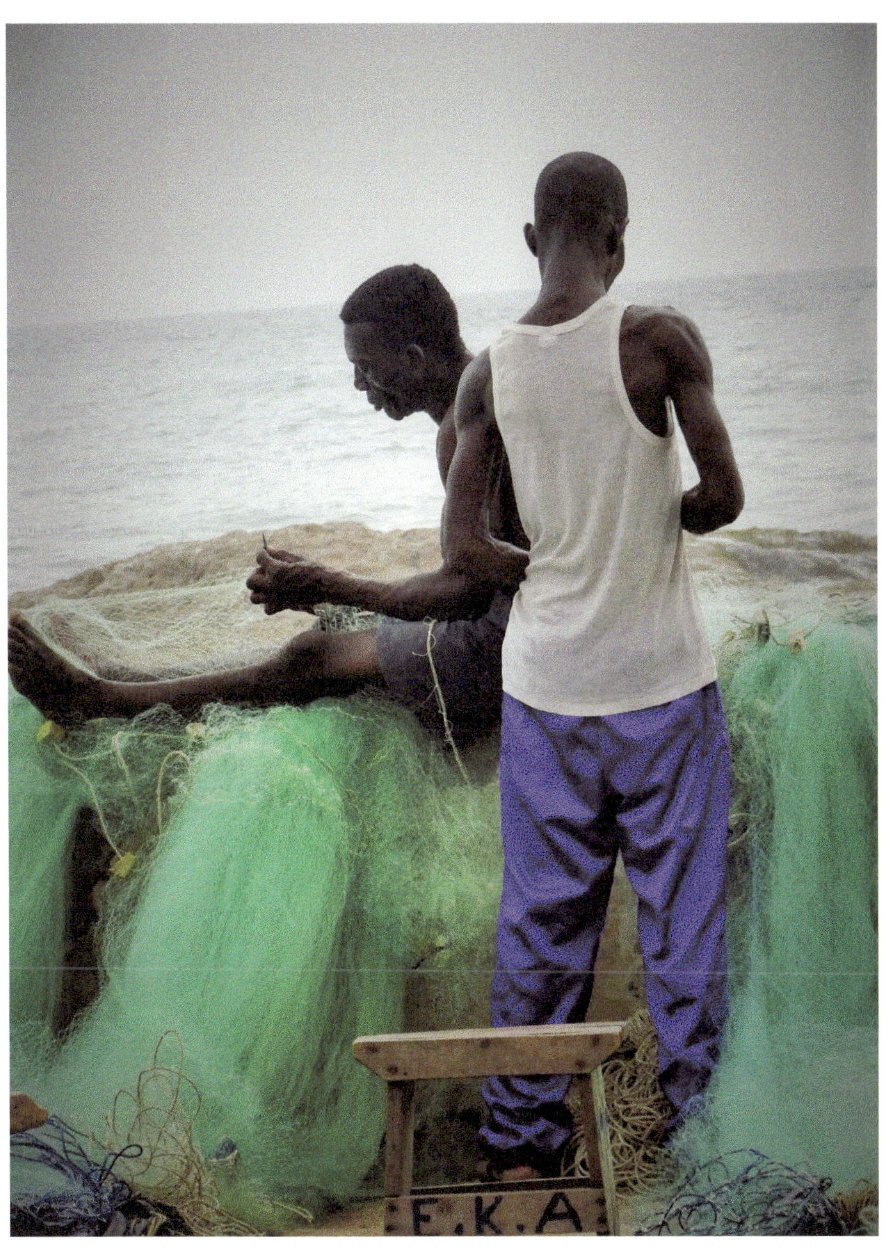

"Preparing for the Catch," digital photograph, 24 x 22 inches, 2016.
Elmina Dungeon. Ghana, West Africa.

"Elmina Village," digital photograph, 24 x 22 inches, 2016. Ghana, West Africa.

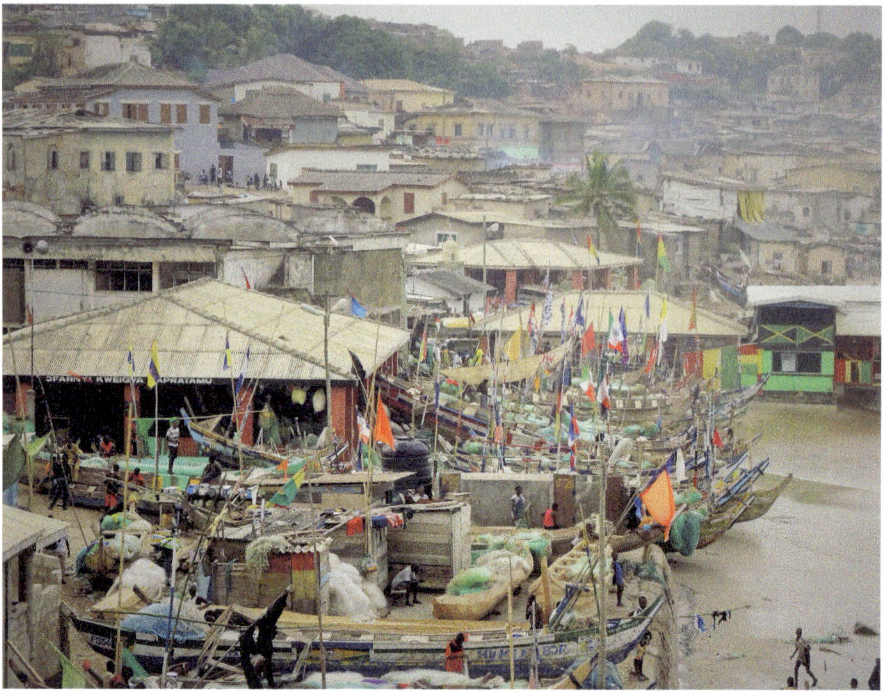

A PANTHER IN AFRICA

We are on the elder's property where he is holding court with the younger warriors. All Diaspora men—there are four men, one Ghanaian, one from the Caribbean and the third, Black American. All arrived in Ghana 20-25 years ago looking for the bush and found it here.

These Diaspora men were looking to get away from the complications of structural racism, noisy capitalism, and modernity. They'd stepped off the grid, yet when I arrived in 2016, they described how the precious bush was being chopped down, land gone, cultural treasures leased and discarded, sold to the highest bidder.

"Progress" keeps these men on the move—when the road gets too close they sell or rent out their houses ... and seek another spot where they will be left alone.

Off the grid, they use solar power, rainwater irrigation. They make small, small carbon footprints. They live sustainably and have tried to share this way of life with the Ghanaian people. Unfortunately, the West is a more attractive option to most of the youth, who wield chainsaws like the cowboys of the wild, wild West brandished pistols. The boys chop down trees—clearing the land of

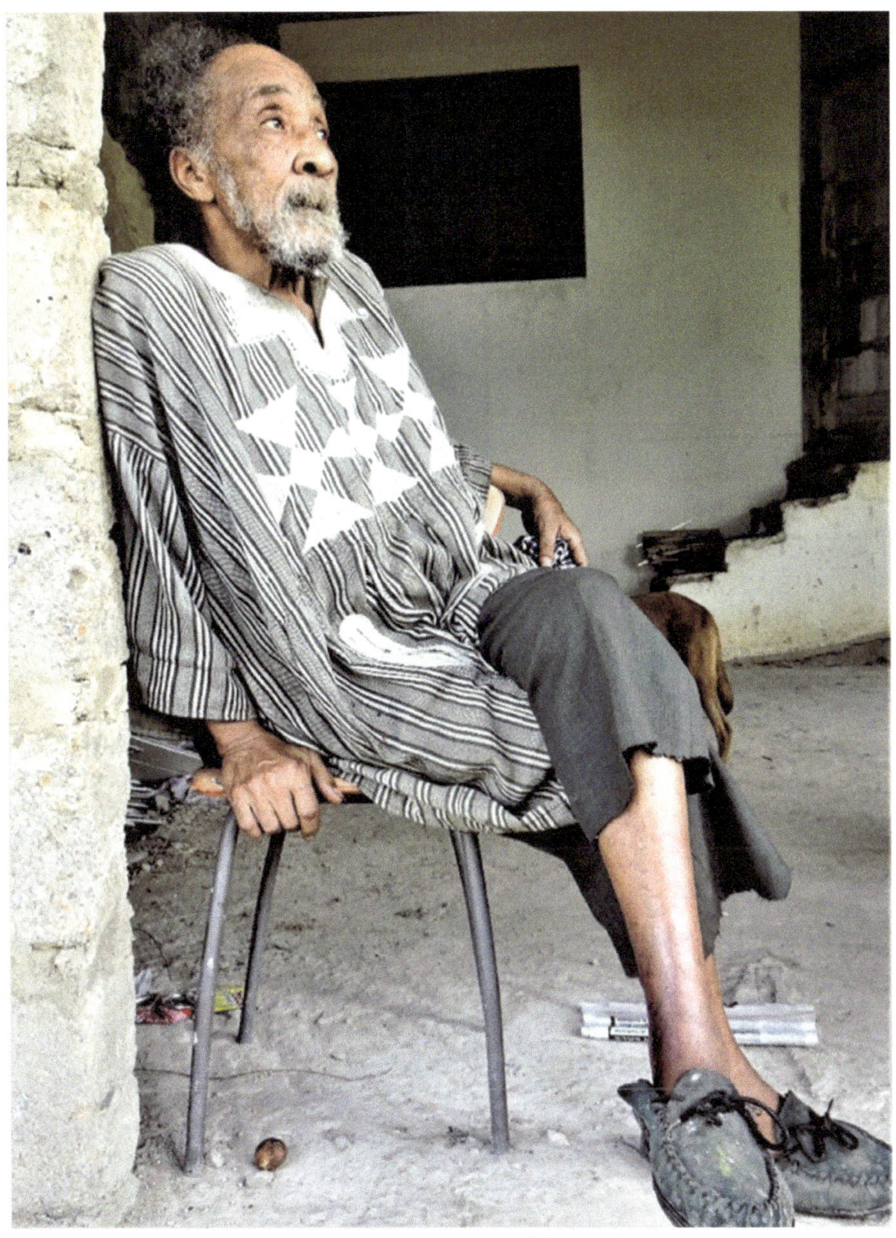

"Brother Muhammad: A Panther in Africa," from the series *A Panther in Africa: From St. Louis, Missouri, to Ghana, West Africa.*

their ancestors for European, Indian, Asian, American outsiders to develop.

The day I visited, it had been storming; we walked carefully around muddy spots on the hillside where three houses stood. A garden flourished, covering the landscape with edible and decorative plants—many of them medicinal.

The outdoor porch where Brother Muhammad sat was like a classroom. We were all eager to listen to his stories about the movement, his first visit to Ghana, and his return for good 30 years ago. Inside his home, I was surprised to see lovely marble floors and walls—spacious and open, with beautiful art in each room.

Another house, further down, was round, with walls tiled with beautiful seashells and mosaic glass.

I think about my Daddy and what it might have meant to his life if he'd had an opportunity to visit Angola, Southwestern Africa, rather than Angola, Louisiana, the largest state prison in America. In the African bush, he would have finally known "how it feels to be free."

* * *

I am now mining my indigenous American heritage—New Orleans and San Francisco. The ancestors are calling me home, home to the red clay that I see in my face—the etchings carved from ships made holy with ceremony, a rite of passage I am still navigating as I get closer to the "return." I am walking with ancestors, the Mothers who stayed and the ones who left … knowing that if we are our ancestors, that they live in we, then no one is gone or forgotten or lost. I am just trying to stay "wombful" and gathered and safe and free and in motion—relative and relevant. Facilitating Wombfulness Gatherings for Black wom(b)en is my goal and my call.

Acknowledgments

A version of "Growing up Black in San Francisco" was first published in *Re(i)magining*.

"A Panther in Africa" is adapted from an artist statement for *A Panther in Africa: From St. Louis, Missouri, to Ghana, West Africa*. https://richmondartcenter.org/aotad2021/wanda-sabir/

Shizue Seigel
HOMELAND INSECURITY

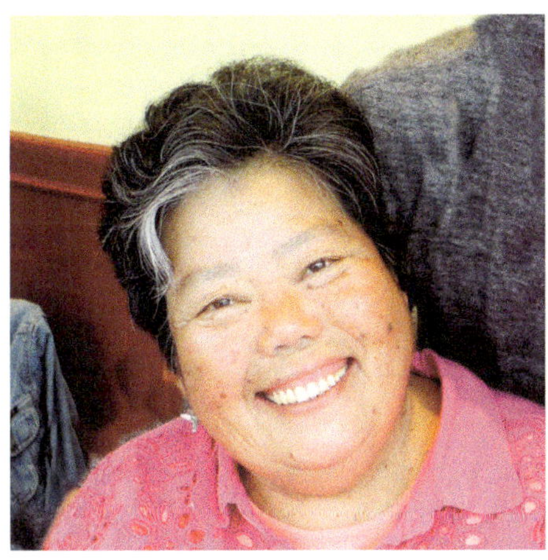

Shizue Seigel, founder/director of Write Now! SF Bay,
is a third-generation Japanese American writer, visual artist,
and community activist whose passion for social justice arises
from growing up in segregated Baltimore, Occupied Japan,
California skid rows, and sharecropping camps.

A largely self-taught college dropout, single mother and
grandmother, she abandoned an advertising career in the mid-1990s
to help tell community stories. For over 25 years, she has worked
with public housing residents, formerly incarcerated Japanese
Americans, and emerging and established BIPOC writers and artists.

She is a Jefferson Award winner, three-time recipient of San
Francisco Arts Commission Artist Grants,
and a VONA/Voices fellow. Her seven books include
*In Good Conscience: Supporting Japanese Americans during the
Internment, My First Hundred Years: The Memoirs of
Nellie Nakamura*, and four Write Now! SF Bay anthologies.
Her prose and poetry have been widely published in
anthologies and journals.
writenowsf.com and shizueseigel.com

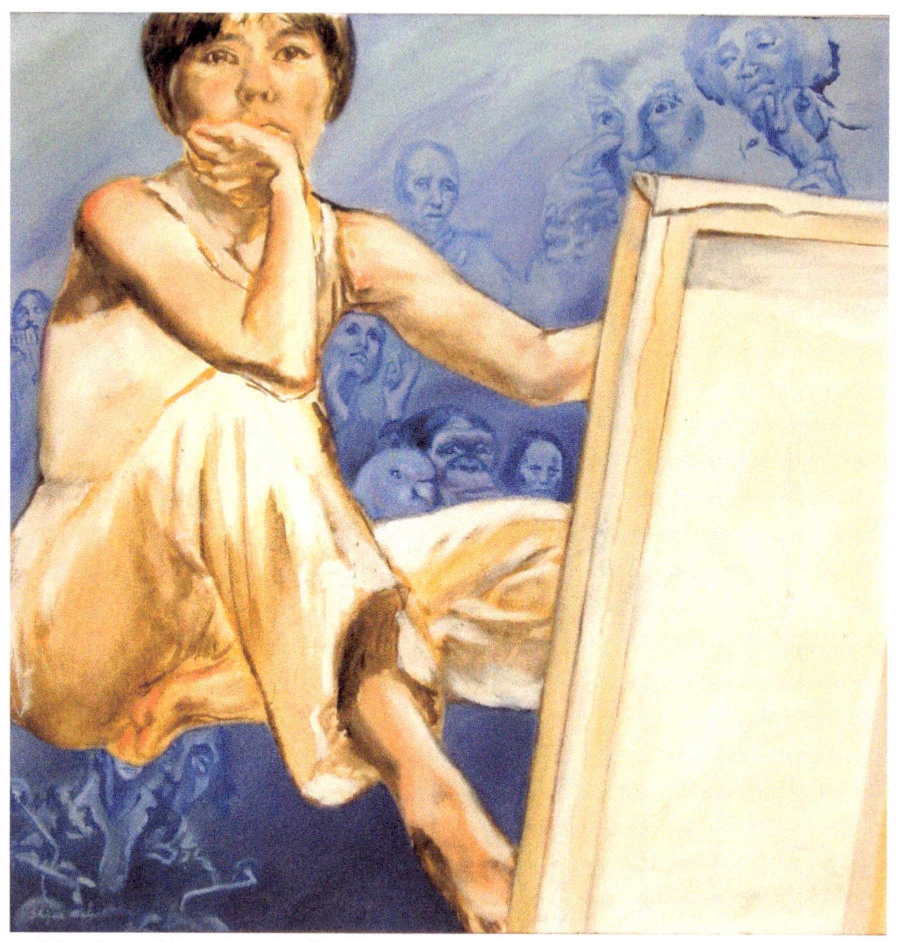

"Burden of Imagination," self-portrait, oil on canvas, 24 x 24 inches, 1978.

My first self-portrait assignment in community college
explored the artist's responsibility to the blank canvas.
I'm sitting on the living room floor because I can't afford an easel,
letting newspaper images float through my mind.
Not a single Asian face—we were invisible.
From top right, Emmet Till's mother, an Appalachian storyteller,
a 100-year-old ex-slave, an Andean playing an antara panpipe,
a nun engaged in charismatic prayer,
a bird, a chimpanzee, and an Amazonian Indian whose habitat
are being destroyed—and whites seem far more concerned about
the welfare of animals than of indigenous people.
Down in the netherlands, constructs of pop culture:
the Wicked Witch of the West and a Hells' Angel.

HOMELAND INSECURITY
Shizue Seigel

I felt like an exile in my own country from the night I was born.

Born in the segregated border town of Baltimore, Maryland, just months after my Japanese American family's release from the American concentration camps of World War II.

Born half a world away from a father drafted into US Army military intelligence and now witnessing the aftermath of firebombing and nuclear attack in his ancestral homeland.

Born to a drugged and dissociated mother under the influence of "twilight sleep." Swaddled by morphine and scopolamine, she did not know she'd given birth until I'd been alone in the world for more than 12 hours.

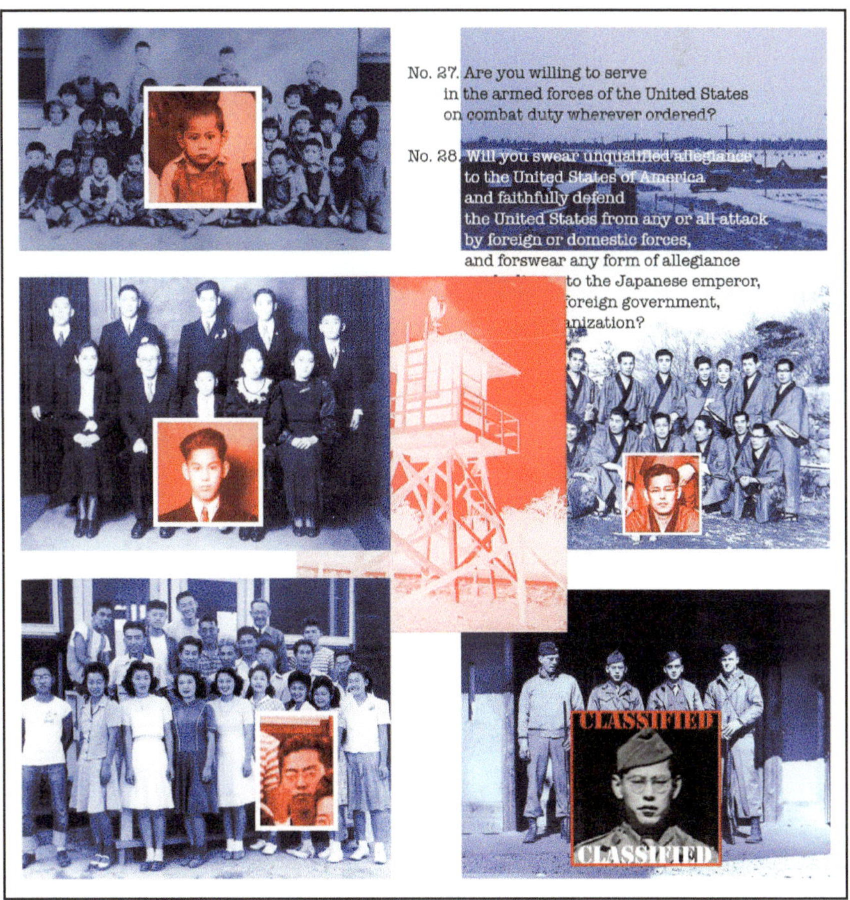

"Classified," photo collage, 24 x 24 inches, 2010.

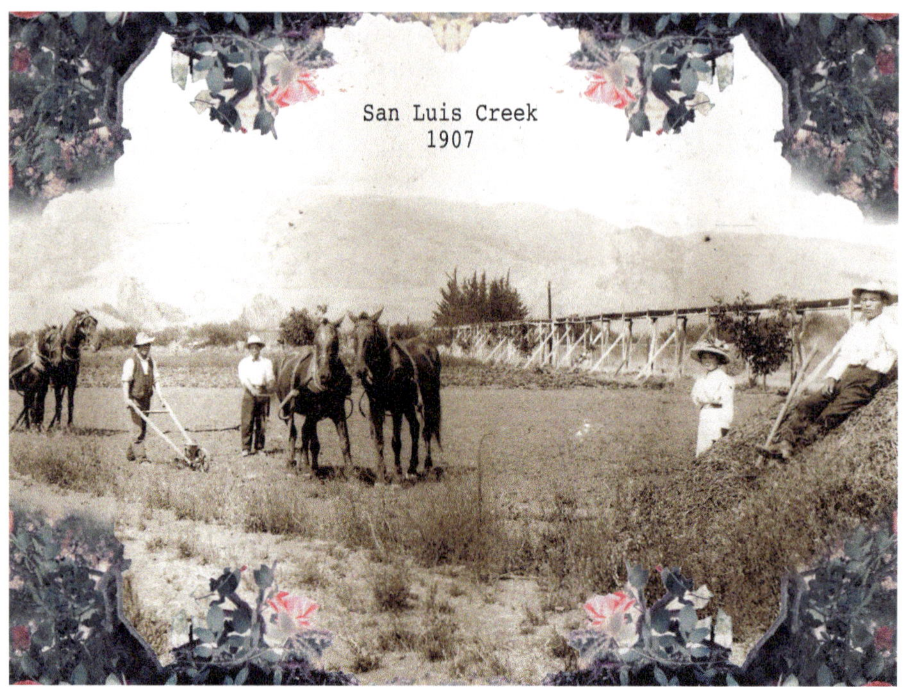

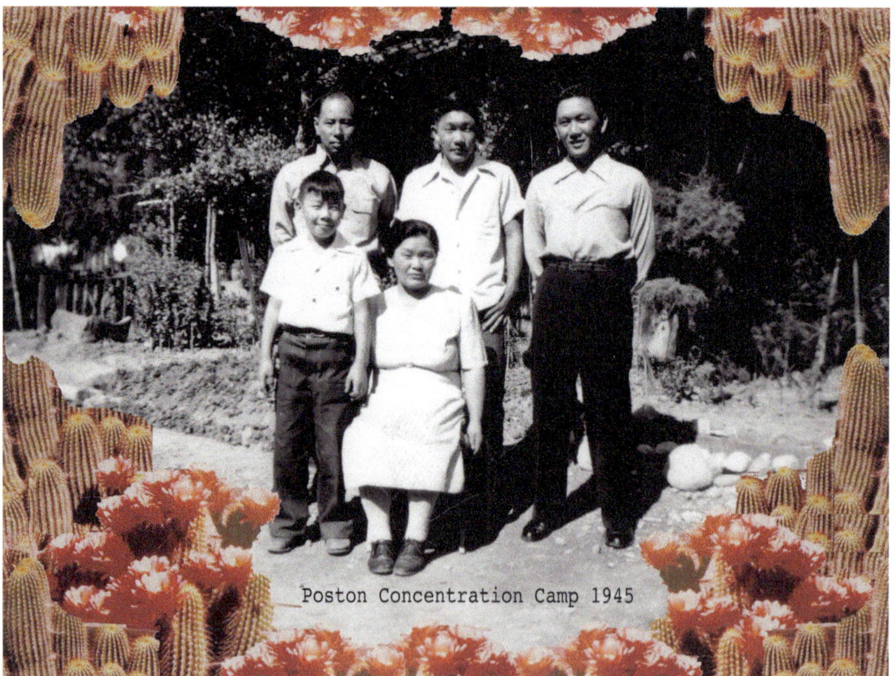

"San Luis Creek, 1910" (my grandfather and partners on their first produce farm) and "Poston Concentration Camp, 1945," (my grandparents and uncles incarcerated), photocollages, 18 x 24, 2018, from *Agrarian Pioneers* series.

Born not long after my grandparents, uncles, aunties, and cousins limped home to California from concentration camps in Arkansas and Arizona. 18 family members crammed into three jalopies that kept breaking down as they drove across a hostile white America, camping by the side of the road and living on peanut butter sandwiches.

I grew up on family stories of loss and displacement—immigrant grandfathers taken away in the dead of night by the FBI after Pearl Harbor, my grandmother forced off her farm, house set ablaze, $80,000 in storefront properties sold under duress for $2000 cash… But I also grew up witnessing resourcefulness, resiliency, and faith.

My first-generation grandparents and their friends left the narrow confines of post-feudal Japan to seek a wide new destiny in America, a new world—a racist world that denied them naturalized citizenship and the right to buy land, work, live, or marry as they chose. They created parallel worlds of their own, with churches, language schools, businesses, and loan clubs. By 1940, they grew 40% of California's produce. They were targets of envy, targets of exploitation, then targets of incarceration after Pearl Harbor. Transformed from "aliens" to "enemy aliens" overnight, they lost everything. But even behind barbed wire, they created community: churches, cultural presentations, gardens in the desert. When they were released, they were in their 50s, starting again on their knees as farm laborers, gardeners, and maids.

My second-generation parents, American citizens by birthright, were traumatized on the threshold of adulthood—simply for looking like the enemy. Citizenship meant nothing compared to the color for their skin and the slant of their eyes. My parents were traumatized for the rest of their lives. They sought safety in the model minority and a middle-class lifestyle, but fear, anger, and insecurity leaked through their pores, subtly infusing into mine. They sacrificed community for upward mobility—and carried with them their private hells, locked in the mental prison of discrimination. "Know your place." "Don't rock the boat." "The nail that sticks up will be hammered down."

I was a third-generation child in the 1950s, growing up with a Japanese sense of Both-And. In the face of the Either-Or, winner-take-all stance of white Christian America, my family raised me to embrace contradiction and paradox as facts of life. American first names AND Japanese middle names, Buddhist AND Shinto shrines, New Year's Day and Obon dances AND Christmas trees and Fourth of July flags. We could be loyal to American ideals of justice and equality while honoring the spiritual and cultural values of our heritage.

But I believed in progress. I thought America was leaving the bad old days behind for good. Weren't we all created equal, with inalienable rights? I wanted to bust out of the invisible cages that trapped my relatives.

SOME GIRLS

What do you mean, "Go for it"?
How can you say, "Speak up"?
Nobody taught me how.

Nice girls are agreeable. / Nice girls are patient.
We don't make mistakes / or act without permission.

Nobody taught me / to love the terrible freedom
the wild solitude. / I did everything they told me to.

"Be patient," they said.
"Compromise
        co-operate,
            wait your turn."

Hesitant and yielding, / gentle flutter of downcast eyes.
Inside resentment builds
        drop
            by bitter drop.

Inside the wild bitch screams.

And yet, during our California visits to my relatives' tight-knit enclaves in Stockton's skid row and Santa Clara Valley farm labor camps, I felt embraced and sustained by temple bell, incense and sutra chanting; spring berries, summer corn, autumn persimmons, and winter frost; sunrise and moonset; birds gathering to roost each night before wheeling skyward toward a new day.

I loved the work-stooped shoulders and sun-creased eyes of everyday; and of the lacquer boxes and silk kimono of holidays. I couldn't understand my grandparents' nihongo, but their deeds and their eyes spoke volumes. The lived reality of their values were golden threads woven into the fiber of my being: gambatte, go for it; gaman, never give up; shikata ga nai, accept what you can't change; and shinjin, abiding faith. Compared to their quiet strength, I felt hopelessly baka, stupid.

I grew up as an Army brat in perpetual exile, moving every two or three years from one strange environment to the next. Physically separated from my extended family, emotionally distanced from my workaholic parents, I was on my own in school, usually the only Asian in a sea of white.

TINY ARROWS

You tell yourself it doesn't matter but it does.
You tell yourself you're not hurt, but your heart chills
You tell yourself you're not scared but your breath freezes.

When did it all start?
Who was the first to put gum in your hair
kick the chair out from under you
prick your nape with jeers
slice your smile with dagger tongues?

Who screamed fear and pain into your face
or slipped it to you silently
cut you off and cut you out
shredded what was left of hope and trust?

But somewhere beneath the debris
your soul's intact.
You can tell your enemies'
memories to leave any time now
Any time now
Any time.
NOW!

Books became my sanctuary and my key to other worlds. Alcott, Austen, Dickens, Tolstoy, Dostoyevsky, Steinbeck wove compelling characters into the larger social, political, and moral context of their times, with social justice at the core. I couldn't see my literal self as a Japanese American female in their work, but they wrote about things I cared about, and it was easy to imagine myself as the protagonist, absorbing their strengths.

Museums fed me, too: African bronzes, Maori fishhooks, Ming porcelain, wabi-sabi bowls… I leaned across the ropes at the National Gallery and saw that the gleam in an 18th century matron's eye was nothing more than intuitively applied daubs of color. Painting was alchemy, and I wanted to learn it.

As much as I loved learning, by senior year of high school, grinding out the A's had turned me into a heaving mess of self-conscious, resentful misery. I was a painfully shy, sweaty-palmed nerd in an intensely competitive environment: one of five or six "smartest" of a thousand seniors, the 99.99th percentile, perched on a meaningless pinnacle in a tiny little world, without a clue about how to get down.

After a summer away taking college courses, I could not make myself pay attention to contemporary, male-dominated literature. I wanted to know how to live a good life, not to become a famous alcoholic. I could no longer hear the words issuing from my teachers' mouths. My classmates were horn-rimmed ants crawling up a ladder, and the life my parents planned for me looked like a life-long desert of dutiful boredom. What did I have to look forward to but mortgages, old age, and cancer? Why not cut to the chase and end it all now?

A week before JFK's assassination in 1963, I took an overdose of sleeping pills and woke up from a coma in a military psychiatric ward. Freudian therapy and two rounds of shock treatments did nothing to make me want to live. The

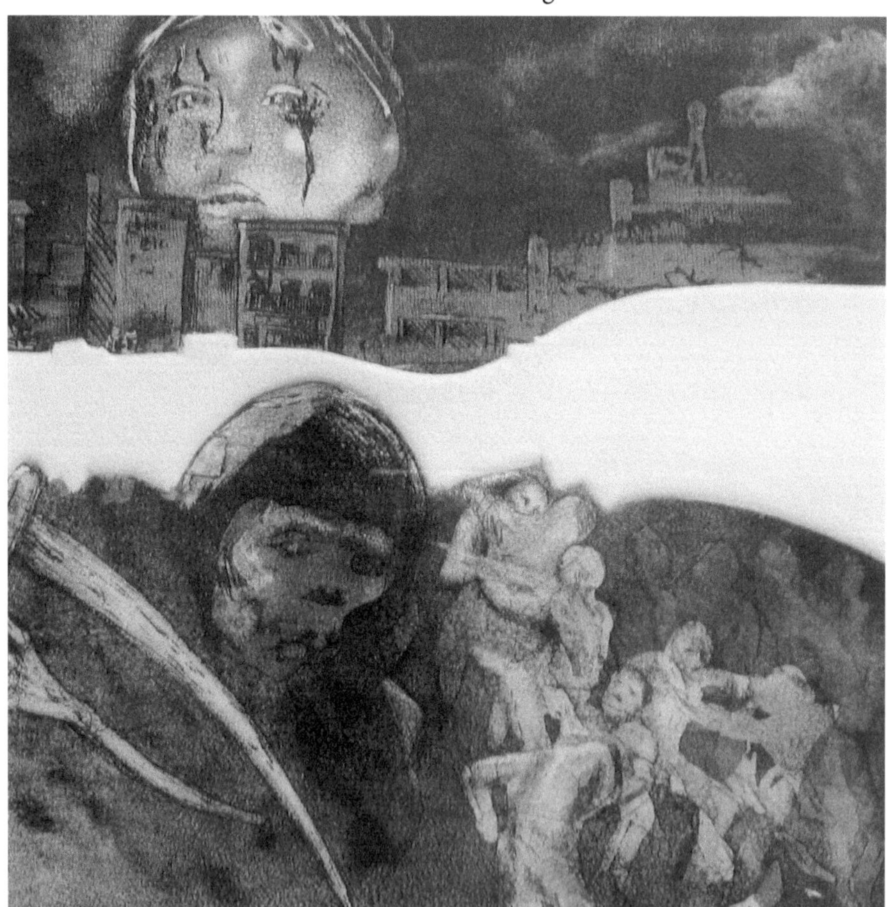

"Blood on Your Face," mezzotint, 10 x 10 inches. 1980.

medical corpsmen did me a lot more good. We were exiles together; these lonely young men were barely older than I was—recruits from rural New England, Virginia, and Navajo Nation. They were training at Letterman Hospital before being sent on, possibly to a place called Viet Nam, which was just beginning to send home casualties. They made me sort of a mascot; occupational therapy meant taking me bowling, teaching me to play pool, and discussing our favorite foreign movies.

I got patched up enough to start college at Dad's alma mater, UC Berkeley, an educational factory where I was supposed to regurgitate received wisdom for another four years. Explain Zeno's arrow… write an essay in the manner of Jonathan Swift… make a cubist collage… I dropped out after three weeks.

My parents gave up on me. After secretarial school, I got a job as a typist clerk, hung out with folk singers, and married the wrong man to get out of the house. In 1966, I was married at City Hall in a black dress by a judge named

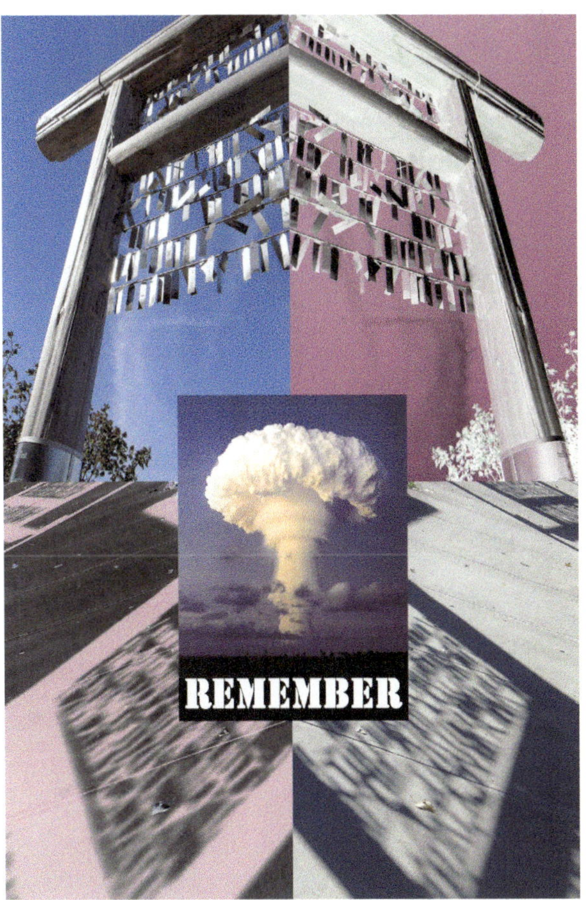

"Remember," photocollage, 12 x 16 inches. 1980.

Loveless, whose beady eye telegraphed doubts about the longevity of our union. It lasted eleven years, beginning with a glorious Summer of Love in the Haight Ashbury where my creativity expressed itself in hand-made clothing and jewelry, acid-fueled drawings, and dancing at the Fillmore every weekend.

After I read that one should write from life experience, I decided to stop trying until I had something to write about.

* * *

For the next twenty years, I was too busy exploring—and then surviving—to write. As a child, I'd been moved from place to place by my parents. As an adult, I became an accidental nomad. Every few years, my life changed radically. It was terrifying yet exciting. But I grew into myself by throwing myself wholeheartedly into each new situation, looking for life lessons.

I'd grown up during the nuclear arms race. It was laughable to think that hiding under our desks during air-raid drills was going to save anyone from mutually assured destruction. By the assassinations and mass demonstrations of 1968, it was clear that the decline and fall of the American Empire had begun. How would we live through turmoil and change with integrity?

I resonated with counterculture values. LSD and mescaline led me to transcendent visions of a timeless, interconnected universe. I felt I'd glimpsed the wordless truth of the universe, and I wanted to deepen that connection without drugs. But my conscious mind didn't quite trust my intuition. I still viewed myself through others' filters: Mom's fear, Dad's secretive cynicism, and my husband's insecurity.

I thought of myself as mousy, timid, living a forgettable life. But in retrospect, I realize I was a pioneer like my grandmothers. I made the most of limited opportunities: I walked barefoot through two years of San Francisco fog and Indian heat to straighten my spine and open a connection with earth and sky. I dragged my husband to Steve Gaskins' Monday Night Classes, the Monterey Pop Festival, and the Holy Man Jam; bought a "back-to-the-land" Russian River cabin; and took a bus alone through Mexico in search of a Yugoslavian yoga teacher. I found faith in an Indian ashram's pilgrims shed, located a midwife at a San Francisco quilting bee, baked bread, grew a vegetable garden, and nurtured children amid sand and fog.

But my husband and I stopped traveling the same road. I had to cut him loose, and my mother's anxious, smothering love as well. How was I going to make my own life with three young children and no job skills?

A new boyfriend, a musician, introduced me to the lure of creativity and gave me confidence to follow the muse. My heart sang as I took painting classes at community college. But it didn't take long to realize that fine art wasn't going to earn me a living.

I switched to illustration and then advertising classes at the Academy of Art College. There, a couple of grizzled mentors gave me something my father

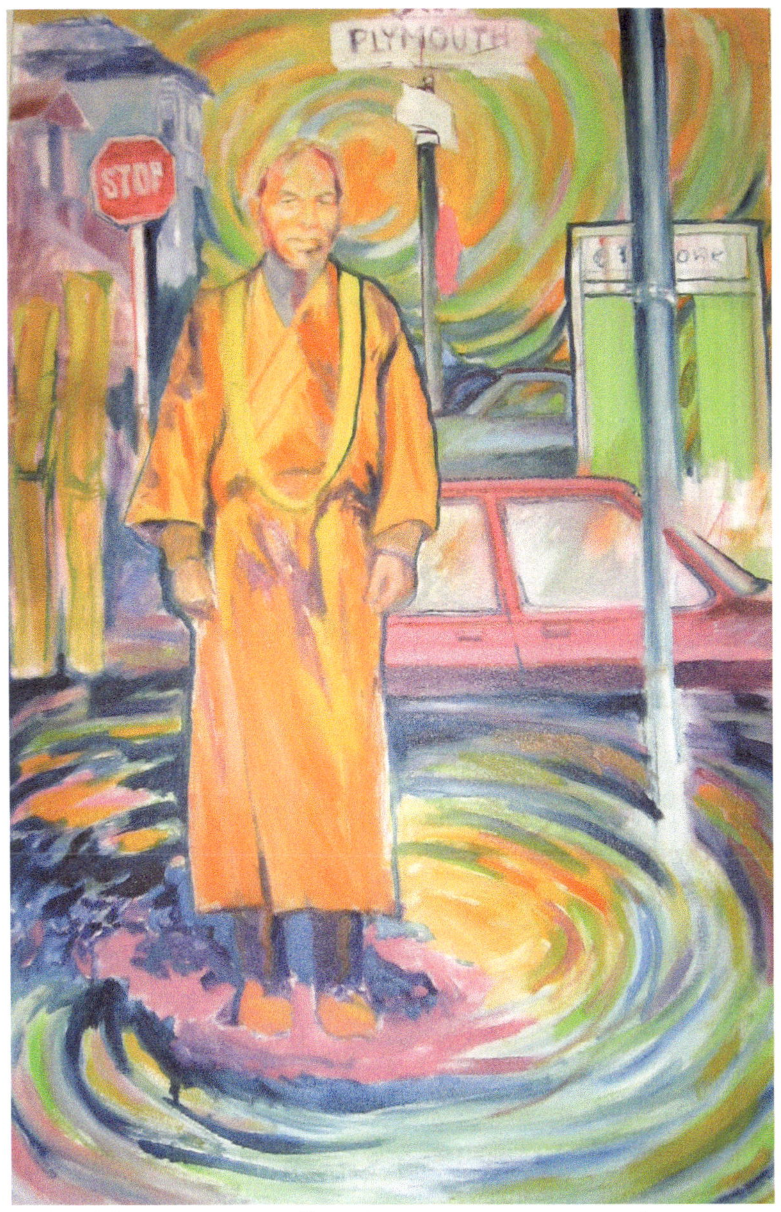

"Buddhism in America," acrylic on canvas, 24 x 18 inches, 1981.

could not: they punched me in the arm and told me I could make it. I felt profoundly empowered—they were not easy to please. A chance conversation with a neighbor led to a job as assistant art director at a big agency. I was a hippie mom abruptly tossed into the shark tank of corporate advertising.

To survive this glossy, high-pressure environment, I had to talk as loud and fast as any white man and crank out visual-verbal ideas by the dozen. Creativity was exciting, and so was thinking in new ways. Who was our customer, what was their psychological profile, and what emotions did we need to trigger to sell them products they didn't need?

Making a living through art was intoxicating. I learned to trust the muse and become a channel for ideas flowing through me. I gained skills and confidence with every assignment—how to put ideas on paper, sell them to account execs and clients, and then bring the ideas to life. Working in advertising felt like being in a war—hunkered in the trenches with creative and production teams I could count on. Bombarded by incoming demands from the "suits," we literally created product out of thin air.

We were the ones who created something out of nothing, so why didn't the "suits" give us the respect that we deserved? Account and Media departments viewed life in terms of money and power, not art or humanity. One boss declared, "Why should we pay you more? Wannabe copywriters and art directors are beating down the doors to work for us." In a world that ran on

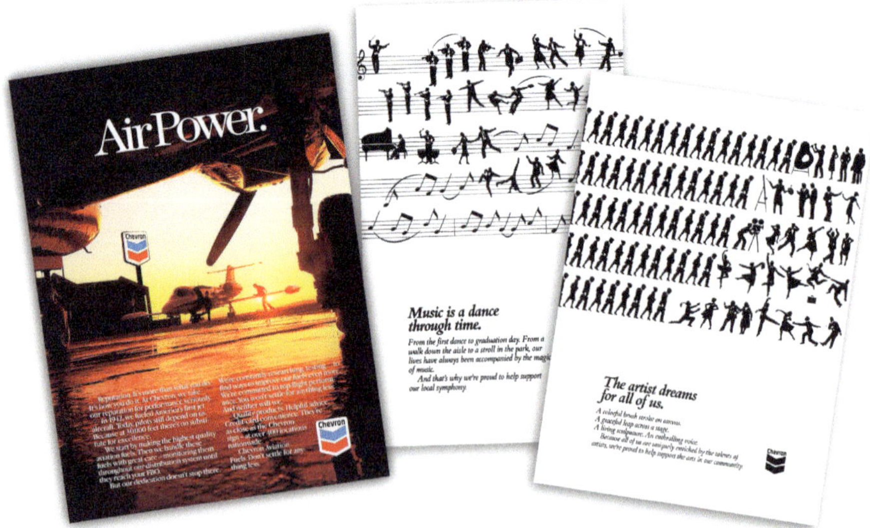

Aviation fuel and public affairs ads art-directed by Shizue Seigel.
The arts ads ran in opera and theater programs for over twenty years.

money, manipulation, and male supremacy, I made 62 cents for every man's dollar, and a male judge let my ex off with only $15 a month child support.

I was the token Asian American woman, pinned in place as an overworked, underpaid but oh-so-hard-working underling in the service of competitive white folks busy chasing big accounts, SUVs, wine-country weddings, and suburban dream homes. The agency literally could not see the value of my thinking, even after I won an HMO account that three senior teams failed to woo. I quadrupled billings in six weeks, but management didn't give me a promotion or raise because they thought my winning pitch was too simple. They didn't understand that my campaign was purposefully simple to reach ordinary people who wanted their health-care paperwork to be simple too.

It was ironic that I found the muse and gained confidence in such an alien environment. But I loved the fast-paced creativity and teamwork. And I acquired portable skills that I could take with me anywhere. More important, I was learning not to be shaken by the opinions of people I didn't respect. I began to trust my own thinking and that of people whose values I shared.

ETHNIC ADJUSTMENTS

Get this. I'm only going to say it once:
I am not nor have I ever been / a Cherry Blossom queen
I did not / nor do I plan to / bomb Pearl Harbor
I do not / nor will I ever / wear a camera round my neck.

No, I won't walk on your back / Or serve green tea,
Hell, I don't even like rice.

Look closely. I'm not yellow inside or out.
My eyes don't slant.
        And I'm sure you've noticed / I'm not polite.
So let's go for a walk
but don't expect me / ten steps behind.
In my world,
men follow me.

Advertising is first to be cut in an economic downturn, so in the early 1990s I was unemployed when I found the job that changed my life—developing community-based outreach campaigns to increase HIV/AIDS awareness among at-risk Black women.

Suddenly the totality of my previous life made sense. I'd learned about the job from the token Black woman at my first ad agency. I'd acquired the requisite copywriting, design, and production skills. And, I realized, I'd been code switching with Black folks all my life—in Baltimore, Stockton's skid row, the Fillmore District, and sorting parcels for the U.S. Postal Service. My life experiences resonated with working-class African Americans in significant ways—racism, mutigenerational trauma, living on welfare as a single parent, losing partners to depression, infidelity, or drugs… Working in the projects was like a homecoming. I was leaving the land of pretense and returning to real communities of people who did not hide truth behind a façade.

I was disillusioned to discover that the nonprofit sector was layered by class, race, and privilege. At the top were educated white women who felt underpaid and under-appreciated at $80K a year, half-time. At the bottom, Black outreach workers were paid $18K a year full time to implement a program dreamed up by white bureaucrats who never set foot in the projects. I was in the middle, an Asian American with special skills making $35K, a third less than my last corporate job.

I'd lost touch with Black people since tourism and drugs overran the Haight, and redevelopment decimated the Fillmore. I was horrified to learn many were worse off than they'd been in the 1960s. To do my job, I persuaded the bosses to get me training for community health outreach and let me go out on the street. I connected with at-risk women by focusing on our commonalities and by reflecting their own inner beauty back to them. They weren't used to hearing their health was worth protecting because they were worth something.

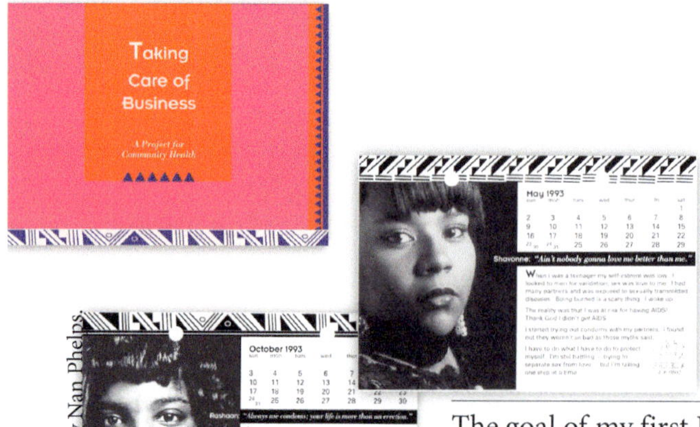

The goal of my first HIV prevention campaign was to gain the trust of at-risk women by affirming their inner beauty and value.

I made plenty of mistakes, but the outreach workers understood I meant well. Together, we produced 24 HIV prevention stories in 18 months, and then the project ended. It was a "research demonstration project," which seemed to mean once a project demonstrated its effectiveness, it was de-funded and money moved to some other crisis—family violence, workfare, or whatever issue of the year.

I was too heartbroken and stubborn to move on. I lived off my savings for 18 months trying to get the program re-funded and visiting the projects weekly to distribute condoms I cadged from the city clinic. I grew hopeful when the Housing Authority asked me to resubmit proposals, but the money was ultimately allocated to policing. I was furious! The residents needed jobs, education, and on-going long-term support, not criminalization.

I decided to become a writer to help end racism. Maybe if people understood the true impact of racism, things would change.

Post-Trump, I'm not so sure… But I had discovered my purpose, the skills I needed to support it, and the faith to let the muse lead me forward. For the next 20+ years, one project led to another. Editing a historical society magazine became a crash course in Japanese American history. I learned the political and legal context of my family's stories. I learned that every aspect of the fight for equity was necessary—demonstrations, legislation, community organizing, education, and creativity… I met historians, activists, and artists who took action time and again in the face of injustice. They were inspiring role models. I was in the trenches again, but this time with folks who were laying foundations for peace and justice.

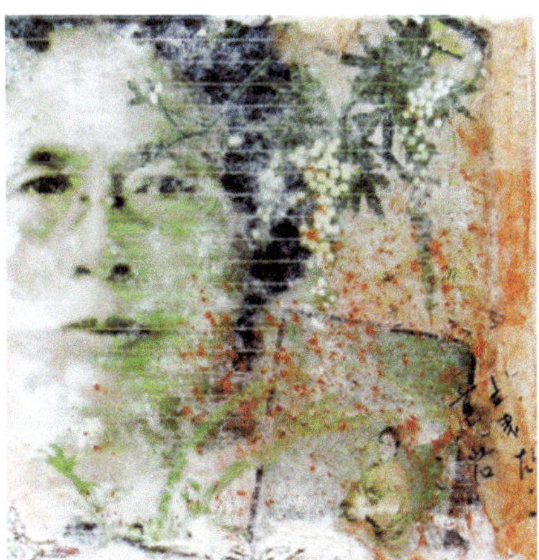
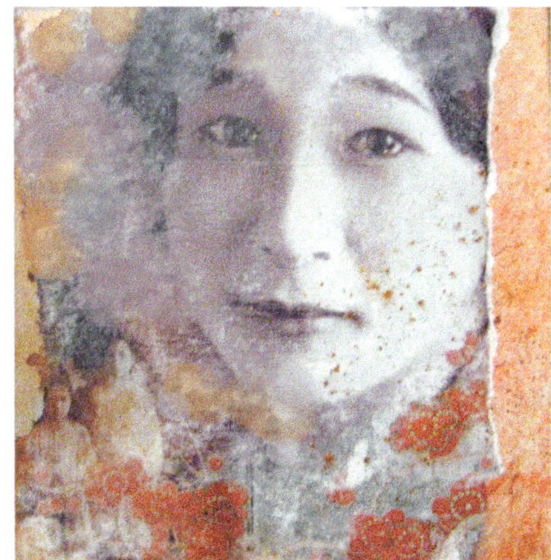

"Rui" and "Nellie," image transfer and mixed media on canvas,
12 x 12 inches each, 2011.

By the late 1990s, my kids were grown and I could afford to live on very little. I'd gained economic freedom just in time to help formerly incarcerated Nisei tell their stories after fifty years of silence. I helped a 100-year-old woman write her memoirs.[1] And researched and wrote a book profiling white allies who stood up for Japanese Americans in their darkest hour. [2]

I was learning to write and edit by doing. To sharpen my craft, I took writing workshops where I was often the only person of color. I was put off by the snobbery and limited vision of middle-class teachers and students. I felt stubbornly out of step until I took my first VONA/Voices of Our Nations workshop in 2010. Faith Adiele, Elmaz Abinader, and other VONA teachers changed my life by affirming everything I'd painfully assembled on my own: Trust your own voice and your own story. Set the narrative in context of culture, history, place, spirituality. And listen: let the story tell itself.

VONA gave me the courage to apply for the artist grant that led to my first workshop series and anthology. Working with Black and Japanese American writers who shared overlapping histories of discrimination, incarceration, and displacement[3] gave rise to a new vision of growing a multicultural community of writers and artists sharing and growing together. I was reconnecting with my grandparents' sense of home. For them, the security of a homebase was not based on external geography, it was an internal stability rising from a sense of integrity—of kokoro—mind-heart-spirit moving as one. Love, faith, and community steadied them in a constantly evolving journey. As they grew to meet the challenges that came at them, they learned they were not alone. Individual craft and discipline were vital, but so was deep faith and the shared endeavor of every voice and hand contributing to a greater whole.

They survived, even thrived, because they valued each person for who they were, working together for common purpose—something contemporary society seems to have forgotten how to do.

Since 2015, Write Now! SF Bay has created a home for 400 writers and artists through year-round workshops, readings, creative showcases, and anthologies. Since its inception, I've carried the organization as lovingly as my

---

1. *My First Hundred Years: The Memoirs of Nellie Nakamura*, Pease Press, 2021

2. *In Good Conscience: Supporting Japanese Americans during the Internment,* Asian American Curriculum Project (San Mateo, 2006).

3. *Standing Strong! Fillmore & Japantown,* Pease Press (San Francisco, 2016).

grandmothers carried infants on their backs. But Write Now! has grown too big to carry alone. It' s ready to walk on its own two feet. It can only survive with practical support from everyone who has benefited from it.

Like my ancestors, I'm not settling for Either-Or. I want Both-And—a multicultural community of writers and artists AND time to get back to finish my own books. Now I get to find out who is ready to step up to sustain Write Now! by becoming working advisors and committee members, qualified and dedicated staff, volunteers and donors. I can't wait for the next chapter to unfold.

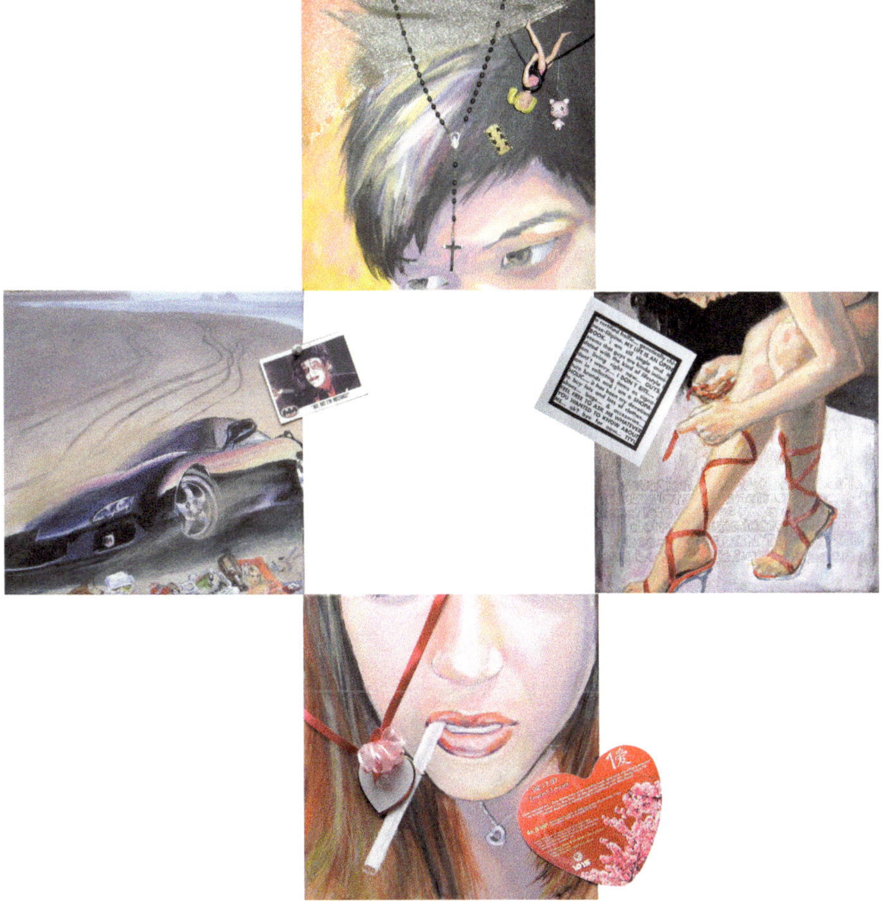

"A-Sim-U-Lation," acrylic and found objects on four 12 x 12 inch canvases,
36 x 36 inches, 2011.

OPEN SEASON • NO LIMIT
Shizue Seigel

Maybe you're not the enemy / today / maybe yesterday maybe tomorrow / Keep your head down /and your bags packed / **You are not white and never will be** / No matter how good you are and you ARE good / skilled virtuous / with grades and / credentials to prove / it or maybe it's / true you are only good / for nothing / as your parents began to say / when you began to think for yourself but still / **You are not white and never will be** You will forever and / ever be / an object / of derision contempt / competition / seduction / You will remain obscure /and inscrutable / finding safety in invisibility keeping cover so / covert jeers and sneers / never erupt into open laughter / open slaughter / So run the gantlet of cruelty / channeled between twin lines of hate / and fear "Rots of Ruck" / your crush writes / in your yearbook / He sees only / girls with hair blonde to their roots / **You are not white and never will be** / You will always be / the one to do the work / with none of the credit / too small in all things / too yellow to matter until YOU become the peril / **But you are not Black and never will be** / You run no daily risk of being stopped while driving / shot for stopping / shot for running / shot for sleeping in your bed / You are no blackbird today / maybe yesterday / maybe tomorrow / When are you going to stop
running?

In solidarity with the Black, Brown, and Indigenous who have been killed by white violence. Dedicated to George Yamasaki, a relative who was shot during World War II near a Wyoming concentration camp. He was on work leave, harvesting sugar beets in an open field when he was severely wounded by a local landowner's son who claimed to be "shooting blackbirds." No charges were filed.

Acknowledgments

"Burden of Imagination," "Buddhism in America," "Rui," "Nellie, and "A-Sim-U-lation" previously published in *Distillations: Mediations of the Japanese American Experience*, Pease Press 2010.

"Some Girls," "Ethnic Adjustments, " and open Season previously published in *Talking to Strangers* mini-publication series., Pease Press, 2021

Sriram Shamasunder
FINDING MY WAY THROUGH MY PATIENTS

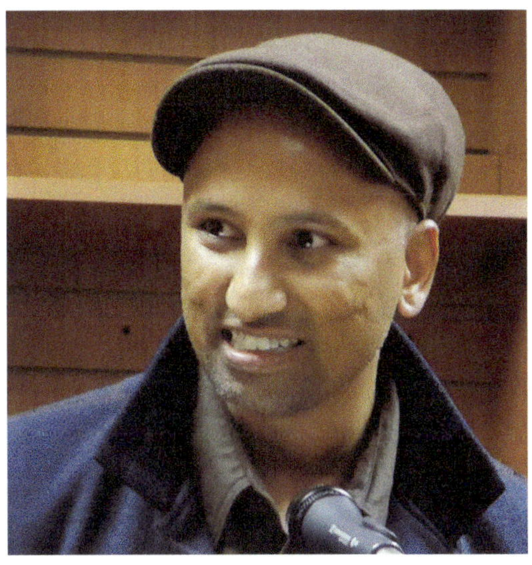

Dr. Sriram Shamasunder is Associate Professor of Medicine
at the University of California San Francisco and
co-founder/faculty director of the HEAL Initiative, an
equity-based global health fellowship working
in Navajo Nation and nine countries around the world.

He trained at UC Berkeley and Harbor UCLA Medical Center
and earned a Diploma in Tropical Medicine & Hygiene
in 2013. He now teaches in the Bay Area and
in underserved settings like South Los Angeles, rural Liberia,
Haiti, Burundi, and rural India. In 2020, he led the
HEAL UCSF response to the COVID surge in
Navajo Nation with 40+ UCSF nurses and doctors and
50+ HEAL fellows in Navajo Nation.

He is a published poet who believes that untold stories
can shift minds and hearts.
healinitiative.org

FINDING MY WAY THROUGH MY PATIENTS
Sriram Shamasunder

STRADDLING WORLDS

I grew up in the small desert town of Palmdale, 60 miles outside of Los Angeles, in a working-poor, largely white community. I was the youngest of three, a son of immigrants. As a child, I watched my mom's interactions with the community. At an "all you can eat" salad bar, or at Sears, my mom would ask an extra question about the soup being cold or a shirt being rung up for a higher price than she expected. Sometimes the response would be a quick "go back to your country" retort by the clerk or waiter. I noticed if my mom raised her voice or pushed just a bit, thinly veiled racism would reveal itself. My father served as a counterpoint. He was quiet and soft spoken and rarely advocated for himself in a public setting. He was an oncologist, one of thousands drawn from their home country to work in rural and challenging settings where most US-trained doctors did not want to work. Every Christmas, a stream of gifts passed through our house from grateful patients. When we ate at the local Chinese restaurant, my father's patients would often come up to our table and speak with immense gratitude about his kindness, expertise, and skill as a doctor. This captured my imagination and awakened me to the possibility of making a profound impact on other people's lives.

Our family was like an island of five in the United States. A small collection of brown skin in a sea of white. We stuck together. My two older sisters and I attended an evangelical Christian elementary school. I accepted Jesus into my heart so many times during the Wednesday assembly. I wondered why he would not stay in my heart, so I accepted him again and again as many times as I was told. At the same time, we heard both overt and covert murmurings about throwing our home religion, Hinduism, under the bus. My parents were treated as if they needed saving—and as dangerous pagans at the same time. They were just a moment away from eternal life if they could just have a "come to Jesus" moment or eternally damned to Hell—depending on who was speaking to us. In high school, my oldest sister came home with questions about why my parents were going to hell, so they decided to pull us out of the Christian school. I started 5th grade in a San Fernando Valley private school, and my dad began a one-hour commute each way that would continue for the next 25 years until he died.

Like so many immigrants, I straddled two worlds. I kept my head down; I was quiet; I played sports. I was good at sports. They were an entryway into a United States that didn't quite accept me. On the field or the tennis court, I could reign equal or superior to my white opponents.

JUNE JORDAN: PASSING THE TORCH

I decided to follow in my dad's steps and was accepted as a pre-medical student at UC Berkeley. There, I found my voice. After feeling disconnected in the poor white community of my early years in the California desert, my education was continued by mentors who showed with their lives and words that another way was possible. They connected me to a lineage of solidarity with marginalized communities. I saw the possibility of learning to walk gently on the planet and align oneself with the most marginalized.

As the child of Indian immigrants, I was a kid with shaky confidence. I came in to UC Berkley with my head down, taking science classes. To fill a humanities requirement, I meandered into Poetry for the People, the course June Jordan conceived of and taught. After taking the course and fulfilling the requirement, I stayed in the class for two years. Not so much because I thought I was a poet but because the class made me feel that even a young person like me might have something to say. I liked the encouragement to craft something that might matter to someone. I became a teaching assistant during my final undergraduate years, running one of the small groups of about 15 students.

June was our professor, both tender and fierce, but mostly someone I admired at a distance. This changed in my last few weeks at UC Berkeley when we studied Arab and Arab American poetry. A disagreement between Jewish students defending Zionism and those supporting Palestinian liberation grew from a murmur to a rumble throughout the semester. In one of our last classes, a teaching assistant publicly accused June—in front of a class of 250-300—of failing to stand up on behalf of Palestinian people. June didn't show up for class next week, without a word.

On the weekend, I went by her house in North Berkeley. We all knew she had breast cancer, but not the extent of her struggle. She was surprised to see me, but she let me in. The morning sun lit up the kitchen and made specks of dust visible. About 20 bottles of medications were laid out on the kitchen counter—to treat cancer, and fight nausea and pain.

We sat at her kitchen table. I tried to find the words to encourage her to come back to class. I stumbled as I tried to convey that the whole class knew her commitment to the Palestinian struggle. June remained unmoved. She was worn. The endless stream of medical appointments and chemotherapy and array of medications on her countertop had blurred into questions about legacy and impact.

She began to talk. She said that her entire career had been brought to a halt in 1982 by the political stance she took in the paper *Village Voice* when she wrote "Apologies to the People of Lebanon" about the Israeli military massacre in the refugee camps in Sabra and Shatila. That same year she wrote the poem "Moving Towards Home" with those iconic words that pushed so many of us to extend beyond our birth demographic to make common cause with the most vulnerable, the most persecuted:

> I was born a Black woman
> and now
> I am become a Palestinian

In the '80s, June's writing life and her career as an author took a beating for her defense of Palestinians. She paid significantly for taking that stand. In some ways she received backlash similar to what Congresswoman Omar gets when she stands up for Palestinians, except June at that time didn't have a social media platform to fight back with. Her bibliography shows a significant gap between the mid '80s and the mid '90s. Publishers refused to work with her. This may in part be the reason she is not as widely read as friends and contemporaries like Alice Walker and Toni Morrison.

That afternoon in her sunlit kitchen, I listened. June was 65, and tired and sick. I was 23. She had already paid a huge price for her solidarity with the people of Palestine. Her willingness to risk stature for solidarity had been questioned by a woman from a younger generation who seemed to be unaware of her personal sacrifice. All of it was hard to stomach.

That afternoon as June got up and moved about her house, cleaning up and doing some chores, we continued to talk. When I played with her beautiful black puppy, he climbed on me and left muddy paw prints all over my white kurta.

I had a white t-shirt under that shirt, so she insisted she keep the kurta, clean it and bring it back to me at our next class. I was hopeful that she *would* return.

The next week she came to class with a new poem and my kurta. She read the poem to the class: "It's Hard to Keep a Clean Shirt Clean."[1] The central metaphor grappled with keeping a commitment to certain values and visions when, inevitably, the original ideal is sullied by the messiness of life. To be *in* the world rather than an observer of it required a pact with the not-perfect—the profound wedded to the practical. Even when we clean ourselves off, none of us are the same, or can claim purity.

Soon after June wrote that poem, I moved to New York for medical school. 2001 and 2002, the last years of June life, were my first years in medical school. We somehow ended up talking a couple times a week across coasts. June navigated the world of oncologists, and chemotherapy and MRI scans as I started slowly wading into that world. It was bewildering to both of us. During our conversations, she recounted her life. I asked questions and she expanded, seemingly grateful to reflect on her experiences.

She recalled sitting next to Malcolm X in Harlem as a young woman, and described how he schooled her on how to convey a message. When he finished answering a reporter's questions, he would turn to June and quiz her on what was asked and when, and how he had responded to guide the conversation down a path that best served his message.

She spoke about her friendship with Fanny Lou Hamer, the great Civil Rights leader who put her body on the line to register Black folks to vote throughout the south. June at the time had a deep aversion to all white people. A hatred even. Period. Fanny Lou Hamer said to June, "Ain't no way, no how you can hate anyone and hope to see the face of God." That shifted June. She realized that bedrock belief enabled Fanny Lou Hamer to face vicious threats and murderous hate and return love—first and foremost for her own salvation.

June recounted her experience with Ralph Ellison when she was in her 20s. Ellison had become disenchanted with the power of words to change anyone's life and publicly taunted a group of luminary poets, including TS Elliot, that their life of words did not make one iota of difference against the violence of the mid 20th century. June didn't have the words to say at the time that she wrote for the *victims* to redeem possibility in their lives rather than for the perpetrators of violence or oppression. Only later did I find that experience described in her book of essays, *Technical Difficulties.*

---

1. www.poetryfoundation.org/poems/48759/its-hard-to-keep-a-clean-shirt-clean

Each conversation unveiled a different time of her life, and the arc of purpose and love that lives at the center of a life worth living. We also spoke of her love for tennis. What struck me was the quality of her listening and her capacity to be loving or indignant or vulnerable.

As June got sicker, the conversations became less frequent until she passed as I entered my second year of medical school. Now when I reflect on what June showed me in that year of conversations, I realize it was the revealing of a committed life, as well as a passing of a torch. She did that for so many of her students. We look to our elders to demonstrate another way of being in this broken world. Another way of extending our circle of commitment to the person in front of us, or to a group, like Palestinian people. *"And" and "Both."* June gave us that.

Now nearly 15 years after medical school, I started and run an organization that trains and transforms frontline health workers from 9 countries around the world, including indigenous communities in the United States. We worked in Haiti after the 2010 earthquake and in Liberia during the Ebola epidemic of 2014. Mostly we work on the non-glamorous task of building the capacity of local health professionals to serve their communities. It is an international solidarity. We get asked from time to time why we work internationally when there is so much need in the United States. There is no "the United States or abroad." We answer, we do *both*. June taught us that.

My experiences in the '80s and early '90s in the California desert prepared me for post 9/11 prejudice in New York City, but the journey to feel belonging, and to make others feel cared for took me first to Berkeley and New York City for medical training, and then led me to work across the world for years at a time in Rwanda, Haiti, Liberia, India, South Los Angeles, and other underserved communities.

MY DARK SKIN, SO MUCH LIKE MY PATIENTS

In medical residency I trained at a Los Angeles county hospital. Black and brown patients lay on gurneys in the emergency room, and lined the halls of the wards. Our patients were mostly poor, often undocumented. The doctors were mostly white.

As residents, we worked and lived in the hospital so many nights. It felt like home.

On one of my days off, in street clothes, jeans and a t-shirt, I went into the hospital to finish dictating some patient notes. There was a metal detector at the entrance of the hospital. Later that morning, a police guard stopped me as I came out of the men's room, suspicious I might have been shooting up in a bathroom stall. I presented my doctor's ID out of my jeans pocket and immediately apologies flowed like water from an open faucet from the guard's mouth.

My dark skin is so much like my patients. Until then, the hospital had felt like home. But that day I learned never to walk around the hospital without an ID. It was no longer a home where I could move freely without question. It was not my home.

A few months later, after a long call shift, I drove to the ocean. Making my way to the water feels like making my way home to where the water is fresh and clean and welcoming and opens the lungs after 30 continuous hours in the hospital.

Redondo Beach and Hermosa Beach are beautiful. It has many bars and the white folks flood them in the evening hours. Beachfront parking is full at 11 pm on a Thursday. I want to bypass the crowds and bars to go sit on the beach to clear my head.

As I circle for parking, I can see a cop car eye me as I come around the block again—my black, beat-up car and my nearly black skin in this dark night. My third time around the block, the cop starts to follow me, a slow dance around a three-block radius before he pulls me over.

The cop is rude. He flashes his light onto the back seat where he suspiciously eyes an ophthalmoscope and reflex hammer. He shines the light in my eyes and asks about the "paraphernalia" in the back.

He doesn't give me a chance to answer. He asks for my driver's license, registration, and proof of insurance, his voice finding its footing somewhere between irritated and angry.

I am nervous. I was living in NYC on 9/11, and immediately after, I saw fear in older white women's eyes as they looked at me. It is a fear I recognize in my dying patients—but it always catches me off guard when I look in someone's eyes and realize I am the thing they fear.

Back in the Jetta, my white coat hangs off my driver's seat. My doctor's ID hangs off my white coat close to the driver's side window. The policeman's flashlight catches the ID and he asks if I am a doctor. I say, yes, at LA County hospital a few miles away.

The wad of papers in his hand—driver's license, registration, proof of insurance—become like a lotus flower as he opens his palms and they flow back to me.

He apologizes and apologizes. He says he didn't realize that I worked at the hospital, the trauma center that takes care of cops when they get hurt or shot.

My doctor's ID becomes a get out of jail free card. An 'I exist' card.

I exist. I exist. I have something to distinguish me from the black, the brown, the sick, the poor, the nameless, the undocumented—from my patients.

What if I had been one of my patients, black and brown and nameless?

What if I had been a plumber looking for the sea after a hard day's work?

Or an undocumented Mexican man who worked and worked for four decades in the vineyards of Napa. I saw him in the hospital when his bone marrow finally failed, exhausted by decades of field work. His body was announcing its existence the only way it could.

If the soul is ignored long enough, the body rebels. A mass in the throat rises to the surface of the skin. A cavity of a lung, riddled with tuberculosis, starts to bleed. The body announces its existence.

Sometimes when I fill out death certificates, I wish I could write the cause of death as poverty. Or American racism.

As a doctor, I am looking to make common cause with the Navajo Nation, where uranium was mined from the earth and left exposed to make Navajo folks fall ill.

As a doctor, I am looking to make common cause with Black boys stopped by the police, shot by police without a doctor's ID to protect them.

I am looking to make common cause with the 11,310 Black bodies who died from Ebola in Liberia! They came into our awareness only in sickness and in death.

Before blood flows from every orifice, can we note their existence?

May we learn their names in life. They exist.

As a doctor, I aim to stand with them before the beautiful fire of their lives becomes ash.

In this country, the only way I know home is through them. I want to reclaim a space for home for the black, the brown, the nameless, my patients, myself. I try to find my home through them.

PAUL FARMER: GLOBAL HEALTH WORK

I was introduced to the work of Paul Farmer and his organization Partners in Health as an undergraduate at UC Berkeley. After my medical training and residency, like so many physicians in my generation, I attempted to follow Paul's example. I wanted to work in Haiti, where he'd started Partners in Health. Instead, he enrolled me to work in a place with even fewer physicians. I began working in Burundi in 2010, then in Rwanda, in Haiti, in India … I have worked in resource-denied communities from South Los Angeles to Navajo Nation to Mexico for the last 15 years.

Early in my career, Paul made me feel that I was making the only career decision that made sense—choosing what he called "pragmatic solidarity" alongside the poor. His words conveyed the irresistibility of social medicine—a model in which health workers aim to address the root causes of disease in their social and economic context. This work is where necessity, urgency and joy become bound together.

From time to time during my work in rural Burundi, I would consult him informally. He would reply with a couple lines at most. But one time, when I asked him what to do with a "non-compliant" diabetic patient who was not taking her medicine, he replied with a three-paragraph retort. He said the onus remained with the physician to figure out what barriers prevented a patient from receiving care. He wanted me to deeply understand the ways in which the health system often conspired against our greatest hopes for the healthy life our patients sought. He refused to allow me to blame a patient, especially one who lived in poverty.

During that last week we spent in Rwanda with Paul, the patient that he was following had an unexpected complication and got sicker and sicker. On a WhatsApp thread with many of the patient's caregivers, Paul turned over and over therapies that might be given, interventions that should be done, possible transfers to other facilities that would give this patient a fighting chance of living.

The patient died. Paul was devastated. He was heartbroken. I remember thinking that this is why he was Paul Farmer. After 40 years, losing one patient was like losing the whole world. Many of us felt the urge to console him.

I told him I could feel his anguish because he loved the patient in a way that we doctors often don't allow ourselves to. He replied that he had unabashedly loved that dying man and had told him so every day.

I sent him a Mary Oliver poem I read with my team when we lose a patient back in San Francisco, where I live and work.

She wrote:

> you must be able
> to do three things:
> to love what is mortal;
> to hold it
>
> against your bones knowing
> your own life depends on it;
> and, when the time comes to let it go,
> to let it go.[2]

Paul said he'd read the poem, but not for years. He said it was beautiful and just what he needed. He thanked me. The next morning, he shared that he'd been friends with Mary Oliver. Of course, he had. He was somehow similar to the poet. He brought deep sacredness to patient interactions, an awe of what might be possible if those who care about health equity worked together, and a bold struggle for a more equitable world rooted in faith in others and in the universe. His life was a kind of embodied poetry of medicine.

I left Rwanda Saturday night. Paul died Monday morning. Even if we must learn to let go of his physical life, we, his students all over the world, will never let go of the example he set for us.

WALKING WITH THE NAVAJO PEOPLE

For the last 7 years, I have worked in Navajo Nation. I have learned a different way of being in relationship with the land, with trying to reach for a medicine that encompasses a wholistic way of relating to the earth, and other sentient beings.

I spent 6 weeks at the start of the pandemic, along with 24 HEAL volunteers taking care of COVID patients in Navajo Nation. I wrote this poem:

---

2. Excerpt from Mary Oliver's "In Blackwater Woods," published in *American Primitive*, Back Bay Books, 1984.

TO WALK IN BEAUTY ONCE AGAIN

Fragility sticks to everything alive like the quiet wetness of morning dew
In this global pandemic
as a doctor
I see this fragility
threatening to swallow so much of what we love
like a large red blanket covering a small bed
And I can't unsee it

In the spring
I spent five weeks in Navajo Nation
an indigenous community in the southwest of the United States
taking care of covid patients
Covid as common as desert cactus in Arizona
blooming like dandelions in an open field

That evening like every other evening
I stood outside a patient room
an emergency room converted into several pods of plastic
cocoons that separate one patient from the next and them from us
all in the hopes of keeping the virus at bay

Blue plastic reflects emergency room light
light like a parking lot at night or a mall
perpetual and yellow glow fluorescent

I methodically don my PPE
Velcro gown clasp
secure the back
face shield
N 95 on
cloth mask over
double glove blue glove pulled over brown skin
no brown skin between gloves and gown
Double-check
Zip up tent step in / zip closed
behind me

He lies left side down
a young Navajo man
Black hair braided down long past his lower back
right down the middle of his back
like a beautiful outer spine
stark against
bleached white sheets

each thick hair knot
dense and strong as rope
like ancestors clasping hands one over the other
Each knot
a closed knuckle
gathering like a prayer at the base of his skull

He has an oxygen mask on.
I watch his eyes closely for signs of fear
And I watch his hands for signs of trembling or what they might reveal
about a life before and up to this moment
He breathes fast
We make small and short talk
a few words between catching his breath
he says real soft between quick breaths
I don't wanna die

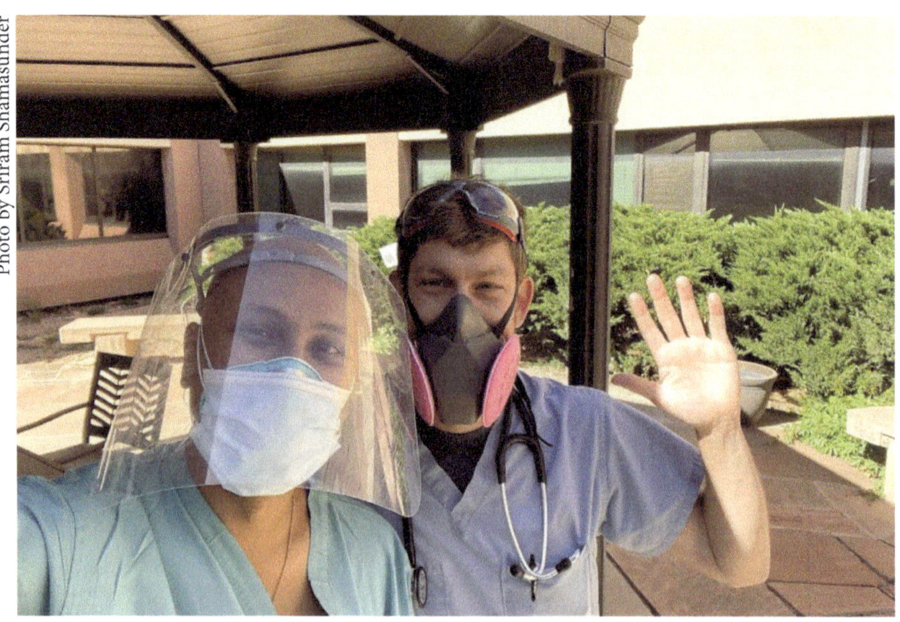

Countering the COVID surge in Navajo Nation, May 2020.

I say we will get through this
and then again louder
the first time for him
the second time for me
We will get through this

I leave the hospital at midnight

The next morning
short coffee run in my rental car
my colleague calls to say that overnight
my patient emptied his lungs like a gas tank
and puttered into the early morning in fumes
exhaustion
He was just intubated
He will be flown to Albuquerque or Phoenix
off indigenous land

My wife calls at that moment FaceTime with my five-year-old daughter
behind her shoulder

I submit to the fact I likely will never see him again
I submit to the fact that he may not survive
I submit to tears that slip down my cheek
And I watch my own hands as they wipe them away

Everything submits to something, I tell myself.

The bears rummage through rotted wood and suck up and slurp up ants.
The ants submit to the bear
The bear submits to winters
Trees submit to fire
the rocks submit to water as it etches grooves across grey
the river water submits to the seasons
thinning out come late summer
and our bodies to time.
And so many black and brown bodies this time.

This is the year of submission
Or surrender
Or survival
I can't decide which

When a patient is about to be discharged from the covid unit
a call goes overhead

from all over the hospital
like a bird migration we descend on the covid unit from
anywhere we might find ourselves in the hospital
All the health providers gather in a line on either side of the hallway
like a sports team
waiting to high five their star player to come out of the tunnel
onto the field

It is this moment a covid survivor gets wheeled out the big doors
into the sunlight
like exiting a dark tunnel
into
their families arms
In those sweet moments, i think
This is the year of resilience
the year of I won't let you go

My Navajo friend tells me with confidence
The Navajo people will walk in beauty once again
And she repeats it again
We will walk in beauty once again
The first time for me
The second time I think she says it to convince herself

Acknowledgments

A longer version of "My dark skin, so much like my patients" was previously published in *Endangered Species, Enduring Values*, Pease Press, 2018.

"Paul Farmer: Global Health Work" was adapted from "With love and tears, my first and last memories of Dr. Paul Farmer." American University Radio WAMU 88.5. https://wamu.org/story/22/02/22/with-love-and-tears-my-first-and-last-memories-of-dr-paul-farmer/

"To Walk in Beauty Once Again" was previously published in *Essential Truths: The Bay Area in Color*, Pease Press, 2021.

Kim Shuck
THIS IS A REAL STORY

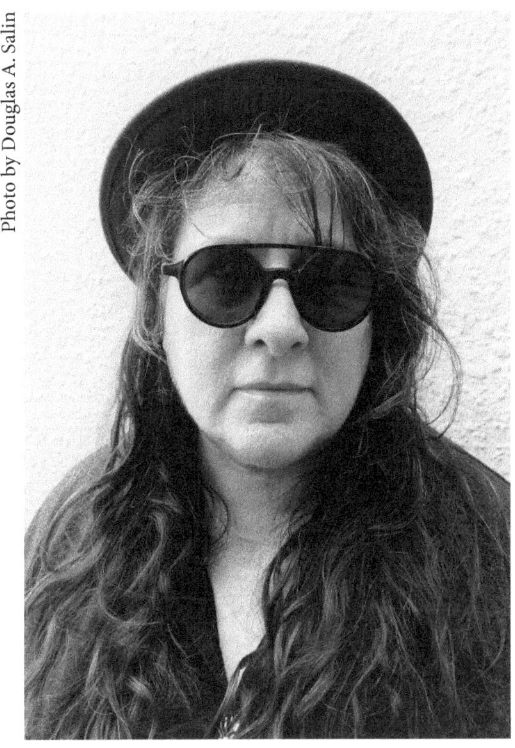

Kim Shuck is solo author of 8 published books. Shuck
has edited another ten chapthologies, anthologies,
and collections. Her publishers have ranged from her own
desktop printer to international publishing houses.
She is a creature of acute obsessions: her
beadwork, string figures, basketry, geometry, history,
and languages. Kim didn't do an MFA in writing,
she rarely submits where she isn't invited, and mostly
likes to sink deeply into her communities of writers, artists, and
San Franciscans. Shuck runs at least three poetry readings
a month, two of them include an open mic.
She served as the 7th Poet Laureate of San Francisco.
kimshuck.com

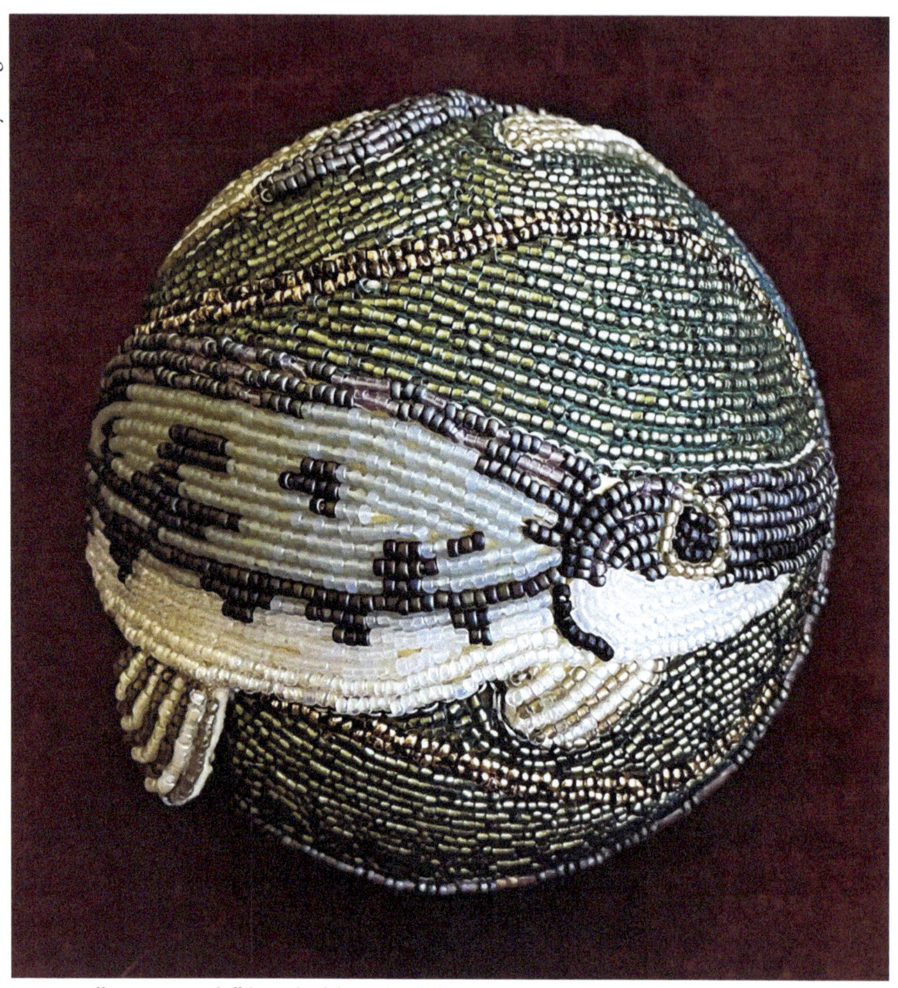

"Nice Catch," beaded baseball from the *Anniversary Balls* series.

Roughly ten years ago I met my current love, Doug Salin. Doug was a big baseball fan and I am a bead artist. The origins of the idea of beading a baseball are lost in time, but we agree that the first idea was something we talked out together. Since then I bead him a ball every year as an anniversary gift. Sometimes I'm a little late on delivery. Neither of us thought that I'd be doing so much writing. The process involves stripping the leather off of the ball and replacing it with deerhide that I can bead into. I have to do the beading on the balls because the surface is curved and otherwise the beading would pull. The beads are very small, size 15 for the most part. Each ball has a funny, baseball related name. Doug enjoys them as much as I enjoy creating them.

THIS IS A REAL STORY
Kim Shuck

I've written three pieces, all published so far, about how and why I ended up poeting. They are all true. They are all different. This one is also different.

My parents are so unlike that they never should have met. Marriage and "till death do us part" is a whole other dance. Dad was in the Navy for all of the reasons: protect, be your best, learn the things, stage your escape from family. Dad did it right based on the stories he was told. Mom is still a bit of an enigma to me. She was born in San Francisco before much of the San Francisco you might be thinking of happened. She had a DA haircut and wore jeans under her skirt when that was seriously not acceptable. Dad was trying to fit into a thing, mom was trying to make the things fit her. They are both geniuses. That word is overused and as a word nerd I try not to use overused words. Genius is still the word I want. Both of mom's parents were culturally tied to the Carpathians. Mom's grandma was from Lvov, when it was Lvov. It may be gone by the time you read this. Grandpa was from the Tatras: the alpine Carpathians. Dad's parents were a career Army Cherokee man and a woman who was adopted early. Grandma Pat still has a somewhat nebulous history. She was a journalist who frequently pointed out that my poems didn't rhyme. Mom is not just from but of San Francisco. Dad is from Oklahoma. My parents are still married and your guess is as good as mine.

Mom used to sing to my brother and me before we fell asleep. Not just as infants but for a long time, well into elementary school. I was a flashlight/book/hiding-under the-covers type. My dad tells long and rambling stories. My grandma Rose told long and rambling stories. My grandpa Leroy would take you fishing and not speak, he still managed to convey long and rambling stories. Grandma Pat (or, in fact any of the names she used at various points) was a scrabble assassin, and talked about the things she imagined about her birth family. I'm related to the first Cherokee to write and star in his own movie. I may actually need stories more than sunlight.

I suppose we're all unlikely.

Before we get too far into this, I should say that I'm not convinced that anyone can explain how to become a poet. It may not be possible to really work out why we become poets. For those of us who really swallow the hook, I suspect that there has been no choice. I can make up a writing prompt and hand it to you. I can tell you what works for me and what doesn't. I can write a thousand poems that you might read or not. I have written more than a thousand poems. You may or may not have read them.

> Feral tuxedo cat
> Pulls self as shadow
> From another shadow
> Becomes part of car shadow
> Tree shadow
> Becomes
> Is verb more than noun
> Is
> Verb
> Flickering from Adrienne's house to
> Our porch
> Where
> Breakfast
> Waits
> In the dark

How many kids, do you suppose, read history books and think, "Well that's not right"? I remember thinking that it was just me. Is that only kids who are strange? Is that the process of defining self as difference? I don't know. I do know that there are more of us than I thought back then.

My great-grandmother was a bootlegger. That's not right. She was, but also my great-grandmother made the best biscuits and gravy.

Once I didn't want to eat the catfish and biscuits that Mae had cooked. Grandpa served me some anyway. Maybe he thought I was saying that they weren't good. Maybe he was trying to tell me I'd long for them someday. Maybe he was just asserting authority.

When I speak to high school students, I point out that I was the school weirdo. I went through a phase where I thought that it might just have been teen anxiety. Then I got older. With the clear eyes of approaching elderhood I can say with authority: I was the school weirdo. Keep in mind that I was part of a maybe 60 person graduating class. There were a fair few eating disorders and cutting behaviors. At least two female students were having sex with teachers. We all knew who the coke dealer was. The level of cheating was a joke. I didn't do drugs. I think that that was mostly fear based. I knew too many addicted adults. I have always eaten a healthy amount. Probably because there had been serious hunger among the parents and grandparents, and love was therefore expressed in calories. I have been cut but I've never intentionally cut myself. Still, I was the strange one. I was told directly by a school functionary, whose actual role escapes me at this point, that I would never be a poet because of something that had happened in an English class. Not worth explaining. I was told by the poetry teacher that my poems were too self-referential to ever be any good. Writing this I begin to suspect that I may be a poet out of an abundance of pique. I can be like that.

For nearly my whole life I've pissed people off when I was trying to make a joke and people thought I was joking when I was trying to start a fight. Another high school era event was the death of my cousin. No one at school believed me when I said she'd died. I evidently didn't look sad enough. I think that what I kept coming up against was a sort of cultural tunnel vision. It might be that if I had darker skin, or looked more like a movie version of an Indigenous woman, I'd have been thought of less as an odd white girl and more as an odd Cherokee girl.

Sometimes I think that I write for the girl that I was. Sometimes I know that I do. I wrote my first book of prose because I'd never read a story about an Indigenous woman who lived in the city, wasn't addicted, beaten by her partner, or didn't end up dead by the end of the book. I'm pretty sure that women like me aren't all the way drawn in for people who have never had to question their cultural ubiquity. Shhh, I never said this, but I wonder sometimes if we're not all the way drawn in for ourselves. Maybe that's just me.

I'm often asked by educational institutions to speak about Indigenous women. I'm not just strange in a rich kid's school in one of the wealthiest cities in the world. I'm strange in my own community too. For example: I get asked how schools should lure in Indigenous students. I have no idea. All I needed to know was that there was a library I wouldn't be able to read my way through in four years. Sometimes I think that I could be very happy with a giant pile of books, a lifetime supply of tea, a sufficiency of nice bubble bath, and a fortress of solitude. From what I can see we aren't all like me.

A student once asked me what poets need to know.

Heading to the poetry conference
We
In the car
In west Marin
Poets all
Folk songs
Silence
Folk songs
Crickets
One poet tells us the temperature based on
Cricket song
Another starts telling us
Star stories
Deep navigation
Braided with
Smells of hot dry grass
Tire crunch
Poet company
A mortar stone

Poets need to know whatever thing snags on their imagination.

School history never fit me. School company never really fit me. My family often didn't fit me. Libraries fit me, but they have hours and we aren't always welcome to stay. There have always been women who lived just outside of town. Recently someone told me, in a sort of strained confidence, that many people think of me as witchy. I laughed. I don't bother to pretend that I'm surprised anymore. Besides there's a book, a piece of artwork, a poem, an event, a tragedy, a batch of cookies, something to do other than to try to align myself with someone else's agenda. I spent some years in an uncommitted effort to fit myself into the shadow of other peoples' expectations. Then I spent time trying to fit myself into a partner's expectations. I was really bad at both of those.

I should probably mention Brian. Brian is the father of my children. I haven't spoken to him in roughly ten years, since our daughter was found dead. Sitting here, trying to be as honest as I can be, I wanted to say that I wasn't angry at him anymore. I think it's more that I hope to not have to talk to him again. I'm not mad, not curious, not even exhausted. We were about fifteen years from friends to over. At the time it was half of my life. I don't know if I wrote one poem while we were together. That feels strange to write. I may have, but when I looked I couldn't find one. I did write chapters for craft books during this time. We went to university, we had kids, we did house things.

And again
Another part of the dangerous poem
Found
The bevels on the brittle edges
Show force from the inside
The poem
The unbound book the
Transformation
Some will look to the skyline
Some
Will look to the skyline to find
Some will find
Their damage in every
Will damage every
Every wall and
Bloom and
Calculation a found
External
An external

I rattled around a bit while collecting degrees. I did a bunch of jobs. I managed a yarn store. The yarn made me happy. I did other things. I spent a lot of time playing a river cane flute under a bay tree on the Berkeley campus. I read a raft of books. I gestated. Men who I didn't know frequently gave me unasked for lectures on the subject of pregnancy. These lectures often began, "When we were pregnant …" Berkeley, California, is an interesting place to grow a baby. We were broke. The neighborhood was changing. I read a metric ton of poetry. I wrote crafting instructions for some high-end, coffee-table crafting books. I wove baskets. I read more poetry. I kept an almost unreadable journal during this time. I was terribly sad and I wasn't keeping it front of mind. My journal knew. I think it was trying to tell me and I wasn't listening.

Here's a small aside: if you write, even if you never share that writing with another soul, it can make parts of yourself easier to see. I think that I was being self-protective by not acknowledging what I was going through, by not writing the poems I have written for most of my life. My writing tells on me. I have access now, 30 years later, reading my own words, to emotions that I wasn't allowing myself to see back then. Everyone finds their way around writing in different ways, finds their way to writing in different ways, learns to distance themself from their writing in different ways. The distance is important for various reasons. If a writer is too tied to their writing then when they submit work for publications a rejection feels too much like a rejection of self rather than work. It's possible to run your career that way, but it's not always good for you. It's not good if you have trouble getting published and it might actually be worse if you are a superstar. It's not easy to be human.

People seem to think that writers know why they write. I think that that's likely unknowable. They also seem to believe that people who do it for a living know how that happened. Part of it is probably work ethic. Part of it is probably luck. The real question is how does a writer become who they are. I don't know about anyone else but I write tiny biographies on a nearly weekly basis. They consist of the least characteristic things I've done. What follows is a more accurate short bio than you will ever read on an event flyer or in a book.

Kim Shuck wakes up before dawn most days. She calls and feeds the two feral cats she has befriended, makes a pint glass of Earl Grey tea, and settles in to write. After writing one unit of work (poem, short essay, bolus of paperwork), she sorts her email and makes a plan for the day. If there is an impending reading she picks poems. If there is an upcoming workshop she thinks about writing prompts. Shuck then does triage on overdue projects, whatever one looks likely to die without care goes first. Pre-Covid she was more reliable, but the lockdown seems to have gummed up her think mechanism. Kim's partner wanders by from time to time and puts food next to her. Eventually darkness comes and she reads non-work things and returns to bed.

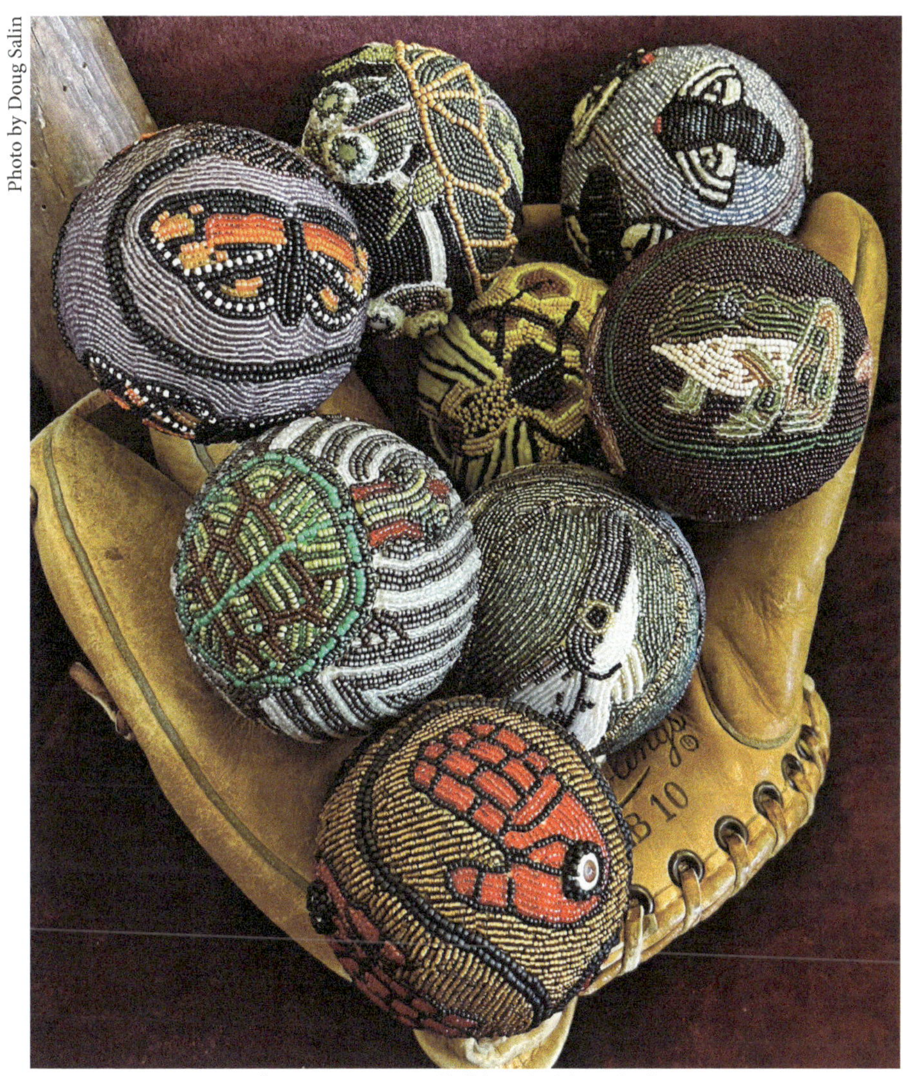

"Anniversary Balls," beaded baseballs.

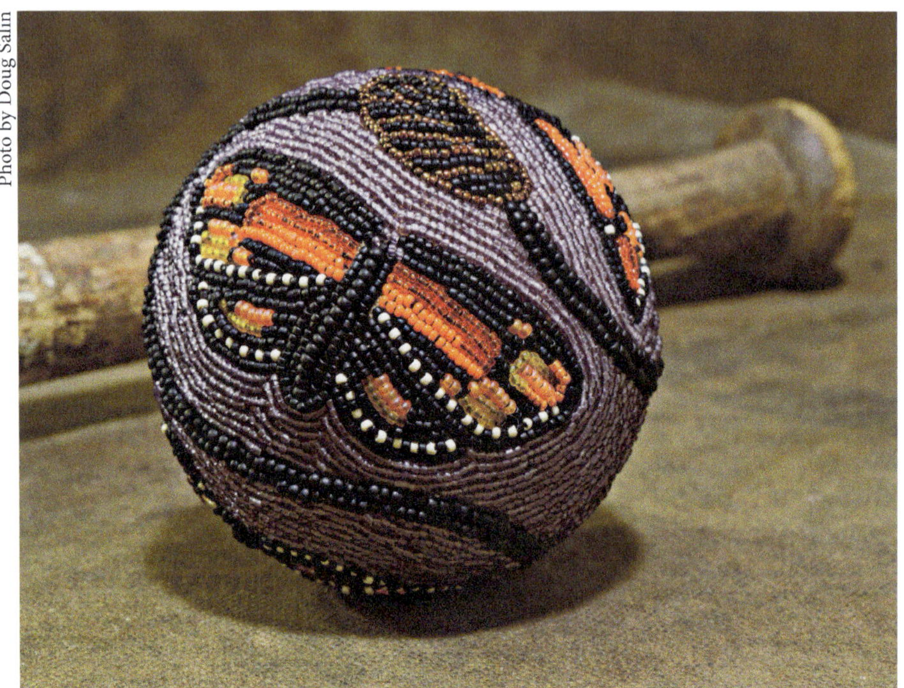

Kim Shuck, "With a Sweep of His Wing," beaded baseball, homage to Satchel Paige, the first Black pitcher to play for the American League (Cleveland Indians, 1948). He played for the Negro League's Kansas City Monarchs from 1940 to 1947, helping sweep the 1942 Negro World Series.

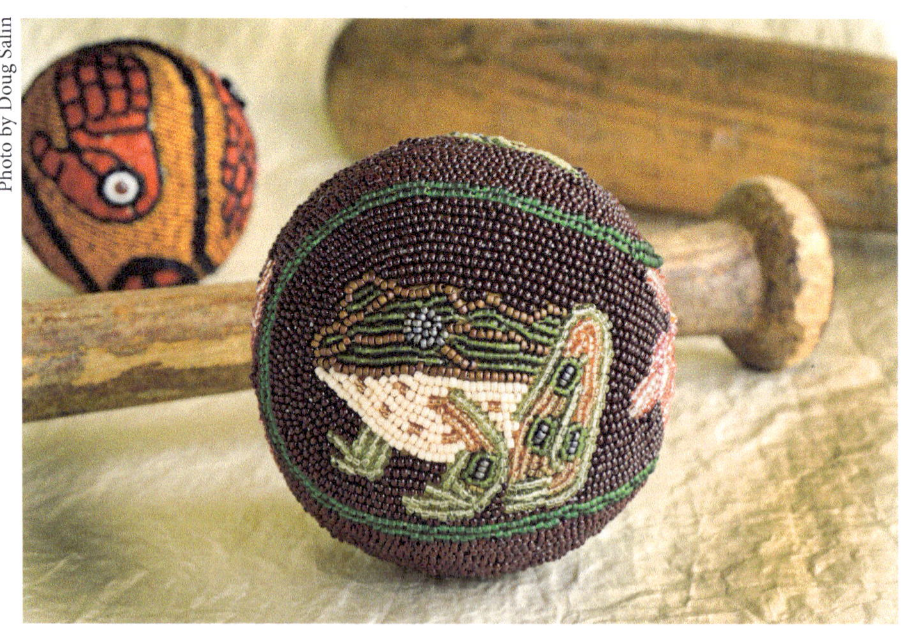

Kim Shuck, "Funny Hop," beaded baseball.

Kimi Sugioka
FORMATIVE INFLUENCES

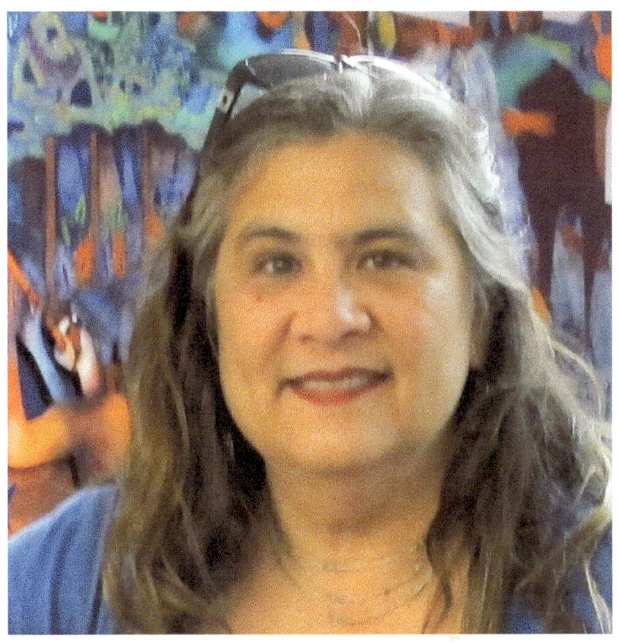

Kimi Sugioka is a mother, educator, and
poet. She earned an MFA
from Naropa University and has
published two books of poetry;
the newest of which is *Wile & Wing*,
published by Manic D Press.
She is the poet laureate of Alameda,
California, and her work appears
in numerous anthologies,
including the upcoming anthologies
HerManos and *Beat Not Beat*.
She loves cats and birds and spending
time with her son. She believes that
creating community through art is a
revolutionary act.

FORMATIVE INFLUENCES
Kimi Sugioka

I was born in the southern comfort of Chapel Hill, North Carolina, into a mixed race family: Japanese Scots-Irish. I was relatively comfortable until age seven, when the family broke in two. Moving to Berkeley, California, in 1965 shifted my world from the quiet rural south to an urban revolutionary powder keg.

It was not unusual to see tanks on Telegraph Avenue. It was not unusual to see cops striking peaceful protesters with their batons as they silently walked by. I also experienced school integration and began to be alternately harassed and accepted as one of the few members of the cultural melting pot. It was during this pivotal time that I learned what it meant to live between two worlds. It set the stage for the rest of my life and became the fulcrum of my artistic expression.

HALF PRIVILEGED

Half Japanese
Half Scots-Irish
Half upper middle class:
coca cola in the fridge,
tempura or roast beef on the table,
apple pie in the oven

Half neglected: garbanzo beans, olives or popcorn
scavenged because my mother was too broke or broken
to shop or cook
Half North Carolina demure
half California dissident
half exotic lily,
half merchant marine pin-up girl
half loved

Half privileged to go to college, get by,
inherit enough for a condo downpayment
half terrified of not being able to pay the mortgage
but making sure to buy 20 pairs of socks
for my son so he wouldn't get the bleeding feet
I had as a child
because of the one pair of socks I wore all week

Half self absorbed and self indulgent
half plagued by madness, depression and guilt

half nihilist
half stubborn
half brilliant
half penitent
half teacher
half sinner
half you
half otter

half optimist
half acquiescent
half broken
half impudent
half poet
half seraphim
half me
half tree

Half salmon
   swimming
      out to sea

As a mixed race woman, I never felt safe or at peace in either world—or in any world really—though I did not realize it until I began my peregrination: treading water between cultures when I moved from Chapel Hill to Berkeley. In Chapel Hill I'd felt more or less accepted as a member of the only Japanese American family in residence. Racist antagonism appeared to be reserved primarily for Black people. As that niche was already filled, we became objects of curiosity as opposed to targets of hatred.

My father had become highly acculturated to post WWII America. He had never been to Japan and, I believe, because he was so mistreated, did not feel compelled to share the culture of his heritage. I was not aware of this until much later in life when I became close to one of my aunts. She was an Ikebana master who communicated love and respect for familial Japanese traditions. My exposure to, and impression of, Japanese culture was initially gleaned from the movies of Kurosawa and the novels of Obata and Mishima.

UPON KUROSAWA'S DEATH

Your departure
severs a cobweb filament
that has hung for decades
between my mind's eastern
and western hemispheres
in haunting half remembrance

A silence made palpable by
the ticking of an ancient clock
long since broken
evocations of the way roses bloom
and fall from my mother's fingers
a camellia's last sigh
in a clear glass bowl
on my favorite aunt's
kitchen table
a decades old rice paddle
the scarred lacquer writing box
my grandfather carried from Japan to California
my grandmother's tattered lavender kimono
the slight bowing of my sister's neck
beneath a full cherry blossom moon

What of the hand
brimming with emptiness?
Seven samurai or
seven grains of rice
A fox wedding
in a forest of dreams

Look to the east
and speak to the rising sun
Tell the rooster
that now
is the time to crow

All of the upper middle class families in Chapel Hill had maids. With my father working from 7am to 7pm, my mother studying art history or otherwise preoccupied, and my siblings in school, I was with Rosa all day, five days a week. I was extremely attached to her. She was a black woman who graduated at the top of her class in high school. She wanted to become a nurse but couldn't afford to attend college. One day, my father drove me to her house in Moncore. Until then, I was not aware of the huge discrepancy between her life and mine. Unpaved muddy roads lead to a group of houses that looked like they were patched together with plywood, next to a river that had been poisoned by the neighboring paper company. Rosa and the maids of my moderately affluent neighborhood lived in a world far different than mine.

The move to Berkeley with my mother began my process of straddling two worlds; I spent the school years in California and summers in North Carolina. In Berkeley, separated from my father, brother, and sister, and living with a depressed and narcissistic mother, I became a sad, self-sufficient, and industrious daughter. I learned to sing to soothe myself to sleep and release feelings of loss and loneliness. I also began to write, journaling at first, then poetry, but in school I encountered skepticism and disbelief from teachers at every turn.

In the 9th grade I wrote a sonnet. I had been reading John Donne and Lord Byron and getting headaches, but I wrote a sonnet as a kind of a romantic imitation. It was in rhyming iambic pentameter. My creative writing teacher, who was a middle aged white woman, did not believe that I had written it.

When I attended a short story writing class at SF State, I wrote an autobiographical story about my friendship with a boy in the Appalachian mountains. I wrote his words in dialect. It was very accurate. The teacher did not think that anyone spoke that way and implied that he did not believe my story.

When I attended an MFA program in writing one teacher told me to write haibun. Another said that, if I wanted to understand the Japanese aesthetic, I should read all four volumes of Blythe's Haiku. He seemed irritated by a sestina I wrote about my Japanese family.

When I think about it, many people have disbelieved my stories, my life experience, and my voice. When I was younger I continually questioned myself as to whether or not my experiences were real.

I could have said that I am not a home for your assumptions and don't have the patience to explain what they are and why you have them. I would rather talk to the pelicans; even the gulls are better conversationalists and certainly more insightful. I learned to share my lunch with blackbirds and crows; they understood what it is like to be hungry and alone.

Theater and chorus were what kept me engaged in high school. I frequently skipped other classes and returned after school for rehearsals. Most often, I was cast as a prostitute in school plays. I aspired to be an actress, but this was the time before blind casting, and, as I learned after high school, I was not a desirable candidate for community plays such as *Oklahoma*. But I learned to love the taste and music of words and continued to write and sing.

My early education in the arts came from various boyfriends: a photographer, a painter, and musicians. Though these relationships were transient, I was exposed to multiple artists and art forms and feasted on them. They stimulated feelings of intense joy and curiosity, and became integrated into the developing architecture of my own aesthetic.

Beginning in my twenties, and continuing throughout my life, I was most strongly influenced by writers of color. For example, Zora Neal Hurston celebrated language that did not conform to the traditional writing by the canon of the white, male writers that I had been exposed to. Anthologies such as *This Bridge Called My Back*, *The Midnight Birds* and *No More Masks* gave me—an unidentifiable exotic who was constantly questioned as to my race, ethnicity, and origin—permission to write in my own voice.

Working from the time I left home at 16, I was determined to be able to provide for myself, but after being a waitress and a residential childcare provider to autistic children for $2.50 an hour, I realized I needed skills. My mother's inability to hold down a job instilled fear that I would be unable to do so. My father partially subsidized my education and I got a teaching credential in Special Education. I continue to support myself and my son to this day. Except for one year of graduate school and one year after my mother died, writing has always been something I squeezed in on the side.

My education in the systemic traps of poverty, abuse, and racism I learned from my students. I have worked primarily with black and brown children from poor and working class families. Teaching students labeled Special Needs, I found myself constantly questioning whether there was something actually wrong with the students or with the systemic oppression that created or informed their family situations and, in turn, their behavior.

DOUBLE DUTCH

On buckling playground asphalt
candy wrappers
pink bunny barrettes
headless plastic monsters
bow-shaped buttons
melting bubble gum

donut skid marks
used condoms and bullets

A salamander
(at first mistaken for a bug)
is ecstatically fondled by 54
nature-deprived
six-year-old hands
until it is finally
loved to death

No slides
        jungle gyms
        swings
        tunnels
        wooden bridges

but beneath three
netless, graffiti-covered backboards
child ghosts
sweat and swear
pound hoops
haunt the streets
fill shopping carts with aluminum cans
or hover about liquor store transoms
where their supple bodies
succumbed to the gun
while out youngest
valiantly continue
to play
        kickball
        four square
        hopscotch
        double dutch

How many little girls
sent to the store for ice cream
survive
behind the dumpster rapes?

How many little boys from
this overcrowded

understaffed
quote driven
text deprived elementary school
outrun the cold metal
drop top
speaker bumps of
this street slumped tomb?

At 8:10 a.m.
eleven-year-old Damian says
Life stinks, Miss Kimi,
I wish I was dead

Dante tells me
he's going to run away from home
leaves me 3 suicide notes
in as many weeks
This time, you'll never see me again
Pigeons coo, tires screech
sirens follow gunshots
and two-inch obituaries
follow hapless youths
on the wrong street
at the wrong time
when all the streets
are the wrong streets
all the time …

When I was 29 my dear friend Susan, also a teacher and poet, encouraged me to get a master's degree in poetry. I didn't believe that I was truly a poet, but I was tired of restraining and being assaulted by children—and by impossible administrative expectations.

I applied and was accepted to the Naropa University, Jack Kerouac School of Disembodied Poetics. Enthralled by poetry and the study of language, I began to dream and sing poems. The Latinx revolutionary poets inspired me to write poems of protest. They gave me the courage to say what I had previously believed to be unspeakable. Unfortunately, I was the only poet of color in the program (a Black woman dropped out). Again, I was the exception to the rule.

MEETING GWENDOLYN BROOKS

She'd come cross country
on a train, cause she didn't
trust hollow metal bodies with wings,
to Boulder, Colorado
to read and greet
the new poets at the
Jack Kerouac School
of Disembodied Poetics

We had lunch together
the student and teacher
poets
As we gawked and spluttered
something half heartedly
half witted
she suddenly stopped
and looked from one
to the next
through her long worn
stained and history
steeped
glasses
and asked
"Where are your dark skinned
poets?"
Everyone looked at me
like I was suddenly
representing all the
absent colors
Anne volunteered,
"She isn't well and couldn't come"
as though that might do

I wasn't so much upset
by Ms. Brooks question
but embarrassed as I
failed to be
dark enough

to make up
for all those absent blossoming
minds

It was a great honor
to meet
Gwendolyn Brooks, I still
have a battered,
autographed copy of her
Selected Poems
Still read
Too Cool For School
to some of my
more wayward
charges

Know that Gwendolyn
paid overtime, double time and
time and a half
for her slice
of literary pie

Ms. Brooks
finished her lunch
and paid the bill

Despite receiving some recognition as a poet, I have always felt like an imposter. Severe anxiety, moderate depression, social anxiety, and high levels of self doubt have plagued me throughout my life. As I look back on my early journals, I see that they served primarily as a therapeutic conduit to my inner turmoil. My writing process is informed by my history of emotional abuse and abandonment as a child. Even though I write from my own experience, I frequently feel alien from the process itself. It is as though the poems are somehow channeled through me and I experience a kind of dissociation. It is usually not until after the poems are written down that I reconnect with myself, recognize and identify myself within them.

My Naropa professors taught me the craft of poetry and gave me the tools to revise and refine my work. From Diane di Prima I learned key elements that I continue to use to scaffold my writing: logopoeia, mythopoeia, phanopoeia, and melopoeia (meaning, mythology, image, and music).

After three semesters at Naropa, my mother became ill. I had to return to Oakland to take care of her with one semester left. She died within a year. Her death was devastating and disorienting. I stared at the walls for months. But, after a time, I felt as though I had nothing to lose and began attending and reading my poems at various poetry venues around the Bay Area.

Before long I was selected to be on the San Francisco Poetry Slam team and traveled to Boston to compete. Though we lost, I made friends with poets from Boston and parts east. Patricia Smith, a well-known and searing slam poet, came to visit me. She read her poems to my students in East Oakland. It was one of the few times when poetry intersected directly with my life as a teacher and with the lives of my students. They experienced vast numbers of deaths in the community; gunshots and lockdowns were common there. Patricia's father had been shot and killed and she read and spoke about this. The children were enrapt, hearing their own stories in her poems. I was very grateful for her presence there.

I met Piri Thomas, a poet from the Nuyorican school, and invited him to read at another school where I taught. After using inane reading texts that were void of people of color with my students from the East Oakland projects, it was gratifying to see them laugh and recognize themselves in Piri's stories.

I was approached by Jen Joseph of Manic D Press to publish my first book of poems in 1994. She hosted a San Francisco poetry series at the Paradise Lounge and I, briefly, co-hosted the Cafe Babar series with her. Surprised and gratified that she saw promise in my work, I was thankful that she published my first book, *The Language of Birds*, and much later, a second book, *Wile & Wing*. I was fortunate to be solicited for publication instead of having to submit my work to multiple publishers. Though my poems were published in various journals, left to my own devices, I am not sure when, or if, I would have attempted to publish an entire book.

I was performing my songs and poems solo, often accompanied by a talented, shakuhachi player, until International Women's Day in 1992, when I became a founding member of a five-woman, spoken word group known as Bloodtest. I stopped performing solo as we wrote, arranged, rehearsed, and subsequently performed throughout northern California, and in Texas and Florida. The content focused on themes for and about women, as well as poems about my students. After the group broke up I became pregnant with my son, but I continued to write and perform throughout my pregnancy.

A LIFE IN TWO PARTS

1.
Before my son
I twinkled, twiddled, danced Caribbean
dreamt in Greek
ran with the bulls of whimsy
spun and stumbled
spittled and mumbled
riddled with words that spilled like fountains of nickels
from the frozen, frothy muzzle of a carousel horse
I was here for the ride
discipled to word
song and circumference
Listened to Van, Bruce, and Bob
like there was no tomorrow
never dreamed tomorrow
was another day

no down payments
strictly cash and carry
and I took only what I could carry
I wasn't into love nests
hearth and home tests
I was up til 3 and slept til noon
yacking and cracking wise
swooning and waxing that big
poem in the sky
my lullaby
my syncope
my salud y dinero
I was sculpting and molding
each day as it came
it was bonafide
pay as you play
and play
and play

Don't get me wrong
I wasn't a rocker or a dime bag doper
I wasn't a reefer suckin', cold duck smoker
No, I was more of a moper and all the time
was dreamtime

studying the path of the Green Ant and
the Red Road
Always late
or giddy
with the guilt of the
self-condemned, I the
poet
prosecutor
jury and
hangin' judge

2.
After my son
I climbed on that pony
and held on tight
learned to wake
to someone else's cries

I was asleep by nine
up by six
(and two and four and maybe more)
I was sleep: walkin', workin', and payin' dues
to the babysitter, doctor, baby gym proctor

The world suddenly shifted
from solipsism to rock hard work
It was work to eat,
eat to work
navigating cries
of hunger
cries of pain, or just plain
too tired to cope
we both just sat down and wailed
like hound dogs
with baleful pleas
for some kind of peace

He cried
I cried
we all cried
for three long months
until he smiled

the wide and worldly, wondrous smile
of one who'd fought and won
his painful withdrawal from
my anti-depressants;
the ones psychiatrists now say
may cause grave, neurological damage
to the unborn …

And I tried to become the mother
I never had
Like a child with some blocks
intent on building a castle
with only a vague intuition
of architecture

But there I was
parenthood upon me
like a hurricane on a sparrow

and suddenly, there was no time
for dreaming and moping and
reading and writing
or even dressing
It was all I could do to
take a shower
with my son strapped into
some baby contraption
beside the tub

I, with the starring
part of supporting actress
without lines or rehearsal
learned to work without sleep
dream with time
play in the sand
and roll in the muck
of every kind of human fluid
learning to be fluidly human

And so it was
he grew me up
taught me the true measure
of sacrifice
that somehow still wrung
the dew from the roses
at dawn

After my son Kai was born, as a single working mother, I was unable to balance teaching and caring for him with performing poetry. After putting him to bed at nine, I wrote Individual Education Plans or lesson plans until midnight. I continued to write poetry but stopped attending readings for about 15 years. I attempted to be fully committed to teaching and child rearing. I say attempted because I found myself to be alien to both the culture of elementary teachers and to the societal strictures of the conventional families in my community. For years I tried to find and become friends with the mothers of my son's peers, but because they were primarily nuclear-family oriented, and because I was far more politically radical than they were comfortable with, I often found myself in a state of social isolation.

Fortunately, a communist and political scholar became the godless (but spiritual) father to my son. Between him and my dear friend, Kathleen, who was also his wife, I continued to receive love, support and limited, but regular, infusions of political ideology that informed my poetics.

THANKSGIVING

Chestnut & sweet rice flour pie crusts
Roasted pumpkin
Allspice ground with mortar and pestle
Juiced lemons
Cardamom coffee
Heritage turkey
The eminent domain of flavor
Extracted,
Pressed
Massaged

Metered interlocutions
4/4, 3/4
Staccato interjections

Tectonic shifts of socio-political
And psycho-social paradigms
An insistence to examine
The labyrinthine interplay between
denial, tolerance and rage

The table is laid
With Mexican & Italian ceramics
And the once prized china
Of relations born
To tin bowls and factory enslavement

Assemble are assimilated
Mongrel African, Chinese, Japanese, European
Progeny
Of the eager or desperate or forcefully displaced
Without complacency
With conviction
That ultimately we must all
Face the blind trajectory of bullets
From the xenophobic supremacists gun
And rise from bus, train, plane or theater seats
As the righteous many
Against the pernicious and cowardly
Few

When my son became a teenager I began to attend readings once again. Shizue Seigel supported and promoted my work with her Write Now! groups for BIPOC folks. She opened a path back into the world of writing that I believed was lost to me. I was surprised at how easy it was to be accepted and appreciated by writers and audiences. The current community of writers is much more inclusive and embracing than the writers that I first encountered in the early '90s. Cafe Babar and the Paradise Lounge poets were highly and loudly critical of the poets who came to these readings.

In 2020 I was named the poet laureate of Alameda. Creating literary platforms and exchanges has been challenging due to the pandemic. Until recently, all readings and discussions were conducted over Zoom. My motivation to nourish and cultivate community through poetry has grown exponentially stronger during this period. I believe that the only way through the sociopolitical and ecological maelstrom that we are in is to learn to trust and support one another.

My politics and poetics are distilled from the worlds I've traveled through: seeing the impoverishment and degradation of Black people in North Carolina, teaching high income privileged students in Marin, witnessing the democratic socialist governmental financial support freely given to my Danish friend, and working with impoverished and marginalized students who rarely left their neighborhoods in the projects of San Francisco and East Oakland.

I found my voice listening to the stories of friends and acquaintances who have had to withstand the oppression and dangers of living in a sociopolitical structure that exploits them and holds them hostage to the capitalist hierarchy. I witnessed the impoverishment of my Appalachian friends who spent their entire lives working low paying night shifts in Levi's or pharmaceutical tubing factories, and I became familiar with the immigration struggles and poverty of the Latinx families in the East Bay. I saw the Bay Area houseless population grow from a handful at the closing of psychiatric hospitals and group homes during the Reagan era, to thousands with the replacement of SRO by hotels and high priced condos. I am inspired by the strength, courage, and tenacity of these people whose paths have crossed with mine. We may all be broken in some ways but when we share our stories with one another, and show our love for each other, we become whole.

Acknowledgments

"Half Privileged," "Double Dutch" excerpt, "Meeting Gwendolyn Brooks" excerpt, and "A Life in Two Parts" were previously published in Kimi Sugioka's *Wile & Wing*, Manic D Press, San Francisco, CA, 2019.

Elizabeth Travelslight
RECTANGLES GO ROUND

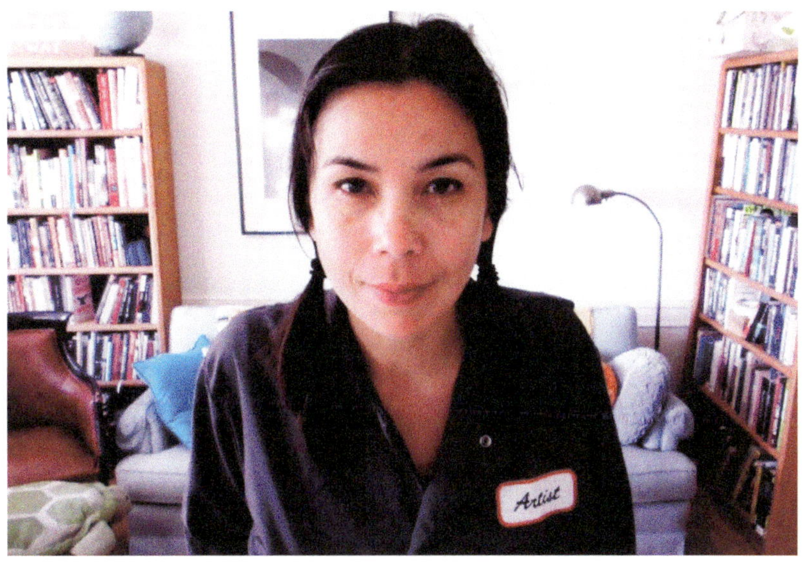

Elizabeth Travelslight, who draws on
transnational Filipinx and White roots, grew up in
San Francisco, where she still lives.
She's currently adjunct professor of Critical Studies
(Math/Sciences) at the California College
of the Arts and of Media Studies at the
University of San Francisco. Previously, she taught
at the San Francisco Art Institute's School of
Interdisciplinary Studies, winning an Outstanding
Faculty Award in 2016 and 2021.
She's worked as a teaching artist from middle
school to university level, served on the board of
directors and the Anti-Oppression Working Group
as a member of the Rainbow Grocery Cooperative,
and was an organizer of the Bay Area Society for
Art & Activism.
elizabethtravelslight.com

RECTANGLES GO ROUND
Elizabeth Travelslight

It is nearly spring. The sun's warmth is returning with force. We've shifted our clocks ahead. Magnolias throughout the city have been in bloom for weeks. Petals scatter in disheveled layers across the ground like pastel party dresses, stained and cast off after a joyful night of dancing on the town. In the lull between tidal waves of novel coronavirus, we celebrate new life. It is an unfamiliar time of beauty and grief. We start to count Year Three since SARS-Cov-2 found good soil in our human bodies.

What a demonstration of capitalism's cruelty this virus makes of us. The careless evolving violence of our economy. The high tolls paid by those who can least afford to pay them. It has been a very long stress test.

In the light of Spring's new life, I am making space for some relief. I set aside my rage but keep it where I can see it. Grief grabs me less but stays in the room, protecting me. My heart aches with lessons to be remembered forever. Who can and cannot be trusted. Who will protect each other and who can only take care of themselves. Shattered by disappointment, I am retooling every expectation with freshly sharpened edges of awareness.

Because uncertainty persists. Long equilibria give way to increasingly rapid changes that exceed predictability and escape reversibility. Some things cannot be undone simply by command. Earth's average temperature continues to rise. Global superpowers and local police flex their weapons. The media thumps with the drums of war while COVID variants keep up their melancholy chorus just off stage, the song a promise to return. The earth rebels. We fight.

"It is time to plan for the increased difficulty of planning."[1]

My beautiful daughter is almost nine. My mother has recently died. I try to handle the future more gently now, like a newborn.

* * *

I have worked as an adjunct college professor for nearly a decade. Through the pandemic, I have taught at the San Francisco Art Institute, the California College of the Arts, and the University of San Francisco.

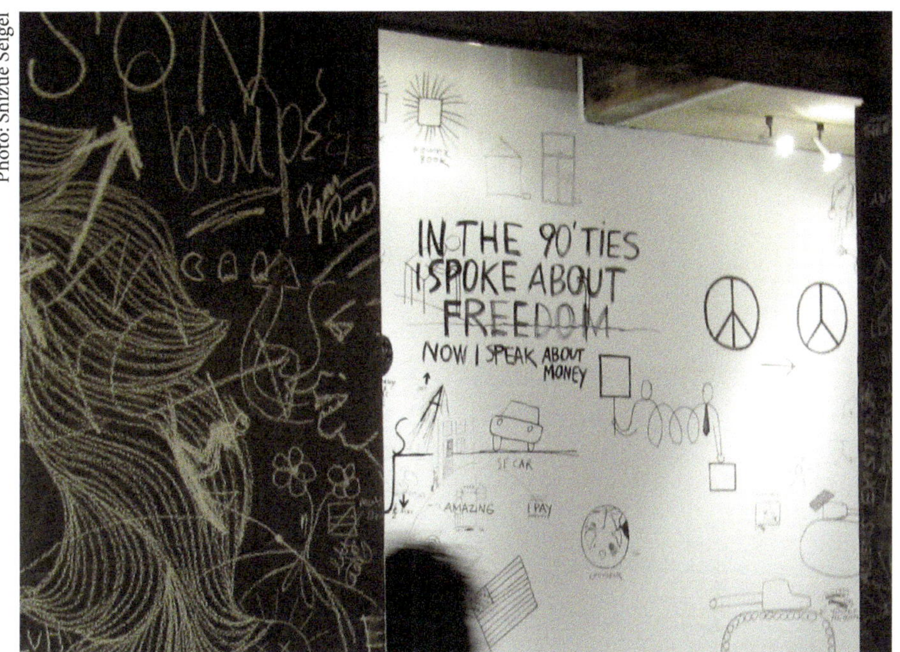

Student exhibition at the San Francisco Art Institute, 2010.

As lifelong users of internet-connected, mobile devices, my students possess unprecedented creative capacities. Unleashing powers of empathy, imagination, and intelligence, they are urban natives of world wide webs and digital megacities. Craving context, they devour histories to make sense of who, what, where, why, and how to be, the reasons for and within our shifting conditions of vulnerability.

Removing obstacles and strengthening their self-expression is rewarding work. But I find that I have lost the strength to bridge the gaps between expensive institutional expectations and what the pandemic has left on the field of possibility. I cannot hold it together. I believe in my students but have lost trust in the institutions around them. A school is not sustainable if students, staff, and faculty are disposable. I cannot consent to a system determined to maintain the historical privileges of the wealthy at the risk and expense of everyone else. And so I prepare to give up a long and once cherished line of work. It is a difficult decision to leave something that has sheltered and rewarded me for so long.

1. Andrea Steves of the Museum of Capitalism, SFMOMA public talk: "The Redirect: Technology after Capitalism," April 25, 2019: https://www.sfmoma.org/event/the-redirect-technology-after-capitalism/

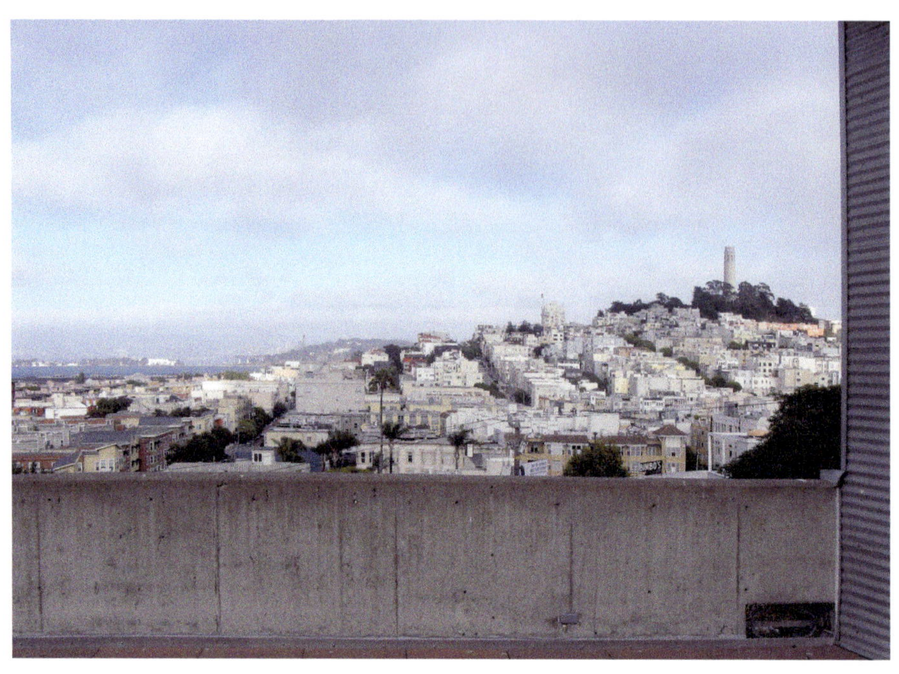

✳ ✳ ✳

Fifteen years ago, "teaching math to art students" at the San Francisco Art Institute (SFAI) became my most daring, heartfelt ambition.

It began in the summer of 2007. Though I was not enrolled there, I had been "sneaking" into SFAI's Anne Bremmer Memorial Library to work on my master's thesis for the European Graduate School (EGS).

EGS was a distance learning program capitalizing on the culture and degree granting capabilities of the early internet. Its website was search-engine optimized for the names of a strategically curated roster of uber-cool faculty, a Top 40 list of European + American critical contemporary thought and practice: Judith Butler, Donna Haraway, Slavoj Zizek, Jean Luc Nancy, Tracy Emin, Atom Egoyan, Paul Virilio, Giorgio Agamben, Manuel Delanda, Catharine Breillat, Helen Cixous.

As students, from October to May we corresponded our course work through an online bulletin board where we familiarized ourselves with the work of people who would become our living topics during a three-week summer residency in the Swiss Alps. It was an experiment in globalization that had me exploring libraries all over San Francisco. By the time I was finished with my degree, I was thoroughly steeped in unfiltered continental philosophy and contemporary critical studies. Poststructuralism and *A Thousand Plateaus* clung to me like rich French perfume.

One afternoon on a thesis-writing break, I walked uncertainly across SFAI's rooftop Zellerbach Quad. Insecure about belonging there, I hoped I was unnoticeable while I took in the most spectacular view. From the roof, San Francisco's sea-city-and-landscape sweeps imperially from north to east—a full embrace of bridges, bay water, and dense sparkling skyline. It is a breathtaking position in time and space.

Intoxicated, I asked myself, "How could I possibly get a job here? SFAI would be a beautiful place to come to work."

I was pursuing a master's degree because I was considering an academic career. Working at Rainbow Grocery Cooperative was wonderful, but after eight years, I was restless and ready to explore other ways to make a living.

Captivated and breathless, I began a dialog with myself:

"How do I get a job here?"

"What could you do here?"

"Math teacher?"

"Everyone needs math," I reasoned.

"Art students need math."

"I bet artists hate math."

"Everyone hates math."

"I bet I could get them to like it."

"With art!"

At that moment, a lightning strike of epiphany coursed through me. I rewired my dreams. This could be fun.

* * *

From a young age, I'd been placed in schools and programs for "gifted children" where I was encouraged to play and practice mathematics. Whatever affinity I had for the formality of it, I trace as a family trait. My father gave it to me and he got it from his mother. Puzzles, probability, precision, complexity, the powers of abstraction, measurement, concentration, and careful calculation—surefire dopamine when a hard problem demands solutions and releases secrets.

In college, I continued to study mathematics because it felt usefully evergreen but also free and untethered. Universal in application and limitless to the point of irrelevance, a math degree also freed my schedule for classes in other departments: Psychobiology, Anthropology, Physics, Psychology, Education, Politics, Women's Studies, History of Consciousness. Interdisciplinarily was the only way I knew how to learn.

Also, I hoped mathematics might help me resolve the pressure of the existential contradictions I felt forming inside. It was a romantic expectation with uneven success, but it did lead me into the history of European and American "scientific" thinking and provide me with critical perspectives on how and why we live in worlds ever more reliant on measurement and numbers, and the violent limitations this reliance entails.

I don't think anyone would consider me especially talented at mathematics anymore. Smart is as smart does, and complex computations rarely come up in my daily life. And I was never very mentally fast, if that's a metric of talent.

But I can be a confident thinker, unintimidated by numbers. Bookkeeping, datasets, codes, and complex dynamical systems can light me up inside. I love stories with numbers. The very idea of numbers! It's fun to try to figure things

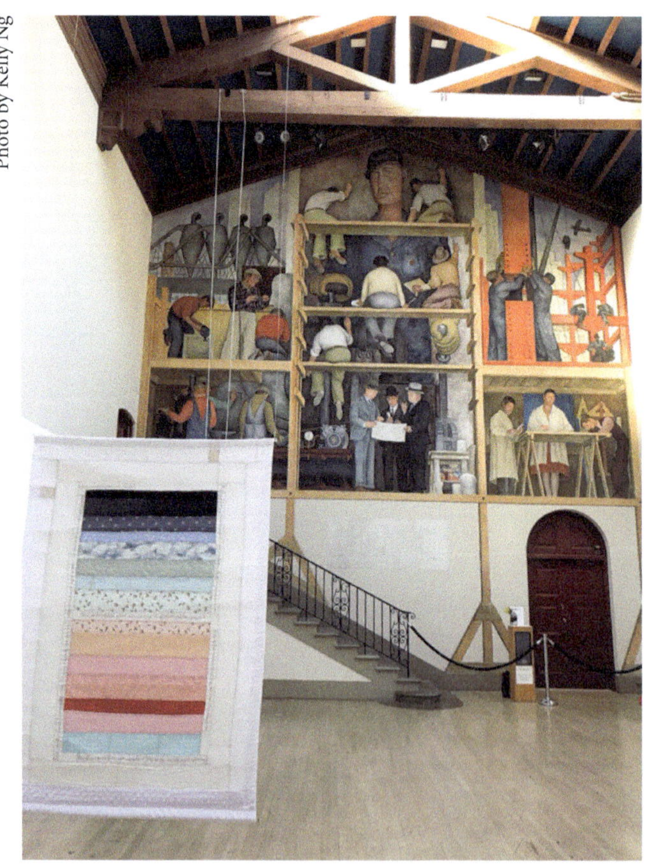

Elizabeth Travelslight's "Security Blanket: Variations (bulletproof)" on display in foreground. On the wall behind: Diego Rivera's mural "The Making of a Fresco Showing the Building of a City," SFAI Gallery, March 2019.

out. But in the end, I am interested in more than the merely mathematical methods. Mathematics is not enough. The reality behind our symbols and beneath our models matters. It's what's the matter. L-I-T-E-R-A-L-L-Y.

We detach entirely the symbolic from the real at our peril. Virtuality is simply and only ever that; it cannot grow food or keep us warm and dry.

* * *

In that moment on that rooftop, SFAI appeared as a tall and glamorous tower. Mathematics. Art. Academic. Education. Interdisciplinary Studies. Studio Practice. Many seductive mysteries could come together here.

With a destination discovered, I felt a path rise up to meet me. Days later, when I mentioned my epiphany to my former math professor, Ralph Abraham, he immediately encouraged me to return to UC Santa Cruz and follow my MA with an MFA in Digital Art + New Media. It would provide both the teaching credential to teach at a fine-arts college and an opportunity to continue my research into the history of mathematics and science.

* * *

Braiding art, mathematics, and teaching felt right—a strong, useful continuation of my path so far, and one that might lead me back to this beautiful view.

I'd been born in Daly City, a daughter of California and the Bay Area, the only child of a Filipina immigrant (my mother) and European-descended white settlers (an American father, and later, a Swiss stepfather). Raised to adulthood by three parents, among three extended families rooted in three cultures on three continents, I found the question of how to be in the world a perplexing one, fraught with cultural paradox and unidentified unspoken traumas.

At college—away from my parents—I was able to start sorting myself out.

"There was a time when you were not a slave, remember that. You walked alone, full of laughter, you bathed bare-bellied. You say you have lost all recollection of it, remember ... You say there are no words to describe this time, you say it does not exist. But remember. Make an effort to remember. Or, failing that, invent."[1]

I began to build an understanding that oriented me meaningfully in time and space.

---

1. Monique Wittig, Les Guérillères, 1969.

∗ ∗ ∗

I look racially mixed, a light-skinned, dark-haired, dark-eyed mestiza Pinay. Over time, I have acquired the apparent confidence and uneasy vigilance of someone whose proximity and comparative lightness acclimate them intimately but incompletely with whiteness. It is an unbearable comfort to know how white supremacy works and how to play along, never knowing when my difference might be wielded against me. I can be a sensitive shape-shifter, finely attuned to the power dynamics in a given situation. Survival can be a reward of successful simulation. But what shape do we become when mimicry smothers our soul?

∗ ∗ ∗

The never-ending contradictions and subsequent friction of being "mixed" reveal that all being is traversed with fault lines where stability cracks. The surface we call identity is a shifting layer of façades. Rubbing against one another over a fluid molten mantle, tectonics are the source of forces from which earthquakes and volcanoes erupt, and seas and mountains emerge. Any solidity to being is a matter of time and perspective. Like the earth, we are more liquid and dynamic than we tend to presume.

I spent years of my childhood roaming Daly City where the San Andreas fault slips into the sea. Countless hours scampering across buckling sidewalks, knocking on doors, ringing bells, picking flowers, collecting rubber bands, buying candy, climbing fences, digging for bugs, chasing waves, pulling ice plants, and breaking things with remarkable impunity. I was a stray string of code run wild in Doelger's candy-colored midcentury fantasy, a rectangular world blanketed in gray fog, a cold palm tree on every lawn.

If I describe my upbringing as middle class, it's to acknowledge the middle of class as another constantly shifting ground where economic stability is as accessible as it is ephemeral. I was raised in a tumultuous middle made steep and precarious by unhinged neoliberal policies that deregulated the American economy in the decades after I was born. I am always a little afraid that whatever I have accomplished (through luck, effort, skill, legacy, privilege, and/or proximity) could evaporate at any moment in a tragic act of chance or carelessness.

The fear may also be a family legacy. Spanish and American empires in the Philippines left a wake of inequality and desperation so pervasive it inspired my mother to cross an ocean to marry a handsome stranger. Combine this with the toeholds of wealth provided by my white fathers and I find myself situated on a sliver of privilege placed at the maw's edge of destruction, where living becomes a dramatic dance of survival, dreams, and calculated risk.

* * *

I have called the San Francisco Peninsula home my entire life. It is my friend and my teacher. It is my favorite, most familiar shape, my best answer to uneasy questions of how to be.

The spiritual foundation and intellectual freedom I was granted as a child, to connect and figure things out, is a legacy I can trace from my mother to her mother to my great-grandfather, Calixto Miranda. Born a century before me in the region of Luzon where the Pampanga intersects with Concepcion and Tarlac, Calixto refused Catholicism and aligned himself with the Unión Espiritista Cristiana de Filipinas. Tired of the casual beatings he experienced from the Catholic Church, Calixto with his wife Sesing, founded a Christian Spiritist community in our family's barrio in Balutu.

While the culture of the Philippines is informed by centuries of Spanish Catholicism, my family has not been Catholic for over four generations.

Spiritism is a speculative and philosophical exploration of spirit that involves methodical investigation and mediumship. It's a sort of Enlightenment-fueled early global Pentecostalism that emphasizes structured inquiry and intimate experiences of interpretation and spiritual connection. A gentler, generous culture of dialogue and inquiry.

My great-grandparents fostered a spiritual sanctuary and political community that fed and protected its members, sheltering them from at least some of the violence of colonialism. The hand that hits was held back. By the time my mother was raising me in California, I took this nurturing protection and spiritual liberation entirely for granted, unable to distinguish its source from our Filipino American way of life.

* * *

My rooftop epiphany was forgotten in the fraught turbulence of economic recession and recovery until, remarkably, I was hired to teach mathematics at SFAI in the Spring term of 2014. I learned that even after many years, our forgotten dreams can come back for us. My daughter was 6 months old. My mother watched her on the one day a week I went to campus to teach. The course was called "MATH 108-1: The Shape of Space." Envisioned as a survey of the history of mathematics and geometry, it was a harmonious rejoinder to the thesis I had been writing in that library seven years prior.

At the time I was hired, the adjunct faculty was organizing a union drive with Service Employees International Union Local 1021. I wanted nothing to do with them. I had a baby, a dream vocation I aimed to take Very Seriously, and Art to Practice. It seemed best to leave the union folks well enough alone and not waste my time.

The union organizers were clamorous and loud. Disruptive. Confrontational. Polarizing. They disturbed the polite veneer of "academic" collegiality by claiming noisily that adjunct faculty, among the lowest paid members of the community, deserved better salaries, stronger job security, and clear pathways to advancement and benefits. They scheduled so very many meetings.

I felt that I didn't have time for it and prepared the awkward excuses that would leave others to do the work. Also, I was good at getting along with white people. If I wanted job security and the opportunity to advance, I could succeed on my own.

My husband had more clarity. He encouraged me to go to meetings. He adapted his schedule and took care of our baby so I had more time. He supported me so I could get involved and come to see why I should.

We won our union NLRB election despite the administration's pleas to wait, and the president's promises that we did not need a union. I learned that those in charge are not necessarily competent nor compassionate. SEIU 1021 by contrast turned out so much support on our behalf. I was permanently transformed by the solidarity of the fast-food workers who showed up to demonstrate with us. I have been organizing adjunct labor ever since.

Organizing more equitable, accessible conditions for art school labor has become an integral part of my creative practice. Beyond making art, it fosters new conditions for belonging in these creative communities, transforming institutions through which so much art does, or does not, get made.

* * *

Our household began to brace for the impact of a viral pandemic as early as January 2020. At the time, my husband Eric was working for a nonprofit preparing to send 2 million N95 masks from the Bay Area to China. An epidemic of a novel virus in Wuhan was serious enough to cause this odd reversal of the global supply chain. It wasn't yet clear that the virus had spread globally, but we understood that a pandemic was a looming possibility.

Back then, I still hoped the nation-state apparatus might be able to do some good. It was colonial and imperfect, but had the advantage of being already in place. Today, I'm not so sure.

Our daughter, Miranda, was halfway through first grade, eighteen months into her life with the community-run public creative arts charter school a mile down the street. Elementary school initiated big changes for her and me. She was forming more friendships, developing her creativity, and learning to count and read. After six years with a lively child, I finally had attention for longer, more uninterrupted thoughts, and the prospect of life and work beyond parenthood. I began to invest more attention on that thing called a career.

When the lockdown came, Miranda and I were once again home together for hours upon hours all day, every day, like when she was small. For months, with wires coming out of our ears, we conducted our lives through masks or Zoom.

* * *

SFAI, already heavily debt laden and cash strapped, buckled instantly under the stress of the early pandemic. The gilded "radical" veneer instantly dissolved to reveal pure white self-preservation underneath. The administration announced a "suspension" of operations. They began to lay off staff. They requested that every student transfer out. They served notice to every single teacher, adjunct and tenure/tenure-track faculty alike.

The tower had become a death trap. In the earliest confusing throes of a lethal viral pandemic, the board and administration started throwing community members out, denying them their livelihoods, their health insurance, and their homes. Those with access and power tellingly confused "saving the school" with securing their own high-salaried positions above all else. It was the most tragic and revealing failure of imagination and leadership I have ever witnessed. I found it unforgivable. If I had any wonder left about the mysterious logic at the heart of their "Art," it was now extremely clear: Preserve white privileges at all costs, above all else.

I understood then how privilege destroys courage and imagination, and how illegitimate hierarchy smothers intelligence. I saw how white mediocrity thrives in white affluence, and I understood why so many of our institutions are stuck. These people seem to know how to do only one thing: Protect and enrich themselves even while others face death. I won't ever be fooled into thinking otherwise again. Beware of liars and cowards.

Since the previous summer, I had been methodically preparing our union for the upcoming contract re-negotiation and was increasingly invested in the school's Strategic Plan. I hadn't had a pay increase in over five years. Salaries across the school had flat-lined while the cost of living grew. Enrollment was in dramatic decline. The situation was starting to undermine my work, my growth. The only thing more appalling than the widespread attrition of faculty and staff of color was the impact this deterioration had on students. Well before the pandemic hit, SFAI was already revealing clear signs of structural violence. The pandemic was simply an opportunity to double down. And so with sad, but certain, reconciliation, I set aside my most hopeful ambitions for SFAI's future and focused on organizing with SFAI's community of students and adjunct faculty to fight for our stakes in SFAI's survival.

One year in, by January 2021, the school was in such dire financial circumstances, the board discussed selling SFAI's famous Diego Rivera mural, *The Making of a Fresco Showing the Building of a City*.

What follows is an excerpt from the public comment I made to San Francisco's Land Use & Transportation Commission in support of landmark status and protecting the mural from removal:

We are here because careless philanthropists failed to follow through on a promise to raise $19M for SFAI's campus expansion to Fort Mason. They gambled their fundraising goals on a loan leveraged against the school's Chestnut Street campus—the buildings, the artworks, and the livelihoods of its community members.

Their failure to follow through on this promise first left students and faculty to shoulder the burden. Now they want to remove and sell a landmark work of art to compensate for their shortfall. This reckless so-called "philanthropy" needs to be stopped, and this site-specific mural must be protected from their negligence.

Students have paid the price for this debt by covering high tuition with student loans. Faculty have paid the price by enduring stagnant salaries and the indignity of part-time, precarious adjunct positions year after year. And SFAI's ongoing inability to support and retain significant representation of faculty and staff of color has been an unacknowledged loss for San Francisco's entire arts community.

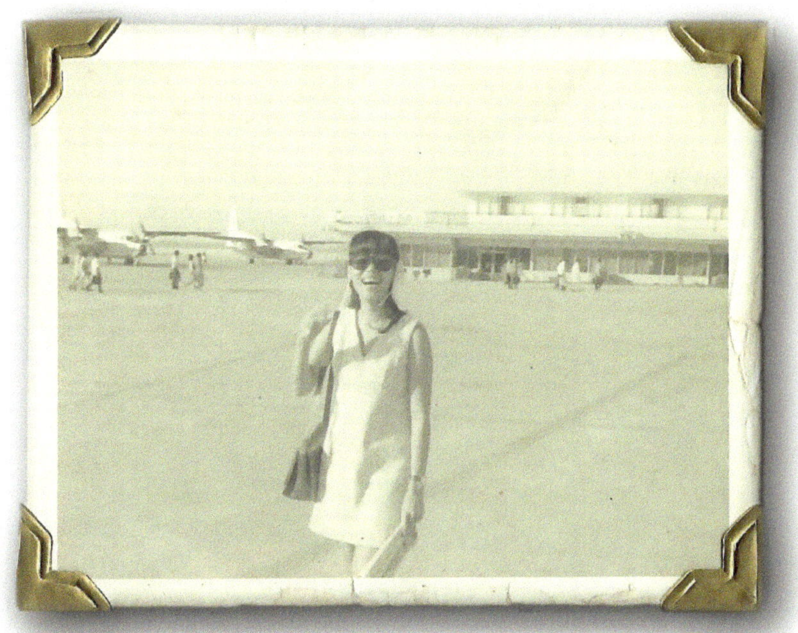

My mom, Angelita Miranda de Leon, laughing at the airport circa 1969.

These so-called "trustees" left a gaping hole in a deeply important institution of learning—gutting a community that has served San Francisco and the creation of art around the world for 150 years. Only they know why they abandoned and now try to obscure their fiduciary responsibilities. Someone should really investigate that. Seventy adjuncts laid-off, three hundred students forced out. And now the removal and sale of this monumental work of art? These are considerable costs for philanthropic hubris.

This mural is a testament to the purpose of art and the importance of essential workers by one of the world's most celebrated artists of color. To use it to cover and compensate for derelictions of duty by SFAI's trustees is unethical, and it's an unforgiveable slap in the face to every artist of color that has ever called San Francisco home.

A year after those remarks, I finally signed SFAI's Adjunct Faculty Union's second Collective Bargaining Agreement, while my mom was on her deathbed.

* * *

Showing signs of stroke, my mother went into the emergency room on January 1, 2022 just as the winter Omicron wave began a rapid upward climb of infection, illness, and death. My mother endured 10 days alone in the hospital due to heightened COVID protocols while her stroke expanded, shutting down her ability to swallow, speak, or move. After about a week, she was still fully cognizant, but had irrecoverably lost almost complete control of her body. My mother's always clear and oft repeated advanced health care directives were invoked. The hospital removed her IV and feeding tubes and discharged her into hospice care. My mother came home to die.

The eldest of twelve siblings, Angelita Miranda de Leon was the first of our family to immigrate to California from the Philippines, and she was the first to pass away here. She was a bridge for multiple generations of people to the Bay Area and a path breaker into Silicon Valley wealth. And she did it with so much style and joy. She was a woman of courage with many talents and complex intelligence. Her lessons were profound to the very end.

Through her marriage to my father, my mother left for the US in the 1970s. Marcos-era social and economic sanctions against Aquino supporters had rendered my grandfather largely unemployable and made my mother, his oldest child, a key strategic breadwinner.

After her arrival, my mother adopted a mantle of casual Republicanism, professing to support Reagan and later Trump, in what appeared to me as a kind of strategic drag. Superficial but seemingly earnest, it was subconscious self-defense against American sexism and racism through the pretense that they didn't matter. My mother would succeed through effort and assimilation. She would adapt to the system as she found it, simulate the terms, reap and redistribute the rewards.

In her heart and actions, my mother was a kind of communist. She dedicated her life to maintaining strong, mutual, interdependent social relations. As someone who had known hunger and need, she loved to give, especially food. Thanksgiving was her favorite holiday. She would prepare and cook for weeks, and invite anyone and everyone to the most wonderful tables of food. Ask the thousands of people across the world that she has fed in her lifetime.

She was impatient with superficial spiritual or political gestures. "Always talking, talking, just talking!" she would say. She understood that shared meals nourish strong spiritual and material communities. My mother aspired to a world where everyone's stomach was full. "Did you eat yet, anak? What did you like?"

Over time, I grew to understand, even if I did not agree, that the ratchet demagoguery of Fox News Republicanism soothed her fears, simplified complex colonial histories, and affirmed her successful assimilation. But it did not resolve the underlying crisis.

Accessing the dream of economic opportunity on those terms turned her repeatedly against immigrants, against women, against the poor, against people of color—against herself. I saw the toll this double consciousness took on her, and in the end, I think the contradictions killed her. They exhausted her, they isolated her. She couldn't bear them alone and she could not ask for help.

More than any other person, my mom's way is the closest to my own code, though not my politics. Her courage and determination shaped me as much as her laugh, the way she sweeps the floor, rests her feet, or reads the room. Her way is the strongest force—innate—and, therefore, that which I test and resist, and embody most deliberately in my own way. Same. Different. How to be.

The weeks of my mother's hospitalization and hospice care were unlike any other. Her dying initiated me into an unforgettable place of timelessness and immanence. Alongside our culture, our technology, our medicine, we are still deeply wired wild mammals.

Two years of pandemic frustrations reached a peak of fury. I could not bear to know that my mother was forced to be alone. Cortisol and adrenaline flooded my body. My legs, chest, and shoulders ached with grief and rage. I was as tense as the pulled-back string of a bow, quivering with the constant restraint of fight or flight reflexes, ready to protect my dying mother with all my sharpness and strength.

For days and nights on end, I did not need much food or sleep. My hearing and vision became exceptionally acute. I was connected to alternative sources of energy. It came to me

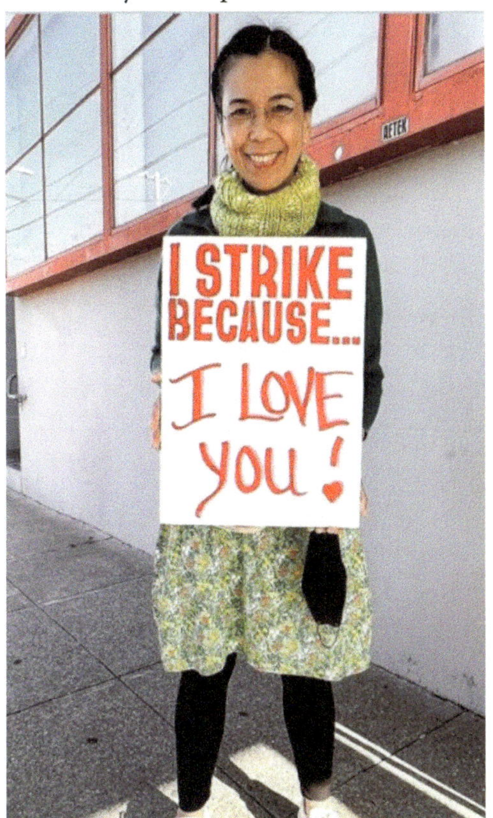

Photo by Ana Llorente, @1dollaraminute

On strike with CCA Staff
& Adjunct Faculty Union,
February 8, 2022.

from my mother, the house she lay in, my cells, our family—her brothers and sisters, my cousins, our children, our ancestors. It came from the land, the sky, the sea, the stars, our memories, and our love. From the Philippines, now we were here. How to be. I was attuned to her and everything around us on a molecular level. Raw wild human life. While it was without a doubt the most difficult thing I have ever endured, it was also the most beautiful and life affirming.

Weeks after she died, I walked the picket line at the California College of the Arts, to push for staff and adjunct contracts there. What I see happening at CCA seems to be a slow motion version of what happened at SFAI. I see white people, high-salaried administrators, institutional debt, high tuition, shallow marketing, uneven risks, increasing precarity, and greater obstacles for those who have always faced systematic exclusion. I keep asking others to tell me how CCA is different from SFAI and they can't.

As Andrea Steves said, "It's time to plan for the increased difficulty of planning."

As summer approaches, life feels more generous, the risks more tolerable. How will Year Three unfold when equilibrium is more clearly the exception than the rule? One sign: Union membership is on the rise. It is increasingly clear that we will have to take care of each other.

I've recorded these events to set down my rage, as a guide, a memorial to what went wrong, for whom and why. To remember where in a crisis it was possible to find strength and imagination, courage and care. The heart of the matter is not an ivory tower. It is a mystery dressed in molten lava, earth, sky, stars, and tides. My mother was a bridge. In planning ahead, I strive to be more present, to handle the future like a newborn—wild, gentle, fragile and strong. How to be. This is what I hope to remember most.

Elaine Chu & Marina Perez-Wong

Twin Walls Mural Company

PAINTING OUR DREAMS BIG!

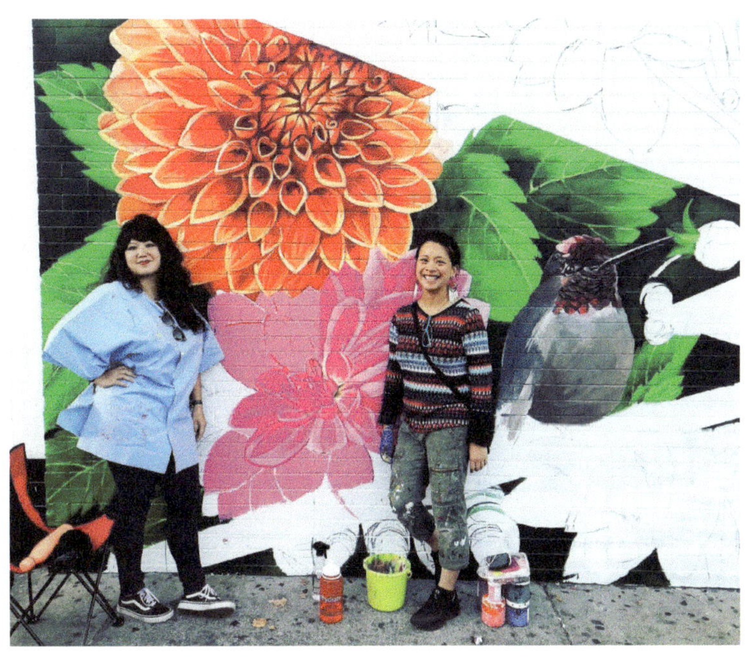

Elaine Chu and Marina Perez-Wong formed
the mural arts collaboration Twin Walls Mural Company
in 2013. Using the power of visual narratives to
capture and reflect a community's history,
struggles, dreams, and intentions,
they have designed and painted over 30 murals in
the Bay Area and New York City. They work like twins
when painting, and ideas flow like water between them.
They work to heal past and present trauma and
to transform the viewer and themselves
through visual language, color, and collaboration.
Though they may be small in stature, they paint their dreams BIG!
"The smaller the world expects us to be, the larger
the surfaces we'll paint!"
twinwallsmuralcompany.com

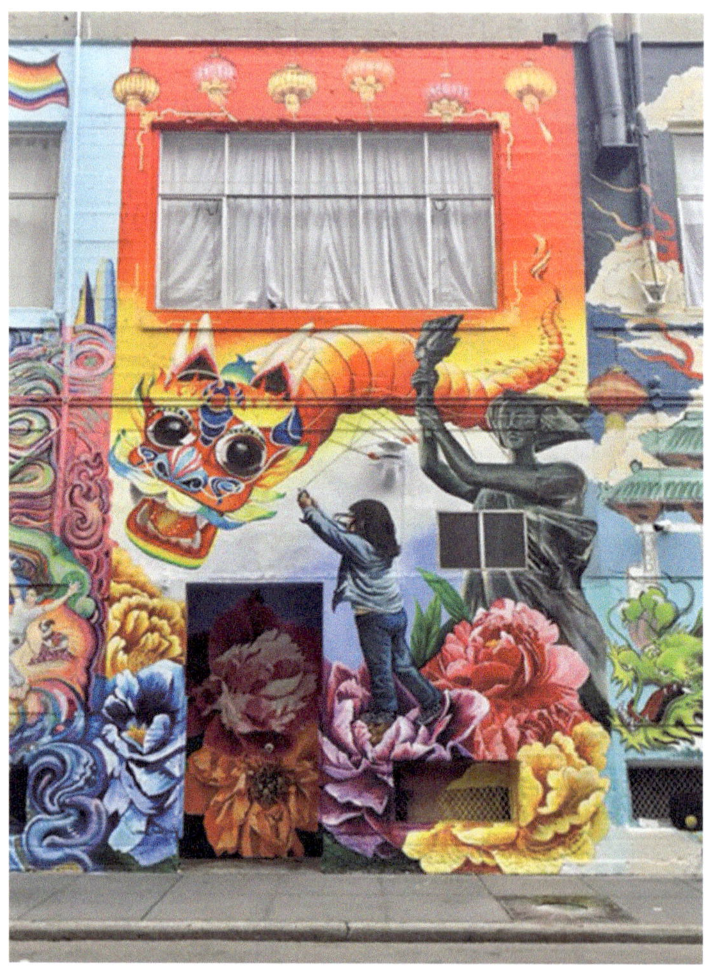

"Hope, Act, The Fight For Freedom" 2017
In collaboration with Chevalier Partners and Interstice Architects.
Sponsored by the San Francisco Mayor's Office of Economic and Workforce
Development and the Lower Polk Neighbors' Association,
Hemlock Alley, San Francisco CA.

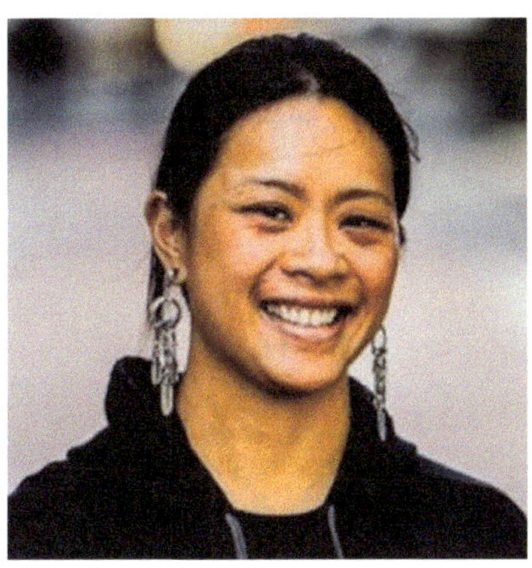

MY VOICE IS IN MY PAINTING
Elaine Chu

I consider myself lucky to have been born and raised in San Francisco because my perspective on life has been shaped by the unique diversity and creativity energy that this city cultivates. I was raised by my mom, Lai Wah Chan, an immigrant and single mother, who worked all the time to support me and my sister. I struggled with finding my identity, often feeling not Chinese enough or American enough. It mirrored my mother's own upbringing which was unique in that she was born and raised in Zanzibar. She often told me she spoke broken Chinese, broken English, and broken Swahili. We were a family that didn't quite fit in anywhere, always outsiders.

My mother is naturally creative and encouraged my artistic side which provided me the outlet I needed to express myself. Drawing made me feel seen, giving me a skill that I could use to make friends and build my confidence. I attended School of the Arts High School where I met Marina Perez-Wong, my best friend and Twin Walls mural collaborator. One summer I interned at Precita Eyes Muralists, and that experience changed my life. I had grown up seeing murals around San Francisco, but being immersed in the world of muralism shaped my entire foundation and led me on the path I am today. I found an art community that was patient enough to teach me and accept me as I was. I learned how to collaborate and work with others because painting on such a large scale requires a team. Precita Eyes is in the heart of San Francisco's Mission District and there I felt at home. There I was surrounded by murals, color, music, food, community, and family. I owe much of my growth as a muralist to my mentor Susan Cervantes who not only patiently guided me in the art of mural making but taught me how to work with and guide community.

By working and painting with different communities, I learned that I was not alone. Through shared stories and experiences, I learned more about the city I grew up in and the beautiful people that make up the Bay Area.

I've spent the last 12 years painting murals professionally, and with each mural I find myself rediscovering and embracing my own unique identity. The power of art drives me and gives me purpose, to continue to create monumental public art that is healing as well as preserves what is important in this world. I believe in painting what I want to see in the world, to make a statement, give a voice to the marginalized and to uplift and inspire the viewer, especially the next generation of artists. Marina and I share the same outlook on life and together our mural collaborations are explorations on life, growth, and the connections that link us. With each project we are able to explore different aspects of ourselves in every stage of our lives.

I finally feel seen the way I want to be seen. My voice is in my painting. My goal now as a mother is to break the chains of trauma that bind us to oppression and self-hatred. In the hope that she and other children will live in a world where they can be seen as they want to be seen.

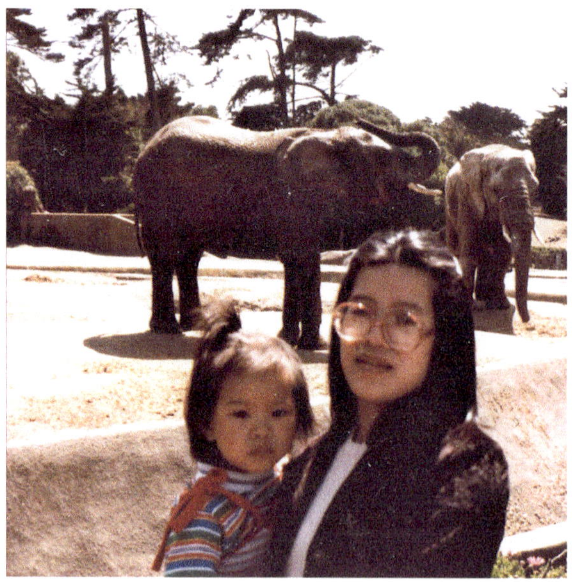

Elaine Chu with her mom.

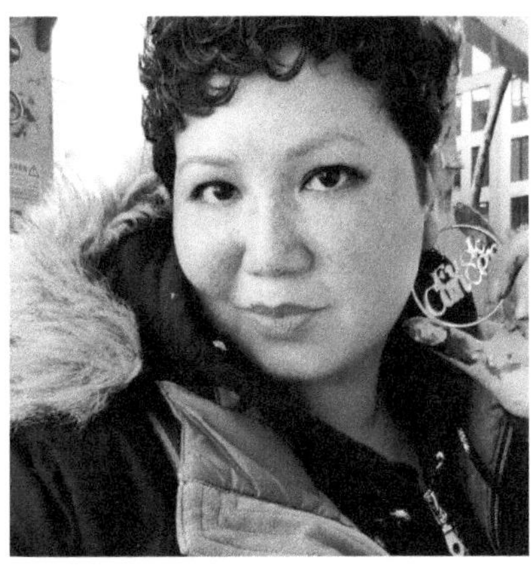

DAUGHTER OF THE MISSION
Marina Perez-Wong

I have a lot of incredible formative influences, but my greatest is definitely my mom. Before you go writing that off as being cheesy and thinking everyone thinks their mom is the best, let me explain. I grew up with a young single parent who survived my having a childhood cancer that almost killed me twice. Well, actually three times now that I've been diagnosed again a couple of years ago. Justine Perez is an incredible artist and human (though she'd say that the two are married). Beyond having survived a lot of abuse, hate, and miseducation, she's maintained her strong sense of spirit and childlike fervor. Growing up, she had many jobs that influenced me, but two stand out the most. She was a photojournalist who was invested in her subjects and a teacher who deeply cared for her students. To this day she continues to work on helping her community, healing her family, and being a student of life.

I'd say this actually began with my grandfather, though, who learned it from his parents. He taught us all what it meant to be a proud Chicano, to learn from history, and fight for our culture and people. He took me to some of my first protests, which were for the union and Cesar Chavez. We were proud to stop eating grapes and strawberries. He taught me about Jazz (he was an upright bass player), health (he was a marathon runner), and how to have a sense of humor. He was so incredibly charming that he could strike up a two hour conversation with a telemarketer and did on several occasions. Really, from all my immediate family—including my real aunties and my mom's best friends who helped raise me—I've learned that the capacity to love and laugh is strength. I also learned to forgive, and got what work ethic really means (unfortunately often to a fault).

As a kid, my home life was for the most part solid. It's not to say that I didn't have my own set of challenges, but in my eyes, I had it easy. We were poor but I wasn't made aware of it until I was in high school. We were rich with what mattered, and I never lacked for anything. My mom and my family would always provide for anything I needed. I grew up in the hospital on and off until I was five years old due to a rare childhood cancer called a Wilms tumor. It was at the hospital that I learned to draw even before I could speak. My mom says it was my way of communicating, but I also think it was my way of escape.

When I finally did come home, we lived in the Mission District. I imagine that coming from the hospital, it looked like a colorful paradise—at least on the walls. My mom had many friends who were artists, muralists, writers, activists, and musicians. One of them, Johanna Poethig, was my very first teacher and is still one of my greatest artistic influences. She taught me to fill the page, which has ultimately translated to filling a wall. Mike Rios, Michael Roman, and Carlos Loarca were also friends of my mom. She would take me around to their murals or to view their work, and she encouraged me to ask them my little art-nerd questions.

There are plenty more influences that I could bring up in this context, but I have to include the Mujeres Muralistas, Susan Cervantes and Juana Alicia as my greatest influences. The narrative nature of all of their work made a sizable impression on me as a kid and a youth—especially Juana's, which reflected the perspective of women—particularly from the lens of a Chicana living through it all. From Susan (whom Elaine and I call our art mom), I've learned

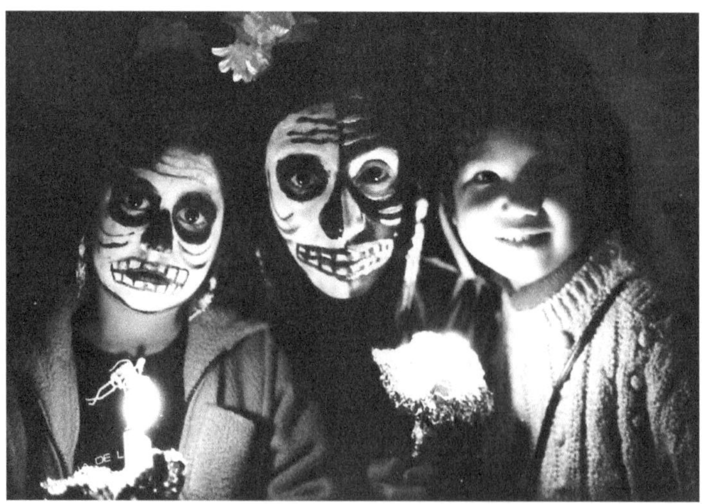

Justine Perez photo of Marina with her Buena Vista teacher
and her daughter at Día de los Muertos.

the importance of community on a greater scale. I've learned that it's our responsibility as visual storytellers and magic makers to be the visual voice for those who have no voice or are overlooked. Also that we have the power to help change whatever we don't like by using our visual art as magic. She's also taught us the importance of educating and supporting youth. But I think the greatest gem she's passed down as a mentor is that she taught me how to collaborate. This is by far the most challenging skill a community muralist must have. Many people have asked me how I do it, as if they can't even fathom it.

Growing up, my elementary school (Buena Vista) was great—full of Mission perspectives, that is to say, community minded, diverse, and full of art. However middle school was hard. It was there that I learned about divisions of race and culture. In high school and college I learned more about these divisions, along with the barriers of class. Between the standardized tests, linear, molded, academic methods of education and being a mixed-race art nerd Mission girl (before it was cool), I never felt like I fit in anywhere. I was lucky enough in high school to meet two people who would change my life forever. Elaine C. Chu. My better half. The yin to my yang, the sugar to my salt! We both went to School of the Arts (now Ruth Asawa SOTA) and had Marsha Pannone as our senior art teacher. Both of these incredible humans have taught me to appreciate, love, and trust my own lens. They taught me to value myself as a whole, and also planted the aspiration to be like them, some of the greatest humans possible.

"It was scary, but life was good, in my neighborhood"

— Raphael Saadiq

I grew up in the heart of the Mission, which is another way of saying that I grew up on the dividing line between two gangs. Being a survivor of life, I didn't understand (and still don't) the violence that ate at my neighborhood. I wasn't allowed past the end of my block. Girls were getting raped, people got jumped, robbed, there were drive-bys, drugs,

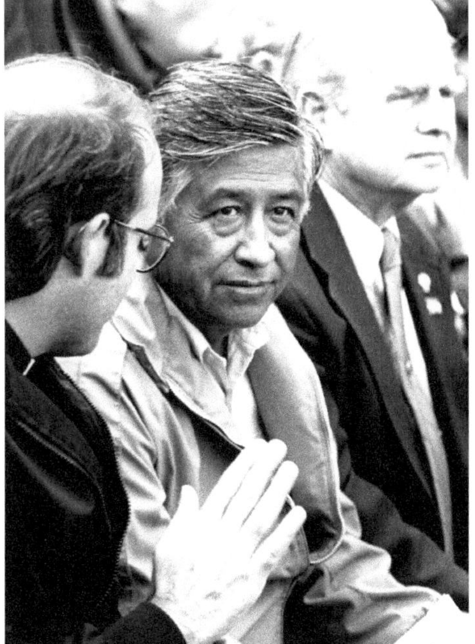

Justine Perez photo of Cesar Chavez.

and poverty was peak. This was a very real part of what it was like in the 1980s and early '90s. On the other hand, there was people pride, a strong sense of community, survivorship joy and triumph, and color everywhere. With other kids from the neighborhood, I went to an arts and crafts class down the block from where I lived. It was taught by Kate Connell, who was an incredible influence on my teaching later in life. I went to Jamestown Community Center after school. So many Mission kids in one spot. My mom helped gut the building so that the Mission Cultural Center could open. One of my aunts and uncles started Carnaval with their friends. We danced in the processions and celebrated Dia de los Muertos together. We could walk down any street in our neighborhood and run into friends or people we knew. This was home.

As a child and youth, I used to have the "bluest eye" syndrome, yearning for the white, middle class world. I used to accept things and feel helpless against a lot of obstacles. Now I realize this acceptance and hopelessness is implanted by the system of oppression. Now I realize I can help change things even if it's only through my craft, showing up, and/or putting my energy into positive change, however small.

I could easily say that one day I volunteered, and the next I felt responsible for helping youth come up and access knowledge that my friends and I couldn't

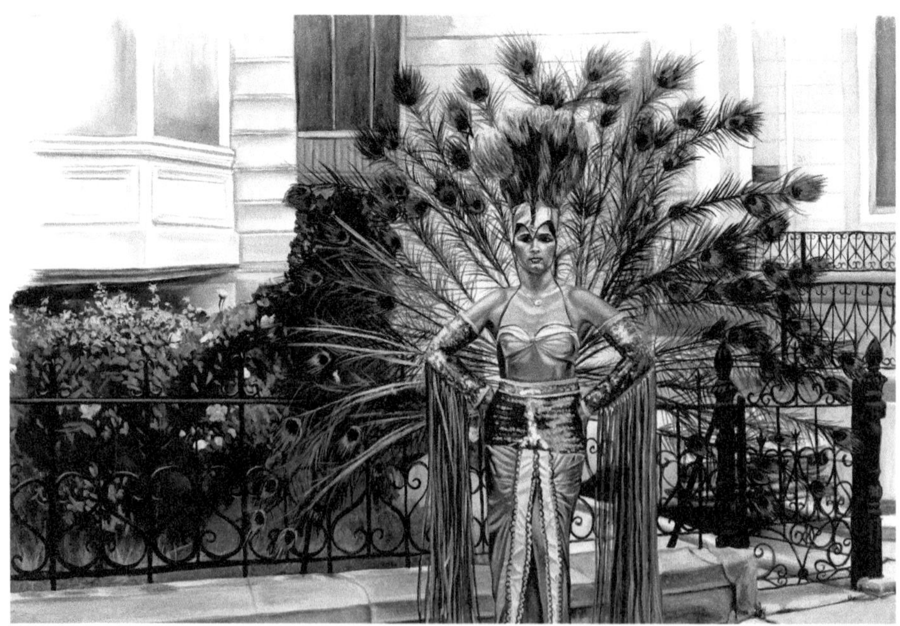

Marina Perez-Wong, "Hill Street" acrylic on paper, c. 2005.
Margaret DeJesus, a family friend in her regalia for San Francisco's first Carnaval, of which she was one of the organizers.

afford. That's partially true, but realistically, my family and my friends and their families were all rooted in an activist mindset (even if we didn't know that's what it was). We are just following our hearts and trying to do what is right for the betterment of society. We care about the oppressed, the overlooked, and the underappreciated because there are too many of those in comparison with the 1% who clearly are only about themselves.

It's incredibly hard to balance life. We might make our work look easy, but it's taxing to give so much energy all the time. Not just on the wall, but in the creation of the initial design, in talking to people as we work, in executing it, and then in letting it go and readjusting ourselves. There is no other way, though. The alternative would just be paint on a wall, divorced from heart and community—and there's already too much of that going around. Like fighting cancer, I just have to take it day by day and aim for the positive. Some days are easier than others, but I'm always growing, always learning. I make a lot of mistakes and sometimes I beat myself up about it, and on my better days I remember to forgive myself and move forward. Try not to repeat that mistake. I realize I'm best when I listen to my intuition and I remember that I have people who will always have my back no matter what. Especially my twinsie, Elaine.

What I do now: I'm a muralist on my better days; an educator when I'm fortunate enough; and the rest of the time, an artistically heartfelt human just trying to heal, be balanced, and project positive energy into others and into the cosmos.

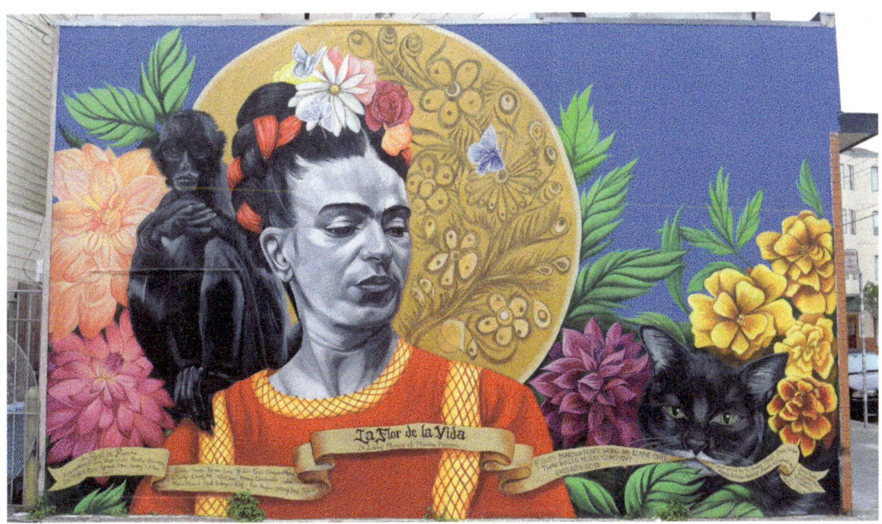

"La Flor De La Vida" 2015.
25th Street between Valencia Street and Bartlett Street.

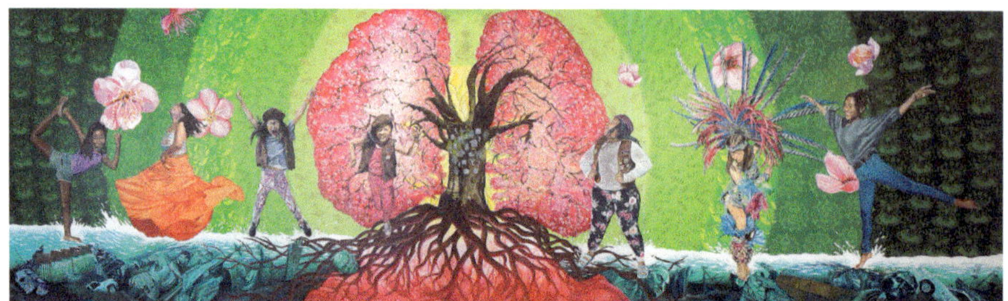

"Our Ancestors' Wildest Dreams" 2020. Assisted by Priya Handa and Lisa Max, San Francisco Museum of Modern Art, 151 3rd Street, San Francisco CA.

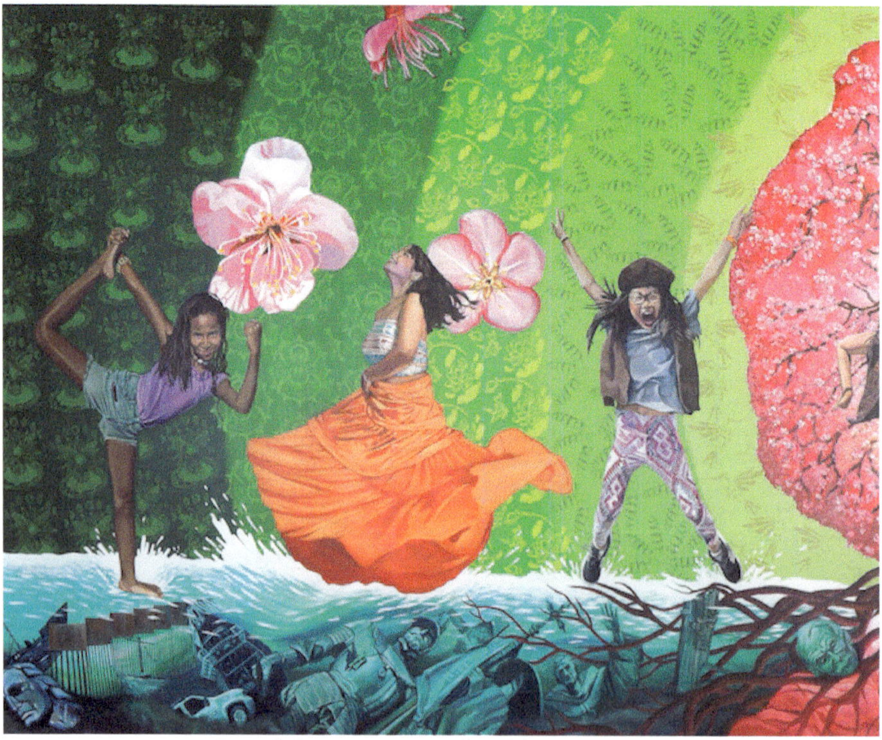

Detail, "Our Ancestors' Wildest Dreams."

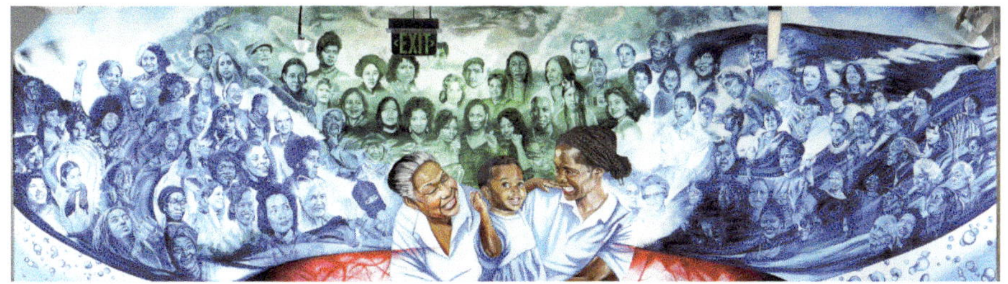

"She Inspires Me—Bringing Her to Light" 2018.
Twitter HQ, San Francisco CA.

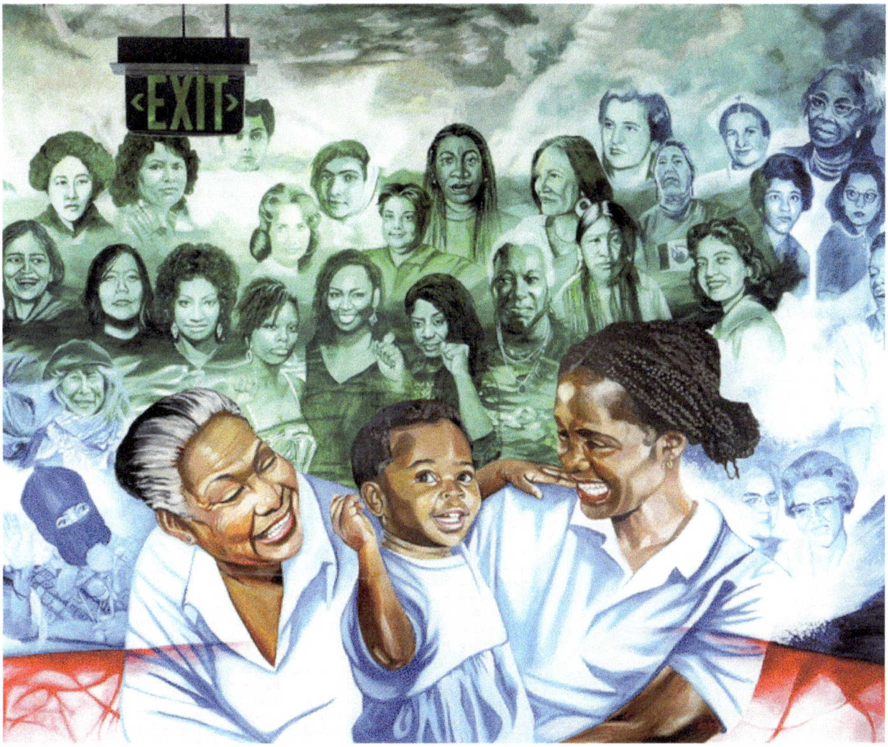

Detail, "She Inspires Me—Bringing Her to Light."

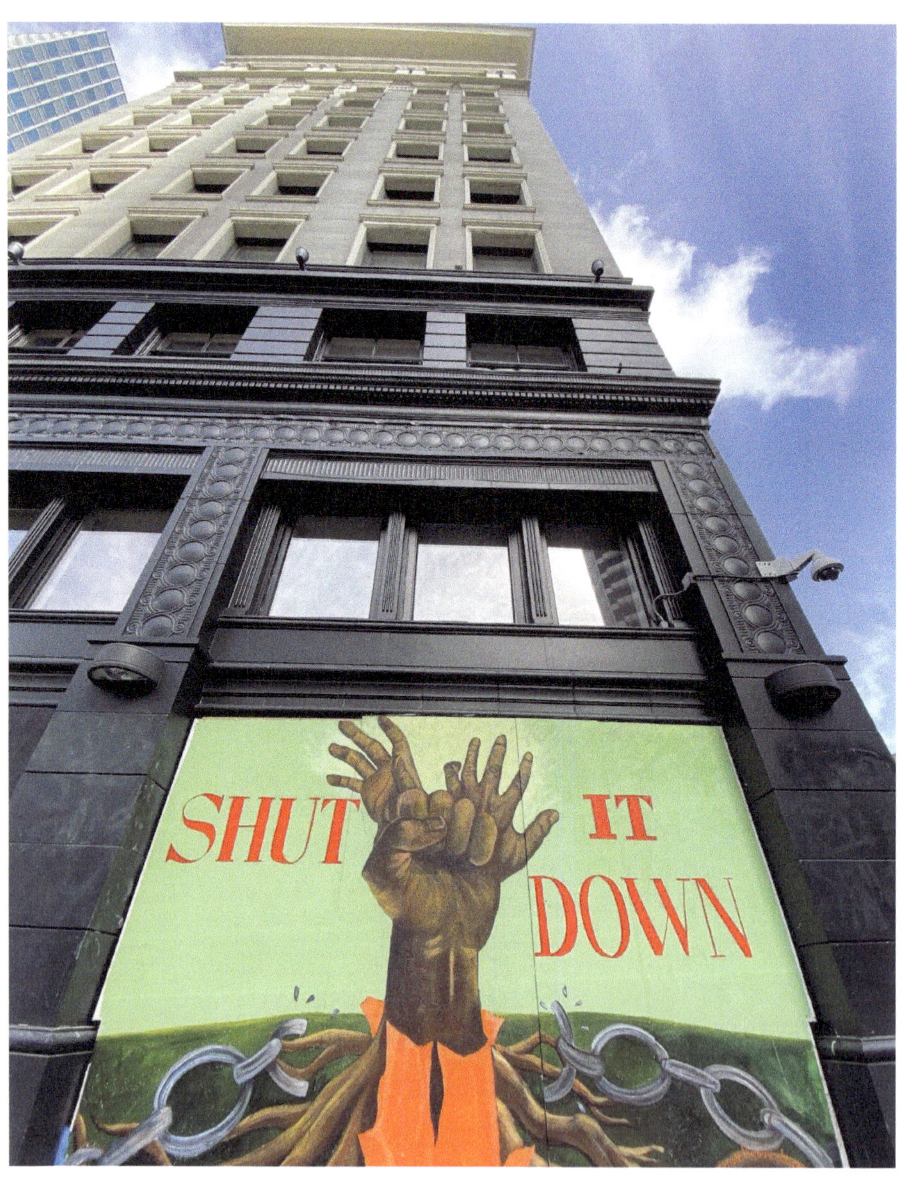

"Shut it Down" 2020.
In support of Black Lives Matter
14th and Broadway, Oakland CA.

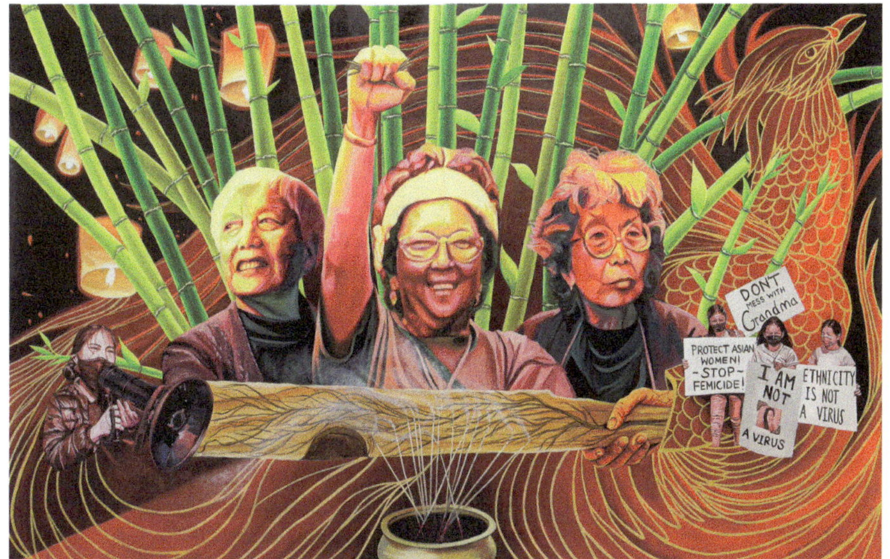

"From the Ashes of a Fiery Red Revolution Will Arise a Third World Phoenix"
2021.

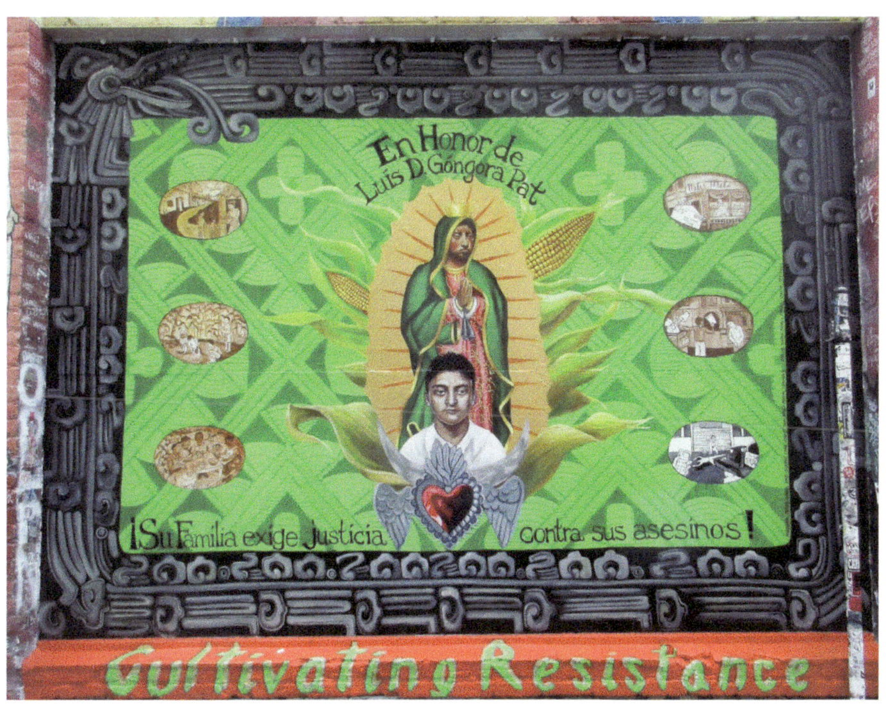

"Justice for Luis Gongora" 2018.
Clarion Alley, San Francisco CA.

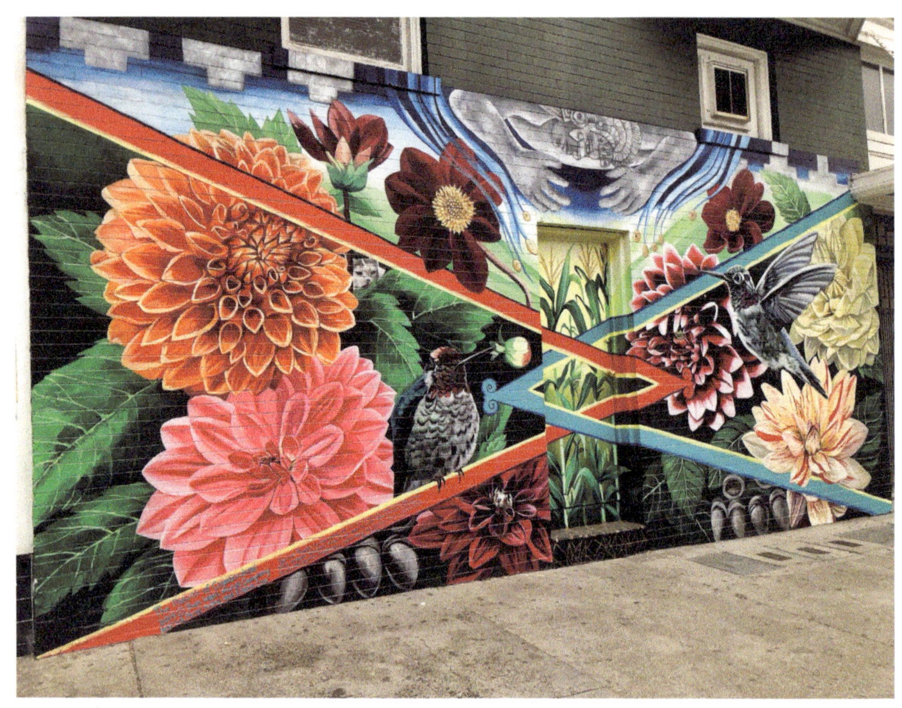

Elaine Chu and Marina Perez-Wong (Twin Walls Mural Company),
"The Rebirth of Coyolxauhqui," 2019.
Sponsored by the San Francisco Arts Commission and
Intersection for the Arts, 18th and Valencia Streets, San Francisco, CA.

André Le Mont Wilson
TRAJECTORY

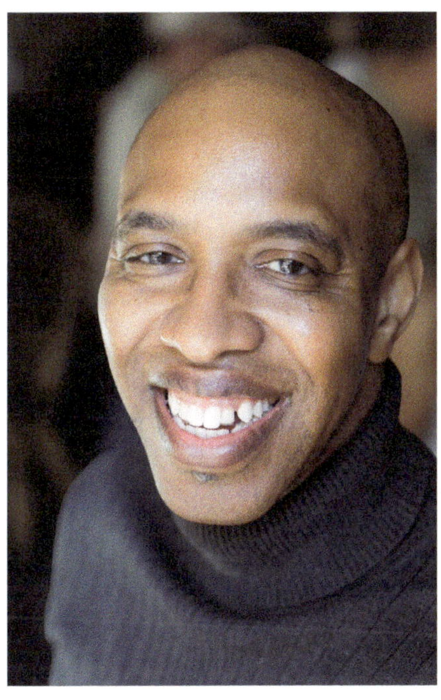

André Le Mont Wilson is the winner of the 2022
Newfound Prose Prize. His chapbook, *Hauntings*,
interweaves racial violence past and present and will be
published by Newfound in the spring of 2023.
Essential Truths: The Bay Area in Color,
Civil Liberties United: Diverse Voices from the San Francisco Bay Area,
Ina: A Queer Erotic Anthology, and
Changing Harm to Harmony: Bullies & Bystanders Project
have anthologized his work locally.
Forthcoming publications include *The Vincent Brothers Review,*
RFD Magazine, and *Obsidian Literature & Arts*
of the African Diaspora. He teaches storytelling and writing
to adults with disabilities in Oakland.

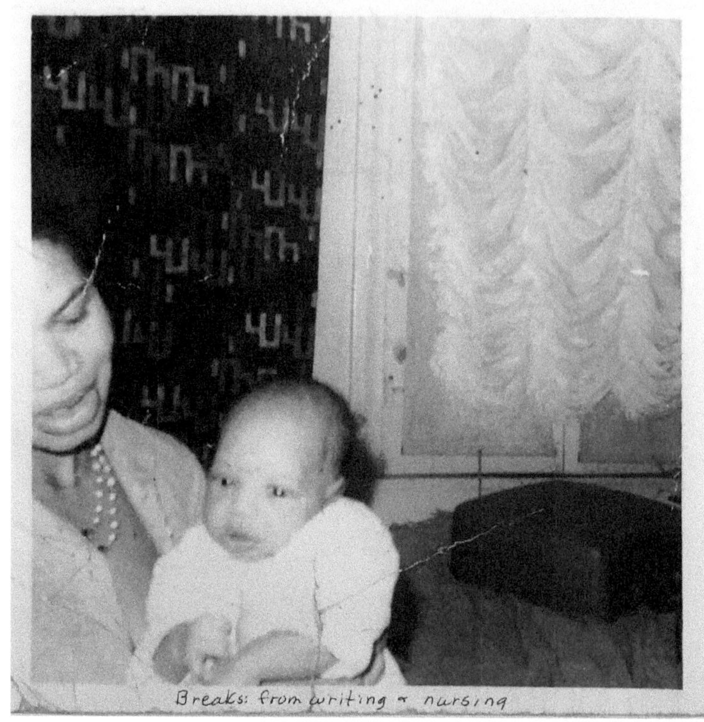

TRAJECTORY
André Le Mont Wilson

1: the curve that a body (such as a planet or comet in its orbit or a
   rocket) describes in space
2: a path, progression, or line of development resembling a
   physical trajectory // an upward career *trajectory*

—www.merriam-webster.com

My mother, Jessie Lee Dawson-Wilson, was the most significant formative influence on my life's trajectory as a creative person of color. She determined my culture, community, and spiritual values. I have written such a large body of work about or inspired by her that it warrants its own focus. Nearly a quarter of the poems and essays I had published for five years between 2017 and 2022 featured my mother in a starring or supportive role.

2022 also marked the tenth anniversary of her death from a heart attack at seventy-five in Los Angeles in 2012. Ten years later, I can now discern my life's trajectory since her death launched me as a poet and writer. Just as NASA mathematician Katherine Johnson was the "hidden figure" behind astronaut John Glenn's orbit around the Earth, my mother was the "hidden figure" behind my orbit.

I will make the hidden known and show how she contributed to my becoming a writer by sharing several published essays and poems. These may not be my best pieces, but they are the ones that tell a fuller spectrum of my evolving life trajectory. I will introduce each by describing the calculations I made in creating the piece and how my mother impacted them. I will follow each piece with a brief afterword describing its legacy.

DEAD BUTTERFLY AND SLEEPING GIANT

Introduction: One of the things I did to process my mother's death was read through her letters to me. I bought a special file box, sat on the floor, read her notes, and filed them chronologically. I discovered a wealth of material I could turn into poems and essays. I also found her consistently urging me to write after I had stopped writing when I left home in 1993. She had described me as a "sleeping giant." In one letter, she predicted that I would "wake up between 45 and early fifties." I found her prediction eerily prescient, given that I only resumed writing at forty-eight after she passed. These letters also created a narrative arc. She envisioned a clear trajectory for me long before I saw the path myself.

She was also a poet, writer, and teacher. She taught everything from haiku to grade school students to creative writing to college students. In 1984, she self-published a haiku chapbook, *Pearls of Wisdom*, featuring her distinctive four-line, seventeen-syllable haiku. *The Four Seasons* (Peter Pauper Press: 1958), a collection of four-line haiku, probably influenced it. Perhaps sensing her end, she quoted her haiku in a letter a year before her death:

> This butterfly,
> whose silent wings
> no longer sing,
> quietly says, "Thank you"

Five years after her death, I answered with a haibun that combined prose poetry and haiku with details quoted from her letters.

Dead Butterfly And Sleeping Giant

Mom told me once, twice, a thousand times, the story of how my kindergarten teacher had visited our home. She had interrupted the poet: "Mrs. Wilson, Andre's not learning at the same pace as his peers. He's quiet in class and doesn't know his numbers. Maybe it would be best to hold him back a year to repeat kindergarten."

My mother led my teacher to a doorjamb where I had crayoned numbers from one to ten: "Andre knows his numbers. Just because he doesn't write them on paper in class doesn't mean he doesn't know. The boy's a sleeping giant and will learn at his own pace."

My teacher retreated from our home and advanced me to first grade.

As I grew, I groaned whenever Mom told me this story: Mom, I'm not a sleeping giant. I'm now a man of below-average height. I want to be normal and not a poet like you, scribbling poems on paper scraps that clutter the house like confetti at a convention.

Like Jonah fleeing the presence of the Lord, I fled home and got a nine-to-five job: I don't want to be a poet like you, Mom.

When she called, she asked: "Have you been doing any writing?"

"The only writing I do is type the staff meeting minutes."

Undeterred, she wrote: "I still say you're a Sleeping Giant. Look out, World!"

Closing her letter, I thought: "Yeah, right."

Years later, Mom wrote again: "Expect some changes or a Divine Stir. We late bloomers usually wake up between 45 and early fifties."

Closing her letter, I thought: "Yeah, right."

She then gave me a gift subscription to *Poets & Writers* and died.

Several months later, at the age of forty-eight, I started writing poetry.

I reopened and reread Mom's letters: How did you know I would start writing after you died? I did not believe your Cassandra-like prophecy. Not until I felt poetry in my heart, lived it in my body, and scribbled it with fingers bloodied from their thrust into your wound.

Mom, you possessed the faith of a butterfly. You laid your egg, well-knowing that you will never live to see your child emerge from his cocoon and fly.

> after laying eggs
> butterfly quivers and dies
> wind blows confetti

Afterword: At one in the morning in February 2022, I logged onto a Zoom event. Marcellus Nealy, a Black poet living and teaching in Japan, greeted me from the crowded Tokyo bar Haretara Sora Ni Mame Maite half a world away. "Konbanwa," he said into his laptop camera. He and co-editor Biankah Bailey had accepted two of my poems about my mother for publication in the anthology *Umoja: ToPoJo Excursions: Black Diaspora Edition*. And now, I would read my poem "In My Backyard" before a virtual audience in Japan. The previous week, I had performed an

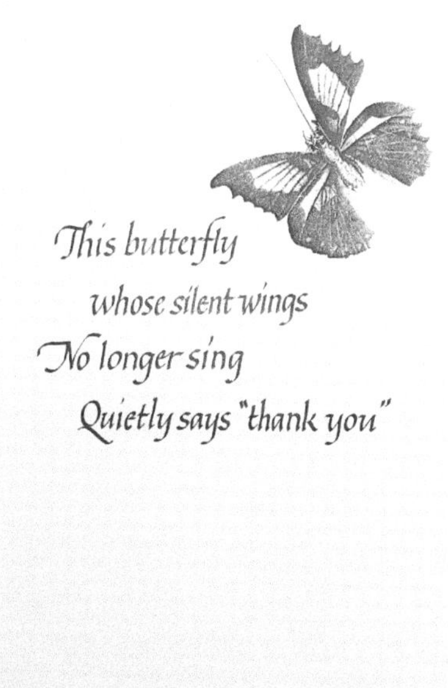

African American folktale before a virtual audience in India.

When I reflect on my trajectory as a poet, I owe a debt to my mother. She wanted to travel the world, and she wrote about universal themes. This yearning inspired her to study Japanese culture, taking up brush painting, haiku, and home decorating. While this yearning may seem incongruous for a Black woman who grew up as a sharecropper's daughter in Texas, she spent many afternoons imagining the world beyond the cotton patch. When the *Tokyo Poetry Journal* put out a submission call for Black poets, writers, and artists worldwide, I answered.

HAUNTINGS

Introduction: To this day, I have not watched the entire video of officer Derek Chauvin murdering George Floyd by kneeling on his neck. I had too many of my own traumas to process. And as more reports arose about police killing one unarmed Black person after another, I simply could not absorb any more and function reasonably. Instead of hitting the streets to protest, I studied my mother's written and oral narratives of lynchings. Seeing a correlation between her stories and what is happening today, in the summer of 2020, I wrote a series of five flash essays. Each one focused on a different lynching story she told me. Published in *Quiet Lightning* in 2021 and the title essay in a yet-to-be-published prose chapbook, "Hauntings" is one of these stories.

Hauntings

When she was a girl, one night before or after World War II, my mother saw a ghost. For whatever reason, perhaps a sixth sense, perhaps chance, she looked out the window of her sharecropper's shack in Somerville, East Texas, and spied a figure gliding across a field. The figure of a man. A Black man.

Fuzzy around the edges, the cloud-like apparition appeared to run, but its feet made no sound. They touched no ground. With wide eyes, the girl tracked its movement.

Years later, when Mom told me this story, I asked, "How do you know it was a ghost?"

"Well," she said, "there was a fence at the end of the field. The ghost didn't climb the fence. It passed through it."

I instinctively knew the ghost was that of a runaway enslaved man who didn't make it. Whether he was running for refuge with an eastern Indian tribe or south to the Mexico border, he ran during a time before fences subdivided the plantation into sharecroppers' plots. Although years have passed since Mom told me this story, I still cry when I think of it. I question not whether she saw something or imagined it. I question not whether it was smoke or shadow. I don't care whether the ghost was real. A ghost is a series of unanswered questions. I will address the questions I have to the ghost himself:

Why are you still here? The Civil War ended. Juneteenth came for every enslaved person but you. No doubt, if I were to return to Texas today and stand on the plot of land where my mother's shack once stood, you would still cross that field, night after night. Why? Something is unresolved. I'm struck that my mother's story is essentially the same as today's stories. The places, names, and details change, but they are the same story. A rope around a neck; a knee on a neck. Blood on the earth; blood on the street. A jogger who never made it home; an enslaved man who never made it to freedom. These are all the same story. It seems that you, that we are doomed to repeat the same story, day after day, century after century. You, we are stuck in a loop. No, even worse, a Möbius strip. We keep going around and around, repeating the same story. Sad to say, a fleeing Black man can still be shot in the back today. I confuse which century I'm in—the nineteenth or the twenty-first. Is there a way that you, that we can break this cycle that is stronger than the chains that once held you, that once held us?

Violence and racism haunt our land to this day. Must we create new versions of the same old story to tell future generations? Can we tell a new story? Can we create a new ending? Perhaps your hauntings will cease when the living achieve the freedom you ran for.

Afterword: In 2015, after a San Francisco solo performance at the Marsh Theatre of my family's slave narrative, several White audience members came up and thanked me. "They don't teach us about slavery in school," they said. "Your story helped make slavery real."

I was stunned that schools then taught little about slavery. This amnesia that our country suffers motivates me to share my mother's stories. Literary journals have published several of them. *Litro Magazine* published "Hanging from the Family Tree," and *Quiet Lightning* published "Br'er Terrapin." My mother had gathered stories of racial trauma. I am using every tool available to disperse her stories as widely as possible. If I did not have this foundation of family stories, my trajectory as a poet, writer, and activist would be different.

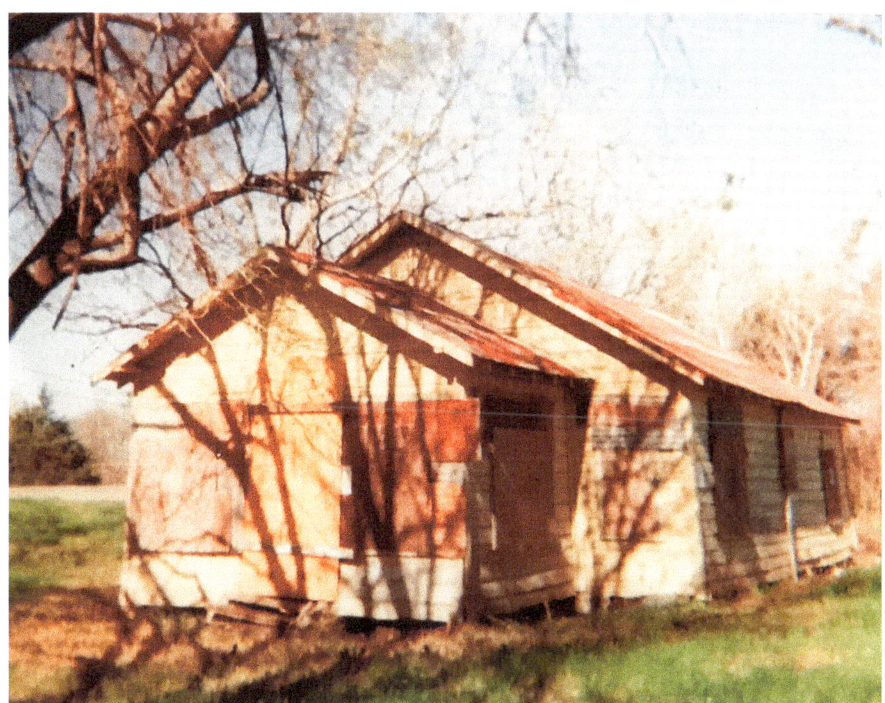

Childhood home of the author's mother in Somerville, Texas, shortly before its demolition for a widened highway, c. 1970.

THIS PLOT

Introduction: In 2019, the *Alexandria Quarterly* held its First Line Poetry Contest for a poem inspired by the first line of a renowned poem. The contest chose as inspiration that year William Carlos Williams' poem "Dedication for a Plot of Ground," which opens with "This plot of ground …"

I can find no plot of ground more worthy of dedication than the plot at the corner of 7th and Brush streets in West Oakland, where her family's apartment once stood. I am keenly aware that my mother lived in Oakland when her family worked in the shipyards during World War II. Long after moving away from West Oakland, she frequently asked me to conduct research at Marcus Books or the African American Museum and Library to help with her writing. I wrote my own dedication poem, which the *Alexandria Quarterly* editors selected and published as one of eleven finalists.

This Plot

This plot of ground,
at the corner of 7th and Brush streets
in West Oakland, welcomed my mother,
nicknamed Yeller Gal,
whose family of Texas sharecroppers
migrated to work in Oakland's shipyards
during World War II.

This plot of ground
provided the first home
for that little Black girl
outside of the Jim Crow South—
a one-bedroom apartment
where her family also slept in the kitchen and the hall
while Yeller Gal and her sister slept in the closet.

This plot of ground
offered this little girl
a closet window so high
she stood on her bed to look out at

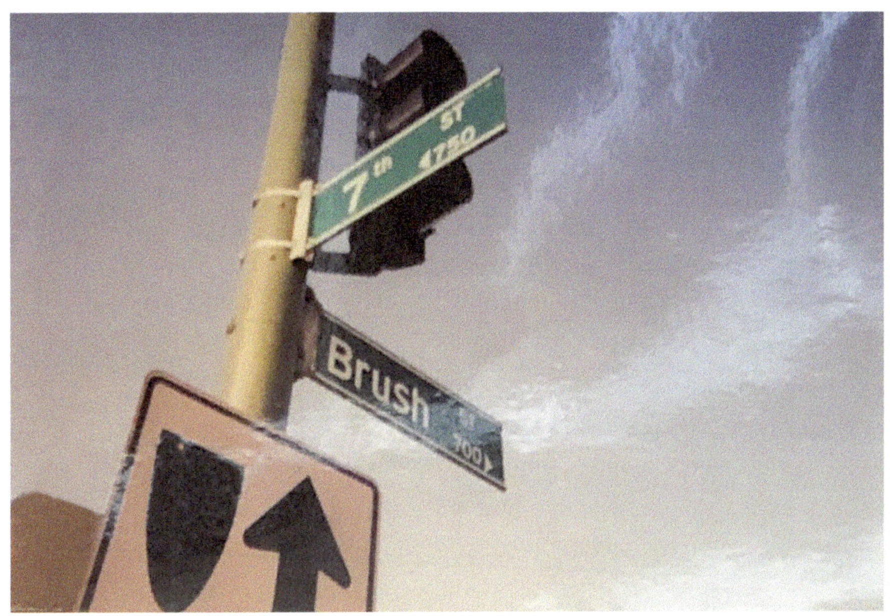

the sailors, shipyard workers, and nightclubbers
who walked up and down 7th Street
to visit the bars, blues clubs, and jazz joints.

This plot of ground
bid farewell to this girl and her family
who moved to the segregated
Harbor Homes Housing Project
next to Moore Shipyard
before returning to Texas after the war
when shipbuilding slowed.

This plot of ground
witnessed the bulldozing of its buildings,
including the girl's first apartment in the state,
to make way for I-980,
leaving nothing
but tree saplings and ivy seedlings
behind the freeway's chain-link fence.

This plot of ground
watched the son of this girl, now grown,
visit to try to surprise her for Christmas
with a photo of her first California home
only to find "there is no there there."
So he photographed the green and white street signs
at the corner of 7th and Brush and gave her that.

This plot of ground
observed the son of this woman, now dead,
make pilgrimages to it
to walk in his mother's footsteps around the block,
to peer through the chain-link fence
at the homeless encampment amid the trees and ivy
where his mother's apartment once stood.
And when he passes it on his way to San Francisco
for his poetry readings, he waves for her blessing.

Afterword: Frequently during the award season, be it Oscar, Grammy, or Tony, several winners will inevitably hold their shiny trophies aloft, look to the ceiling with tearful eyes, and say something to the effect, "I wish my mom and dad were here to see this. I know you're looking down on me. This one's for you. Thank you." The audience gets all choked up, knowing that the departed parent never lived to see their child achieve a dream. They hope that if there is a heaven, the parents will look down on their child with pride and joy.

Such sentimental moments at award shows are so familiar that they are almost cliché. But I get what the award-winners are saying and feeling. Whenever I get published or win an award, I think, "I wish Mom were here to see this." Her absence makes my publishing or winning bittersweet because the one person who inspired me is not here to see my accomplishments. If I had my druthers, I would give up writing if I could have my mother back. But that is not the trajectory she imagined for me. She knew she wasn't going to be around forever. The best that a parent can do as they go to the grave is to plant a seed and hope.

After my mother died, I became suspicious about why *Poets & Writers Magazine* started arriving in my mailbox suddenly when I never subscribed to or read it. I had a hunch and called the company's subscription department in

Palm Coast, Florida. I asked, "Did Jessie Wilson of Sun Valley, California, give me a gift subscription to *Poets & Writer*?"

The clerk checked her computer and said, "Yes."

"When did she give it to me?"

"On December 30, 2011."

I immediately thought *My mother had made a New Year's Eve resolution for me to resume writing.*

"Thank you," I said before hanging up, stunned that my mother knew she was dying way back then, and threw a Hail Mary pass to get me to write again. Maybe she had mentioned the gift subscription to me, and I didn't pay attention.

But when I learned what her dying wish was, I began to dust off and read the growing pile of magazines. Ultimately I began to write and submit. Sometimes I publish more work in one year than she did in her lifetime. But I know I will never be a fraction of the poet, writer, educator, and activist she was. After she lit my ignition, the best I could do was go as far as possible with my writing. That would have made her happy. When her gift subscription ran out in December 2012, I renewed.

Acknowledgments

"Dead Butterfly And Sleeping Giant" was first published in *Failed Haiku: A Journal of English Senryu*, 2019.

"Hauntings" was first published in Quiet Lightning's *sPARKLE + bLINK*, 2021.

"This Plot" was first published in *Alexandria Quarterly*, 2020.